PENGUIN BOOKS
CÉLINE

Patrick McCarthy was born in Wales, of Irish parents, in 1941. He earned his B.A. and Ph.D. degrees at Oxford in 1963 and 1969 respectively (having received his M.A. at Harvard in 1964), and he has taught at Cambridge and, in the United States, at Vassar, Cornell, and Haverford. He is presently attached to the Johns Hopkins School of Advanced International Studies and is at work on a book about Camus. Of his *Céline*, he says: "I have always been extremely curious about World War II because I am too young to remember it but was surrounded during my childhood by adults who had lived through it and talked of nothing else. This was the origin of my enthusiasm for Céline."

CÉLINE

PATRICK McCARTHY

PENGUIN BOOKS

Penguin Books Ltd, Harmondsworth, Middlesex, England
Penguin Books, 625 Madison Avenue, New York, New York 10022, U.S.A.
Penguin Books Australia Ltd, Ringwood, Victoria, Australia
Penguin Books Canada Ltd, 2801 John Street, Markham, Ontario, Canada L3R 1B4
Penguin Books (N.Z.) Ltd, 182–190 Wairau Road, Auckland 10, New Zealand

First published in Great Britain by Allen Lane 1975
First published in the United States of America by The Viking Press (a Richard Seaver Book) 1976
Published in Penguin Books 1977

Copyright © Patrick McCarthy, 1975
All rights reserved

Printed in the United States of America by
Offset Paperback Mfrs., Inc., Dallas, Pennsylvania
Set in Monotype Fournier

ACKNOWLEDGMENTS:

Dell Publishing Co., Inc.: Excerpts from *Castle to Castle* by Louis-Ferdinand Céline; Copyright © 1968 by Dell Publishing Co., Inc. Excerpts from *North* by Louis-Ferdinand Céline; Copyright © 1972 by Dell Publishing Co., Inc. Used with the permission of the publishers/Seymour Lawrence.

New Directions Publishing Corp.: Louis-Ferdinand Céline: *Death on the Installment Plan*, translated by John H. P. Marks; Copyright 1938 by Louis-Ferdinand Destouches, © 1966 by Mme. Louis-Ferdinand Destouches. *Guignol's Band*, translated by Bernard Frechtman and Jack Niles; Copyright 1954 by New Directions Publishing Corporation. *Journey to the End of the Night*, translated by John H. P. Marks; Copyright 1934, © 1961 by Louis-Ferdinand Céline. All reprinted by permission of New Directions Publishing Corporation.

Except in the United States of America,
this book is sold subject to the condition
that it shall not, by way of trade or otherwise,
be lent, re-sold, hired out, or otherwise circulated
without the publisher's prior consent in any form of
binding or cover other than that in which it is
published and without a similar condition
including this condition being imposed
on the subsequent purchaser

Contents

Introduction

Céline is one of the loneliest figures in twentieth-century literature. At his death in 1961 the French newspapers gave him less space than Ernest Hemingway who died the same day. His funeral had none of the pomp of Valéry's or Mauriac's. Post-war critics had virtually excluded him from French literature. Yet he is a great artist. Sartre once thought so and so did Henry Miller. *Voyage au bout de la nuit* (1932) was a revolution in novel-writing. In *Mort à crédit* (1936) Céline created a new language to express his nightmarish vision.

He was neglected because of his political opinions. He wrote anti-semitic pamphlets, sided with Hitler and fled to Germany in 1944. He belonged to an era that Frenchmen preferred to forget. Camus, Sartre and the writers of the Resistance dominated the post-war period. A curtain of silence was drawn over their opponents. *Voyage* and *Mort* were admired but ignored. Céline's later books were greeted with slight enthusiasm. The pamphleteer had brought the novelist into disrepute. Céline had been paid – so Sartre said – by the Nazis.

The truth is harder and stranger. Céline was a creature of violent contradictions. A First World War hero, he went on to write *Voyage*, the most pacifist of novels. A life-long hater of the Germans, he threw himself into their arms at the moment of their defeat. Trotsky praised his writings, but so did the Nazi review *Stürmer*. Céline was a Celt from Brittany with the Celtic love of language and talk. He was also the epitome of lower-middle-class France: modest, cautious with money, a very private person. He lived a turbulent life caught up with the great events of his age. He fought in two world wars, worked as a doctor for the League of Nations, visited Russia in the 1930s, took a stand on fascism. Along with this he pursued his personal quest for beauty: falling in love with dancers, trying to introduce their art into his novels.

Here lies the problem. Among so many Célines, which is the real one? One must separate the man, the pamphleteer and the novelist. In his life Céline was anti-semitic but he was not as obsessed as in *Baga-*

telles pour un massacre. He immersed himself in his novel-writing, but
he was not as demented as the narrator of *Mort.* The 'I' of the pamphlets is not the same as the 'I' of the novels. One must look closely
at Céline's life and work and undertake the prosaic task of sifting the
evidence. Céline did not want us to do this. When biographers asked
him for details of his past he grew angry: 'Invent them,' he snapped.
One must deliberately go against him.

In discussing Céline's life one encounters two kinds of problems.
The first is obtaining information. Céline was almost forty when he
published *Voyage* and his earlier life is badly documented. It is very
hard to find out anything about his childhood and adolescence. The
second problem is to distinguish between fact and invention. Céline
gives a distorted view of his life in his fiction. He blackens himself. He
did travel to Africa, as Bardamu does in *Voyage,* and he did spend
months in Sigmaringen, as Ferdinand does in *D'un château l'autre.*
But he also went through years of stability, which his narrators do not.
He did not always fail, as they do. When the ageing Céline talked to
journalists about his life he portrayed himself as an innocent victim. He
would not admit he was anti-semitic or that he had collaborated. He
cried to high heaven that he was a blameless scapegoat thrust into the
desert by a million enemies: Resistants, Communists and Allies. At
other times, switching his role, he would lead people to believe that he
was indeed a monster. He praised Hitler and condemned post-war
France.

The facts are more complex than any of these inventions. Céline was
Jekyll and Hyde: successful author and hunted refugee, kindly doctor
and anti-semite. He was a passionate, tough man. It is tragic that he
convinced so many people with his legends because the truth is so much
more interesting.

The pamphlets are an embarrassment to Céline's supporters. The
editor of the *Oeuvres complètes* refused to include them. But they cannot
be ignored. Appeasement is an integral part of Céline's thought, anti-
semitism is another: it is an escape-hatch from his pessimism. Céline
needed to become a pamphleteer. He had to distort the reality of the
1930s into a hallucination where he could hate and be hated. In the
pamphlets he could explain to himself the evils of Communism and war.
The explanations he offers are appalling and they contradict the values
of his fiction. He has cut himself off from his readers and fallen into a

solipsism that *Voyage* condemns. But the pamphlets must stand as Célinian works.

They are less important, however, than the novels. As a novelist, Céline gives free rein to his tragic vision. Evil has dominion, man is trapped, he can do nothing to alter his fate. *Voyage* depicts a hero who comes slowly to understand and feel the horror of his condition. But, at the end of the night, there is also beauty. *Mort* introduces the artist into the book and poses the problem of transforming the world by style. Céline's first two novels have overshadowed the others. One of the aims of this book is to show that *Féerie* and *D'un château l'autre* are no less exciting than *Voyage*. If Céline had written only his later novels he would stand as a great artist. He goes through a clear evolution. Each of his novels goes a little further than the previous one, each presents a new map of hell. *Guignol's Band* (1944) is a world of black magic. *Féerie pour une autre fois* (1954) shows that the black magician is the artist himself, his creative power closely linked with destructive forces. In the final trilogy (1956–61) all worlds disappear into an eternal nothingness. Céline's style, the vehicle of his hallucinating imagination, changes too. He does not stop at the innovations of *Mort*: the tide of *argot*. In *Guignol's Band* he plays with language: he creates long images, builds fantasies. In *Féerie* he goes much further: neologisms abound as he mixes rhetoric and poetry to convey the creativity he is describing. By contrast the trilogy is written in short, bare phrases: language dissolves as reality does.

The purpose of this book is to separate the pieces – and then to put them back again. Céline's life and thought centres around his unrelenting pessimism: his vision of a world where the deathshead stands behind every human face. There are various reasons that explain why he should be pessimistic. The poverty of his upbringing and his experiences in the 1914 war are one kind of reason, the crisis of European culture in the 1930s is another. They are unsatisfactory explanations because the pessimism lies deeper. It is not determined by anything, it determines. It is the driving force behind Céline's work as a doctor and behind his stylistic innovations. Each of his many selves is a mask that he adopts to deal with this tragic vision. For this reason one must accept Céline as he is. One must not whitewash him. One must not preserve a 'good' Céline and banish a 'bad' Céline. That would be easy and Céline hated easy solutions – here one may not go against him. In his life, his pamphlets and his novels he sought out the worst because only there did he find truth. He is a mythological figure of our times. He ventured into the night of modern life to bring back the hidden secrets that most men prefer to ignore. This is the real reason why he is such a lonely figure.

[1]

The First Forty Years

When *Voyage au bout de la nuit* appeared in 1932 its author was completely unknown. Overnight Louis-Ferdinand Destouches, who wrote under the pseudonym of Céline, became the sensation of the reading public, the object of anathema and admiration. His book recounts the journey of one Bardamu across battlefields, hospitals and jungles. The Fall is everywhere, Redemption nowhere. The only relief is Céline's laughter as he mocks his wretched characters. *Voyage* represented something quite new.

The story of its discovery belongs to literary mythology.[1] One morning in 1932 Robert Denoël, one half of the Steele and Denoël publishing house, found on his desk a brown-paper parcel containing two novels. One was a love-story of a hundred and fifty pages, the other was the five hundred pages of *Voyage*. Denoël started to read the longer novel. Once he had begun, he could not put it down. On the spot he decided to publish it. He called in one of his writers, Robert Poulet, and waxed eloquent about his new discovery who was the equal of Dante, Shakespeare, Cervantes . . .

Denoël was just the man to appreciate *Voyage*. A 'little publisher of no account',[2] he had made no money but had already discovered Antonin Artaud. Poulet, a talented author who was to become Céline's friend, describes Denoël: 'Lots of ideas, not so many scruples, a quick intelligence, one part sensualist and polite impostor.' Denoël was an adventurer who had fled from his devout Catholic family in Liège to the excitement of Paris. His innumerable publishing ventures had brought him debts and near-bankruptcies, but he had always managed to escape and start again. He was famous, Poulet notes wrily, for promising his authors pots of gold that never materialized at the end of the rainbow. Still, he had not made money himself either. He was 'half comic valet, half ship's captain'. Supposedly secretive but incapable of silence, he was full of schemes and intrigues. He had 'the ear of a cat that pricks up at the slightest sound'.

Denoël had a flair for what was new. Amidst the confusion of his office on the rue Amélie, he could pick out good, original writing. Undeterred by Céline's coarse language and his attacks on France's sacred cows – the Army and the colonial administration – Denoël saw that *Voyage* was a great novel. Whereas Poulet thought on first reading that it was an immense farce, brilliantly funny but without depth, Denoël was convinced that he had a masterpiece.

His next problem was to discover its author, no easy task since the manuscript had been sent anonymously. A messenger was dispatched to the authoress of the love-story, who lived in Montmartre. When he arrived burbling about masterpieces she thought he meant her novel. Finally she realized that the other book was being praised. Deeply disappointed, she directed him to the home of one Dr Destouches, who lived on the rue Lepic and worked in the Clichy municipal clinic. Céline had just received a letter from the illustrious firm of Gallimard to whom he had also sent *Voyage*. The reader, Benjamin Crémieux, thought the book had possibilities, but it needed to be shortened and rewritten. If this were done, then perhaps ... Denoël was left alone in the field.

Poulet remembers Céline's first visit to the rue Amélie: '... a big devil with an inscrutable face and a scornful mouth, rigged out like a café owner on holiday'.[3] There was no trace of the conventional writer. Shy and unsure of himself, Céline hid his insecurity behind long harangues. He dressed in well-worn suits and his flat on the rue Lepic looked like any other lower-middle-class home. He worked long hours on the Clichy night-service where he tended the destitute, the alcoholics and the men beaten up in street-fights. He had picked up their slang, which sounded strange in the publishing houses of the Left Bank. Fanatically independent, Céline resisted Denoël's attempts to soften the language of *Voyage*: 'they want to make me write like François Mauriac' was his rebellious cry.[4] Yet he paid no attention to the details of publication. He refused to correct the proofs himself and, when the book appeared, he had to be persuaded to talk to journalists. He seemed to care only for his royalties. On this subject he had bitter disputes with Denoël. Max Dorian, one of the publisher's henchmen, remembers Dr Destouches as the most bizarre of writers: a 'strange character with a big nose, huge feet in huge shoes, timid in spite of his stentorian voice, talking, whether naturally or by affection, in a lower-class Paris accent'.[5]

One problem remained before *Voyage* could be published. As Denoël had no money of his own, he had to appeal to his partner. Bernard Steele was a pleasant, francophile American, an expert on wines, 'who knew nothing about publishing'.[6] He had no money either and he had to contact his mother in New York. After a series of transatlantic telephone calls she agreed to finance *Voyage*. Ironically, Steele's family was Jewish and he was to part company with Denoël over *L'École des cadavres*. But for the moment he was delighted with Céline.

Voyage appeared in November 1932. Céline, who was still professing not to be interested, went off to Germany in December on a mission for the League of Nations. He was to study the effect of unemployment on the health of the working class and he was going to Breslau to visit a young girlfriend, Erika Irrgang.[7] But Denoël was not the man to let *Voyage* gather dust in the bookshops. He sent a copy to Léon Daudet, one of the leading lights of the Action Française. Daudet, whose literary tastes were broader than his political opinions, was so famous a critic that he could make or break a book with one article. He read *Voyage* and wrote a glowing review. Success, both literary and popular, followed. The novel made an enormous impact. Poulet, on second reading, called it 'the cry of a real man appearing in a crowd of dummies and automatons'.[8] The young Lucien Rebatet, whose path was to cross Céline's, devoured the opening chapters, while sitting on a bench in the Boulevard des Italiens.[9] *Voyage* was praised, analysed and denounced. Readers wondered about this strange author who worked among the Paris poor and wrote in their language. The shrewd Denoël had been proved right.

Voyage aroused controversy. In January 1933 Albert Thibaudet notes: 'It is a long time since a book was discussed as much as *Voyage au bout de la nuit*.'[10] The debate was heated, often acrimonious. Conservative reviewers found the novel iconoclastic and obscene: 'M. Céline expresses with unrelieved baseness the disgust he feels for humanity' (*Candide*). Another opponent found *Voyage* 'extremely weak' (*Revue de Paris*). Another disliked Bardamu: '. . . no sympathy for this character who delights in coarseness and is eternally cynical' (*La Presse*). Favourable critics found Céline's pessimism strikingly honest. They commented on his 'appalling lucidity, on the verge of madness' (*Le Rouge et le noir*). They called his novel 'a long tunnel full of mists and terror' (*Nouvelles littéraires*).

One of the most interesting reviews came from Georges Bernanos. Despite his Catholicism and the left-wing stance he was to adopt in the late 1930s, Bernanos was not unlike Céline in temperament. Both men reacted violently against the lies of conventional life, both were extremists. Bernanos found the pessimism of *Voyage* attractive because it corresponded to his own vision of a world without God. He too loathed the smug optimism of the French bourgeoisie and the dawning age of American industrialization. But Bernanos saw beyond all pessimism a rebuilt Christianity that could conquer darkness: 'The end of the night is God's gentle pity.' There is no such hope in Céline.

The debate about *Voyage* assumed political overtones. The anarchist right wing like Daudet might admire Céline; the conservative right did not. Most of his supporters came from the left. Georges Altman, sometime communist, sometime fellow-traveller and friend of the veteran socialist Henri Barbusse, called the novel 'the cry of a man flayed alive'. The left appreciated *Voyage* because it portrayed capitalism in its agony: 'Céline's chaotic book, full of despair and revolt, reflects the decomposition and the death throes of French bourgeois society' (*L'Humanité*). *Voyage* was translated into Russian by Elsa Triolet and Louis Aragon, poet laureate of the Communist Party. The left did have its reserves. In *L'Étudiant socialiste* a then unknown young man called Claude Lévi-Strauss noted that Céline was 'not one of us'. The positive side of socialism was absent from his book. But Lévi-Strauss agreed with Altman that the pages on the war were a splendid criticism of the military spirit. He concluded, correctly, that socialists and Céline had a 'common enemy'.

The scandal that *Voyage* had aroused continued – decidedly it was Céline's role to create trouble. Denoël hoped the book would win the Prix Goncourt. When the committee met on 30 November the vote was tied with five votes for Céline and five for Guy Mazeline's *Les Loups*. But, as the committee's president Rosny voted for *Voyage*, the award was to go to Céline. Then, when the committee met on 7 December to make its official decision, the Rosny brothers switched sides. The Prix went to Mazeline by seven votes to three. Céline's only champions were Léon Daudet, Jean Ajalbert and Lucien Descaves. Descaves, an old admirer of Zola and future friend of Céline, was so enraged that he walked out of the meeting, slamming the door behind him.[11]

Rumours flew around Paris. It was said that the jury had changed its mind for reasons of national prestige: what would foreign readers think, if the Prix Goncourt were bestowed on a novel as obscene as *Voyage*? Other people said the jury's motives were not so idealistic: financial pressure had been brought to bear on the Rosny brothers. In *Le Petit Crapouillot*, a muck-raking newspaper full of new writing, black humour and polemic, Galtier-Boissière railed against the committee's decision and was sued for slander. He took on the law suit with his usual vigour and managed to avoid being convicted. Meanwhile Céline had been given the consolation award of the Prix Renaudot. The controversy died down slowly.

To the public Dr Destouches remained an enigma. He continued to work on the night-service at Clichy and to shun the publicity his book had brought him. But beneath the mask of unconcern he was watching anxiously. He was very eager to get the Prix Goncourt and the decision hit him hard. Jeanne Carayon, an ex-neighbour who corrected his proofs, accompanied him back to the rue Lepic after the announcement. In a rare moment of frankness he appealed to her: 'Do not leave me alone.' His façade of irony broke down and he spent the evening in a daze of disappointment: looking at the drawings his young daughter had done, watering his geraniums, trying to find comfort in living things.[12] The intense emotion of which he was capable showed itself here. He never forgave the committee for its decision and the word 'Goncourt' became his favourite term of abuse: 'a little Goncourt' meant a trivial, conventional novel.[13] On the other hand he was deeply grateful to his supporters Descaves and Daudet – even if he did turn on Daudet in the pamphlets.

This nervous, passionate side of his nature was kept well hidden. To the newspaper-readers Céline seemed reserved. Photographs show a tall man with a bony face and deep-set, piercing eyes. He is dressed in badly-fitting suits and shabby overcoats. He is polite but weary and there is an uneasiness about him, as if he is always on the verge of running away.

One reporter, Elisabeth Porquerol, became a friend. She describes a conversation they had after his return from Germany.[14] Céline paced up and down the room waving his arms and talking incessantly. Instead of answering her questions, he poured out a series of complaints. Denoël was cheating him of his royalties and getting him involved in a lot of publicity he did not want. He was not a writer at all, but a doctor who had turned to writing because he needed money to buy a flat. He had been inspired by the success of Eugène Dabit's *Hôtel du nord*. A good, popular novel was what he had wanted to write and he was not interested in discussions of philosophy and style. Not surprisingly Elisabeth Porquerol thought he was putting on an act. His virulence, she felt, masked timidity. His confidences revealed only his loneliness. But she felt the man's power: the wave of nervous energy that swept along the jumbled resentments.

This power was evident to Poulet, Max Dorian and all who met Dr Destouches. It set him apart from ordinary writers. Céline continued to shock. When Denoël read his second novel in 1936 he discovered that it was much more frank than *Voyage*. *Mort à crédit* had to appear with blanks instead of the obscenities Céline had written. Even worse, the anti-semitic pamphlet *Bagatelles pour un massacre* appalled precisely the left-wing admirers of *Voyage*. Altman broke with Céline,[15] *L'Humanité* denounced him. Céline did not care; secretly he was pleased. He was jealous of his independence and anxious to go to extremes.

Even in 1932 it was clear that the *Voyage* controversy was more than a storm in a teacup, more than another of the endless feuds in the introvert, literary world of Paris. What was so special about Céline and his book? Throughout the preceding decade the Surrealists had flaunted their contempt for public opinion. They had been outrageously bad-mannered, they had attacked such venerable artists as Paul Claudel and they had paraded bizarre inventions like automatic writing. This kind of outrage is a normal feature of the Paris scene – quarrels, reconciliations, manifestos. The emotions Céline aroused were more profound. In part it was *Voyage* itself. The novel struck a new note in French literature – the note of stark tragedy, random and violent. Nothing written since 1900 conveyed this sense so directly. Proust was deeply pessimistic, but he expressed it in a subtle, civilized way. *Voyage* was the start of a new and harsher era, as young writers like Sartre were quick to realize. The only comparable event during these years was the early translations of Faulkner: *Sanctuary* came out in 1933, *As I Lay Dying* in 1934. But a translation could not make the same impact. The other difference lay in the character of Céline himself. He was no Cocteau. He did not flirt with the salons of the *seizième*, an 'enfant terrible', malicious but always pardoned. The Flanders trenches and the Clichy hospital beds lay between him and his readers. His feelings of rejection went deeper, his brooding sense of injustice contained real violence. He had something in common with Genêt, whose years in prison have left him with a special brand of loneliness. But Céline was more aggressive than Genêt.

The clues to his strange, complex temperament must be sought in the early years of his life. As already stated, no biographical information can really account for his agonized vision. But one can learn something about the author of *Voyage*, if one looks at his childhood, his war wounds, his first marriage and his wanderings.

Louis-Ferdinand Destouches was born in 1894.* His grandfather had been a teacher in the *lycée* at Le Havre and a member of the town council. Monsieur Destouches, a well-educated man with a university degree, worked for an insurance company. On his mother's side Céline came from a line of shopkeepers. His grandmother had an antique shop in the rue de Provence where she specialized in old and precious lace. She was an imposing woman and her acquaintances remember seeing her wearing long strings of diamonds.[16] Her daughter Marguerite Céline followed her into the lace business. In 1893 she married Louis Destouches and they went to live at Courbevoie, the Paris suburb where Céline was born.

In *Mort à crédit* Céline has left a remarkably unpleasant picture of his family. The young hero Ferdinand is trapped in a home that is a

* The problems of learning about Céline's early life are great. The only facts that can be ascertained with certainty are those contained in official records – date of birth, war experiences and the like – and those that can be learned from reliable witnesses – very few – who knew Céline at the time. There is all too little information of this kind. A second kind of information can be drawn from people who knew Céline later. This is valuable but suspect, because they draw on what Céline has told them and because, following in his path, they create legends of their own. A third category of information comes from Céline, and is subject to the distortion discussed in the following pages. In this chapter the bare, provable facts of Céline's early life are set out. Facts and opinions from other sources are given and the value of the source is discussed. The aim of the chapter is twofold: firstly to set down what can be learned about the young Céline; secondly to look at the relationship between the man and the writer. Where it is possible speculation – it can be little more – is made about how such-and-such an event may have influenced the author of *Voyage*. On the other hand, Céline's portrayal of his life – in his first three novels and in his conversations – is often contrasted with the facts. This too enables one to get at the writer: it shows the way he transformed his experience.

triangle of hatred. His father is a petty tyrant, perpetually on the verge
of madness, and his masochistic mother wallows in her suffering. This
portrayal reflects the transformation that Céline imposes on his life in
his writing. In reality Monsieur and Madame Destouches were not the
demented figures of their son's imagination. Céline's father was 'a man
of honour and completely honest'.[17] He was 'jovial and very frank'.[18]
He loved the sea and ships and transmitted this love to his young son.
He liked 'to fish with a rod and line and he went sailing wearing a
commandant's peaked cap for he had always dreamed of going into the
navy'.[19] He and his wife lived happily together. They were 'nice, quiet
people, ordinary and retiring'.[20] And they were devoted to their son.

Not long after he was born they moved from Courbevoie to the
Passage Choiseul where Madame Destouches had a lace shop. As the
Passage is the setting for *Mort à crédit* and as Céline grew up here, it
merits description. It stands, then as now, in a maze of little streets close
to the opulent Avenue de l'Opéra but worlds apart. Tourists who
admire the beauties of Paris know nothing of this neighbourhood,
which is a hive of small shops and cafés, of bargains and basements.
Ancient women hover behind dusty counters and haggle with customers. Gossip flies through the air. At lunchtime each café has its
clientèle of harassed shopkeepers who devour their *croque-monsieur* and
flee behind their narrow doors. The Passage, its glass roof admitting
a murky light, offers to the shopper a cobbler's, a watch-maker's, a
tailor's and a second-hand bookstore that does not have a single volume
of Céline. It lives and breathes the fetid atmosphere of slim profits,
fatigue and bankruptcy. It is a shrine to that most powerful of French
gods – the *petit commerce*.

Near the entrance stands a television-shop, sole emblem of modernity. The tiled roof, narrow corridor and tiny flats above the shops
have not changed since 1900. The young Destouches grew up in this
'sinister passage where the sunlight never entered'.[21] His parents
taught him their values: honesty, industry, and self-effacement. Céline
rebelled against their code, but he never shook it off. It explains why
he was not at home in the publishing-houses of the *Quartier latin* and
why he was so worried about money. It accounts for his well-worn
suits and his abstemious habits. Even his writer's vision was shaped by
his background. The Passage was the home of people who, caught between the twin blocks of Capital and Labour, were frightened of the

modern world. Céline took their anxiety and raised it to the level of genius. His eternal sense of frustration reflected their feeling that they had no control over what was happening to them. They, despite their tenacity, could see no future for themselves, hence perhaps his depiction of a society in permanent decay. He could hope neither for a flowering of capitalism nor for socialism. Céline's parents thought themselves quite different from the industrial proletariat. Their son, although he would hate the rich, could not join with the workers in a political strategy, could not even share their class-based view of society. Most of all Céline, the pamphleteer, drew on the Passage. Although it did not blossom until later, the seed of anti-semitism was sown here. In *Bagatelles* he would excoriate the Jew and extol the merits of the lower middle class. He would defend their old, safe France against everything that was new and threatening: communism, internationalism and the like.

Céline's earliest memory was of the shop – 'I was born in a shop,' he says with some exaggeration.[22] The life was hard but it had flashes of beauty. He remembered his mother's exquisite lace-work that took so much time and effort. He watched the elegant ladies who came to buy it – this, he later claimed, was his first glimpse of feminine charm.[23] He played in the Passage with the children of the other shopkeepers and he attended elementary school at the nearby Place Louvois and the rue d'Argenteuil.

The first outside event to impinge on his consciousness was the 1900 Exhibition. He was taken to see the huge, triumphant gate that had been erected on the Place de la Concorde. He was marched along a 'moving pavement that went creaking up to the gallery of machines' and he was taken around the exhibits from the different countries. For a six-year-old child it was like a fairytale. It was also his first exposure to the contemporary world: 'Modern life was beginning.' He remembered the crowds that jostled around him, 'especially the feet, feet everywhere and clouds of dust so thick you could touch them'.[24]

News of another public event filtered through to him. The Dreyfus case was making headlines in the press and dividing the country. Monsieur Destouches was ardently anti-Dreyfus and he bewildered his son with 'great speeches' about the army and national honour. On a conscious level at least, Céline was unimpressed.[25]

More real than Dreyfus's supposed crimes was the first journey that he made in 1904.[26] The Normandy beaches were then fashionable resorts to which Parisian ladies retreated from the summer heat. Madame Destouches, whose business came to a standstill in July and August, decided to follow them and to ply her wares on the promenade in Dieppe. With her went the ten-year-old Ferdinand who helped to carry the bundles of lace and push the handcart. He eyed the pretty daughters of the rich who came along the promenade with their maids. They stopped to buy from his mother, but they haggled like people who were penniless. The young Destouches felt, as yet, no social resentment. The rich were glorious beings from another planet who graciously provided his family with a living. But later, when his resentment did grow, it fed on his memories. His bitterness would be all the greater because it had been slow in awakening. It had not been diffused by the various experiences of growing up. It would weigh in his stomach like a ball of lead that he would keep trying to vomit up.

Meanwhile he attended school. The only lesson he remembered in later life was a natural-history class dealing with the fermentation of seeds. A bean was placed inside a jar full of water that was then exposed to the sun. As the bean swelled up the jar broke, illustrating the tremendous forces of nature.[27] May one deduce from this memory that the child was already turning towards natural science? Scarcely. But Céline claimed that from the earliest age he wanted to become a doctor: 'I had a great admiration for doctors ... I thought they were wonderful fellows who cured people.'[28] At school he did nothing to further this ambition. The bulk of the lessons made no impression on him. As it was a state school no religion was taught and Céline had little contact with the Catholic Church: 'I made my first communion and then I never thought about it again.'[29] As for his classmates he remembered them as boys much like himself, the sons of lower-middle-class families. Two or three had rich fathers and they stood apart from the rest.[30]

What sort of a boy was the young Destouches? According to Brochard, he was 'a child full of the devil, undisciplined, freedom-mad'.[31] From the start he was a problem to his parents. Despite his keen natural intelligence and a definite bent for learning, he could not settle down in school. At the age of eleven he left, having obtained his leaving certificate but without going to the *lycée*, as his father and grandfather had done before him. There is an important distinction to be made here. It is not that Céline's parents were too poor to think about sending their son to the *lycée*, the gateway to the professions. They expected him to go. It is rather that he, rebellious, resisted their pressure on him. Without knowing it, he was already pushing himself down the social scale, going lower than his grandfather and father.

His worried parents decided he was too restless to follow his father into a desk job. He would have to follow his mother into commerce. They started him as an errand boy in shops. They hoped that he would rise to become a salesman, and then a buyer or a manager in a department store.[32] To give him some specialized skills they sent him to Germany and to England to learn the languages. In 1908 he attended the *Volkschule* in Diepholz in Lower Saxony, where he was the only French child. It was a painful experience: 'There the young Destouches ran up against the hateful, unyielding chauvinism of the children his own age who insisted on making his life unbearable.'[33] The next year he was sent to a school at Rochester – which became the Meanwell Academy of *Mort à crédit*. Marcel Brochard sums up Céline's first journey abroad: 'You are sent to Germany at the age of fourteen to study the language and learn about the commercial world. A precocious boy, you sleep with your landlady and are sent home. In 1909 you are packed off to England where, after the same kind of exploits, you are "returned" to your parents.'[34] Brochard may well be exaggerating. But his account fits in with the picture one has of a troublesome boy.

From the time he left school until the age of eighteen, Céline had a series of jobs which he left or lost. When he was eleven he was sent to work at a silk shop, 'Raimond Frères', in the rue du 4 Septembre. Later he was employed as an errand boy for jewellers: at 'Lacloche', on the elegant rue de la Paix, and at 'Robert', in the equally fashionable rue Royale. These were responsible jobs because the young boy used to carry through the streets jewels that his lifetime's wages would not buy. In the winter of 1910, when Lacloche's customers moved to the Riviera, Destouches was sent to the shop's Nice branch on the Boulevard Masséna. He went around delivering 'treasures, diadems to Russian princesses'.[35] At the time he was earning sixty francs a month out of which he had to pay for his keep. It was a hard life – although not exceptional by the standards of pre-1914 France. Céline did not keep any of his jobs for long and his parents grew more worried about him. After leaving Lacloche he went to work for a goldsmith, 'Wagner'. His task was to take specimens of the firm's work around to jewellers. He describes his day: 'We went to all the jewellers on the boulevard with the skip and then we all met, all the sales representatives met on the steps of the Ambigu, you know the steps going down. We all met there and our feet hurt because our shoes . . . well my feet always hurt.' [36]

Clearly commerce did not suit him. He had no taste for overseers or customers. But he was studying on his own, preparing for the *baccalauréat*, making up for the years of secondary schooling he had not had. Although he disliked formal education he was keen to learn. He describes how he studied: 'I bought the school curriculum and the books with my pocket money; I used to mug them up in corners, wearing out my eyes that were burning with lack of sleep.' [37] It was a hard, lonely task. In 1912 he sat and passed the first part of the *baccalauréat*, a remarkable achievement for a self-taught student.

He had no clear vision of his future, even though he still hoped vaguely to become a doctor. What was clear was that life at home was growing impossible. The crisis came to a head not long after he passed his *baccalauréat*: 'At the age of eighteen you clash with your exasperated parents and, as you are exasperated too, you take it into your head to join the army.' [38] The rebellious feelings welled up inside the adolescent Destouches until he could check them no longer. This was another reaction against the ordinary, stable life that his parents were offering him. Danger seemed more attractive.

He enlisted in the cavalry and was sent to join the 12th Cuirassiers at Rambouillet. He soon discovered that the army was not what he had hoped it would be. A diary that he kept in 1913 gives some insight into his first year.[39] Inevitably he disliked the discipline. His officers did not inspire him. Baron de Lagrange, his commander, was a 'good and sincere' man but prematurely aged by debauchery. Most of the N.C.O.s had 'crushing manners' and one man, Servat, was a 'rogue and a brute', always picking on Destouches. The daily routine was oppressive to a youth filled with 'a deep nostalgia for freedom'. He hated waking up in the morning to the sound of the trumpets and having to clean out the stables. He even admits to 'an innate fear of horses'. His unhappiness was so great that he thought seriously about deserting – 'the only escape from this calvary'.

His diary portrays a young man imbued with a pessimism deeper than the usual crisis of adolescence. There may be a naïveté about entries like this one: 'How many times have I come up from stables and all alone on my bed, filled with depression, I have, despite my seventeen years, cried like a girl making her first communion.' But Destouches is aware in himself of a more permanent sadness: 'I am stamped with melancholy, I live and move in it like a bird in the air.' He bears within him 'a wealth of unhappiness' that he cannot shake off. His melancholy is not really to be explained by his harsh upbringing – especially since he says his time in the army is 'the first really painful [period] I have endured'.

Destouches does not give in. He wants to escape from his pessimism through action: 'what I want most of all is a life full of incident'. This, after all, was why he had joined the army. He is growing aware that his escapades must have some direction. What is he searching for? 'I want to dominate,' he says. He explains more precisely: 'I want to know and understand.' He is searching for truth and action is a way of uncovering his real self. He will look for 'the detours which allow you to get a moral education'.

He is aware of his exceptional temperament: 'I am a man of complex and delicate feelings,' he boasts, like a young Romantic hero. He wishes to study himself so that he may understand the movements of his mind. But he is not content with introspection. He wants to be transformed. He notes the change that has taken place in him since he joined the army: 'I have seen my soul suddenly stripped of illusions.' He has an ascetic awareness that by submitting to the burden of life in the cavalry he is becoming a tougher and better person. He has been lonely but he has learned to face it. Truth is seen as a willingness to confront the worst without flinching.

Destouches's first year in the army involved a domination of himself and his environment. He became a good soldier, efficient with horses and at ease with his comrades. He acquired a relish for military life, that would have surprised Altman and Lévi-Strauss. When he took part in the grand parades at Longchamps on Bastille Day, he was delighted with the coloured banners flying in the air and with the precision of the manoeuvres. He had no scruples about the army's role: he helped without a twinge of regret to put down a group of striking workers in the rue des Pyramides.[40] A photograph, taken around this time, shows a tall, gangling youth with strong features and a determined mouth. Rather gingerly, he is holding on to a horse's bridle. One of his comrades has left a description of him: '. . . a likeable companion, the first thing one noticed was his attitude of modesty and polite reserve, he was a quiet observer, sometimes a rather mocking look about him, a subtle smile'.[41] This is the first mention of Céline's redoubtable sense of humour. In the cavalry he was too shy to reveal it, but soon his flair for mockery would show itself.

When Kaiser Wilhelm's troops drove into Belgium, Destouches had been in the cavalry for nearly two years. He had been promoted to sergeant. Now he was to taste action. Patriotism was running high as France prepared to resist the second German onslaught in a lifetime. In *Voyage*, cowardice is the only military virtue, not so in reality. On 25 October 1914, Destouches's regiment was in action at Poelkapelle near Ypres. A message had to be transmitted but the regular messengers were reluctant to set out under heavy enemy fire. Destouches volunteered.

He set out on horseback and was fired on. Although struck by a German bullet, he delivered the message. The bloody trench battles of Flanders had only begun and disillusionment had not set in. Destouches's exploit made him a hero and a model of patriotism. His action was portrayed on the front page of *L'Illustré national*. Even as he was carried off to hospital his praises were being sung. He was mentioned in dispatches and awarded the military medal. An official letter, signed by no less a personage than Joffre, describes Destouches's deed: 'In liaison between an Infantry Regiment and his brigade, volunteered to carry under heavy fire an order that the Infantry liaison units hesitated to transmit. Carried the order and was gravely wounded in the course of his mission.'[42]

Céline remained delighted with his action and his medal: 'he was proud to have gone through the [war] with courage and distinction and he was always proud too of the grave wounds he had received in the service of his country'.[43] An old-fashioned patriotism and a liking for things military were henceforth to be a part of his character.

In later life he talked much about his wounds. Again and again he claimed that he had been struck in the head and that the doctors had inserted a plate into his skull. Jean Ducourneau, editor of the *Oeuvres complètes*, has unearthed the surgeons' report.[44] He finds no mention of a head-wound. Destouches was treated for an arm-wound and the operation left him with a stiff right shoulder. His friends recall seeing the deep scar that ran down to his elbow.[45] But the head-wound is pure invention. Yet medical matters are not that simple. Céline suffered from headaches and buzzings in his ears, on this point his friends agree. Whether these pains should be called psychosomatic, or whether the nervous shock of the bullet did physical damage to the eardrums, is hard to say. The experience of being wounded was to exert great influence on Céline. He became an ardent pacifist, ready to make any and every concession in order to avoid war. At the same time he felt a secret attraction to violence. He became acutely conscious of bloodshed: terrified that fresh holocausts might break out, yet willing them to do so. In the 1930s he would see the danger-signals early and he would cry out, like some modern Cassandra: fascinated and horrified by the collapse of the fragile European order. In *Voyage* he would describe not just the tortures of war but the violence that lay just below the surface of everyday life. And yet one is aware here of the limits of biography. Thousands of men who were wounded in Flanders recovered and went on to lead normal lives. They were not haunted by ambivalent nightmares. They did not see every passer-by as a potential executioner. One can only conclude that Céline's nervous, melancholic temperament led him to dramatize his experiences.

The young hero spent weary months dragging himself from hospital to hospital. In December he was at the Val-de-Grâce for observation. He was operated on at Villejuif. After convalescing at Vanves he returned to the Val-de-Grâce in March 1915 for electrical treatment. Then the clouds lifted. On leaving hospital he was sent to London to work in the passport office run by the French government. He remained in England nearly six months.

This stay forms the autobiographical basis of *Guignol's Band*. But Céline has systematically deformed his life. The hero, Ferdinand, is surrounded exclusively by low-life characters like Cascade, the French brothel-keeper, and Boro, the bomb-throwing Russian anarchist. He is permanently on the run from the English police, the French army, everyone. In reality Destouches had a sober desk job, read hard in the evenings and spent only part of his time wandering around Soho and the East End.

Georges Geoffroy, who shared a room with him on Gower Street, has described their life together.[46] Their work in the passport office consisted of granting or refusing visas to people who wished to go to France. Doubtful cases they referred to their superiors. Most of the applicants were ordinary men and women, but they did meet 'lots of strange and dubious characters who delighted Louis Destouches'. Céline loved to study people who had trouble with their visas. He probed them, trying to find out what they were hiding, which disgraceful actions lay concealed in their past. He was especially pleased one day: into their office came the ill-fated Mata Hari. She was made to wait for her visa.

In the evenings Destouches liked to read: 'He used to read aloud to me passages from Hegel, Fichte, Nietzsche, Schopenhauer', difficult authors for a twenty-year-old with no formal education. Céline had not yet started to write and his long-term ambition was still to become a doctor.

Many evenings the two young men did prowl the streets. Destouches was an adventurous youth – he liked the dockland pubs with their drifting population of seedy characters. But even more, he liked to pursue women: 'we went out in London, often around Soho and as we had an appetite for women we knew quite a lot of girls, English, French and many others'. They did not have much money but being French had its own advantages: 'the French pimps and their protégées were nice to us, always ready to buy us dinner'. Even better than brothels, Destouches liked music-halls. He visited them a lot, using his military medal to get in free. Geoffroy had a girlfriend who was a dancer and who introduced them to theatre-women: 'Louis was wild about dancers. He had a passion for dance.' This is the first mention of what was to become a lifelong enthusiasm. Céline did not care whether his young friends did classical ballet or striptease. He admired them for their sheer physical beauty. He was fascinated by the graceful sweep of an arm and by the strength of a leg. It was a sexual attraction and yet there were other elements: liking for the animal good health of the trained body and a genuine aesthetic pleasure. This love of pure beauty was fostered, ironically enough, in the popular variety shows of wartime London.

On 2 September 1915 Sergeant Destouches was officially declared unfit for military service. He went back to France. Over the next few years he turned his hand to anything in order to make a living. He took all kinds of jobs. He seemed to be drifting but he was still studying on his own. In 1916 he set out for Africa as a representative for the Sangha-Oubanghui company. He was sent to the Cameroons. Nothing is known of this trip except that it was unsuccessful.[47] Destouches fell ill and had to go to hospital with chronic enteritis. He returned to France, his head full of tam-tams and tropical jungles. Once more he had to look for a job. For a while he was secretary to the inventors' magazine *Eurêka* and did a translation from English of a scientific article.[48] He worked as an errand boy in an experimental school that was being started outside Paris.[49] These two incidents put together are the basis of the Courtial des Pereires episode in *Mort à crédit*. In reality neither job lasted for long. Destouches was repeating his pre-war experiences. But he was less shy now. He knew how to bluster and to persuade. With immense self-confidence he proposed himself for jobs – as a lecturer, a teacher, a propagandist.

One of his most daring pieces of bluff succeeded. As the war ended the Rockefeller Institute set up a group to fight tuberculosis.[50] Céline, seeing the announcement, applied for a job as a propagandist. He got it. He was part of a team that went around Brittany teaching the people how to fight T.B. by improving their hygiene standards. The job had its comic side and Céline calls it 'Charlie Chaplin' business.[51] As the project was run under the auspices of the American army, he used to dress up in the uniform of an officer in General Pershing's command. The other people in the team were stray eccentrics in need of a job. One of them, an artist, wore a smock and beret. No one had any clear idea what they should have been doing. Confronted with such weird creatures the Breton villagers 'stared at them wide-eyed'.[52] The Bretons understood little of what they were told – many of them did not even speak French. They were amazed to hear that their time-honoured custom of putting the well next to the cesspool might be bringing disease. The team had a simple routine: 'a documentary film that broke down every five seconds; speeches, always the same right down to the commas; handing out of tracts'.[53]

In Rétiers a young boy, Henri Mahé, who was to become Céline's friend, remembers seeing the tall, gangling Destouches wandering around the village in his American uniform. Behind him came hordes of curious children. In the evening the American officer showed magic-lantern slides of microbes to a horrified audience, which had never suspected that such creatures existed. Then came a harangue from Destouches. He screamed at the villagers to boil their milk and water before drinking. He frightened everyone so much that the parish priest came up. He asked whether his well might not be infected since it stood next to the cemetery. He brought some of his water to be analysed. 'What you're drinking isn't water, Father, it's concentrated meat juice,' bellowed the delighted Céline.[54]

Beneath the farce he was pleased with his job. It gave him contacts and intellectual status. In June 1919 he went to Bordeaux and passed the second part of the *baccalauréat* with the grade of 'good'.[55] At Rennes his work for the Rockefeller Institute had put him in touch with Monsieur Follet, the head of the medical faculty. He had also met Follet's daughter, Edith. On 11 August he and she were married at Quentin. Edith wore a white dress and veil, Destouches an impeccable dark suit with a white handkerchief sticking out from his top pocket. In the autumn he began his studies at Rennes University

The sarcastic Marcel Brochard puts it simply: 'Louis Destouches could only study medicine at Rennes by marrying Edith.'[56] Dr Follet was not just head of the medical faculty. He was a T.B. consultant with a lucrative practice, one of the leading citizens of Rennes and a rich man, 'very rich, the bugger', said his son-in-law.[57] He was able and willing to help Destouches. One year after entering the university Céline obtained degree certificates in physics, chemistry and natural sciences. As he was an ex-serviceman his period of study was shortened. He began medicine proper in 1920 and in three years had completed all the requirements for the degree except the thesis. The years of working on his own had borne fruit. He had become a doctor. There is no better example of the role of will-power in his life. 'I want to dominate,' he had said. Now he had done it. When he had left school the professions had seemed closed to him. While he was wandering around Soho, Monsieur Follet would have seemed a remote figure. Yet by work and a certain ruthlessness he had achieved his great ambition. Nothing can better illustrate his determination to survive and succeed. It will show itself time and again. He will battle through war and imprisonment, he will hold out against the contempt of the entire French nation. In his writer's vocation he will be equally strong. How, one might ask, could anyone who held such a pessimistic view of things go on writing long novels over a period of thirty years? The answer lies in Céline's tenacity. Despite critics' hostility and readers' neglect he never stops working.

The Rennes years were his first period of settled living. He had a profession, a home and a family. Edith was conventionally pretty and sensible. She had had a sheltered upbringing and her aspirations were ordinary. In 1920 she gave birth to a daughter. Colette Destouches was baptized in 'a baby's robe that had belonged to Napoleon's son', a present from Céline's mother.[58] Yet the medical student Destouches was the same man who had prowled around the London music-halls. He had not turned 'bourgeois'.*

People who knew him at Rennes did not think he was staid; quite the reverse. A fellow-student remembers him as 'a very attractive spirit, happy, mocking, interested in everything, with original ideas on all problems'.[59] He impressed his class-mates by his ability to hold forth on matters that had not yet been discussed. He was rebellious and delivered diatribes against the university authorities. Beneath the noisy façade there were glimpses of real emotion, of a sensitive man 'disappointed by the lack of human warmth'.[60] The shy, lonely adolescent had not disappeared, he had merely gone underground. Destouches did not mention the war or his wounds. He covered up his feelings with a welter of activity. He was attached to the Rockefeller Institute as a translator and occasional lecturer. He was corresponding with the famous physiologist Alexis Carrel, who had won the Nobel Prize for his work on tissue-grafts.[61] Carrel studied the way that grafts could survive outside the human body, a subject that appealed to Céline. Although only a student he was conducting some research of his own.[62] He was interested in the hibernation of silk-worms: he wondered whether they might in this way prolong their lives. He also examined a certain kind of sea-worm that takes on the colour of the algae in which it lives. Does it sacrifice its own identity? All these problems have to do, in one form or another, with death. There is little scientific value in Céline's curiously amateurish experiments. One cannot really imagine him doing the highly disciplined teamwork required by modern science. He was too much of a lone wolf. But his work bears witness to

---

* Poulet considers the Rennes years Céline's bourgeois period. Brochard stresses that Céline did not conform at Rennes. One may conclude that however little Céline conformed it was too much for him.

his inquiring spirit. He wanted to penetrate the secrets of the natural universe.

To the citizens of Rennes, Destouches was a striking figure – 'the foe of conformity in his manners, conversation and dress'.[63] He would stride boldly into a salon, wearing his hat over his ear like a cowboy. Without waiting to be asked, he would sit down, put his large feet up on a chair and start to talk. He dominated any group he was in. Brochard describes Céline's ascendancy over him: 'I was conquered, subjugated, bewitched by this unrivalled and already gigantic spirit.'[64] Certainly Céline dominated Edith. Her father, who had made it possible for his son-in-law to study medicine, did not interfere. It was recognized in Rennes that Céline must be allowed to go his own way.

Brochard stresses his gift for words: he was 'startlingly curious, versatile, scoffing, rude, inspired, irritable, a great spinner of yarns'.[65] A born actor, he could mimic his friends, change his accent, demolish an opponent. From the Rennes period on, all Céline's friends testify to this verbal magic. In conversation he would remain sullenly silent and then burst into passionate speech. He could talk about anything, the words dictating the content. As he went along he grew more and more excited. He was drawn into the spell he was casting over his audience. He would get angry or start to laugh, depending on his subject. Meanwhile the words continued to roll forth. This is the closest one can come to establishing a link between the man and the artist. At such moments Céline, carried away by language, entered the world of his imagination. By mimicry he created different characters, by his mockery he created comedy. He was not yet a writer, but in the Rennes drawing-rooms he was talking novels. Looking at it the other way around, his books may easily be seen as giant monologues. Not only do some of his creatures – Courtial, Sosthène – hold forth for pages on end; in general his novels are shaped by the torrent of language which spills over chapter endings, creates and discards characters and is itself the order and meaning of the work.

In 1923 Destouches began his doctoral thesis and went to work as a houseman in a Paris maternity hospital. There he studied under Professor Brindau, a specialist in obstetrics. The next year he completed his thesis, which was accepted by the University of Paris. He was now a professional man of good standing. He opened his surgery on the Place des Lices at Rennes. The future seemed bright and settled.

If his wife and father-in-law had read his thesis carefully they would have known he was no ordinary doctor. It is already a Célinian novel in miniature – angry and despairing. The historical Semmelweis was a brilliant hygienist who discovered that sterilization would kill germs and prevent infection. His contribution to medicine was immense and it stood, according to Céline, in direct proportion to the misery of his life. He searched for a truth which no one wished to hear and which finally destroyed him. Semmelweis is the first of Céline's many fictional selves. He is a more extreme version of his creator, made to incarnate tensions that Dr Destouches fought against and sometimes overcame.

The analogies between writer and hero abound. Like Céline, Semmelweis was brought up in a troubled world – the French Revolution and its aftermath. He had little taste for formal schooling and preferred the wisdom of the streets to the classroom. He had a deep love of music, which opened up for him a world more real than his physical surroundings. Like Céline he was an independent-minded scientist who fought and suffered for his beliefs and who made powerful enemies.

Semmelweis suffered at the hands of society. Klin, his superior at Vienna hospital, persecuted him because Semmelweis's ideas were right and they made his own seem stupid. The archaic structure of Metternich's Austria could not tolerate the impact of genius. Semmelweis tried to help destroy the old world in 1848, but reaction triumphed and he was disgraced. Yet his greatest foe was not society but himself. There is an integral connection between his ability and his downfall: the passion that led him to his discovery drove him to madness. His interest in medicine was not a rational matter but 'a penetrating lucidity, emotional like jealousy'.[66] His single-minded pursuit of truth damaged his health and reduced him to poverty. His end is worthy of *Voyage*: demented, he rushed into a dissection theatre, cut up a corpse, infected himself and died in agony. Céline's verdict sounds like the closing lines of a Greek chorus: 'Shame on the man who cannot choose the path that is appropriate to the destiny of our race.'[67]

To the university jury Destouches's thesis had no personal significance. It was his passport to prosperity, nothing more. For a while he did seem to settle down. He practised at Rennes, returning home in the evenings to his wife and child. But the calm was superficial, the restlessness remained. Brochard describes a conversation they had: 'I can see him still, showing me the pretty little fluted curtains of his surgery and telling me: "Out there, my friend, is freedom."'[68] In 1925 Céline fled. He abandoned his wife, his practice and Rennes. Edith divorced him and married a more suitable husband. Destouches resumed his wanderings. He left behind a rich father-in-law who would have assured him a comfortable life.

'My mad passion for independence made me shake free from that haven where I had only to sit back and let things come,' he states later.[69] The limits placed on him had not been great, but they had been too great. Monsieur Follet put up with his son-in-law's outbursts and his rapid changes of mood. Céline could not put up with Rennes. He made the same kind of decision he had made when he joined the army. He opted for danger over security.

His revolt was not a simple one. He did not believe that freedom led to happiness – the example of Semmelweis was there to prove the opposite. Young Frenchmen of the 1920s were imbued with the doctrines of André Gide. They listened to the siren song of revolt. 'Families, I hate you,' cried Gide. He taught his youthful readers to abandon home and church in order to discover themselves. The path of liberty led to undreamed-of wonders. Céline, child of the Passage, had no such illusions: Gide's doctrine was a game for the pampered children of the rich. In any case Céline was not looking for happiness but for his own brand of truth, which meant facing up to the worst. He left Rennes because it was a bad choice.

So far he was taking the same road as Semmelweis. But there was a difference. In his writings Céline blackens the world. His novels make no mention of the comfortable years at Rennes. The Klin of his thesis is a more malicious figure than Dr Follet. It is the same with himself. He was not following Semmelweis to the extremes of madness and destitution. The will to succeed asserted itself even as he was making his deliberately bad choice. On leaving Rennes he did not return to the jobs he had held before. He obtained a much sought-after post with the League of Nations. He got the job partly through his connections with the Rockefeller Institute, partly through his usual bluff and partly, strangely enough, through his father-in-law's influence. He was stationed at Geneva, but he was sent on medical missions all over the world. Versatile as ever, he became an expert on hygiene. He studied the social aspects of medicine, the links between disease and poverty. This work interested him more than his comfortable Rennes practice.

And it was now that he started to write. He began work on the play *L'Église*.

Perhaps it is unnecessary to ask why Céline started to write. The need to create was there: it showed itself in his conversations. Excitable, tormented by a too vivid imagination, he was always on the verge of entering his own nightmarish world. But there are two more specific reasons: the need to create beauty, which will be discussed later, and the need to pursue the truth which he felt to be near. By now his life was taking shape: a series of revolts, a belief that only the night-side of life counted, an exploration of what most people fled from or hid. With his writing he could probe further, as he was doing with his scientific experiments and his medicine. *Semmelweis* was there to point the way. Now he would turn to more personal forms of creation. He would give free rein to his agonized vision, confront it directly and, who knows, perhaps even banish it for a while.

The milieu of the League made a bad impression on him. It was his first exposure to a certain kind of modernity and he loathed it. 'Babel, number two', was his favourite word for the Geneva headquarters.[70] Later he summed up his views: 'you have to live for some time at the League to understand the ... "commissions", the emasculation by speeches, the flight to theory'.[71] To Destouches, brought up in the emotional hot-house of the Passage, rooted in lower-middle-class Paris, Geneva was abstract, hence unreal. In *L'Église* he mocks it as a muddle of international officials, multi-lingual meetings and involved planning. There is no place for individual humans and ordinary common-sense. He depicts a Balkan colonel, who has changed nationality three times since 1900, and a Balkan people, so confused by their changing frontiers that they cannot recognize their national army. To Céline nationality was something one felt: it was personal roots, the language one spoke, the flag one fought under. The League was a jumble of slogans – internationalism, progress, modernity – that had nothing to do with anything he could understand.

Presiding over this muddle was a demon-king – the Jew. Céline dated his anti-semitism from his days in Geneva. 'At the League I could see clearly that that was how things were wangled.'[72] This does not explain everything. Céline's childhood in the Passage during the post-Dreyfus years played a part and anyway anti-semitism is an attitude that is chosen, not imposed. But the Geneva years were an important influence. Céline saw the Jew as the rootless incarnation of modernity, who was at home nowhere except in the League. His superior made a deep impression on him: 'Dr Ludwig Rajchman – a Polish Jew – a man of lofty and splendid political culture and skill ... he is the Yudenzweck of *L'Église*.'[73] Yudenzweck is a grotesque, brilliant creature, who uses the complexities of the League to manipulate international affairs and advance the position of the Jews. In one scene he and his collaborators discuss how to start a war between two countries called Blagamore and Brame. Here again one must not fall into the trap of thinking Céline's writings are the direct expression of his experiences. He was much more at home with Rajchman than Bardamu is with Yudenzweck. But he did begin, while at Geneva, to blame the ills of the modern world on the Jew.

As yet his anti-semitism was fairly mild. This is not meant to excuse him but to make an important distinction. The Nazi persecution during World War Two has innoculated post-war Europe against anti-semitism. But in the France of the early nineteen-hundreds a mild anti-semitism was common – there were also more virulent brands, witness the Action Française. In literary circles, for example, the expression 'he writes like a Jew' was used to mean 'he writes badly'. Even before 1914 a contributor to the *Nouvelle Revue française*, Jean Blum, used to sign his articles with the name of Jean Florence. Had he not done so, he would have been published anyway. But this disposed of the problem. Anti-semitism grew in strength during the 1930s, partly because of the Stavisky affair, the influx of Jews from Eastern Europe and the controversial figure of Léon Blum, and chiefly because, as political difficulties increased, the need for a scapegoat became more intense. In this sense Céline was of his age: his anti-semitism built up over the next decade. But he went far beyond almost anyone else.

Destouches did not enjoy writing up his reports or socializing at League cocktail parties. All that was quite alien to him. He did like the missions he was sent on: in 1925 he went back to the Cameroons, which Britain and France were administering under a League mandate. He studied the methods being used to combat sleeping sickness and yellow fever.[74] The next year he made his first visit to the United States, a country that was to fascinate him.

He was sent to Detroit to study the health conditions of the Ford workers. It was his first glimpse of another form of modernity which he hated – American industrial life. Detroit was to Céline a new kind of hell and he describes it in a grimly ironic article. Despite its flat style, this is another personal piece.[75] He studies the way that Ford take on sick people, give them a small task and provide them with on-the-spot medical care. But his real aim is to describe a proletariat wandering hopelessly in a world of machines. 'Naturally all the down-and-outs of existence come to ask for a job at Ford's,' he begins. He tells how they are chosen: 'We saw the hiring-process: the candidates the management likes best are those who are the most down-and-out, physically and psychologically.' This is because they are the most loyal. Anyway, since the workers are required to perform only simple tasks, their state of health does not matter. Machines do the important work and men are reduced to serving them. They are not really human beings at all: 'The doctor ... confided to us that what they really wanted was chimpanzees.' Céline describes the numerous blind, sick, epileptic workers. He cites the case of a seventy-two-year-old man with hernia, who can do nothing but open and close a door. The employees work amidst the endless throbbing of machines: 'There is an infernal hubbub in almost all the workshops.' The management is invisible and serene. It looks down on its servants with 'immense indifference'.

Detroit's real significance was that it presented a model for Europe: 'There is not much chance that we will avoid this trend.' Céline watched horrified as the Ford factories unveiled to him a vision of what industrial man would become. It was an affront to his passionate, anarchical character. He examined every detail of the Detroit inferno. As he linked truth with misery, he exaggerated the workers' dehumanization. The medical man tried to cope with it – as will be discussed later; the observer of America concentrated on this modern kind of suffering. The Ford workers lived in 'a state of humility'. They were a truer representative of the human condition than French people, who were still hiding from industrial reality. 'Nothing that constitutes our pride exists over there,' Céline wrote later to Eugène Dabit.[76] He welcomed this, because man's pride prevented him from understanding his condition. On the Ford assembly-line men were stripped of conceit as of deceit.

America was more than a dehumanized society. Céline's picture was nuanced, even contradictory. On his 1926 trip he stayed in New York where he wandered around Broadway and Times Square. He picked on the commercialism of American life, the anonymity of its cities, the ruthlessness of its people. All this was conventional enough, the most common reaction of the European traveller. Céline was more unusual when he commented on American women. He was a great admirer of their 'feline quality':[77] their beauty and physical vigour. They were the highest form of the feminine beauty he had pursued since he was a child in his mother's shop. He noted their 'divine winged gait' and their 'prodigious legs'.[78] On the streets of New York he stopped and wondered as crowds of goddesses flocked past him. What was the secret American women possessed? It was 'the appeal of youth (even extreme youth – healthy and joyous) that was why I liked America so much'.[79] American girls were free – from ugliness and decay. As the representatives of a young and energetic country, they were the most vigorously human women Céline had known. They strode among the crippled proletariat, across the dreadful cities. Here again Céline's special slant is evident. He has turned America into his imaginary kingdom – beautiful and hopeless.

In 1928 he left the League. He was bored with the Geneva circus and he returned to Paris. He moved to Clichy, one of the northern suburbs to which the Parisian working class had been migrating for the previous half-century. Driven out of the city by Baron Haussmann, they had taken over the area that stretches above Montmartre. Quite different from central Paris, this conglomeration of industrial communities became, in Céline's words, 'a doormat thrown before the town where everyone wipes his feet'.[80] Dr Destouches was choosing his patients among the poor. He found a flat on the rue d'Alsace which 'stretches on out monotonously'.[81] He lived at number 36 and on the door was a blue plaque with the inscription 'Doctor Louis Destouches – General Practice – Pediatrics – First Floor, left'. Inside, the flat was ordinary enough except for the African masks that hung on the wall and the wooden statue of an African god in the corner. This was enough to make the neighbours curious. One of them was Jeanne Carayon who fell ill one evening and had Dr Destouches come to visit her: 'He is handsome. Grey eyes, sailors' eyes ... His rapid, clever gestures contrast with his vigorous frame, they show the same sensibility as his look and voice.'[82] Jeanne was to become a friend and, as she worked as a proof-reader, she would help with the final drafts of *Voyage*.

Dr Destouches's companion was even more intriguing: 'a young woman who smiles when you meet her – tall, very thin with strong legs'.[83] This was Elisabeth Craig, the 'empress'[84] whom Céline had met in Geneva and who was to live with him for the next few years. She was an American and a dancer, so she personified his ideal of beauty. Marcel Brochard remembers her as 'tall, beautiful, statuesque'[85] and Henri Mahé, another connoisseur, has left a vivid description of her: 'Big, cobalt-green eyes ... a delicate little nose, a sensual, rectangular mouth ... long reddish-gold hair falling in ringlets on her shoulders ... Small breasts, firm and arrogant'. Like Céline, Mahé was fascinated by her gait: 'She does not walk, she glides, very upright.'[86] Elisabeth was no intellectual. A letter she wrote to Mahé shows that her French was fairly fluent but incorrect. That did not matter. Céline was never interested in intellectual women. Anyway he felt that a dancer's movements expressed more than other humans could say or write. Temperamentally Elisabeth was high-spirited, an independent American girl enjoying Paris life. She was often away on tour and, when she returned, there were uproarious evenings for the African god to behold. The neighbours asked shocked questions. 'I'm sure they dance naked,' said the butcher's wife, outraged.[87] Elisabeth was sexually uninhibited and generous with her favours. She was willing to oblige 'old male friends and young girl friends if it amuses Louis ... it amuses him often'.[88] Nor was she jealous for she introduced him to her dancer friends. She flattered his complicated sexual needs. Céline enjoyed her instinctive liveliness which was the antithesis of his moodiness. He liked her sense of humour and described it as 'Molièresque'.[89] Beyond all sexual game-playing, he loved her: 'I would never have been anything without her,' he said later.[90] Molly in *Voyage* owes something to her but Céline cared more for Elisabeth than Bardamu does for Molly. And in the early years they were happy together.

Clichy suited Dr Destouches well, but he had no talent for private practice. He disliked making up his bills and sending them out. In 1931 he went to work at the municipal clinic where he was paid a salary by the town council. He left his flat on the rue d'Alsace – the bugs were too bad, says Jeanne Carayon[91] – and moved to Montmartre. He found a place to live on the rue Lepic and travelled to Clichy each day. He was very busy. In the mornings he went down to Montparnasse where he worked with a chemist friend, Robert Galliez. He made up prescriptions and invented new medicines with strange names like Kidoline and

Basdowine.[92] He was doing this work chiefly to make money. But it was another kind of amateurish scientific research, like his Rennes experiments. In the evenings he went to the clinic and took turns with the other doctors tending the factory workers. He was now bringing *Voyage* to an end. He worked on it in the afternoons and frequently late at night. Elisabeth was still living with him and he had numerous friends who made claims on his time.

Who was he really, this strange Destouches-Céline? He was the brooding pessimist, nursing his head-wound, at home amidst Clichy's grim poverty. This was the man who shocked Jeanne Carayon by telling her that it was only natural to think every day about suicide.[93] But there was the other side of the coin. The Destouches whom Mahé knew was a fine athlete who loved to tramp the Paris streets and go sailing on the Seine. He had many friends from all walks of life: painters like Gen Paul, writers like Marcel Aymé, an old doctor, Dr Camus; yet he remained deeply lonely. His conversation continued to be bawdy and brilliant, ranging from ancient history to medical obscenities; but he spent long hours toiling away alone on *Voyage*. He pursued long-legged dancers in the back-stage of variety shows and he spent entranced evenings at the ballet. He could not live without women, even though he could not take them completely seriously. Then there was the man of extreme sensibility who hid behind the noisy façade, afraid to show himself. This was the Destouches who befriended the stranded German girl Erika Irrgang and who devoted himself to his poorest patients.

So many masks for one man. Each was a way of coping with the nightmare which by now he carried around with him. With every one of his friends he was different: riotously bohemian with Henri Mahé, talking over old army days with Dr Camus. In this chameleon quality – as in his ability to mimic – lies the artist's talent. He divided himself up: now he was as cynical as Robinson, now as spellbindingly confident as Courtial. As he played out his different roles he realized that they were not enough. They left too much time for loneliness. There was always a moment when he had to stop talking, leave the clinic, push Elisabeth away. He would go one step further – into the novelist's world. There he would create fresh selves: soldiers who were completely pacifist, doctors who could not, for one moment, forget their patients' sufferings. His friends too would be exactly as he wanted them – Molly less bothersome than Elisabeth, the Jules of *Féerie* more evil than Gen Paul. Their roles, like his, would be deeper and richer.[94]

In the meantime he went on living. In some ways he was still the child of his parents. He lived in the style of the Passage. The rue Lepic, which winds its way around Montmartre hill, was an unpretentious street and many of Céline's neighbours were the same lower-middle-class people he had grown up with.* His three-room flat – living-room, small study, bedroom with kitchen and bath – was done out simply: 'Middle-class furnishings in the style of a country doctor ... Rustic table, Breton cupboards, shining and waxed, stylish armchairs, large sofa'.[95] A later visitor notes 'no trace of artistic or intellectual life'.[96] Destouches disliked both elegance and artistic pretension. His tastes were simple: he ate sparingly and drank no alcohol. When he dined out he went to the cheap restaurants of the neighbourhood, often to the 'tabac' on the Place Pigalle. He wore suits that were bought to last and he rode around on a motorcycle, complete with goggles. Only a Degas picture of dancers that hung on the wall hinted that he was different from his parents.

Each workday he went off to his clinic – the 'witches' cauldron', to which patients of all kinds found their way.[97] Dr Destouches listened to them all. He let them tell their weird tales, harangued them and helped them. *Clochards* came in and he prescribed for them a liquid diet of water. Workers sought him out because Dr Destouches was good about recommending sick-leave with pay. There were stranger cases like the man, so Céline told Mahé with gales of laughter, who lived on a diet of roquefort cheese and whose face had turned yellow with little blue spots. Then there were innumerable girls who came in wanting abortions, and one girl whose mother brought her in, so that the kind

---

* It might be useful to point out that Montmartre, despite its reputation, has never been solely a bohemian neighbourhood. The artists, who migrated there, came because it was cheap. It was cheap because it was poor. At the time of the Commune it was a staunchly working-class and left-wing area. It grew as a night-club centre when rich people from other parts of Paris came 'slumming' to the Moulin Rouge. In this century Montmartre grew gradually more prosperous. By 1930 it had acquired a varied population: a preponderance of working-class and lower-middle-class people, a few of the very rich, large numbers of night-club entertainers and street-girls and a smaller number of artists. Céline drew on all segments of this population. He had a strong sense of 'belonging' to Montmartre. But so did many other people who lived there.

doctor would introduce her to some 'nice men'. Dr Destouches helped as best he could. He did take some girls out of the factory and sent them to make an easier living posing for Mahé. A colleague attests that Céline lavished time on his patients with no thought of personal gain.[98]

What did medicine mean to him? He had a high concept of his profession and he always referred to himself as a doctor first and a writer second. He studied many facets of his subject: he had begun with T.B., he moved to hygiene, he specialized in pediatrics. He read the medical journals and kept up with research, although he was more interested in looking after patients. On a personal level he was proud of his medical diploma because it symbolized his triumph over obstacles. But, as he later told an interviewer, his main interest was in easing pain.[99]

Céline defines medicine in an unpublished preface to *Semmelweis*: it is 'perhaps the only kind of really human thought in the world'.[100] This is because the doctor confronts the patient when 'happiness, that absurd, arrogant trust in life, gives way to truth'. The sick person must face the essential fact of human life: that he must die. This is the moment the doctor sees. Naturally the patient does not wish to hear what the doctor tells him. He wants to be restored to health and to the illusion of happiness. He responds to the doctor's diagnosis with 'ingratitude and insolence'. The doctor must expect to be hated.

What is left to him is pity. In *Semmelweis* Céline defines medicine as 'a pity that is more active than others'.[101] It is informed by knowledge and results in deeds. Unlike most people the doctor is not blindly optimistic. He knows that health is a fragile thing and that the patient will soon die anyway. But he has specialized knowledge that enables him to relieve pain. While others stand around uselessly he can help. Dr Destouches's methods reflected his temperament: he used simple techniques and hoped for small gains. 'Drink no alcohol, exercise regularly,' he told his Clichy patients. He expected no miraculous solutions, no wonder drugs to cure cancer. He believed in few drugs except morphine, the painkiller that allows a man to die in slightly less agony. On the other hand he had no patience with people who were not seriously ill. He was never interested in the sicknesses of the rich. Not for him the bedside manner and kind ear lent to imaginary complaints. He preferred the witches' cauldron.

All this implies that he was extremely sensitive to pain. He had defences in his professional etiquette and in his obscene jokes. But he suffered with his patients. He had, after all, seen hospitals from both sides: as wounded and healer. This may also help to explain his pacifism. Since there was already so much pain in the world, why add to it?

When he wrote about hygiene he drew on his experiences. But there is an important difference: not only does he blacken the picture, he dehumanizes it. A piece he wrote about the social services reveals this.[102] He insists that his Detroit description of workers slaving in the factory, living in abject poverty and having to work while ill, is the only correct view. In the name of truth he cuts through utopian projects of social reform. Nothing will be done to improve wages or housing, so it is useless to suggest medical schemes which presuppose a well-fed, well-housed proletariat. It is foolish to deal with the workers as if they were free, when they are chained to the assembly-line. 'Our humanitarianism ... is out-of-date and harmful' and it causes only 'bankruptcies and confusions'. Dr Destouches proposes a harsh solution. He insists that the problem must be considered 'solely from the point of view of work', without the pretence that anything will be done to alter the industrial system. Workers must be kept at the factory as long as possible, so that they can earn money. Doctors should not let them linger at home on minute pensions, because their housing is insanitary and they will waste their money in cafés. The doctor's aim should be to make them work and tend them at the factory. This, according to Céline, would be the 'real, experimental beginning of a genuine, preventive medicine'. The doctor should go into the factory and have 'permanent contact with the people'.

Some of this is sensible. The notion that a doctor should understand his patients' social background is more widely accepted today than in 1930. Most of Céline's argument is unconvincing. One could easily maintain that the gloomy picture he paints is incorrect and that social conditions could be and have been improved. But that too begs the question of what Céline is doing. Once he puts pen to paper he identifies the worst with the truest. Here he has gone a step further and started to propose solutions. In order to do this he has to think in abstractions. The kindly Dr Destouches becomes 'the doctor', the Clichy sick 'the patient'. But the saving grace of Céline's novels is that they deal with the concrete. Bardamu is not just a medical man but a bundle of emotions; Bébert, his patient, is a child whom he sees on the street. *Voyage* is full of feeling, of pain and of pity. Bardamu could not possibly write this piece on the social services. He could not join in a scheme which presupposes a disease-ridden working class, huddling in factory corners. Céline's pessimism has become brutal as well as dogmatic.

He is already writing as a pamphleteer. In *Bagatelles* a similar dehumanization takes place. No longer will the main actors be Ferdinand Destouches and his Jewish friend Jacques Deval. They will be abstract entities – the anti-semite and the Jew. So any solution, even a final solution, will be possible. One might approach the problem the other way around. Why does Céline feel the need to suggest solutions when he denies in his novels that there are any? The answer is that the pain becomes two great, the nightmare too bad to be tolerated. He could not live with the Detroit conveyor-belt or with a Europe at war. Any escape was good enough. If it was a bad escape, then so much the better. Already by 1930 the pamphleteer was present within Destouches-Céline, alongside the author of *Voyage*.

In his life he was much more humane. Erika Irrgang remembers that, when she was staying with him on the rue Lepic, he would wander through the Montmartre streets late at night: 'He talked to old drunkards and pale prostitutes, he gave an entry ticket for one of the municipal shelters to some poor devil whose lungs were ravaged.'[103] Since his war-wound Destouches did not sleep well. So he went out to see the other side of Montmartre – the suffering that lay behind the tawdry glamour of the Moulin Rouge. This was a kind of travel – comparable to the journey to the United States. Destouches's return to Paris did not mean that he wanted to settle down. He was still looking for a 'life full of incident'. He sought out the people of Clichy and made them his companions. He used to walk back from his surgery with Vivette, a lively young girl who would tell him all the dramas of her love-life. She had a woman-lover who was trying to murder her husband so that she could live with Vivette. In the meantime Vivette carried the red flag in the Communist Party demonstrations, and battled heroically with the police when they tried to take it from her.[104] Such stories delighted Céline. He was fascinated by the working class: by its wit, slang, the wisdom of the streets. He was deliberately slumming. He chose friends of whom his mother and the Passage would not have approved. Montmartre alcoholics and Communist Party standard-bearers did not count as respectable people. This was precisely why Céline liked them:

they wore no masks. They were closer to the human condition as it really was.[105]

Céline did not merely observe people – although the urge to observe was strong in him. He helped too. He had a long string of protégés, who had to be assisted in one manner or another. There was Marie Hémon, the little Breton dressmaker. Céline persuaded Elisabeth and her friends to have Marie make their clothes. There was the male dance-couple the Harger-Howell: Mahé was supposed to go around and get them some publicity. Then there was the accordion player Marceau Verschuren, whom Céline thought had great talent, but who needed to be introduced to theatre managers. The list of such people is endless. They bear witness to Céline's kindness. Convinced that life was desperately hard, he tried to lighten the burden. In his letters he is full of schemes, calling on one friend to help another. Gen Paul was supposed to encourage people to buy Mahé's paintings, Robert Galliez was supposed to find a chauffeur's job for a Clichy protégé who could no longer work in the factory.

His role as Benedictine monk – albeit of a very human kind – is seen in his friendship with Erika Irrgang. She was a young German girl who came to Paris to study and to work. In the spring of 1932 she had spent all her money and had no job. She was wandering in a daze of hunger around the Place des Tertres, when Céline saw her. He took hold of her, put her into a taxi and drove her straight to a restaurant, where she devoured a large plate of macaroni and ham. Her first impression of him was of 'a gentle face which inspired confidence in me at once'.[106] After she had eaten he took her back to the rue Lepic, where she fell asleep. She stayed with him for some weeks. He made her eat regularly at the Pigalle 'tabac', drink lots of milk and go for walks. She considered him 'the most extraordinary man I had met'.[107] Sometimes he talked to her about *Voyage*, which was almost finished. He never dwelt on it for long and she had no idea it was such an important book. Their relationship was a blend of friendship, father–daughter protectiveness and sexual attraction. It contained what she calls 'a certain erotic value'.[108] Céline enjoyed her young girl's appeal and he was glad that the affair went no further. When she returned to Germany he continued for four years to write her long letters full of parental – and sometimes not so parental – advice.

'The only thing that keeps us alive is the affection of beings and objects,' he wrote to her.[109] He himself was both affectionate and easily hurt. His father's death in 1932 hit him hard: 'My father is dead. I did not send for you. I like to reduce sadness to a minimum. It is not easy. I am at an age where nothing can be forgotten,' he wrote to Mahé.[110] The impression of a man struggling with pain is striking. Céline was an alarmist who saw mountains behind every molehill. 'I am leaving for Rennes, my daughter is ill' – at each of Colette's childhood sicknesses he would drop everything and fly to her help.[111] Nervous depression was never far away. 'Look closely at the cemetery. It contains everything you can say or feel,' he once observed.[112] Yet he had a virile, mocking strength that sustained him. It is described eloquently by Henri Mahé.

Mahé was a fellow Breton, a lover of ships who lived on a houseboat called the *Enez Glaz*, which he kept on the Paris *quais*. Periodically the police would come along to tell him he was breaking one of the innumerable regulations and he would move his boat to another spot. Mahé was a painter, most famous for his huge erotic murals. His patron saint was Toulouse-Lautrec and he had a similar knowledge of Parisian night-life. His best-known work was a series of erotic paintings he had done for a rather intimate house – 31, Cité d'Antin. He produced a book of sketches representing these paintings and Céline wrote a preface for it, but it never appeared. Talented, talkative and bohemian, Mahé possessed innumerable friends from all walks of life, one of them being the future Resistance hero Colonel Rémy. As his work involved doing nightclub murals he used to sit up most of the night, absorbing the atmosphere and waiting to talk business with the owners. At daybreak they would count their takings, discuss the paintings they wanted and leave him to go home to bed exhausted. Such evenings left Mahé with a wealth of experience; he knew the proprietors of music-halls, the dancers in variety shows, the pimps and the prostitutes. His friendship with Céline was many-sided. He lectured Céline on painting and confirmed him in his love of Breughel and Goya. They went sailing together and held uproarious parties on Mahé's boat. Sometimes he went up to the Clichy clinic, put on a white coat to look like an orderly and listened while Dr Destouches harangued his patients. Then the two would walk back to Montmartre, sometimes with Vivette, while Céline shouted out the verses of his ballad 'Long live the harlot Katinka'.

They had other friends, like Dr Camus an admirer of writers and artists who succeeded in getting Mahé declared unfit for military service. Then there was painter Gen Paul, a real Montmartre bohemian who lived in the shadow of the Sacré-Coeur. Paul was a restless creature with a passion for Spain and for sunshine. Whenever he sold a painting, he would dash off to the Pyrenees, abandoning his usual haunts and friends. He had lost a leg in the First World War but it did not dampen his aggressive spirit. He had a flair 'for attracting outlaws' and, when the Spanish Civil War came, his flat was bursting with Republican sympathizers.[113] At other times Paul was often drunk and always noisy. Céline had friends of a different kind, who were not artists. He liked the local people – the garage-mechanics and café-owners. He would sit with them for hours on end, talking in *argot* and commenting on girls who passed in the street. Some of his writer-acquaintances were surprised at his taste for this company. Perhaps Céline found relief in such mindlessness. Certainly a need for male friendship and gossip was an important part of his character. Not for nothing has he been called the writer of the P.M.U.* He used the term Mafia to describe his band of followers.[114] They used to prowl around Montmartre in a gang. Often they went to the cinema, for Céline was a keen film-fan who could watch the same picture through twice without getting bored. Sometimes he found his way to the Lapin agile, which Picasso had made famous. The proprietor Max Revol was an old friend and they would sit around until late telling stories.[115] And then, often, there were women.

With Céline one always comes back to women, and especially to dancers. Their names run through Mahé's book: Dréna, Mona, Karen ... When Elisabeth was on tour Céline chose his friends among the Clichy girls, the models who posed for Mahé and especially those he found backstage in the Paris theatres. He explored different nationalities: Danish, English, American. 'I have lived by Priapus all my life, either as a pimp or as a patron and always for fun,' he writes later.[116] A woman's body was a source of unfailing delight to him. Most of all he liked young girls. He describes Margaret Severn, whom he was bringing

* The *Pari Mutuel Urbain* is the French betting system run by the cafés (*bureaux de tabac*). It is a pursuit for males and goes together with local gossip and conversations about sport. Maurice Clavel refers to Céline as the writer of the P.M.U. in *Arts*, 12.7.1961. Robert Poulet laughs about Céline's liking for this form of café-life. It is a trait that Céline shared with Marcel Aymé. But Aymé liked to drink, Céline did not.

to pose for Mahé: 'She is incredibly sensitive ... but you should see her thighs and buttocks.'[117] Of another friend he wrote: 'She knows good stories. She is eighteen now. She only puts out for hard cash.'[118] Mahé and Céline used a maritime jargon to describe women: a very young girl was a 'skiff', an adolescent a 'schooner' and a girl over twenty a 'three-master'![119] To Mahé's boat came floods of young girls, willing and eager in sexual matters, who drifted on to other towns and other dance troupes. There was Mona, a 'melancholic beauty'[120] from New York, who had an act in which she balanced by one hand on the top of a walking stick. There was Dréna, a striptease artist, who had the sinister and surely unfounded reputation of having been Al Capone's girlfriend. Mahé exaggerates his stories, exaggeration being part of the sexual game.

What precisely was Céline's interest? Certainly he enjoyed physical love, but he did not want too much of it. His comparison of himself with a pimp is intriguing. The pimp is the girl's protector. She is at his disposal, but he does not have to satisfy her. He looks on while the customer makes love to her. One remembers that Céline liked to watch Elisabeth play with her girlfriends. A remark he made about himself later throws light on this: 'A voyeur certainly and an enthusiastic consumer a little bit.' He is more direct: 'I do not consume much, alas, concentrated as I am on my terrible work ... I have always liked women to be beautiful and lesbian – very nice to look at and not wearing me out with their sexual demands.'[121]

It is clear that he found a woman a burden. Again and again he protests that he does not believe in love: 'I have never taken seriously all the everlasting nonsense, pantomimes, eyes to the heavens.'[122] One thinks that the gentleman doth protest too much. Love was a danger. It threatened his freedom and left him – he who had such a low opinion of human nature – vulnerable to another person. Retrospectively this throws light on his marriage. For a 'voyeur' there could be no greater horror than the marriage-bed. It may have been this, rather than a rejection of Edith's bourgeois world, that caused him to leave her. This explains too why Elisabeth, whom he was really tempted to love, could be a threat and why he was not displeased at her long absences. It was easier to have short-lived affairs with girls who would soon be gone. The friendship he showed Erika Irrgang was easy too. It acted as a barrier against greater intimacy. None of this was so clear-cut in

Céline's mind. He needed women to protect him against loneliness and he loved Elisabeth – at least for a time and in his own way. But love over a long period was another matter. He was not sure that he wanted or could give it.

In any case it was a barrier to his main passion: enjoyment of female beauty. He defines physical love in a way that excludes the woman: it is 'a delirium (copulation is a delirium)'.[123] No mention of a moment of contact between two people. It is an outbreak of ecstasy for the man and, as such, it is not really different from the contemplation of women. The line of a dancer's leg was as enchanting as the woman herself. In any case the dancer remained on the stage, quite separate from the man who watched her. Céline's passion was at least as much aesthetic as sexual – Bardamu will go much further down this road – and women were glimpses of a beauty he dreamed of.

This is the crux of the matter, because it leads to Céline the writer. One does not wish to stress the abnormality of Dr Destouches's sex-life. By most standards it was normal enough. He was married twice, fathered a child, loved at least once and had a string of short affairs. What was unusual about that? Certainly a psychoanalyst might start talking about emotional instability, inability to form lasting relationships, and the like. One might just as easily say that Céline's eager response to pretty girls and the kindness he showed them were healthy, life-giving traits.[124] Either way the reader of *Voyage* focusses on the point where the sexual interest became aesthetic.

Céline said repeatedly that there was a close connection between the two. He talked about writing in sexual terms: 'you need more brutality than you have, more sexual boldness, if I may say so. Because sex is at the basis of all these things', such is his advice to a would-be authoress.[125] But the two do not go happily together. The energy that goes into sexual love is taken from literature and the enjoyment of women is not compatible with the task of creating. Baudelaire had put it succinctly: 'The more man cultivates the arts, the fewer erections he gets.'[126] By the time Céline was writing *Voyage* the flush of youth had passed. His work as an artist was starting to replace everything else. Around 1930 he sent a postcard to Marcel Brochard: 'The "dreadful" age is here.' Brochard understood: 'At thirty-six the "dreadful" age! Impotence? The result of the evenings in the rue Lepic where after the frugal meal at old Maria's – with only water to drink – Louis settled down to write.'[127] No claim should be made that Céline was physically impotent, either now or later. But the sexual urge went into creating characters.

What then of Elisabeth? As Céline worked she sat in the other room alone. Not surprisingly she could not stand the neglect. She went off to America for a long stay. The love-affair began to break up. This was the price of *Voyage*. Yet she was playing an important part in its creation. The beauty that she displayed so generously was a spur to Céline. One is reminded of Proust's Bergotte who wanted to pay pretty girls to sit around him, so that they would inspire him to write better. This is the secret of Céline's endless adventures with dancers. His novels set out to reproduce the beauty of their gestures. Not that his female characters are always beautiful, much less loving. Quite the contrary. The enchantment lies in the creation itself: the rhythms of his sentences retrace the movements of dance; one of his books, *Normance*, has the very structure of dance. The distance that lies between the London music-halls and the writing of *Voyage* is not as great as it seems.

When Denoël came to tell him that *Voyage* was a great novel Destouches was a mature man. His writing career was starting, but his formative years lay behind him. The next two decades would be hectic and he would take major stands in literature and politics. But his character was already shaped. The man who, in the late 1930s, deliberately destroyed his novelist's career and exposed himself to danger, had done so before when he left Rennes. Conversely, the Destouches who saved himself in 1944 was showing the flair for survival he had shown in his various jobs before and after 1914. Many things repeat themselves. He returned to the United States for another important visit. He volunteered for the Second World War as he had done for the First. He remained in the literary world of Paris the troublemaker he had been at Rennes. His women friends change their names but not their profession. Behind his erratic switches of direction lay the quest for his own kind of truth. He did not always succeed in finding it: he fell into the crime of anti-semitism. In his novels he succeeded better. Unlike his creator, Bardamu never flinches from a truth he knows to be tragic.

[2]

Voyage au bout de la nuit

Voyage begins in Flanders where Bardamu is a reluctant soldier who seeks refuge in hospitals and lunatic asylums. Later he goes to Africa to discover a colonial system that pillages the blacks without benefiting the whites. He flees again: to the skyscrapers of New York, loneliest of cities, and to Detroit where cars pour off the assembly-line in endless, pointless streams. America, despite its new forms of horror, is not the end of the night. Bardamu returns to Paris and becomes a doctor at Rancy. Squalid and poverty-stricken, Rancy is populated by murderers, abortionists and wife-beaters. It is excellent terrain for Bardamu and his mysterious friend Robinson to study human depravity. Then Bardamu runs away to another lunatic asylum, while Robinson murders an old woman and is himself murdered. Bardamu is left gazing at the boats on the Seine: they carry off all life into the night of death.

This résumé hints at *Voyage*'s agony but not at its complexity. Céline's novel is rich in landscapes that range from the sunbaked, malaria-ridden colony of Fort-Gono to Wall Street, shrine to the god of the dollar. It has a cast of eccentric minor characters: the obsessively greedy manager of the rubber company, the pornography specialist, the head of a lunatic asylum who goes the way of his patients. The restless Bardamu seeks out the strangest people and societies, as he strives to understand life. Even more important, *Voyage* is a fertile book that contains in embryo the themes of Céline's later writing. The problem of madness, touched on in the closing pages, is a central theme of *Mort à crédit*, which is told by a narrator who suffers from fits of madness. Bardamu raises questions of language that are the main preoccupation of *Féerie pour une autre fois*. Other matters like the role of the narrator and the shifting levels of reality are probed more deeply in the later novels. These questions will not be analysed in detail in this chapter. In discussing *Mort à crédit* and *Guignol's Band* one will refer constantly back to *Voyage*.

In other ways Céline's first novel draws a picture of life that he never changes. His particular brand of pessimism – his view of the world as dominated by triumphant evil – is the same in his last novel as in his first. His vision of human beings as hateful puppets pulled by an invisible hand remains unaltered. His gloomy treatment of sex is no different in *Mort à crédit* or *Guignol's Band*: men and women destroy one another in what ought to be their most intimate moments. And Bardamu's quest is repeated, although with variations, by all Céline's narrators who are determined, like him, to uncover the worst. In this chapter *Voyage* will be discussed as the foundation-stone of Céline's work. Stress will be laid on the features that do not change. What is the particular agony that the Céline character – and reader – must face?

Céline's art aims at turning life into a series of random catastrophes. *Voyage* has no preamble to explain why Bardamu went to fight. If Céline had given the historical causes of the war, or if he had traced the reasons Bardamu might have had for joining up, the battles would have seemed logical. Instead Bardamu starts out with 'It all began just like that'. In the middle of a café conversation he rushes off to join the army. When he travels he has no clear goal. He leaves for Africa because he has some idea that he can make his fortune; he is carried off to America on a galley-ship. Céline omits explanations and emphasizes that Bardamu is acting more or less at random. When he returns to France he is not re-establishing an order in his existence – 'You pick up the thread of your sticky, precarious life where you left it straggling behind you,' he says. The other characters appear, display their eccentricities and vanish. What happens to Lola when Bardamu leaves New York? Does Baryton continue to travel around Europe speaking English to everyone he meets? Neither the reader nor Bardamu knows: 'everything was . . . a matter of chance', we are told. Céline's tale has no neat conclusion: Robinson has just died, Bardamu will have to go on living. As far as one knows, he will continue on his 'sticky, precarious' way.

By this technique Céline destroys cause and effect. The different episodes of the book have no internal logic. The war is fought in a wasteland with neither conquerors nor conquered. The French soldiers, who do not dislike the Germans, loathe their own officers. There is no strategy: the men are sent out into the dark and told to look for their units, which they usually cannot find. 'The war, in fact, was everything that one didn't understand,' concludes Bardamu. When he goes to Africa he finds the colonial administration dedicated to tasks of stunning futility. The Fort-Gono engineer builds miles of road that no one uses and that are swallowed up by the jungle. At Topo, Alcide's militia, which is training with non-existent weapons for battle with a non-existent enemy, capers in 'a pattern of intricate and prodigiously futile movement'. These are not isolated examples. The whole cruel enterprise of colonialism is irrational, because the whites suffer as much as the blacks. The whites are devoured by insects and racked by disease, but they toil away. The 'natives after all have to be bludgeoned into doing their job – they've still got that much self-respect. Whereas the whites carry on on their own.' The colonial system, like the war and the Detroit assembly-line, knows no logic.

The supremely irrational fact of life is death. It is everywhere in *Voyage*: 'Behind all music we ought to try and catch that noiseless tone that's made for us, the melody of death.' The book begins with the Flanders' slaughter and ends with Robinson's murder. On the way countless people have died in Africa, Bébert has been struck down by typhoid and Madame Henrouille has been killed. None of the characters – except perhaps Robinson – is ready to die. They are obliterated casually and meaninglessly. 'The truth of this world is to die,' says Bardamu. As he treks across continents, this is the most important piece of wisdom he acquires.

Death is ugly as well as arbitrary. It reduces man to an animal screaming with pain. The soldiers of Bardamu's regiment are slaughtered like pigs while their blood runs out in pools sticky as jam. Céline likes to pile up gruesome details: Robinson's captain dies 'holding himself and spitting ... pissing blood'. He suffers no more than Robinson who dies horribly, his face blue, his heart broken by a huge haemorrhage. Sometimes death comes in a grotesque form: Madame Henrouille tumbles down the steps of the crypt and falls among the mummies that have lain there for centuries. In *Voyage* there are no famous last words, dignified mourners and graveside eulogies. Such things would lighten the burden. Céline stresses that death has absolute dominion.

Two examples show how he does this: the colonel and Bébert. The colonel is a hero who writes out orders for his men, while German bullets whizz around his head. He believes in the conventional values of war: gallant officers, faithful soldiers, medals for patriotism. In the reversal of values that takes place in *Voyage* such heroism is stupid. It prevents the colonel from understanding the only truth of life. Bardamu notes that 'like a dog, he had no idea of death'. The colonel is worse than an animal because he stands there 'adoring his own madness (which no dog does)'. He is committing the sin of hubris by displaying his contempt for death. When the messenger arrives he is angry with him for his cowardice. When he hears that the quartermaster has been killed, his only concern is for the bread supply. He is sure that death cannot touch him. Fate strikes quickly. It does not bother to come in the form of an enemy soldier: the anonymous shell is sufficient. This is how the colonel dies:

As for the colonel I didn't have any grudge against him. Still he was dead too. For a moment I couldn't see him. He had been tossed onto the bank, the explosion had stretched him out on his side and thrown him right into the messenger's arms – he had had it too. They were locked in an embrace for now and always, but the messenger had no head, only an opening above his neck with blood in it, that was swishing around like jam in a pot. The colonel's stomach was wide open, his face was twisted into an ugly grimace. That must really have hurt when it came. Tough luck for him. If he had run away when the shooting started it wouldn't have happened.

The description is casually horrible. Now the colonel is as insignificant as he had been glorious. Human aspirations are no more than arrogant fictions to be shattered by death.

Bébert commits no crime of vanity. He is a child who dies of a disease he cannot understand. Here Céline emphasizes that man can in no way resist death. From the moment Bébert is born in Rancy, he is in death's grip. He is an orphan, he is so sickly he looks like an 'emaciated monkey' and his aunt takes him for walks to the local cemetery. He learns quickly about Rancy's evils. He knows that at night many a man is found with his 'throat slit across by a razor'. Small wonder that Bébert falls ill and struggles weakly against the typhoid germs. The focus switches to the people around him. At first his aunt and her neighbours are full of suggestions for remedies. Nothing works and gradually they fall silent. Dr Bardamu enters the fray and uses all his skill, but 'nothing that I tried was any good – baths, serums, dry diet, injections ... Do what I might my efforts were in vain.' He turns to the scientist Parapine, the world-famous authority on typhoid. Parapine's science is useless: 'Amidst so many unstable theories, so much contradictory data, the reasonable thing, when it comes down to it, is to make no definite choice.' Science is impossible in a world without cause and effect. Each of Parapine's theories is as good as the others, none can explain what typhoid really is. The disease lies beyond human comprehension. Parapine gives up, Bardamu leaves him and Bébert dies. One last defeat is in store. Bardamu picks up a copy of Montaigne and reads how the essayist's son dies. To console his wife, Montaigne sends her a letter by Plutarch advocating stoicism in the face of calamity. Bardamu is not impressed: there is nothing in Montaigne that can make Bébert's end easier to bear. The consolations of philosophy and literature have failed. In the Bébert incident Céline runs the gamut of man's attempts to resist his fate. None of them works.

This is why death dominates *Voyage*. It is not just that all men must die, but that each moment of their lives is rendered futile. Everything they do is ridiculous. Bardamu might as well not have tried to save Bébert, might as well not have tried to become a doctor. The novelty of Céline's conception is that man's habitual state is to be dying. The African episode shows a continent given up to decay: swamped by the jungle, burned by the sun. All the inhabitants are as miserable as the Spanish soldier who watches while the red ants march through his hut eating everything in their path. In *Voyage* people merely wait around to die. 'You get old without noticing it. I know what it's like,' says Robinson. Old age, physical illness and mental disorders fascinate Céline because they are forerunners of the end to come. The African colonials boast about their fevers. Bardamu's T.B. patients are obsessed by their disease, from which they have no wish to recover. Bardamu himself is a trained observer of death, who cannot look at a beautiful woman without seeing her as a shrivelled hag. When he sees Musyne two years after she has left him, he is struck by the change: 'Two years is just the interval that is needed to make you aware at one glance, irrefutably and as if instinctively, of the ugliness that has come over a face.' The ugliness is inevitable; what is surprising is that Musyne should have succeeded in looking beautiful.

The most frightening – and important – moments of *Voyage* come when Bardamu confronts his own death. In New York he encounters a new kind of solitude:

In Africa I had indeed found a sufficiently frightening kind of loneliness but the isolation of this American anthill was much more crushing.

I had always been afraid that I was nearly a void, that I had no single, serious reason for existing. Now, confronted with this, I was quite convinced of my personal emptiness. In this place, so different from the one to which I was, in my shabby way, accustomed, it was as if I had at once fallen to pieces. I felt that I was, quite simply, close to not existing at all. I discovered that from the moment that there was no one to talk to me about the things I was familiar with, nothing prevented me from falling into an insuperable boredom, a sickly, terrifying collapse of the mind. A disgusting experience.

Without the protection of habit, Bardamu is thrown back on himself. But he finds nothing. He is not the traditional *homo sapiens* endowed with reason and will-power; he is an empty creature who hovers between being and nothingness.

The experience recurs in different forms at every stage of the novel. On the battlefield Bardamu feels his thoughts disintegrate into fear: 'Never have I felt so futile as among all those bullets in that sunshine.' In the African jungle he has to flee before he is overcome by the climate and vegetation. In the Detroit factory he has the feeling that humans have vanished and machines are all there is: 'Life outside must be put away; it must be turned into steel too ... it must be made into a thing.' In each case Bardamu is faced with the extinction of himself. Stripped of its façade, life is nothing more than this 'disgusting experience' where one's personality breaks up.

This being so, it is inevitably dreadful. There can be no question of enjoying oneself while awaiting one's end; no question, as in Camus, of the North African sunshine offering a period of happiness before the cemetery claims its victim. Death is omnipresent: 'Endless waves of trifling human beings come drifting down from the beginning of the ages to die all the time under our very noses.' Bardamu's window at Rancy offers him 'a spectacle of unrelieved hideousness'. The word 'unrelieved' is important. There is no way of avoiding or changing the family tortures and alcoholism that fill the Rancy day. Occasionally Bardamu meets people who are good like Alcide, the Topo sergeant who is devoted to his crippled niece, or Molly, the kindly prostitute from Detroit. Such people are both rare and powerless. Alcide cannot alter the colonial system and Molly does no more than console the Detroit workers. They are islands of goodness in an ocean of misery. Nowhere in *Voyage* is there the sense that man can alter his condition. The experience of feeling himself disintegrate is precisely what makes him a man, so it is ludicrous to expect him to rise above himself. Bardamu is convinced that 'we get nowhere. It's been proved.' A student of history, he reads about Napoleon and the Cossacks, who came from Russia to France to fight against him. Napoleon achieved dizzy greatness and then fell. The anonymous Cossacks lie buried in a Montmartre cemetery. They are no different from the Emperer. 'And yet we persist in hoping for certain things,' says Bardamu bitterly. His medical skill cannot save Bébert, his friendship cannot help Robinson to die in peace and he cannot make Molly's dream of love come true. Man is governed by an inexorable fate. Any action is mere hubris, like the colonel's heroism. In Greek tragedy, Fate is personified in the figures of the gods. They punish the arrogance of such men as Oedipus who rise above their station. The gods are harsh and arbitrary, but they are not blind. They incorporate a moral order that the chorus and Oedipus recognize. In *Voyage* there is no such moral order. Death strikes down the good and the bad, the weak and the arrogant, indiscriminately.

Why then are human beings not innocent? If they can do nothing about death, surely they are not responsible for its havoc? This plausible argument is absent from *Voyage*. Bardamu's mother puts the matter simply when she describes how the ordinary people have helped to bring about the war: 'They must have done a lot of foolish things, without realizing it of course, but they were to blame nevertheless.' This is a very Jansenist view. Although men are not aware of what they are doing, they must bear responsibility. They have committed some undefined crime and they are guilty. This over-simplified philosophy is not necessarily Céline's; but Bardamu too feels guilt: 'I never felt quite innocent of any misfortunes which came along.' Like Oedipus, he is guilty although he has not knowingly done evil. He blames himself for Bébert's death and for being unable to help Robinson. Without knowing how or why, man is aware of original sin. When Bardamu is forced to realize his 'personal emptiness' he describes it in moral terms as 'disgusting'. He does not accept it as a painful fact. He feels responsible for it.

The Céline character wants to escape from his lonely misery into hatred. The mechanism of hatred will be analysed later; but one must note here that it springs from the fear and guilt that death inspires.

Hatred is rampant in *Voyage*: 'Five francs are enough to make one hate a person.' Cocorico hates the manager of the rubber company, Parapine hates his chief Jaunisset, the list is endless. By hating, men participate in evil. From the Rancy patients, who show Bardamu 'all the horrible deformities hidden away in their hearts', to Pomone's customers and their 'disgusting cartloads of commonplace passions', humans bear witness to the Fall. 'There's no doubt about our having been turned out of Eden' is Pomone's conclusion. At war the N.C.O.s, who send soldiers out to die, have become 'even more brutish, meaner and more odious than usual'. In Africa the whites exploit the blacks but the blacks are only too willing to exploit one another. Life is polluted by the presence of death. Humans do not need gods to oppress them. 'It is of men, and of them only, that one should always be frightened,' says Bardamu. Far from being victims of fate, men are their own executioners. They bear witness to the all-corroding power of evil.

The sense of evil marks Céline's lonely place in modern writing. His awareness of death as a crushing force and his view of man as eternally guilty and malicious, inspire his work with a pessimism unique among his contemporaries. He may be seen as the forerunner of the writers of the absurd, and yet he is not one of them. Sartre, for example, was impressed by *Voyage* and a Céline quotation stands at the head of *La Nausée*.[2] Up to a point the two authors are in agreement: man is living in a world hostile to him and over which he has no control. There the resemblance stops. For Sartre the universe is a painful enigma, but, once man has realized the truth of his condition, he can change himself. In *Les Mouches* Oreste gives shape to his life by his act of revolt against Jupiter. He may achieve little for his fellow-citizens and he may be condemning himself to the Furies' revenge, but his action is significant. Before, he was an empty shell wandering around Greece and imbibing his teacher's abstract ideas. Now he is a man with passions, loyalties and remorse. This represents a kind of triumph over the universe. In creating Oreste, Sartre – at least the Sartre of 1945 – shows that, far from despairing of human nature, he thinks it has great possibilities. Man retains a certain freedom from the restrictions of an absurd universe. In *Voyage* there is no such margin of liberty. Bardamu is part of the absurdity. He feels the misery that is man's lot and he knows that he cannot act. The same gulf lies between Céline and Camus, another writer obsessed with death. Camus maintains that man is capable of limited virtues. Rieux struggles against the plague. Although he achieves little, the reader of *La Peste* feels that there is value in his efforts and in the fraternity he feels for Tarrou. In *Voyage*, the friendship between Bardamu and Robinson offers no such grounds for hope.

Neither Sartre nor Camus has the sense that evil corrodes human nature. In Céline's writing it is ludicrous to talk of freedom, revolt and fraternity. Transformation of the self – as practised by the Malraux hero who turns to political commitment – is impossible because man's nature is fallen and it will remain so. The only French writer whose pessimism resembles Céline's is – despite great differences – the exiled Irishman Samuel Beckett. He too has abandoned the search for values. Molloy knows that he must just go on living. He makes fun of Camus's notion that Sisyphus is happy – 'as the fashion is now'[3] – because he is aware of the absurdity of his task. In Beckett's work such awareness does not lead to change, any more than it does in Céline. Beckett insists on the illogicality of life, Céline on its malice. But neither admits that there can be any road that leads beyond nihilism. When Bardamu travels he meets no Rieux. Like Baudelaire he encounters only 'the weary spectacle of immortal sin'.[4]

The use of theological language is deliberate. Céline's thought has a religious strain, which explains the differences between him and the Existentialist writers. Although he was no believer in any kind of Christianity, he had – as Robert Poulet pointed out[5] – a religious temperament. He feels that there is a flaw in life which is inherent and which cannot be altered by political change or philosophical argument. His belief in fate, guilt and sin reminds one of the pessimistic side of Christianity – of thinkers like Augustine, Pascal and Baudelaire. He is a writer in search of a divine grace that eludes him. Like his wretched character Pomone, he feels that men have been driven from the Garden of Eden and that there is no way back to God. 'Never had I felt the way of men and things to be so implacable,' says Bardamu on the battlefield. Since humans can do nothing for themselves, there remains only the Redeemer in whom Pascal believes. But Céline does not believe, so for him there is nothing. Like Beckett, he uses the language of theology to indicate the absence of God.

The characters of *Voyage* are left to face their existences as best they can. Most of them – except Bardamu and Robinson – exhaust their energies in passionate, random pursuits. The manager of the rubber company has one thought – to cheat the firm. Nothing else interests him – neither women nor alcohol. Bardamu is amazed: 'I wouldn't have believed that there was one single human carcass in the world capable of such a maximum intensity of greed.' Monsieur Henrouille spends his life scraping and saving to pay for his house; as soon as it is his, he forgets about it and starts to worry twenty-four hours a day about his health. Whatever they do, Céline's characters go to extremes.

They are constantly changing their course. Baryton spends years building up his hospital. Then he suddenly starts to learn English, forgets about medicine and takes the train for Dover. Like Henrouille he passes easily from one extreme to another. Why does he begin to learn English? It is just that he is bored with his old passion and needs a new one. Up to a point Céline's characters are like Balzac's. The *Comédie humaine* is rich in powerful passions: Hulot's lust and Goriot's paternal devotion are only two that come to mind. But Balzac's characters are like huge trains which, once put on a track, cannot leave it. They do not switch the object of their devotion from medicine to English, from houses to health. There is a randomness in *Voyage* that is absent from Balzac. Why does Madelon, scarcely the most faithful of fiancées, cling with such tenacity to Robinson? Why does old Madame Henrouille agree to go off to Toulouse with the very Robinson who has tried to kill her? The answer is that the characters of *Voyage* have no control over their destinies. Driven on by the fear of death, they seize every opportunity to prove they exist. Any pretext is enough to unleash their torrent of energy.

The key to Céline's psychology is the Pascalian concept of *divertissement*. According to Pascal, the need for *divertissement* springs from 'the natural unhappiness of our condition which is weak, mortal and so miserable that when we think about it clearly nothing can console us'.* So men plunge into hunting, gambling and other available amusements. The object of the hunt is unimportant, the hunt everything. If the aristocrat were offered the hare he pursues so ardently, he would not want it. He wants to be diverted from his real situation: the

* Pascal, *Pensées*, Éditions du Seuil, Paris, 1962, p. 89. Céline does not himself use the term *divertissement*. He uses the vocabulary of the theatre – 'role, scene' and the like. But the metaphysical dimension is clearly present when he talks of characters who have no roles: he uses terms like 'anguish' and '*ennui*'. So the use of the Pascalian terminology does not distort his thinking.

torment of a spirit deprived of God. The *divertissement* is a false activity which allows man to avoid his condition, but not to remedy it. This view of human behaviour is not peculiar to Pascal. It plays a central role in *Les Fleurs du mal*, where Baudelaire's various enthusiasms for wine, hashish and feminine beauty are no more than a series of amusements that help him escape his underlying *ennui*.

Céline follows in the same path. As Bardamu puts it 'Life's a classroom and Boredom's the usher' – here again the French word is *ennui* which denotes not just boredom but a deep anguish. The characters cannot face the loneliness that Bardamu endured in New York so they try, as he did, to escape. Bardamu takes refuge in the cinema: 'You plunge straight into an atmosphere of warm forgiveness. You have only to let yourself go to feel that the world had at last become indulgent.' Naturally this is an illusion because New York is not in the least indulgent. The sex on the screen is enjoyable precisely because it is unreal. Outside, the New York women are frozen goddesses more anxious to exploit men than to please them. After Bardamu emerges from the cinema he is as lonely as ever. But the hours he spends inside enable him to pretend that he really exists and that he is happy.

This is not a complete case of *divertissement*, because Bardamu is conscious of what he is doing. He uses the cinema to survive, but he has no hope that it will do more. Pascal insists that a man who engages in a *divertissement* must believe that it is real. The gambler will not replace money with counters because he would be forced to realize that he is involved in a sham, whereas his aim is to make his game into a genuine existence. Most of the characters in *Voyage* do not question the reality of what they are doing. It is left to Céline to point out its falsity.

A recurring symbol of the *divertissement* is the fair-ground, mecca of the poor. It has 'an organ that isn't even gold, behind a shooting gallery where the eggs are only shells. It's the fair for duping people over the weekend.' The alternative would be for the Rancy poor to face the reality of their lives: their grim exploitation at the hands of the rich. As they cannot do this any more than the New Yorkers can face loneliness, they rush to the fair-ground. Spurring them on is the fear of death: 'You must choose: either dying or lying,' notes Bardamu. As most people prefer to lie, there hangs over *Voyage* a huge air of charade. The colourful extremes of passion are just games that people play, while Bardamu looks on ironically. He sets the tone at the start when he is sitting in the café with Artur: 'Everybody in Paris seems to be busy but actually they only walk about all day.' The most common *divertissement* is alcohol and the saddest sight in Rancy is a workman 'without enough in his pockets to go and get a drink – and come alive again'. In *Voyage* the choice is hopeless: to face the useless truth of death or to catch at the illusion of life.

As well as the mass *divertissements* there are the individual roles that the characters find for themselves. Dr Bardamu witnesses many family dramas, all of which are genuine dramas: fictions that people invent and play out, because they do not wish to cope with sickness. When Bardamu goes to visit an unmarried girl who has just been aborted, he finds her mother screaming hysterically about family honour: 'she had the leading part as intermediary between her daughter and myself – she was having a wonderful time'. The mother does not want to face the fact that her daughter will die unless she is taken to hospital. But there is more. Normally the mother ekes out a drab existence in an ugly home with a nondescript husband. Now excitement has come her way and she can live more fully. She is delighted: 'the theatrical side of the disaster absolutely thrilled her'. The same is true of the unmarried mother whose child Bardamu visits. She 'accepted with delight the great sorrow which had been meted out to her, and the ravages of Fate became, as a matter of fact, a dramatic godsend to her'. The woman has found a special role; amidst millions of people exactly like her, she has become an exception: an unmarried mother. She plays the part to the hilt, talking freely about her 'new responsibilities' and weeping over her fatherless child. The moral issue does not bother her; she has a role and that is what matters. In the world of *Voyage*, moral values are not important: heroes, scientists and unmarried mothers are as good as one another.* The important thing is to have some pretext for living. Parapine, the supposed typhoid expert, is playing out his part. His publications are revised versions of one short article and his days at the laboratory are spent whiling away the time. No one occupation is better than another since all are lies.

Behind all of them lies the desire to live. Like the Rancy workman the characters of *Voyage* want to emerge from the state of dying. The

---

* Moral values are not important to most of the characters. They are, of course, to Bardamu and Céline.

best example is old Madame Henrouille, whose new life-span comes about very strangely. Before Robinson's first unsuccessful attempt to kill her she has withdrawn to a little hut in the garden. She spends her days fighting off the death that may come at any moment from the outside world. Suddenly she discovers that she has been the victim of an attempted murder. Now she has 'a profitable role which she found extremely exciting ... The wish to live came back to her old carcass'. She screams insults, threatens to bring the police and bemoans her fate. Before she was a neglected old woman, almost dead. Now she comes back to life and she is convinced that she will live for ever: 'She wasn't going to let herself die.'

Of course she does die and the agent of her destruction is the same Robinson who had helped her to live. The *divertissement* does not replace reality, it provides death with a new weapon. In 1915 the French are playing the game of heroism and even Bardamu is joining in: 'The whole thing was pure theatre; you had to play a part.' The décor is music-hall songs, uniforms and smiling women; the actors are soldiers who talk of brave deeds: 'We were living a tremendous saga in the skins of fantastic characters.' Things grow more and more unreal. Bardamu recounts his exploits, quite fictitious, to an actress whose friend, a poet, makes them into an epic, that she recites with great success at the Comédie Française. A complete fiction has been created. Bardamu is actually a coward, the poet is carefully avoiding becoming a soldier and the actress is pursuing her pre-war career – except that the spectators have forgotten about the illusion inherent in her profession. The reason for this frantic activity is clear: unwilling to believe that they will soon die, men drape corpses in flags and indulge in orgies of patriotism. Paris is the scene of the *divertissement*, Flanders of reality. But the *divertissement* hastens death. The rhetoric of bravery encourages men to enlist and go forth to battle. By taking their minds off slaughter, it stimulates bravery and hence massacre. The *divertissement* proves itself a dangerous illusion. This is not an isolated example. The alcohol, to which the Rancy workers have recourse, serves to kill them. Old Madame Henrouille plays her role of victim until she becomes a real victim, while her son undermines his health by worrying about it. In *Voyage* each person has to find 'his own way towards Death'. The *divertissement* makes the road shorter as well as seemingly easier.

There are frequent moments when the illusion breaks down, leaving the character helpless. Céline describes this in theatrical terms: 'People move from one piece of play-acting to the next! When the stage isn't set they cannot envisage its form or what their proper part is, so they stand there, doing nothing . . . reduced to their simple selves, reduced to nothing.' The fear of death takes possession of them and they must find another role quickly, if they are to survive. This is the fate that befalls the Duke of Monmouth, who fascinates Bardamu and Baryton as they read English history in the mental hospital. Defeated at Sedgemoor, Monmouth drags himself uselessly around England: 'Monmouth the pretender no longer quite knows what it is he pretends,' comments the ironic Bardamu. He is a false king who cannot sustain his role. He has to look around for another and the only one he can find is to become a royal exile. But his ships sail without him so he is stranded again. He can only wait to be executed. Céline draws the conclusion in Pascalian language: in Monmouth's situation 'all the pitiable absurdity of our puerile and tragic natures is exposed, so to speak, in the face of eternity'.

When the *divertissement* breaks down, the Céline character has one last defence: hatred. As already mentioned, the men and women of *Voyage* need to hate. It allows them to emerge from their isolation and make contact with others. More important it gives them a concrete, if illusory, explanation for their unhappiness. They are miserable because they are the prey of malicious enemies. If only they could destroy these enemies they would be happy. This piece of reasoning is quite false, but that does not matter. Hatred is the last escape-hatch. As long as they have enemies to hate, the characters of *Voyage* can project their guilt and fear on to someone else. The characteristic trait of Célinian hatred is that it is gratuitous: one does not dislike because the object of dislike has harmed one; one hates because one has to.

This mechanism is analysed in the account of Bardamu's voyage to Africa. He is travelling on the *Amiral Bragueton* with a body of soldiers, civil servants and schoolteachers who are returning to the colonies. At first all goes well and then Bardamu finds himself the object of vicious animosity. How does this come about? The passengers are quiet until the ship passes Portugal and then an 'ugly despair' settles on them. They realize that they are returning to Africa, land of death. The colonial is nothing but a 'crawling carcass', who is terrified of the 'frightful loneliness' which will engulf him. He would like to take refuge in *divertissements*, but on the ship there reigns an 'unbelievable boredom ... a cosmic boredom'. The passengers feel their existence reduced to nothing. Although they resort to alcohol and sexual flirtation their plight becomes desperate.

Hating Bardamu is a relief – 'I was a source of entertainment'. The passengers have been reduced to their last *divertissement*, which is murder. Why do they pick on Bardamu? Of what can he be guilty? The answer is of nothing. He is slightly different from them because he is paying his own passage, whereas their fare is paid by the government. A homogeneous group, united by alcoholism and stupidity as well as by profession, seizes the crumb of difference. Bardamu goes out of his way to avoid giving offence but that does not help. In a short while rumours are circulating that he is an insolent fellow, a homosexual, a pimp, a drugtaker and a criminal. The passengers are inventing reasons that will permit them to hate him. Truth and falsehood are irrelevant: pretexts must be found, so that they can forget their misery.

Bardamu understands perfectly: 'I had begun to take the part of the necessary "infamous unworthy wretch", the scorn of humanity, pointed at through the centuries.' (He is playing the traditional role of the Jew.) What qualities are required for this part? The important thing is that he must be weak, so that there is 'no risk attached' to hating him. The passengers are seeking to avoid reality, not to face it. They do not want a difficult, much less a genuine target. Secondly the hate-object must be so vague that he can fit any set of circumstances. The 'infamous unworthy wretch' is 'assuming always a different shape, so fugitive on earth and in life as to be actually indefinable'. Bardamu fits the bill. The fact that he has no evil characteristics leaves the passengers free to invent them.* So the men curse him in the evenings, as they get boringly more drunk, and the frustrated women look forward to the bloodletting as a form of sexual excitement. For the time being *ennui* is banished.

---

* Perhaps the real reason is that Bardamu incarnates the death they do not want to face. He is still carrying the Flanders trenches around with him. But at this stage of *Voyage* he himself he is not fully aware of this, so the theme is implicit rather than stated. In *Féerie* it is much clearer. The Parisians hate Ferdinand because he is a walking corpse, who has been condemned to death by the Resistance.

As the hatred reaches its climax, Bardamu's death begins to resemble a ritual sacrifice. He will be offered up to propitiate the gods. He will die and the others will be saved. On the great evening the soldiers are decked out in full uniform, while the women wear evening gowns. The bravest warrior challenges Bardamu with 'full dramatic ceremony' and the other officers accompany him to the deck, like 'an escort to Fate'. The passengers are acting like a primitive tribe engaged in human sacrifice. They are equally irrational, equally futile and equally determined to turn their own fear against another. Bardamu is the scapegoat who will be driven out into the desert, so that the tribe may be purified.*

In this case the drama turns to farce. Bardamu escapes by making a frantic appeal to his executioners' vanity. He utters a long tirade about the soldiers' bravery. He takes them down to the bar, plies them with liquor and listens to grotesquely exaggerated accounts of their heroism. He is offering them a new *divertissement*: alcohol mixed with the heady wine of 'self-glorification'. He is trying to remove their need to hate. Only the women, who are shut out of this new game, eye him malevolently.

In another sense Bardamu has not escaped: he continues to be the victim because he has to pander to the soldiers' vanity. He feels that this is inevitable: 'One human being can only tolerate another human being and rather like him, if he plays the part of an admiring doormat.' Decent relationships are impossible in a world where each person is alone with death. Men can only exploit their fellows: as listeners for their fictions, as amusements for their boredom, as targets for their hatred. They cannot meet a friend or lover on equal terms because they have nothing to offer. In *Voyage* most relationships assume the executioner–victim pattern that Baudelaire talks about so often. The strong exploit the weak and the weak turn on the weaker.

At Rancy marriages follow the Baudelairian model. The great moment comes after Saturday lunch: 'Father wields the chair, my God, as if it were a battle-axe, while Mother flourishes a stick of firewood

* Very often in Céline's work themes may be explained in terms of primitive religion and mythology. For other examples see the treatment of madness in Chapter Three and of anti-semitism in Chapter Five. This approach can be misleading. Céline was after all a twentieth-century Frenchman and not a prehistoric Celt. But his tendency to see the world in terms of primeval myths is an important part of his vision.

like a sabre ... The littlest one gets it in the neck.' Such is the reaction of the poor to their lot. The deprived worker beats his wife who thrashes the children. Instead of analysing their situation objectively, the Rancy inhabitants seek out weak targets. The poorer classes cannot face their collective misery any better than the individual passengers on the *Amiral Bragueton* can face their loneliness. This explains why the common soldiers in the army 'rarely, if ever, ask the why and the wherefore of what happens to them ... They merely hate the sight of one another.' While inferiors sometimes hate their superiors, it is more common for hatred to be random or to be the reward of kindness. As a doctor, Bardamu finds that his generosity is repaid with dislike. He charges his patients little – 'for which you are not easily forgiven'. This is natural enough, since any kind act puts the recipient in an inferior position. Inevitably he responds with hatred. A gratuitous malevolence is the Céline character's normal reponse to the world he lives in. As well as expressing his guilt and projecting his fears, it gives him some hope that his life may not be as bad as it seems. Céline's characters need to hate as Graham Greene's characters need to love: violent emotion banishes the feeling of 'personal emptiness'.

Not surprisingly, *Voyage* abounds in cruelty. Bardamu's officers send him out on useless, perilous missions, while Lola and Musyne encourage men to be killed. The colonialist brutalizes the blacks and the Ford management looks with indifference on the workers' misery. Horror has become so banal that the family Bardamu meets in Flanders forgets their child's death to sell him a bottle of wine. Violence is so comic that Robinson mocks the dying captain.

The insistence on cruelty is another of Céline's special traits. He has seized on the most appalling tendency of our age: the willingness to slaughter millions of people. Inventions like the hydrogen bomb or germ warfare would have come as no surprise to Bardamu, who sat through weekends at Rancy while his neighbours conducted their rituals of torture. He knows that men are happy to slaughter their fellows: 'One might as well realize that in everyday life at least a hundred people thirst for your miserable life in the course of a single ordinary day.' Since violence is rampant in modern life, it is not surprising that there are wars. Céline is the chronicler of the two world wars: his first novel begins with the trench warfare of Flanders and his last novel ends with the fall of Hitler's Germany. He sees mass slaughter as an integral part of contemporary life. World wars are not exceptional periods of bloodletting; they are general manifestations of the hatred individuals feel for one another. When Bardamu meets the officer who is to conduct his execution on the *Amiral Bragueton*, he calls him 'a further fragment of the war confronting me again, purposeful, murderous, inescapable'. And what is Rancy life if not a ceaseless battle?

After torturing others the characters of *Voyage* torture themselves: 'To kill others and to kill themselves, that's what they wanted,' notes Bardamu. Like other *divertissements*, hatred leads to death. In Fort-Gono 'vital energy ... was consumed by hatreds so bitter and insistent that many of the residents used to die in their tracks, poisoned by themselves, like scorpions'. They wear out their vitality without realizing it. Projecting their emotion on to others, they forget that they are exhausting themselves.

There is a still closer connection between hatred and self-destruction. Dislike of others is the expression of a man's dislike of himself. The Céline character is trying to escape from his burden of guilt. As he can never do this for long, he is filled with self-hatred. Then he can no longer turn on those around him, he turns on himself. Usually he does both at the same time. Masochism is common in *Voyage* where many of the characters resemble the African who walks through the bush for three days to be flogged. He has 'God knows what sorrow on his mind' and it can only be lifted by punishment. The Detroit workers compete to become robots and the colonials are 'pleased, yes quite pleased to carry on until the ten millionth mosquito had sucked from them the last red corpuscle'. Men are attracted by the very death they run from.

A psychologist would not find this surprising: hatred lies close to masochism. The Céline character wishes to die because existence is such a tiresome chore. Death becomes yet another form of escape. Few men see the matter this clearly or else they would commit suicide, which they do not. Suicide is too rational an act for people like Pomone or Baryton. They continue to seek for amusements and hatreds, even while they are pursued by the death-wish. There is no real contradiction between their desperate attempts to live and their secret desire to die: both are the products of their guilty fear. Bardamu, who is himself not immune from the self-destructive impulse, watches the people in the fair-ground: they enjoy the bumper cars because of 'the terrific jolts they give your head and your insides'. These people, who are supposedly drowning their fears, have to be 'dragged away from their destruction'. But then Céline himself shares their feelings. In the preface to *Voyage*, written later, he says that he 'would destroy everything'.[6] He would like to publish nothing more, suppress his past writings and plunge into the silence that is a writer's death. His characters feel the same urge.

As men are unable to cope with death, their dealings with one another turn out badly. Céline's treatment of sex, which is the most intimate kind of human contact, leads back to the central flaw in life. The themes of *divertissement*, hatred and self-destruction recur here. Between men and women the need to be amused is great, so they use one another as objects until their intimacy gives birth to enmity. Céline is at his most pessimistic when he portrays Bardamu's relationship with Lola, or Robinson's with Madelon. Yet there is a new theme: beauty. Céline is a great admirer of feminine beauty and Bardamu lingers over Molly's long legs and Sophie's generous curves. In sex there are rare flashes of beauty – bought at great expense – which constitute Bardamu's happiest moments. They point to a whole new level in Céline's work: the quest for a dream that lies beyond ordinary reality.

In *Voyage* men are tormented by sexual desires: 'I was an appalling lecher,' says Bardamu, and most of the characters are no different. Sex is like any other passion. It is random and men cannot control it. Parapine likes to follow twelve-year-old girls as they come from school, while Pomone, pimp and pornography dealer, ignores the women who surround him but is maddened by masturbation. Women are no better. Pomone's female customers spend hours telling him about 'their intimate charms, the like of which, to hear them talk, you'd think couldn't be found under any other mortal skirt'. In *Voyage* sex is a ceaseless, bizarre preoccupation, from which no one – except Robinson – is exempt. Bardamu tells an anecdote about how Napoleon could think of nothing during the retreat from Moscow, except rushing off to Warsaw to spend the night with his Polish mistress. When the sexual urge came over him, he forgot all about defeat. Bardamu's conclusion is that 'one has to make love as one has to scratch'.

The other person involved in the act is nothing but an object. The sexual desire comes first and the partner is a means of satisfying it. There is little room for love or even for treating the other person as an equal. Pleasure is the prime aim. Women are praised for their bedroom skills: 'a certain salacious ingenuity is as essential as pepper is to a good sauce'. In turn women seek physical enjoyment: the Rancy girl is described as 'a beautiful athlete in pursuit of pleasure'.

Sex is a great *divertissement*. Bardamu explains how in wartime France the brothel queen, Madame Hérote, sells sex to the soldiers, who must return to the front. With death awaiting them they plunge into the oblivion of women's caresses. Baudelaire, whose opinions on women are close to Céline's, explains that love is 'the need to escape from oneself'.[7] Bardamu expresses the same sentiment in different language: 'A woman who can take account of the wretchedness of our nature easily becomes our darling ... We expect of her that she shall preserve our lying *raison d'être*.' The key word is 'lying': men who plunge into love have chosen to lie, rather than to die. Needing a release from loneliness, they accept at face value women's protestations of affection. Madame Hérote is particularly skilled in illusion. She runs an underwear shop where *risqué* books are on display. She creates a décor of perfumed daring, which the soldiers are eager to accept as reality. They are trying desperately to live and she offers them the opportunity. In Detroit, Bardamu will use women as a way of coming to life after his day at the factory. He spends his evenings at the brothel because 'I needed the promiscuous transports of these splendid ever-ready creatures, to fashion myself a new soul'.

For women, too, love is a *divertissement*. Lola, the American Joan of Arc, enjoys being escorted around Paris by heroes. For her, love is walks in the Bois de Boulogne and dinners in fashionable restaurants. Musyne, more prosaic or simply poorer, allows Bardamu to love her, while she makes her way as a high-class prostitute. Both women demand of Bardamu that he amuse them. Madelon is a more complex case because she clings to Robinson, although he does not amuse her and does not want her. She is not stupid and he is quite graceless, so why does she persist? The answer is that to her 'way of thinking you had to love somebody'. Her relationship with Robinson is the only thing that gives her life significance. She is his fiancée, that is her role. 'Do you want me not to believe in love any more?', she asks him, when he tries to get rid of her. The question is rhetorical, because Madelon refuses not to believe in love. If she did she would be left with nothing. So she pursues Robinson.

Small wonder that love-affairs break down: each is asking what the other cannot give. Neither man nor woman can protect his partner against death. Bardamu goes from girl to girl but he leaves them all, even Molly who is a creature of genuine emotion. Lola, after her promenades with heroes, goes back to New York to live a childless life on her own. Sex is a failure: 'Pleasure pretty soon becomes hard work,' says Bardamu sadly. Once again Baudelaire has expressed Céline's view: 'after debauchery one always feels more alone, more abandoned'.[8]

This is the last thing the Céline character is willing to face. Instead he persists in illusion, finds new partners, relies on sexual expertise. As nothing works, love turns to hatred. At Rancy husbands and wives torment one another: 'the female sets the pace, shrilling, calling her mate to battle'. Cruelty lies close to sexuality and it can spur on lagging desire, so the Rancy fights are followed by orgies. In deeper vein cruelty is a revenge for the failure of the partner to fulfil one's dreams. The dreary cycle of executioner and victim takes over. Robinson and Madelon persecute one another, so do Lola and Bardamu. Madelon is infuriated with Robinson because he will not believe in love, Lola attacks Bardamu because he will not be a hero. If the Céline character cannot love, at least he can hate. The bedroom becomes a battlefield.

In this struggle woman emerges victorious. Like Baudelaire, Céline looks at sex from a male point of view. To him woman is the vampire who 'enters like a knife-thrust into my heart'.[9] As she takes advantage of man's need to exploit him, she is always acting as a kind of prostitute. *Voyage* is rich in prostitutes, because they illustrate Céline's theme that, while providing man with his illusion, a woman can 'to a large extent earn her own living'. Musyne personifies the predatory female. By her patriotic songs she makes men believe in heroism. Meanwhile she is making a good living by obliging the war-profiteering Argentinians.

Céline goes further when he suggests that women need to destroy men, because there is a link between female sexuality and cruelty. At Rancy it is the wives who begin the fighting. On board the *Amiral*

Bragueton the greatest danger to Bardamu comes from 'unsatisfied females'. A young schoolmistress spurs the others on: 'Deep down in her wasted insides she was stirring at the thought of some magnificently blood-bespattered scene. The idea of it was as exciting to her as that of being raped by a gorilla.' Perhaps her cruelty is a revenge on the male for his aggression in the sexual act. But it is more obviously a revenge for the failure of sex in her life. Her frustrations will be taken out on Bardamu, his death will provide her with the sexual delights she has never experienced.

Most of the women in *Voyage* are associated with death. Lola and Musyne are Cornelian spirits ready to applaud the carnage of the trenches. The New York girls try to destroy Bardamu by thrusting him back into loneliness. Cold and remote, they are the guardian angels of Manhattan's icy solitude. Then there is the *concierge* who sleeps with the soldiers at the hospital, before betraying their secrets to the authorities. She is wonderful in bed; but her favours are dearly bought because her lovers are later executed. But it is left to Madelon to become a murderess when, unable to possess Robinson, she shoots him. This is the clearest example of a woman who becomes an executioner because men cannot fill the role she has allotted them.

Woman's triumph is short-lived. She is destroyed by childbirth as she has destroyed man in sex. Dr Bardamu tells horrible stories of abortions and miscarriages: the 'beautiful athlete' bleeds her vitality away in her third abortion. The wife with the miscarriage bleeds too and moans 'like a large dog that's been run over by a car'. Despite this the main focus of *Voyage* is on man. There is a self-hatred present in his foolish pursuit of a woman who will destroy him. As Baudelaire pointed out, 'love is the taste for prostitution'.[10] For a man, sex is a kind of death where he prostrates himself before a woman, like the lover who 'looks like a dying man caressing his tomb'.[11] Psychologically it is easy to see the link between the loss of self in the orgasm and the oblivion of death, but Céline and Baudelaire go much further. Céline sees man's obsession with women as an expression of his weary desire to have done with himself and his guilt. Bardamu chases the New York girls, although they make his loneliness even more unbearable. He accepts that they will reject him. Already he had understood all too well what Lola and Musyne were about. Here again there is no contradiction between love as the desire to escape from oneself and love as the desire to destroy oneself. Both spring from what Baudelaire calls the 'horror of solitude'.[12]

In *Voyage*, sex turns out to be disgusting. Céline has an Augustinian strain which makes him insist that the joys of the flesh are sinful. Since all of life is flawed, sex must be especially flawed. *Voyage* is full of sordid descriptions. A Rancy couple tie their little child to the bed and beat her to stimulate their sexual desires: 'That's how they went together, their *concierge* told me, against the sink in the kitchen. Any other way they couldn't manage it.' The hysterical mother is letting her aborted daughter bleed to death, because she 'jealously disapproved' of the girl's capacity for sexual pleasure. At every point the sexual instinct is portrayed as dirty. This makes for another parallel between Céline and Beckett: one thinks of the pages where Molloy describes how he fumbled around with Edith on a rubbish heap. In Beckett, too, women are potential executioners for Lousse tries to hold Molloy captive in her home. He escapes, following in the line of Beckett's heroes who resist women's charms. Already Murphy had ignored Celia although she, like Molly, was a good person. Goodness is not enough in Beckett's work, because the flesh is damned once and for all. There is no possibility that sex can satisfy the mind's agonizing quest to explain an absurd reality. Sex is part of the world that lies outside Murphy's mind and that he wants to avoid; it is the part of the world that Molloy knows he cannot avoid, but that he is not willing to accept.

Whereas Molloy resolves the problem swiftly by rejecting women, Bardamu goes on pursuing them. He sees in them a dream that he cannot ignore. It is one of *Voyage*'s great paradoxes that, alongside the ugliness of sex, there is a thread of beauty. Bardamu is entranced by the frigid New York girls, whom he considers a 'treasure-trove of harmony'. He is happiest when he is making love to the pretty nurse Sophie. One is reminded of Baudelaire's love-poetry where Jeanne Duval is both the disgusting, unfaithful harlot and the mistress whose body is an enchanting delight.

Like his creator, Bardamu insists that physical beauty is what attracts him. For a short time a lovely woman can banish old age and convince even Bardamu, the observer of death, that life can be wonderful. A woman's body is important, her mind is not. When he is with Lola, Bardamu ignores her patriotic ideas and concentrates on her physical charms – her 'body was an endless source of joy to me'.

Yet Bardamu is not convincing when he maintains that his pleasure is purely sensual. There is something non-physical about his descriptions of women. When he talks about Molly's legs as 'lithe and muscular and noble', the third adjective seems out of place. He uses the phrase 'miraculous epidermis' to describe Sophie. In both cases the physical is just the starting-point of the dream. Bardamu recognizes this in the Detroit brothel, when he contrasts his own 'impotent fervour' with the lusty wenching of a visiting baseball team. He knows that he works with his imagination, until the woman's body becomes an ideal harmony that is his own creation. His attitude is less one of physical desire than an 'erotico-mystical' contemplation. He pursues in spite of himself a beauty of which the woman is no more than a part. He talks of his 'vice for seeking after perfection in shapes' compared with which 'cocaine's nothing but a hobby for station-masters'. This is very Baudelairian language. In *Les Fleurs du mal* Jeanne Duval's body is only the beginning of a reverie that creates an ideal aesthetic beauty. Her hair is a port 'where my soul may drink great waves of perfume, sound and colour'.[13] Both Céline and Baudelaire describe women in terms of ships: Sophie is a 'brigantine of tender gaiety', Jeanne a boat following a 'soft, lazy and slow rhythm'.[14] Once more feminine beauty is described in an unsensual manner. The lines and movements of boats have a more abstract appeal, that satisfies the artist's need for pure form – witness Bardamu's descriptions of the boats on the Seine. Women become objects to be contemplated rather than caressed. They trigger off the writer's dream and he transforms them into ships, landscapes or whatever he likes. They personify his aesthetic ideal.

This is why the hours Bardamu spends with Sophie are the summit of his happiness. She scarcely exists as an independent person, she is his creation. To him she represents life in its highest form. She is 'un-selfconscious' because she knows nothing of Rancy poverty or New York loneliness. She does not appreciate the weary troubles of her friends Bardamu, Parapine and Robinson. They admire 'her aliveness', because they know that unlike them she reigns triumphant over death. To humiliate her a little Bardamu goes to watch her as she is sleeping: only then does she struggle to breathe like an ordinary mortal. At other times she is freed from physical and moral corruption.

Here one enters troubled territory. Although Bardamu keeps saying that beauty is the highest form of life, it remains a kind of death. In making love to Sophie he forgets about her not just as a person but as a physical object too. He undergoes a mystical experience – 'You soar up to the infinite plains which stretch out before mankind'. The old Bardamu vanishes to make way for the visionary, who will be absorbed into the new world of harmony. Beauty is death but, paradoxically, it enables man to live more intensely than ever before.

In *Voyage* Céline goes no further than this. The two poles of this thought – disgust for women and love of beauty – are represented by Robinson and Bardamu. The dualism governs his thinking about sex over the years to come. In *Mort à crédit* the young Ferdinand will oscillate between similar extremes of contempt and ecstasy. But the theme of beauty becomes more important. Women will be viewed as merely one manifestation of the harmony the artist is seeking. In *Voyage*, however, the rare flashes of delight are all that is offered to Bardamu to console him for the futility and violence of his existence. They are transitory moments and, when they are over, he must continue on his way.

Bardamu is a strange creature who wanders across the devastated universe of *Voyage* like a modern descendant of the knights errant. He has none of their qualities, for he is neither brave nor handsome neither generous nor faithful. He drifts around, inspired, it would appear, by the simple need to run away. Why does he leave France for Africa and Africa for America? The obvious answer is that he has to. He flees from each place as it becomes impossible to stay. 'Personally I only wanted to get away,' he says, as he stands in the middle of the battlefield. He has no hope that he will find an Eldorado at the end of his travels. New York will be no better than Fort-Gono but, as Fort-Gono is hopeless, he leaves for New York. *Voyage* revolves around these flights: from the war, Africa, the United States and Rancy. Bardamu looks for refuge in hospitals and lunatic asylums. When he arrives at Fort-Gono he twists and turns to find a way of entering hospital. As he cannot he has to go on – to the greater loneliness of Topo and the tropical forest.

He does see some sense in his wanderings: he is not just running away. When he decides to leave Molly he comments: 'I was very fond of her, of course, that's certainly true, but I was fonder still of my own obsession, of my longing to run away from everywhere in search of something, God knows what.' The sense of quest is evident, even if the goal is not. Bardamu's particular Holy Grail is hard to define, but it is a kind of knowledge. 'I wished to know all about this,' he says at each new adventure. Eternally curious he spends hours at his hotel window in New York. At Rancy he listens attentively to his neighbours' battles. Women offer knowledge of another sort. While caressing Lola's 'American contours', he is inspired to visit the United States. Her body sends him 'a message from a new world'. As the book goes on Bardamu becomes more aware of what he is looking for; at the same time he is transformed by it. The Rancy doctor who sees through his patients' theatrical antics is a far cry from the callow youth who went to war.

Bardamu's quest for knowledge is illustrated and parodied in the opening pages. Faced with the war which was 'everything that one didn't understand', he resolves to find out what is happening. 'I felt I wanted to understand their brutal behaviour,' he says of the Germans. He adopts a rational method. He will talk the matter over with the colonel and together they will work out how to stop the fighting: 'two heads would be better than one'. Fortunately for him, the colonel is killed before he can ask such treasonable questions. Bardamu's concept of knowledge is foolish because it implies that life can be understood rationally and that there are clear ways to change it. He soon learns differently. In his few months on the battlefield he discovers that man's soul is 'foul and idle'. As he does so, he becomes himself a coward. There is no question of learning about the war in a detached, analytical manner, Bardamu grasps the mixture of senseless brutality and empty heroism during the long nights when he rides through deserted villages looking for his regiment. 'Never had I understood so many things at once,' he says. When he returns to Paris he is a changed man: 'I'd lost my innocence!' He has a knowledge of war that sets him apart from his flag-waving compatriots.

He has started to unveil the horrors of life. His next step is the exploration of women. Lola and Musyne teach him that women prey on men. They rid him of his illusions: 'I lost my enthusiasm over that slut of a Musyne and that horrid little bitch Lola.' When he meets Molly he has no emotion left.

He becomes a more austere person, because his search has taken him down a negative road. He strips away the lies by which other men live: heroism, love, whatever they may be. His travels across Africa and America are a 'search for this nothing at all'. By travelling he breaks down the fabric of habit which protects people. In New York he has no daily round of work, home and café, so he experiences an 'inexorable glimpse of existence as it really is'. This is a terrifying moment because it means facing the disintegration of the self that occurs on the Manhattan streets. But Bardamu persists because he wishes to discover the truth. He is striving, like an ascetic, to peel away his illusions in order to confront death.

He realizes this when he decides to leave Molly. She represents happiness and love, but they are not what he wants. He is determined to go on to unhappiness: 'Maybe this is what one is looking for throughout life, that and nothing more; the greatest misery there is to feel, so as to become oneself truly before death.' He wishes to be a man, which is to exist in a 'protracted death agony'. It is to feel oneself exposed to random bullets or to be aware that one is a machine on the Ford assembly-line. Bardamu wishes to experience his 'personal emptiness'. He too has his *divertissements*, which take the form of cinemas and women, but they are not important. His real aim is to transform himself – this again is a kind of self-destruction – until everything in him that pretends to live, is broken down. Only then will he know his condition.[15]

Why should he do this? In Céline's eyes it is the only road for a man to take. He is condemned to die in misery, but he has some control over his death. He need not be arbitrarily slaughtered in battle and he need not blind himself with *divertissements*. He can choose to face death, a more painful but more dignified process. 'Man is not an animal because he knows his future,' writes Céline.[16] The future is death, no question about that. But one 'ought not to die ... merely as a dog dies ... one ought to take minute after minute to die'. This is the difference between the colonel and Bardamu.

It explains too why he becomes a doctor. In his travels he had stood outside of other people's suffering: 'Before, one was only hovering around life ... With my medicine, although I wasn't very good at it, I had come into closer contact with men, beasts and creation.' When his patients are dying, they are most truly themselves. The aborted girl and the woman with the miscarriage tell Bardamu far more about death than he ever knew. Their families offer him weird and wonderful examples of *divertissements*. Either way he delves into the human soul.

He quickly realizes that he can do nothing. He fails to persuade the girl's mother and the woman's husband to send them to hospital. His ultimate failure is Bébert. As he listens to the wife-beating among his neighbours he reflects: 'I wasn't any use at all. I couldn't do anything. I simply stood there and listened as always, as I did everywhere.' His knowledge does not lead to action, because the human condition cannot be altered. The gulf between Céline and Sartre is evident. For Sartre, as for Marxists, knowledge involves change. The realization of one's place in the universe brings with it the commitment to revolt. For Bardamu it was 'only inside me that things were happening'.

He undergoes changes of a negative kind. He has lost his self-respect on board the *Amiral Bragueton*. At Rancy he learns he is not a healer. He still has some way to go, when he stumbles on Robinson's attempt to kill Madame Henrouille. Here he acquires guilt. By any legal standards he is Robinson's accomplice, because he knows of the plot and does nothing to prevent it. 'I was guilty,' he explains, 'of being willing in my heart of hearts that this should go on.' He lets the plot unfold because he wants to investigate evil. He wants to see how far Robinson's nihilism will take him, whether Monsieur Henrouille will stand by while his mother is murdered, what part the abbé Protiste, the man of God, is willing to play. His own guilt is part of his exploration: 'You delve deeper into the night at first and start to panic, but you want to *know* all the same, and after that you don't come out of the depths of the darkness.' There is a reversal of conventional values here. Bardamu is committing a crime yet, as guilt is part of the human burden, he is becoming more of a man. In consciously submitting to guilt, he is showing his willingness to face death. Bardamu, who is now more self-aware than in the first part of the book, insists on the ascetic element in his search. He is one of those who 'rid themselves on the way of all the lies and timidity and unworthy eagerness to obey'.

More is in store for him. He returns from Toulouse to work at the lunatic asylum. Madness fascinates him and he watches, as Parapine sinks into insanity and Baryton has a breakdown. In the next chapter the theme of the sane and the insane will be analysed at greater length, here it must be mentioned because Baryton's asylum is the last stage of Bardamu's quest. He sees in madness a 'true manifestation of the inner workings of our souls'. The mad are not really different from so-called ordinary people. They have simply gone further down the same road. Recognizing the gulf between life as it really is and life as men think it to be, they have given up trying to make sense of things. They have retreated into silence: 'Nothing, not even a gold mine, could coax these creatures to venture outside their minds.' To Bardamu they possess a truth that the sane will not admit: they recognize that life is hopeless. Not surprisingly he is comfortable among them, finding them 'easy to manage'. He is himself tempted by insanity, because the inmates have come part of the way he has come. But they have solved the problem by stepping aside from the human condition, which Bardamu will not do. Instead he needs the example of a man who has as bleak a view of the world as the insane, but who will not step aside. This is the importance of Robinson, whose death marks the end of the book.

Robinson is Bardamu's elder brother, another pariah and citizen of the night. At each stage of his wanderings Bardamu finds Robinson ahead of him: more disillusioned with the war, deeper into crime. 'Decidedly, through having followed Robinson in the dark as far as this, I had learned a number of things,' says Bardamu. Robinson is not consciously searching but he too undergoes change. His death is the culmination of a long evolution.

Robinson's character is extremely negative, which in *Voyage* is a virtue. He has the same ascetic strain as Bardamu. His early life has become a complete blank to him, except for one incident in his adolescence. He was working as an errand boy for a milliner when one of the rich customers seduced him. The experience remains in his mind as a kind of original sin. It has turned him away from sex and forced on him the awareness of poverty. His own life has become alien to him. He continues on his way to become a failed deserter and an incompetent murderer, who refuses to believe the lies that other men live by.

When Bardamu first meets him, Robinson is trying to escape from the war. 'I don't want to kill anyone' is his creed and his aim is to be taken prisoner by the Germans. He has not yet understood how hateful men can be and he has not yet arrived at despair. He believes that, if he could only run away from the war, he could live the quiet life he had known before – selling newspapers on the Paris streets. Bardamu finds him interesting because Robinson does not join in the game of heroism. His voice is 'sadder somehow and so more decent'. When they meet again in the African forest, Bardamu finds his friend changed. He has now become a 'brigand'. He treats Bardamu to an exposé of the evils of the colonial system and then, matching action with word, runs off with most of the money. He has entered on a period of revolt. Bardamu notes that Robinson has 'one of those rebellious heads which come up against life too sharply instead of letting themselves be carried along by it'. The romantic phase does not last: there is no room for rebellion in Céline. When they meet in Detroit, Bardamu discovers that Robinson is a failure. He is working, appropriately enough, cleaning out lavatories by night. He has come 'right down to the very heel of people and things'. It is Robinson's failure – his negativeness – that makes him interesting. He symbolizes the absurdity of Henry Ford's brave new world. The people he works with form a 'sort of Foreign Legion of the night'.

On his return to Rancy, Bardamu dreads meeting Robinson. He is busy unveiling the hatreds of the neighbourhood and the people remind him of his friend. As Robinson has always been an example of the worst, Bardamu is afraid to discover how far he will have gone. Sure enough Robinson has become more degenerate: he is ill, embittered and convinced that the poor are damned. Soon he turns to crime: 'The impulse to murder which had suddenly come over Robinson seems to me to be more, in some way an improvement on what I'd noticed till then, in other people, who were always half hating, half kindly.' Robinson has become openly what all men are in secret. He has little practical motive for wanting to kill Madame Henrouille. He undertakes the task for a small sum and completes it for no reason at all. He is bringing to the surface the poisonous but latent hatreds of Rancy. In the topsy-turvy world of *Voyage*, the criminal is more of a man than the so-called honest citizen, hence the 'improvement' Bardamu noted.

There is no shred of romanticism in the portrayal of Robinson as murderer. He is as much a failure in his new career as in his old. He succeeds only in blinding himself. This presents him with a twofold problem. First he must suffer, which he accepts not gladly but with some courage: 'he would manage to stagger on under it a little further, as under some burden that was far too heavy for him, an infinitely point-less suffering'. Then a graver question arises: he has to conform because a blind man cannot reject other people's help. Robinson is sent to Tou-louse where he finds a little job and a fiancée, Madelon. For the first time he begins to drink wine and discuss politics. He even starts to believe in love and he and Madelon make 'plans for the future, a future which was to last forever'. 'You're respectable middle class', Bardamu tells him with disgust. Robinson has found his *divertissements*. His 'account was settled'.

But his sight returns and he sees the trap into which he has fallen. He abandons Madelon, forgets about the restaurant they were to open and returns to Paris. After his period of comfort he is more alienated than ever from life. His whole being is enveloped in 'a sort of already forgottenness, with silence all round it'. Sometimes he grumbles, but he talks less than before. And he too is quite at home in the lunatic asylum.

When Madelon returns to challenge him with the false values of love, he stands firm: 'I've no longer any wish to be loved ... I hate the thought of it.' Robinson shares the Augustinian view of sex: it disgusts him. He knows too that love is just another illusion. He rejects Madelon and she shoots him. It is a ridiculous death – murdered by a jealous woman in a taxi. But it is glorious because Robinson has refused to give way to lies. Bardamu admires it: he hopes 'like Robin-son, to fill my head with a single idea, some really superb idea that was definitely stronger than death'. Robinson has not died blindly, like the colonel or Bébert. He has chosen to die rather than submit to Madelon's charms. He has shown himself free and courageous.

This is why his murder is the culmination of the novel. Bardamu hopes that he too will 'croak superbly ... like Léon had done'. In the context of the Célinian universe Robinson is a kind of martyr. Bardamu has already used religious language to describe him. At Detroit he looked at Robinson's haggard face and commented that: 'Fatigue and solitude bring out God's image in man.' An ironic observation, but one taken up later: 'Robinson was another fellow who was, in his own way, harassed by infinite longings.' Bardamu is not just being sarcastic. Robinson does have a religious view of life. More than any other character, he follows Pascal's dictum that a man should contemplate his condition honestly. When he does so, Robinson experiences the disgust he hurls at Madelon. He is filled with a genuine horror of evil. He has no sense that the world could become better or that he could become better. He merely keeps his eyes fixed on the truth. Honesty is a human, not a theological, virtue so Robinson's last word is not one of redemption but of submission to death. Deprived of the positive side of Christianity, he can do no more than recognize the Fall.

Truth is his and Bardamu's prerogative. It is the reward offered to them for their negativeness, their suffering and their crimes. They speak their truth to others. Fleeing from the battle, Robinson sees a dying captain shout, 'Mother, Mother'. 'Mother, what the hell,' is Robinson's answer. He forces the man to realize that maternal love cannot help him. In New York Bardamu insists on telling Lola that her mother will die of cancer. Doctors have promised to save her; Bardamu cuts through their lies. This is the kind of honesty the other characters do not want to acknowledge. They react with hatred, until Madelon can stand it no longer and has to suppress the truth by shooting Robinson.

After the murder Bardamu is left alone. He seems to have arrived at no particular point. When the book ends he is standing, watching the boats on the river. Céline does not end heroically because it would imply that man can control life. Still Bardamu has achieved something – he has made 'some little progress'. He has borne witness – to war, illness and hatred. He has held fast to his tortured vision of truth. He and Robinson affirm that they are men by failing, and acknowledging their failure.

The last word belongs to death. Not for Céline the 'we-must-be-content' sentiment that ends traditional tragedy. No Fortinbras arrives on the stage to assert that some sort of human order will continue. Robinson dies uselessly, Bardamu is left behind. They offer no solutions.

The reader is left with a nagging question. Who is Bardamu and what is his relationship to his creator? It is clear that Céline is an autobiographical writer. His novels draw closely on his life and he never fails to use the first person narrator. As already seen, his novels are an extension of his life and also a distortion of it. This means that the narrators are neither Céline himself nor objective characters.

When Céline goes into his hallucinated, creative fit he brings out of himself other selves. It is a process of self-transformation, of projecting one part of himself into the realm of his imagination. Characteristically he sees it in terms of death: the man Destouches dies and the fictional character, Bardamu, replaces him. The world of the novel then falls into place, for it is nothing but Bardamu's vision of things. This painful creative process eventually becomes so important to Céline that it enters itself into the novel – which is what *Féerie* is all about. But in all his works his hero-narrators are more extreme versions of himself. They play out roles that he can only partially fill. They are more courageous, more unhappy and more grotesque. And they can be discarded, once they have been used.

Each of Céline's fictional selves is different. Bardamu stands at the opposite end of the spectrum from the Ferdinand of the final trilogy. Bardamu is young and he discovers things; the world is enormous. Ferdinand knows everything already: he watches and suffers as Europe vanishes; the world has shrunk to a heap of ruins. Each self goes further than the one before. Semmelweis possessed nobility, he was a great scientist. Bardamu goes beyond nobility for his task is to learn about death. Ferdinand, the demented narrator of *Mort à crédit*, writes down Bardamu's wisdom. The 'collabo' prisoner-narrator of *Féerie* probes more deeply into artistic creation. And so it goes on. Samuel Beckett's novels follow a similar pattern. His various selves continue down a seemingly impossible road: Watt begins where Murphy stopped, Molloy goes beyond Watt. Each knows of the others, for Moran wonders whether they will not all meet one day, and some of them know about Sam, who is their creator or perhaps only their comrade. These narrators, like Céline's, mark a series of steps in their master's evolution. Even so, one self per novel is not enough for Céline. He splits himself up, giving different fictional names to different aspects of his vision. In *Voyage* there are Bardamu and Robinson, the latter being a more extreme form of Céline's pessimism. In *Mort à crédit* there will be a similar relationship between young Ferdinand and Courtial and in *Nord* between Ferdinand and Le Vigan. Céline plays with the various facets of his many-sided personality. He demonstrates that his world is not static and that there is no one viewpoint from which to look at it. It is far too absurd for that.

A contemporary reader might have wondered which road Céline would take after *Voyage*. One puts down the book feeling that he has said everything. And yet *Mort à crédit* is quite a different kind of novel. It shows much variation from *Voyage*. The portrayal of lower-middle-class Paris replaces the journeys. Courtial des Pereires is a new kind of character, although trapped in the old problems. But it also goes beyond *Voyage*. Céline invents a style of his own, which can express his vision with greater immediacy. At the same time the writer himself enters the book: the adult Ferdinand is a novelist who is writing a novel. *Mort à crédit* is deeply concerned with beauty. The moments of ecstasy that Bardamu experiences with Sophie are transformed into something more important. How can the horrible world of *Voyage* be made into beauty? This is the great question of *Mort à crédit*.

[3]

Mort à crédit

Mort à crédit begins with an adult Ferdinand, who starts in a fever to write the story of his early life. He traces the sorry upbringing of the young Ferdinand from his earliest years to the time he enters the army. The first half of the book describes memories of infancy, jobs in Berlope, a clothes-shop, and Gorloge, a jewellers, and a stay in a school in England. Most important is Ferdinand's tormented relationship with his parents in the closed world of the Passage des Bérésinas. Then, in the second half of the book, the writing changes. On stage comes Courtial des Pereires, a self-styled genius – inventor and philosopher. Courtial believes he can lay bare the secrets of the universe. He tries in a dazzling series of schemes – for perpetual motion, for underwater-diving and for an agricultural revolution. All fail and he eventually commits suicide. Ferdinand is left alone in a state of shock.

Contemporary critics disliked *Mort à crédit*.[1] Having lavished praise on Céline's first novel, they condemned his second. René Lalou sets the tone, when he complains that Céline's view of life is sordid (*Les Nouvelles littéraires*). Another critic calls the book 'mediocre and disgusting' (*La Concorde*), and yet another comments on 'the terrible intellectual and moral nullity of this sad volume' (*Candide*). The Courtial des Pereires section was considered the most successful – 'by far the best part of the book' (*Le Figaro*). The *argot* caused much heart-searching and, if one reviewer enjoyed the 'Villonesque language' (*Paris-midi*), the majority did not. They dismissed it as artificial (*Le Journal*) or inaccurate (*Le Peuple*) or simply boring. Most articles dwell on the details of life in the Passage and say little about the Krogold legend or the entry of the narrator into the novel. One of the most interesting pieces came from Robert Brasillach, who was to become one of the leading lights of the fascist *Je suis partout* and an ardent admirer of the pamphlets. Brasillach admits he 'had a lot of trouble getting through this book', but he admires the 'mock-heroic epic' of the Courtial chapters. He discusses the theme that runs through all the reviews: the problem of realism. Is the book a chunk of lower-class Paris life or 'a kind of obscene epic' (*Le Figaro*)? Most critics stressed the realism and some compared Céline with Zola (*Le Peuple* and *La Tribune*).

Mort à crédit is both more and less realistic than *Voyage*. In one sense it is far removed from the Naturalists. It is not a closed world where, to recall Flaubert's famous dictum, the novelist hides behind his creation like God behind nature. In *Voyage* Bardamu does not appear as narrator. He tells his tale in the first person, but nothing is made of this. In *Mort à crédit* the adult Ferdinand comes on stage as a writer and takes up the first fifty pages of the novel. The writing of the book is an essential theme. The child Ferdinand is already a would-be novelist, who recounts to his friend André the tale of Krogold. Courtial is the author of numerous pamphlets, which bring him some fame and much hatred.

But Céline has also gone deeper into the Paris life that he portrays in the Rancy chapters of *Voyage*. He gives more naturalistic details: the smell of the inevitable noodles that the family eats, the dust of Berlope's shop, the stench of Ferdinand's feet as he tramps through Paris looking for a job. Unpleasant details of excretion abound. Ferdinand is always being punished for not wiping his backside – 'The little beast ... unutterable pig! Why, his clothes are all full of filth.'[2] Such remarks ram home to the reader the sense of a drab, squalid world.

Céline uses another kind of realism: he shows people in the context of their society. He lets them interact with the laws that shape them. The notion of class is stronger than in *Voyage*, where many characters like Parapine and Sophie have no clear social background. Ferdinand's parents are seen as creatures of their lower-middle-class environment. His mother is a small shopkeeper. This governs her attitude towards money – thrift is essential; towards the family – it is sacrosanct; towards the rich – they are always right. When Ferdinand goes out to work he is portrayed – up to a point – as a typical case. The other boys at Berlope are harassed and neglected. They are all oppressed white-collar workers. The women Ferdinand meets are seen in their social context: Madame Gorloge, for example, as an employer's wife. Ultimately *Mort à crédit* may be too much of a caricature to be realistic. But the attempt at realism is evident. Whereas Bardamu stands outside the various societies he encounters, Ferdinand is part of lower-middle-class Paris. He is conditioned by the squalor, which Céline describes in such detail.

The lower-middle-class Paris world is in decay. Horse-drawn cabs vanish, small shopkeepers grow poorer, the imperfect subjunctive becomes obsolete. Such changes may perhaps be seen as the positive signs of a better future? Not so in *Mort*. Changes are death-throes: grandmother Caroline's houses are falling down and Ferdinand's parents have gone bankrupt once already. The 1900 Exhibition is a civic *divertissement* where people go to forget their poverty. Society invades the most private areas of life, poisoning family and sexual ties. The relationship between Ferdinand and his parents illustrates this.

Father and mother refuse to face the fact that their lower-middle-class world is tottering. The father, terrified of losing his poor post as a clerk in an insurance company, trembles before his superiors. He compensates by playing the tyrant at home. His wife knows that each day may bring disaster to her shop. She spreads her brave despair around her. In particular she punishes her son's slightest misdeeds because, in this harsh Paris, they could prove to be his ruin. The family is held together by hatred. Father bullies mother, she infuriates him by her angelic resignation. Ferdinand's view of his parents is simple: 'Personally I have no preferences. Howling rages or plain bitchiness – they're all one to me. She hits less hard but more often. Which would I rather was killed of the two? I almost think Father, possibly'. Their cruelty takes more refined forms than beatings. They insist that he follow in their path. They inculcate him with the virtues of their class which have so signally failed them. After the Paulo incident: 'I had to promise to be very careful how I behaved, not to throw stones at clocks or consort with guttersnipes.' They make him take up a career in commerce when their own shop has been a millstone round their necks. If they could face the truth of their declining world, they could let him work out a different path. But they cannot admit they are wrong. So Ferdinand goes into commerce and, when he fails, it is his fault. His parents project their guilt on to him.

For fail he must. Like the other families in the Passage he is doomed to be a victim. He is labelled lower middle class, 'the son of respectable parents'. He is poor but he cannot enjoy the carefree poverty of the industrial workers, whom his family despises. He has no skills and no trade unions to defend him. He is not educated but he must not work with his hands. His first post is at Berlope. This, according to his mother, is a great honour: 'Berlope and Sons didn't take on just anyone, even for a trial.' He does not last long; he is soon dismissed through the malice of his superior, Lavelongue. After months of searching he finds another job. Again he makes great efforts, again he is dismissed. He scours the Paris streets looking for work. Céline describes unemployment eloquently: the day is spent 'cadging and inquiring . . . hoping and accosting, wheedling and gasping from door to door' until at night Ferdinand is 'dizzy, panting, weak, sticky from haste, drenched to the marrow from rain on the outside and sweat beneath'. He is simply a pawn in the economic game and unemployment and exploitation are the poles of his existence.

Everything in Ferdinand's life is related to his poverty, even his experiences with women. He is seduced and then exploited by Madame Gorloge, the wife of his employer. Nora, who runs from him to her watery grave and thus involves him in her suicide, is the wife of a failed businessman, a schoolmaster driven to ruin by a more enterprising rival. Ferdinand knows a few moments of happiness with Violette, the street-girl: banished by society she turns out to be more honest than other women. Within society all human relationships have been destroyed. The malady of capitalism is everywhere.

In the eyes of an orthodox Marxist this is the essence and error of Céline's pessimism. Ivan Anissimov, writing in the preface to the Russian translation of *Voyage*, maintains that Céline is right to criticize capitalism, but that he is confused.[3] Capitalism has distorted his outlook so that all life appears flawed to him. If he analysed the problem correctly, runs Anissimov's argument, he would realize that life could be different under another economic system. As it is, his nihilism is both an extra proof of the capitalist malady and a shortcoming in his thought. Marxists lament Céline's supposed indifference to the sufferings of the working class. This deprives him of a standpoint from which to analyse society. He is obliged to follow his subjective feeling that something is badly wrong, without having any objective insight into how capitalism works. He condemns without analysing.

Anissimov is certainly right. Céline may be correct in thinking that a socialist society would be no different, but his view of capitalism is distorted. He starts out with the prejudice that men are malicious. Why does Lavelongue dismiss Ferdinand from Berlope? It is not because the shop's interest demands it. It is because he hates Ferdinand more than the other boys. This gratuitous hatred makes sense to Céline but it prevents him from analysing the plight of a young worker in a big store. Why does Céline see the changes in Paris solely as signs of death? This fits in well with his pessimism, but it is a barrier to his understanding of pre-1914 France. This of course does not matter in a novel, at least not to a non-Marxist reader. It does leave Céline very exposed to error when he enters politics. He will incline to irrational solutions. As he does not analyse the situation, there will be no relation between disease and remedy. It is a short step from the arbitrary portrayal of society in *Mort à crédit* to the anti-semitism of *Bagatelles*.

Céline has no historical point of view – Gorki is right. This means that *Mort à crédit* is not, despite appearances, realistic. Céline has concentrated his gaze on a narrower chunk of society, but he has not explained how it works. Despite the abundance of naturalistic detail and the linking of character to social background, his picture of society remains arbitrary. This makes the difference between Céline and Zola. In *Germinal* Zola does portray society accurately. The miners may not understand their situation but the author's comprehension lies behind every page. Zola grasps the exploitation of the workers, the competition among the mining companies, and the effects of poverty on social life. He knows that all men are not malicious all of the time: they are influenced in different ways by their environment. Céline adopts the trappings of realism but his point of view is religious: humans have been abandoned to misery.

The real sense of Ferdinand's childhood is that it repeats Bardamu's mystical quest. Most novelists of childhood describe an awakening consciousness: the child opens out to experience the world. Not so Céline. He depicts pain growing into intense agony. Ferdinand goes through the same stages as Bardamu: he makes gestures of revolt and he resorts to flight. There is no need to describe his evolution in detail but one variant is worth mentioning: his tendency to solipsism. When he is sent to England to learn the language he refuses to speak. In part this is another subtle revenge on his parents who have made sacrifices to pay for his trip. It is also a refusal of contact with others: 'I didn't take kindly to this business of talking ... I was through with confidences and double-crossings, I'd had my fill of such cock for good and all.' Language is dangerous, Ferdinand feels – without realizing the implications of this view. He has been sacked from Berlope for telling André the tale of Krogold. He remembers, when Merrywin tries to be friendly, how Madame Gorloge had made advances in order to betray him. He is happiest when he is alone. 'Keeping my trap shut' becomes his philosophy of life. His solipsism is a kind of flight, that helps him avoid an intolerable reality. It does not work because, like Bardamu, Ferdinand wants to learn. He recognizes that something in him de-demands new experiences: 'I had to keep a sharp look-out, or my imagination ran away with me.' He likes Courtial who offers him 'complicated wheezes and dubious wangles'. Ferdinand is delighted: 'I'd never be happy in any other job . . . it suited me perfectly.' And so he goes on his adventurous way.[4]

But the difference between Bardamu and Ferdinand is that the emphasis is not on the acquisition of understanding, although this is present, but on the pain of acquiring it. Ferdinand does not probe like a doctor, he shrieks like an adolescent. Céline went back to his child-hood for *Mort* because the child can transmit pain more directly than an adult, witness the difference between Bardamu's calm despair at the end of *Voyage* and Ferdinand's breakdown at the end of *Mort*. How Céline achieves this cry of agony is a stylistic question that will be discussed later. Here one may stress that the Passage des Bérésinas is not a Zola piece of documentation. It is a new kind of inferno.

The nightmarish quality in *Mort* becomes evident once Courtial des Pereires enters. Courtial is no social type shaped by his environment. He is a legendary figure who lives out a gigantic myth, far removed from lower-middle-class Paris. At the start Courtial is a triumphant hero whose newspaper, the *Génitron*, is the bible of French inventors. This does not last long. Céline ridicules Courtial: the dedicated scientist spends his time being whipped in brothels, the brilliant analyst loses his money betting on horses. Céline views him the way that Flaubert views Emma Bovary – with some admiration and much irony. He undercuts him, makes fun of his philosophy and leads him through a comic calvary. But he admires him because Courtial, like Ferdinand, tries to cope with an impossible world.

Courtial dislikes systems. When Ferdinand tries to organize the shop, Courtial corrects him: 'you'll never escape from your strong-box of reason, Ferdinand ... So much the worse for you ... It's you who mess up all my disorder with your scurrilous ideas.' According to Courtial the universe is a great creative disorder. He loves to trace the vast, erratic movements of the stars. He designs houses that, instead of resisting the elements, sway in harmony with the winds. He is intrigued by machines for perpetual motion, because he considers the universe to be a flux of ever-changing forms. He also believes – a cardinal point this – that the universe is made to the measure of man. Matter assembles and disperses like a chain of thought passing through the human mind – 'I respect it! It respects me! It's always there, mine for the asking,' says Courtial about the universe. So the search for truth is an easy matter and Courtial 'had in fact in the course of his career explained pretty nearly everything'. He is supremely confident that human intuition can solve the riddles of life.

In one sense his concept of the universe is like Céline's *Mort à crédit* is a world in flux where people wander and objects disintegrate. Céline's remark about the 'flood of things and people and days – shapes passing by, never stopping' could almost have come from Courtial. Almost but not quite. The Célinian universe is not made to the measure of man. It is alien, ruled by death. It is changing and irrational, as Courtial believes, but it cannot be conquered by humans. The net result of science is to assert the absurd, as Parapine has done in *Voyage*. This is why Courtial's search turns out to be false.

He despises death. He takes many risks in his determination to extend the frontiers of knowledge. A pioneer motorist, he is almost killed when his engine blows up. A balloonist, he ascends to the clouds. He hopes to invent a diving-bell that will take him to the depths of the sea. Courtial is a power-house of energy: 'He had to fling himself wholeheartedly either in one direction or another, but in any case all the way, to the bitter end.' He has no sense of human limitations.

Death plays a cat-and-mouse game with him. His balloon flights come to an end when his trusty Archimedes can no longer be repaired. In any case the new aeroplanes are making him obsolete – he the ultra-modern is left behind. He launches the competition to invent a diving-bell, spurred on by a mad priest who hopes to recover the treasures of the Armada. When the competition collapses the inventors take revenge by smashing up his shop. Buried beneath the rubble, he rises again like Lazarus. He resorts to flight – a familiar stratagem. Our in

the countryside he tries to revolutionize potato-growing with radiotelluric methods. He starts a blight that ruins his crop and threatens to
spread for miles. Without knowing it Courtial is drawing near to
truth.

He is gradually being destroyed. He slumps into poverty and his
friends, the peasants of Saligons, start to hate him. The police pursue
him because he lives by theft. Courtial is a failure, all the signs are
there. He contemplates another flight – 'how I wish I were right away
from here! Right away completely'. Instead he faces his situation. He
takes an old rifle, goes out into the cold winter morning and shoots
himself. Céline describes his death in graphic detail: 'He was still
holding the gun. He had it clasped in his arms. The double barrel
went in his mouth, it stuck right through his block. All the mincemeat,
all the pulp on a skewer … in little shreds, in dollops, in strips
… great clots, and hunches of hair. He hadn't any eyes'. His suicide is a conscious act of courage. He recognizes that the world is
not, after all, made in the measure of man. Courtial has devoted himself to knowledge and, when he finds it, he does not flinch from it.
The horror of his death is a sign of his greatness.

Perhaps greatness is not the word, for it would be wrong to idealize
Courtial. Céline makes fun of him. To his wife his suicide is a cowardly
act and his science was just a farce. Ferdinand heaps insults on the
'old chiseller'. One returns to the parallel with Flaubert. Emma is not
a great Romantic destroyed by a full society. She is a mediocre
adulteress, shallow and stupid. She has a touch of greatness: her
aspirations. But her efforts to realize them throw her into the arms of
the provincial Don Juan Rodolphe and the bourgeois clerk Léon. By
focusing his irony on Emma, Flaubert is saying that there can be no
heroines, that people, regardless of their environment, are incapable
of greatness. Céline's irony serves the same end. Courtial's aspirations
are great but he is a charlatan. Céline is showing that man cannot
triumph over the universe.

Courtial becomes a comic character, a parody of Semmelweis.
He sees himself as a genius persecuted by the mob. When the police
pursue him he declaims to Ferdinand: 'Fate overwhelms me. I'm
bullied, baited, hounded, ruined, trampled on, persecuted from all
sides.' Comedy results from the gulf between his grandiose view of
himself and his actual situation: the incarnation of the modern scien-

tific spirit wanders around the Saligons cafés like a shabby peasant.
Courtial's speeches are great flights of empty rhetoric: 'It's like an
ascent . . . I go up; I cross a part of infinite space; I'm about to break
through. I traverse some clouds . . . At last I shall be able to see! More
clouds drift by . . . Thunder strikes me! Still more clouds . . .
I'm scared! I can see nothing!'. Courtial is certainly a verbal hero
(of which more later); but, unlike Semmelweis, he achieves nothing
except a mammoth potato blight. He is trapped in his creator's humour,
doomed to be mocked.

Still the nagging touch of greatness remains, as it does with Emma.
Courtial strives after truth. He does not play the usual games – why
does he not remain the successful editor of *Génitron*? He is tormented
by his desire to know. In one way he is a new kind of character, for
no one in *Voyage* has his energy. But he belongs to Céline's family.
The character who resembles him the most will be Sosthène, the
Tibetan explorer of *Guignol's Band*. Sosthène's magic is like Courtial's
science and its consequences are almost as disastrous. On a more
general level Courtial and Ferdinand are brothers, like Robinson and
Bardamu. Courtial is to Ferdinand a model of how to die. In a strange
way he reminds one of Robinson. They represent opposite poles of
Céline's thought, but they have something in common. The one is
entirely cynical where the other is boundlessly enthusiastic. But they
are both tough men, determined to face the worst, surrounded by
madness and suffering. Courtial too is 'harassed by infinite longings'
which lead him to confront the flaw in the universe. And, like Robinson, he dies bravely.

Madness lies in wait for Courtial: the priest Fleury returns to watch
over his corpse. Madness lies in wait for Ferdinand too and for the
other characters. As a very young boy Ferdinand meets his uncle
Rodolphe who 'laughed uproariously without rhyme or reason',
until one day he vanishes completely. Later there is the idiot child,
Jonkind. Madness takes many forms: Jonkind is pathetic, the inventors
are violent. Some people, like Ferdinand's father, are perpetually on
the brink of insanity and have attacks where they lose their reason
completely. The insane may appear normal, as Fleury does when he
deceives Courtial, and the supposedly sane have breakdowns, witness
Merrywin. Madness is not something that can be labelled and forgotten. In *Mort à crédit* it is so insidious that it finds its way into the

telling of the tale: Ferdinand, both as child and narrator, has fits of insanity. In probing madness, Céline is going far beyond the realistic world of the Passage. He enters an even more sombre territory with different horrors and a new kind of knowledge. He had touched on madness in *Voyage*, but in *Mort à crédit* it is a major theme.

It is not peculiar to Céline. Madness is an important topic of modern literature. A self-confident age like the Victorian could assign lunatics to asylums and forget them; but the twentieth century is less certain that they are alien and reprehensible. At the core of contemporary interest lies the notion that the insane have valuable things to tell us. This is the feeling that draws so many readers to R. D. Laing's studies of schizophrenia. Meanwhile, artists probe what was traditionally called folly for clues to the contemporary condition.

Samuel Beckett, whose early novels play with the relationship between sane and insane, presents parallels with Céline. Murphy, like Bardamu, likes working at mental hospitals and is delighted when the inmates accept him as one of themselves. *Watt* is told from an asylum by a patient called Sam, who describes how Watt, exhausted by the struggle of making sense of Knott's house, has gone mad. Why do Murphy and Watt court insanity? In a world, Beckett feels, where logic and reality never touch, the insane are better able to survive than the sane. Far from expecting reality to make sense, Murphy's lunatics have abandoned it altogether. They are content with the world that lies inside their heads. They play endless games of chess according to rules that they invent themselves. They have their own logic. They fascinate Murphy, because they have a solution to the absurdity of life.

This is what Céline suspects too. In *Mort à crédit* there are three categories of madness. The largest group, composed of people who totter on the brink of insanity, may be called the 'maniacs'. The inventors form part of this group. Although they pass as sane, they can quickly become a 'procession of goblins with their eyes on stalks, screeching at the door, bristling and swollen'. They are obsessed by their ridiculous devices, each of which will save the universe. Diving-bells and machines for perpetual motion are their *divertissements* and, when their cherished toys are rejected, they are left with nothing. Terrified by this prospect they break out into hysteria. As the distance between mask and reality grows greater, the attempt to hold on to the mask becomes more anguished. Finally the Célinian character can juggle no longer, so he tumbles over into madness. Hysteria is a last resort: it is a way of avoiding the truth, but it is a sign that the truth is menacingly near.

Hysteria is usually accompanied by hatred: the inventors vent their feelings by smashing up Courtial's shop. Ferdinand's father is hysterical as he thunders against Jews and Freemasons. One may wonder in retrospect whether the ship's passengers who persecuted Bardamu were not mad – it is hard to tell in Céline. Sometimes the target is legitimate – the inventors have a genuine grievance against Courtial – more often it is not. Ferdinand's father invents enemies, changes them and lives in a world of fiction. His hysteria is one step beyond the normal Célinian hatred because he cannot channel his aggression. The psychological mechanism is the same, but he has no focus. This uncontrolled unfocused hatred is one of the signs of hysteria.

The first category of the insane is not very different from the sane. Ferdinand's father is quite normal for much of the time, although of course normal is a strange word to use about any of Céline's characters. It would be better to say that almost all of them are not very different from the maniacs. They are a little less extreme in clinging to their *divertissements* and their hatreds, but that is all. The natural state of a Céline character borders on madness.

The maniacs' aggression shows that they retain some contact with reality. They cannot, like Murphy's lunatics, live in their world. So they try in their violent way to make contact with others: by assaulting Courtial the inventors admit that he exists. The next step is to sever the link with reality altogether. Fleury ignores the problems he will encounter in recovering the Armada treasure. He has no maps and no equipment, but he does not care. Here insanity has become a refuge for the man who can no longer play the game of pretence. Despairing of fitting the mask to reality, he settles for the reality of the mask. Merrywin stops trying to save his school and slumps into an alcoholic daze, while the removal men carry off his furniture. Ferdinand's father moves from hysteria to this more frightening kind of madness. When his son returns to visit him before leaving for Courtial's farm, he finds him quite different: 'he'd been living in a ghastly dream. He didn't know what he was saying. He couldn't recognize people; he mistook all the neighbours.' There is much less violence now and fewer diatribes against the Freemasons. Ferdinand's father has fallen silent because he is totally preoccupied with himself. He has decided to live only in his inner world. He now belongs to the second category of the mad: the 'exiles'. He joins Fleury and the idiot child Jonkind who, unable to speak, is completely cut off from reality.

The exiles are not violent, because they do not need other people. Instead, the exiles become the victims of the sane. The boys in Merry-win's school torment Jonkind. When they lose a football-game, they revenge themselves on the idiot who has to be rescued – interestingly enough – by Ferdinand. When a character loses his aggression he is persecuted – such is the harsh law of Céline's world. When the police come to arrest Fleury, they tie him up and beat him. This is the price the exiles must pay; but there are compensations.

The mad do not have to play games any longer. They have given up pretending that the world is happy. The process of going mad is a stripping away of the lies that constitute reality. This is what happens to Parapine who goes mad in *Voyage*. The former typhoid specialist and pursuer of little girls begins by withdrawing from his friends, until he ignores them altogether. The intrigues of Bardamu, Robinson, Madelon and Sophie leave him unmoved. Medicine and women interest him no longer. He becomes totally silent – in two years 'he had certainly not uttered more than a score of remarks in all'. He explains to Baryton that he is 'waiting for the arrival of an Age of Mathematics'. This will be the golden age when logic will explain reality. Recognizing that such age is not at hand, Parapine steps outside of time. He gives up the attempt to make sense of the world and retreats into a solipsistic silence. Like Murphy's lunatics, he is content with his own logic. Parapine has taken a big step forward in recognizing that life is a huge deceit.

Does this show that the insane possess a truth the sane will not admit? Céline does not hesitate to say so. The simplest example is the first lunatic asylum in *Voyage*, which is a refuge for men who do not wish to be slaughtered in battle. What an eminently wise point of view! Yet they are considered mad, while men anxious to rush to their deaths are counted as sane. Clearly the mental hospital is a stronghold of wisdom.

This example is too simple because Bardamu and his friends are not genuinely mad. In *Mort à crédit* Céline goes further. When the crisis comes to Merrywin's school Jonkind reacts strongly. He does not understand what is happening, but he is aware that things are badly wrong. When Ferdinand receives the letter telling him to leave, Jonkind goes wild and knocks over the soup-bowls. That night 'he wouldn't shut an eye, I tried ho-hoing him. It did no good, he flapped about, he bounced, he rattled his cage, he growled like a bear. He was afraid I'd run out on him in the middle of the night. He didn't like the idea one little bit'. Jonkind is quite right: Ferdinand does run out on him. Jonkind's idiocy exposes him to the unreason of life. He grasps intuitively that the world around him is falling apart. Although he is plunged into solitude, he has antennae that can pick up the chaos of Merrywin's school.

In particular the mad possess insight into death. In *Voyage* one of Bardamu's inmates leans out of the window on All Saints' Day, screaming that death is everywhere and that he does not want to die. In *Mort à crédit* Uncle Rodolphe is found embracing the rotting corpse of his mistress Rosine. The mad are acutely aware of death – how else does Fleury know when to return to Courtial? Their understanding is limited because they do not know what death is; but they see it everywhere. Their world is arbitrary and irrational so death is not alien to them. They are its companions, as Jonkind accompanies Nora on her last walks. As they have stripped away the false logic of the sane they can know death directly, like Rodolphe, who knows that his dead Rosine is somewhere just 'on the other side of the Seine'. This feeling for death constitutes the exiles' wisdom.

Ferdinand, like Bardamu, is attracted to madness. He alone among the schoolboys looks after Jonkind and he becomes Fleury's companion after Courtial's death. He is interested in the exiles for the same reason as Murphy: he suspects that the madman's world may be an image of the true world. But he and Bardamu have fits of insanity themselves. They are prone to hallucinations, where they lose contact with those around them. During these moments they gain insight into the truth of the mad. For a short time they become exiles, then they return to the ranks of the sane. They belong to the third category: the 'visionaries'.

In *Voyage*, Bardamu has three major hallucinations. As he passes the shooting-gallery with Lola, he sees men being butchered at random; when he leaves Africa for America, he travels in a galley-ship where slaves must row for ever; as he walks in Paris with Tania he sees the dead rising up over Montmartre. Each time he seems to be mad – Lola packs him off to the mental hospital – and each time he is right in the context of the novel. His hallucinations allow him to see a deeper truth that others reject.

Even more important: the subjective reality of madness is depicted in the same way as the so-called objective reality of the rest of *Voyage*. Instead of setting aside a little corner for Bardamu's visions, Céline throws them into the text. Far from being isolated moments of insight they deepen the portrayal of life that the book offers as a whole. At least this is the case with the second and third hallucinations, for the first is different. Here Bardamu has a breakdown that is entirely explicable in psychological terms. He holds the memory of Flanders just beneath the surface of his conscious mind, until the sight of the shooting-gallery releases it. Afterwards he knows himself that he has had a fit. His second hallucination is more complex. He thinks that he has really been a galley-slave and he describes the journey without hinting that it is unreal. True he has just had a fever, so a rational explanation is offered. But Bardamu does not think he has imagined the incident. Even when Robinson tells him in blunt terms, 'You're ill', he does not give way. The galley-slave episode is presented as another part of *Voyage*, not necessarily different from the rest. The Montmartre vision comes into the same category. Here the psychological explanation is evident: the sleepy Bardamu, thinking of Tania's lover's death, sees all his acquaintances rising dead over the city. Surely this is a trick of the mind? But it is presented without comment on the narrator's part and it is never explained away. It stands as Bardamu's final word on characters like Bébert and the Spanish priest.

Madness is part of the reality of *Voyage*, where there is no objective world in the positivist sense. Psychological breakdowns can also be prophetic utterances. There are shifting levels of reality, ranging from the naturalistic Rancy chapters through the stylized descriptions of New York to the Montmartre hallucination. Bardamu's visions are an integral part of his experiences and hence of his narration. As they gather into concentrated form his years as a soldier and a doctor, they illuminate the rest of the book. Madness is not a momentary flash of truth but a deepening of the truth of 'ordinary' life.

In *Mort à crédit* the child Ferdinand has similar experiences. When he is ill with fever, he has a hallucination of a giantess who sweeps through the Passage and starts a riot. This hallucination is true in the context of the novel. But Céline goes much further when he analyses the adult Ferdinand's visions. Here the truth of madness is seen as the truth of art. Insanity is part of the writer's inspiration and it leads him beyond other people's perceptions. The visionaries are the only true artists.

The adult Ferdinand knows the wiles of insanity: 'Madness has been after me, close on my heels, these twenty-two years.' During the first section, when he is preparing to write, he has a fit. He is walking near the Arc de Triomphe with the harlot Mireille when she runs away from him. As he pursues her a crowd gathers and they fight and scream, until the flame of the Unknown Soldier rises up and destroys them. This onrush of insanity is depicted in the same way as the shooting-gallery incident in *Voyage*: Ferdinand has clearly had a psychological breakdown. But his illness continues and out of it comes his novel. When he is brought home from the Arc de Triomphe his mother looks after him. He hears her recounting her version of his childhood and her lies enrage him. In a fresh paroxysm he resolves to tell the truth. 'You're mad, Ferdinand,' she cries, terrified by his outburst. The stricken novelist has another vision: of boats going down the Seine each carrying a 'wee wrinkled corpse hoisting his life-story'. Madness and death go together again, but here they have a third companion: art. *Mort à crédit* is the truth that Ferdinand brings back from the kingdom of the mad. The whole tale of his childhood grows out of his hal-lucination. No longer is insanity just another, deeper kind of reality; it is specifically seen as the creative force. Céline presents Ferdinand as a demented creature lying alone on his bed: this is the author of *Mort à crédit*.

Céline may be seen, without too much exaggeration, as the modern equivalent of the Old Testament prophets who went into trances and returned with the knowledge of God. His novels are full of visions: the Sigmaringen sequence in *D'un château l'autre* is triggered off by another hallucination. Céline keeps on making fun of intellectual truth, because his own truth springs from a deeper source. Ferdinand's account of his childhood has a veracity that no objective historian, much less his conventionally pious mother, could match. So madness plays in Céline's writing the role it plays in much religious experience.

It enables Ferdinand to go beyond the confines of the Passage, to discover the very workings of the universe.

Yet Céline's narrators are no more mad than he is himself. They are visionaries but not exiles and, if they have fits of insanity, they emerge from them. At the second lunatic asylum Bardamu fights to remain sane, as Parapine slips into madness. Ferdinand has madness on his heels but 'it can never quite catch me up'. The elaborate structure of his novel bears witness to conscious intelligence.

The parallel with Beckett recurs. He too rejects the solipsism that Murphy admires. He thinks that there is truth in madness, but that it is only part of the truth he is seeking. After *Watt* the theme of insanity is less frequent in Beckett's writing. Molloy is not at all mad, for he is painfully aware that there is a reality he cannot understand. When he fails to penetrate the problem of his sucking-stones, he does not assume that the problem does not exist. He recognizes that his lonely task is not to understand the unintelligible. By accepting that he is living in an absurd universe, Molloy has gone beyond madness.

Céline does the same: Ferdinand must return from the kingdom of the mad. Between him and the exiles lies the question of lucidity. Jonkind may grasp that Nora is about to die, but he does not know what this means. Fleury does not know why he is returning to Courtial's corpse. The exiles' solipsism has put them outside of the human condition and they cannot appreciate what death really is. Only the visionaries can both see death everywhere and understand what it signifies to man. The adult Ferdinand would not embrace his mistress's corpse because he knows that death is appalling. But then he has rejected solipsism, as he did when he was a child. He is willing to live and therefore to suffer, which gives him a greater understanding than Rodolphe can ever possess. As a novelist Ferdinand uses madness; but he must also be sane so that he can see the truth of the hallucination in the context of 'ordinary reality'. Madness is part of his destiny, but he must have the courage to go beyond it.

Mort à crédit is very much a book about the writer, about his splendours and miseries, of which madness is only one. The child Ferdinand's story is presented as the adult Ferdinand's novel and the novelist dominates the early chapters. While he is preparing to write, he tells us about his job, his friends and the kinds of books he writes. Later he intervenes as a man, to comment on his childhood experiences.

In the middle of the Nora episode he remarks: 'It's years ago, yet I can call up her image whenever I want.' Céline keeps before us the act of writing.

He talks frequently about aesthetic beauty. The child Ferdinand is delighted by the harmonies of fog-drenched England, where he sees a 'battle of rainbow shades ... yellows, purples, pale green'. Nora personifies another kind of enchantment. These flashes of harmony point the way to real beauty – literature, the joy of artistic form. Céline's style is extravagant, no longer a vehicle but an end in itself. Comedy and movement are stated themes of *Mort à crédit*. The consolations of literature, which are the only values in the wasteland of the book, represent the positive side of Ferdinand's writing.

Yet the writer's aim is knowledge. He must tell the truth, however horrible and at whatever cost to himself. This is why the novelist Ferdinand quarrels with his mother. She invents the story of a hard-working family with a devoted father. To Ferdinand this is 'a whole obscene stinking pack of lies', because there never was a 'lousier skunk in the whole world' than his father. His mother is horrified because he has undermined the fiction by which she lives. Like most people in *Mort à crédit*, she has been lying to invent an existence for herself. Now Ferdinand has destroyed it. He has made her realize that her life was just so many years of useless toil. This is his truth.

In order to discover it he must take the road that Bardamu mapped out in *Voyage*. He must abandon *divertissements*, break down the defences of habit, know guilt, madness and suffering. Only by this process of self-destruction can he see death clearly. The relationship between Bardamu and the adult Ferdinand is evident: Bardamu is preparing to be a writer and he ends up where Ferdinand begins. He has not yet taken the final step, which is to give aesthetic form to his experiences but, morally and philosophically, he is already an artist.

Like Bardamu, the narrator of *Mort à crédit* is a broken man whose miseries are all too obvious. Ferdinand is a doctor and he goes about his daily round, which is the usual Célinian brew of squalor and corruption. His cousin Gustin, a doctor at the V.D. clinic, is dying of cirrhosis of the liver and his typist Madame Vitruve is an evil-smelling hag, whose ambition is to become an abortionist. Ferdinand himself lives in poverty and his neighbours are starting to hate him. He is trying to recover from Madame Vitruve the manuscript of his tale of

Krogold. She has lost it and no one cares because Ferdinand's work is not popular anyway. He has other troubles, for he is prey to madness and so obsessed with guilt that he befriends even the fox-terrier he meets in the street. Like Bardamu, he sees death everywhere and can hardly cope with conventional life. Ferdinand is stamped with failure.

Voyage had contained a few scattered observations on writing and these serve as an introduction to *Mort à crédit*. Bardamu repeats that he wants to have done with it, be silent and 'let's hear no more of all of this'. The writer's task is hard; small wonder that Bardamu is weary. But he remarks that 'we shall never be at peace until everything has been said, once and for all time'. Ferdinand too is willing to keep on searching, until he has told the full horrible story: until Courtial is dead, the child Ferdinand shattered, and the novelist himself reduced to sickness and ruin.

Ferdinand's first problem is the temptation of silence. 'So many people have come in here, to my room. They've talked: they've not said much,' says the novelist. As a doctor, Ferdinand has listened to floods of complaints. He has given up paying attention because he knows it is just words. He withdraws into silence as he did when he was at school in England. Instead of making protestations of sympathy he fixes up a toy for the sick child. In his writings Céline pays homage to silence by leaving out the elements of traditional fiction. The lack of brave heroes, of organized plot and of well-rounded sentences marks the rejection of the mother's stories.

But the writer must break the silence and express his knowledge. It will inevitably be unpleasant: an expression of 'all the hatred I feel'. But it will not be a mere description of his experiences. At the outset Ferdinand himself declares 'I'd just as soon tell a few stories.' The book he is working on is a romance about a medieval king, Krogold, a rebel prince, Gwendor, and a beautiful princess, Wanda. He is creating a world of make-believe which seems miles away from the Fondation Linuty. He recognizes that in one sense his stories are like other people's. He enjoys listening to Mireille – 'she was swell at telling marvellous stories' – and he suggests that they work together. There is a contradiction here: Ferdinand dismisses fiction as a *divertissement*, he also enjoys it. He sees it as a false kind of art that does, however, have something in common with his writing. *Mort à crédit* is full of false artists – from Mireille on.

The Passage, seemingly so drab, teems with them. Ferdinand's father 'was an artist at heart . . . Sometimes he'd draw a storm for me in chalk on my slate.' He likes to paint water-colours of ships and he is a storyteller who delights his neighbours with an epic description of the Exhibition. Then there is Ferdinand's mother who loves fine lace, and Wurzem the cabinet-maker who is 'an artist, an unrivalled craftsman'. The list goes on: Uncle Arthur 'used to draw sailing boats on a big board', Madame Divonne has 'the artist's temperament' and she 'played the piano beautifully', Gorloge is 'the proud artist to the life', a worker in gold and jewels. Later there is Nora, who plays the piano exquisitely, and of course Courtial, writer and storyteller.

All these characters have one corner of their lives where they create beauty. While telling his stories Ferdinand's father is raised above his office and family. He lives in a world of 'wonders fifteen times more startling than ten dozen Exhibitions'. Madame Divonne can bring enchantment on the house with her performance of *Clair de lune*. She is trying to dispense with reality and bring magic into her existence. The aesthetic is not the prerogative of a privileged few and it is not a special, separate activity. It is a natural response to the world. The characters are transforming their hopeless lives: they are all, in Baudelaire's phrase, striving to turn the mud of the Paris streets into gold. In the Passage, the lace and antiques form a wonderland where the customer strolls like 'a fairy princess, through a toppling, tinkling avenue of crystal'.

Yet the transformation fails. 'My father regarded imaginative flights with suspicion,' notes Ferdinand. He was right. When he tells his tale of the Exhibition he casts a spell: 'Magic reigns in our shop.' But one evening Madame Méhon comes across with a paper saying 'Liar'. The listeners laugh, the illusion is broken and Auguste must return to his problems. The same is true of the little God of Happiness, fruit of Gorloge's talent and Ferdinand's hard work. It brings only trouble. Art is the most dangerous of *divertissements*. For a short time it enables one to escape; but soon the real world crumbles beneath the storyteller's feet. Nora, for example, plays the piano while her school collapses.

Ferdinand's Krogold legend is a higher example of art, although it too is a transformation that fails – initially at least. The shabby doctor cannot live in the world of glorious warriors that he creates. But, unlike his father's stories, his tale is true. One must return to Ferdinand's initial comment that he will 'tell a few stories' instead of expressing 'all the hatred I feel'. In practice his stories are full of hate, for he never writes about 'the pleasant side of life'. The events of the legend are terrible.

It is governed by death. Krogold, a brutal king whose banner portrays a 'decapitated serpent bleeding at the neck', represses Gwendor's rebellion. As Gwendor lies dying on the battlefield, he understands that the world is hopeless. Death appears in person, shorn of the disguises it wears in *Mort à crédit*. Gwendor pleads for 'a little while ... one day, or two' but Death insists that 'Everything betrays'. Krogold's rule is re-established. The gold crescent, symbol of his temporal and spiritual sway, has been stolen but he recovers it by murdering the thief. He sends his hounds into the cathedral, places his sword on the altar and is greeted by his brother, the archbishop. The people of Christiania tremble before him.

This is the world of *Mort à crédit*. Like the Paris of 1900, Krogold's kingdom is built on cruelty, and his subjects fear him as Ferdinand feared Monsieur Berlope. There are many lesser parallels between legend and novel. Krogold's only threat is his golden-haired daughter Wanda who will humiliate him, as Madame Gorloge deceives Ferdinand. Thibaud, the troubadour, is plotting to kill Joad's father, as Ferdinand tries to kill his father.

Thibaud is an especially interesting character because he is an artist and the story he tells Joad's father is a tale within the tale. Its significance is clear. Thibaud is a difficult creature, an outsider who will not pay the toll at the city gates. 'Frothing at the mouth' with madness he is dragged before the sheriff, Joad's father. He 'screams out his odious story': Joad had murdered an archer years before.

Like Thibaud, Ferdinand is telling the grim truth. But he can still create beauty. The legend presents the theme of beauty, both through the trappings of medieval local colour – fair princesses and noble steeds – and by direct statement. Death says to Gwendor: 'there is nothing gentle on the earth, Gwendor, but the gentleness of myth. All its kingdoms end only in a dream.' As Gwendor dies 'a beautiful dream took possession of his soul'. It can neither save him nor change the bitterness he feels. But it is present in its own right as beauty. The inescapable connection of the dream with death shows that true beauty

– unlike the false art of Ferdinand's father – can be bought only by defeat. This explains the reconciliation in the cathedral. Krogold's rule is absolute, but he pardons the people of Christiania in a scene full of aesthetic and religious ritual: the casting of the sword on the altar, the sign of the cross, the presence of the archbishop and the chanting of the credo. The aesthetic transformation can be lasting only when it faces up squarely to the human condition. Death, when triumphant, has the order of great art.[5]

The way the legend appears and vanishes shows how Ferdinand creates a world that is both imaginary and real, both beautiful and horrible. One may break down the tale into three parts: the pieces that Ferdinand has written and that he tells to Gustin and Mireille, the fragments the child Ferdinand has read in the *Illustrated Adventure Stories* and the parallels with the legend that are present at Courtial's death.

At the outset the legend has been lost. Ferdinand finds it in Madame Vitruve's apartment, its fragile harmonies juxtaposed with her squalor. He recounts parts to Gustin, who is 'suspicious' and then falls asleep out of boredom. Separation of the aesthetic and the real is the keynote here. Dissatisfied, Ferdinand decides not to continue with his legend and instead to tell the story of his childhood. But Krogold and Gwendor do not disappear.

For the young Ferdinand, the legend is not a separate creation but an integral part of his early experience. He learns to read in the *Illustrated Adventure Stories* which recount Krogold's wars. He has not created the myth, which is intertwined in his consciousness with the noodles he eats and the stories his father tells. He pays dearly for reciting to André the reconciliation in the cathedral. Lavelongue enters and dismisses him for telling 'dirty stories'. The myth is playing a role in the plot: legend and novel are one, just as the Passage is both drab and full of fantasy. Later Nora reads to Ferdinand from the same tales – which Jonkind loves – but he rejects them as part of her siren song.

This is the last specific reference to Krogold and his court. When Courtial comes on the stage they vanish. But Courtial is himself a mythical figure, whose 'genius swelled that brain of his all day long', and who could 'have made a thunderbolt pass through the eye of a needle, produce sparks of lightening or have hailstones play tunes in a retort'. *Mort à crédit* shifts to a new level, which is halfway between the Krogold legend and the Passage. Courtial's destiny is seen in symbolic terms right down to his death – the destruction of his brain that marks the failure of the human intellect in which he believed.

The end of the book falls into two sections: the day in Blême-le-Petit and Ferdinand's return to Paris. More is involved than a change of place. In the first section Ferdinand is detached. He looks on while Madame des Pereires is hysterical and, although he is angry at Fleury's capers, he soon recovers. At Blême-le-Petit Ferdinand's calm allows him to see the events following Courtial's death as an ordered sequence. They are presented as a ritual, reminiscent of Gwendor's death or Krogold's reconciliation. Céline reminds us of the legend: the priest Fleury, who replaces the archbishop, has a hunting horn with which he announces Courtial's death. His repeated question – 'Are we going to call on Charlemagne?' – sends the reader back to the Middle Ages. Courtial's suicide becomes an event that possesses the aesthetic order of the legend.

Céline makes us see it as the death of a king who is absurd and yet royal. As Courtial has been 'bitching up the whole face of the earth', his kingdom is dying with him. His shattered body is brought back to the farm on a wheelbarrow. The funeral procession takes three hours and he is attended by his wife and his dauphin Ferdinand. At the farm, villagers, police and journalists form a sarcastic chorus. The orphaned children of the New Race lament and the policemen eat and drink as at a wake. The corpse is wrapped, not in funeral clothes, but in a 'bright red bit' of Archimedes. This is an ironic reminder of Courtial's triumphs and a grotesque symbol of resurrection – 'He used to go up into the sky,' says his wife.

Religious symbolism is important. Society is mocked in the figure of the Public Prosecutor and his frozen feet, but religion is treated in more complex manner. There is an element of pure parody. The priest is mad and his robes are ridiculous. He wears the hunting horn and the Legion of Honour as well as a crucifix. He is aware of some occult forces called the 'Powers' and he does an insane dance around the room sprinkling water, as if at a church funeral. Yet there is a serious attempt to present Courtial as a martyred victim: 'They've martyred him enough,' sobs his wife. Already she has prayed for him, now she wishes to give him a religious burial. Fleury, whose destiny is caught up with Courtial's, is another Christ figure 'with his arms stretched out, making a cross himself'. He too utters incoherent prayers – 'Thy kingdom come,' he repeats.

Céline is expressing his religious awareness: Courtial's death can be understood only by a man convinced of the Fall. If these symbols were not grotesque they could represent a reality beyond futility. As it is they reveal the absence of a God who could bring Courtial back to life. But they also reinforce the sense of ritual, as they did in the reconciliation episode. They form a pattern that makes the reader see the suicide as part of an aesthetic order.

The final pages set this order in its place. The Blême-le-Petit section has revealed Céline's vision of the world as a blend of legend and reality where aesthetic creation is incessant. The Paris pages repeat the lesson that art is a failure. As in *Voyage*, which ends not with Robinson's brave death but with Bardamu's despair, so in *Mort à crédit* Céline never implies that the aesthetic order of Courtial's death is any solution. He leaves the last word to Ferdinand, the boy not the observer. Ferdinand reacts violently to the horror he has seen. Until now he has been calm but he goes through a delayed shock. Finding himself alone he has a hallucination where Courtial appears to talk about the stars and the glories of the human intellect. Ferdinand turns away in revulsion. He knows it is just words and he rejects Courtial, as he will reject Uncle Edouard's conventional optimism. 'No' is his last word. Céline does not bring back the adult Ferdinand as narrator because he does not want to depict art as a triumph over reality. The hysterical child is left behind: he too is an image of the writer.

The kind of artist Céline is presenting is better understood if one glances at the Zola lecture. While reviewers saw similarities between *Mort à crédit* and the Rougon-Macquart saga, Céline insists on the differences between Zola and himself. In Zola's age, so the lecture runs, the horrors of life could be interpreted by the rational mind; by the 1930s this was no longer possible, because contemporary reality was simply appalling. It was useless to analyse it from the outside. What then was the writer to do? Céline explains: 'One must deliberately place oneself in a state of nightmare in order to get the right tone.'[6] The careful realism of the nineteenth-century novelist will be abandoned and the modern writer will use 'symbols and dreams'.[7] Whether or not Céline is doing justice to Zola, he is certainly putting himself in a different tradition: the seer tradition of Baudelaire and Rimbaud. According to Rimbaud, the artist is a *voyant* who tries, by deranging his senses, to penetrate beyond the physical world. The Célinian artist, who courts madness and creates legends, is very much a Rimbaud figure.

And like Rimbaud he is destroyed: the act of writing is 'almost a suicide'. Morally and philosophically Ferdinand is bankrupt. 'I shall be old soon – then it'll be all over,' he says. He expects nothing from his readers who, in true Célinian manner, will respond to his books with hatred – 'they'll come back, on purpose, to kill me, from the four corners of the earth!' His only reward is the consolations of literature. One could say of any work of art that its form redeems its pessimism, but Céline is doing something else. He is insisting that life is an aesthetic matter. Reality involves legend and dream. One cannot separate them any more than one can distinguish Krogold's crimes from Wanda's golden hair. Comedy, movement and style are the fruits of despair. Young Ferdinand is comic because he has gone beyond pity. If one felt sorry for him one would not laugh, but one knows that pity is useless in the world of *Mort à crédit*. Novelist Ferdinand's stylistic innovations are a way of conveying his nihilism. Traditional language cannot express his predicament, so he creates a new style that will embrace death and go beyond it. At every point one returns to the lesson of Courtial's burial.

At first sight this story of suicide and squalor does not appear funny. There are no young lovers, servants with quaint accents and happy endings. Yet Céline considered himself a comic writer: 'my "danse macabre" amuses me, like a huge farce'.[8] His books are not solely comic; they are also sad and frightening, which traditional comedy is not. But one does laugh.

Comedy results from the gulf between the mask and reality. When Ferdinand's father thunders against the Freemasons the reader is amused because his diatribes are so exaggerated. Courtial's attempts to grow radiotelluric potatoes are grotesque because he knows nothing of agriculture. One is reminded of Bergson's comment that comedy springs from man's attempt to impose a rigid order on the flux of life. The characters of *Mort à crédit* keep behaving as if they lived in a normal, rational world. Merrywin is comic because he insists on turning out his football team while his school is falling apart. The situation is always the same: Céline's clowns are grotesque because they pretend to be happy.

Voyage was already a humorous novel and the pattern of comedy was the same. The soldiers trying to find the battlefield and the colonials trying to build roads are comic because they will not recognize that their tasks are absurd. There ought to be military strategy and there ought to be roads but, as there are not, men who believe in them become ridiculous. In *Mort à crédit* Céline has pushed the same kind of comedy much further. The first half of the book is a series of short chapters that take place within Ferdinand's family. Most of them follow the same pattern: the family sets out to achieve some modest goal and fails. Ferdinand's mother tries to make a little money by selling her lace at an outdoor market; Ferdinand ruins everything by smashing a clock with a sling-shot. What happens when the family goes on a trip to England? They lose their cases and are washed away by the rain. The supreme example is the outing in the country. They set out happily on Uncle Edouard's motor-tricycle, but it falls gradually to pieces, leaving them stranded and distributing its parts across the fields. Each of these chapters is exploited for its comic possibilities, although it may add little to our knowledge of the characters. In the second half of the book Courtial's exploits are described in the same way. Céline heaps up accounts of inventions that end in disaster. These chapters are variations on a set theme, rather like a Molière farce. *Mort à crédit* has the structure of a comic novel and large sections of the book are designed chiefly to arouse laughter.

Céline runs the gamut of traditional comic devices – exaggeration, disguise and farce. Courtial is particularly reminiscent of Molière's heroes – he is the *bourgeois gentilhomme* of science. But the first difference that strikes the reader is the absence of norms. In Molière's plays the sensible friends and the witty servants provide a yardstick to judge the hero's folly. In Céline there are no norms, because reality itself is absurd and no one can make any sense of it. Whatever the characters do turns out wrong. The young Ferdinand's solipsism is as amusing as Courtial's enthusiasm. The heroes who try to understand life are as ridiculous as the clowns who hide from it.

One returns to the special problem of Célinian comedy: its relationship with nihilism. Surely the insistence on death will destroy the humour? Surely it will awaken in the reader horror and its con-comitant emotion, pity? It will obliterate the distance that is necessary in comedy. But Céline expunges sympathy. Bardamu comments: 'Maybe I was to be pitied; most certainly I was absurd.' Like the young Ferdinand he knows sympathy is useless because nothing can be changed. When Ferdinand smashes the clock he blames himself for being stupid enough to trust Paulo: 'I'm making no excuses' is his conclusion. People are malicious, he should have known that. Céline's comedy both reinforces and springs from his pessimism. Pity is the last vestige of humanity and, once it is gone, the world becomes a wasteland. Céline's heroes are so degraded that, far from evoking admiration, they cannot even arouse pity. They are dehumanized by his irony. At the same time the absence of sympathy makes possible the aesthetic pleasure of comedy.

This new kind of gallows-humour is one of Céline's special traits. 'I only rejoice in the grotesque on the borders of death', he remarks.* Here again there is a parallel with Beckett. Molloy is a comic character who laughs at himself when he is unhappy. He accepts that pity would be wasted and he knows that he is no longer a human being in the traditional sense. He too is nihilistic. In Beckett the line between laughter and pity is not clear so the reader is sympathetic even as he smiles. But smile he does. Beckett and Céline have created a charac-teristically modern kind of humour. In *Mort à crédit* it is a reward offered to the ruined writer Ferdinand.

Movement is another reward and it too is death's prerogative. *Mort à crédit* is full of movement. The child Ferdinand begins his tale by describing how the nineteenth century 'disappeared along the road beyond Orly to Choisy-le-Roi'. From this moment on nothing is static: short chapters flit by, characters appear and vanish. Ferdinand is rushed through his childhood: 'I always had a dirty behind, I didn't have time . . . we were always in too much of a hurry.' Still he enjoys movement. He is fascinated by the chaos of Courtial's office with its 'sweeping cataract' of papers and its 'deluge of blueprints and proofs'. He knows that the jumble is not as great as it seems, for Courtial can find anything in an instant. Behind the movement of

---

* Despite this 'dehumanization' Céline's characters do, of course, attract pity just as Beckett's heroes do. The characters in the pamphlets are 'dehumanized' in a different way.

Mort à crédit is an ordered rhythm, to which Céline draws our attention. Rhythm, Baudelaire says, is one of beauty's greatest attributes. Ferdinand agrees: line, harmony of colour and the dance of disintegrating objects are a delight to him.

In *Mort à crédit* things are always changing. Edouard's motortricycle sheds screws and bolts along the roadside. This constitutes another difference between Céline and the nineteenth-century realists, who portray things as solid entities in a solid world. Flaubert's description of Charles Bovary's cap turns it into an absurd object that bears witness to the stupidity of provincial life. But the cap stands fixed and immobile, because Charles does not change and because his life resembles countless other lives in contemporary France. In Flaubert's books time is static so things are durable. When they do change, they fall to pieces very slowly like the house in *Un Coeur simple*. This is quite the opposite of Céline whose objects fly apart, like Courtial's car which 'disappeared in a flash'. The family's crockery is smashed, Nora's furniture is carried off, Courtial's shop is destroyed. Disintegration is rapid and ubiquitous.

Ferdinand enjoys swift movement. His father is a great wrecker of objects: 'He raves, he roars, he explodes, he's going to break every saucer in the place. The dresser's empty ... All the dishes are in smithereens, spinning, crashing, hurtling through the air ... He capsizes the table with one almighty boot'. As an observer Ferdinand is not interested in the cups and plates themselves but in their movements, hence the different words to describe how they fall. The phases of his father's temper are another kind of motion – his anger being seen as a succession of changing states. In both cases Ferdinand transforms what is happening into pure movement. Things and people become figures in a dance and they create harmony, not through themselves, but through their motions: the changes in the father's temper form a pattern with the falling crockery. When Ferdinand describes a crowd the same transformation takes place. He watches a group of English sailors: 'They lurch and frolic along. Already tight and ever so happy. They skip and romp and guffaw ... They barge into the crowd. They can't make any headway, their jigs collide around a lamp-post. They get entangled'. The sailors are described not as men but as moving blobs. Ferdinand turns their walk into a dance where they separate, change pace and intersect. As abstract movement the sailors have a harmony which they do not possess as people.

One remembers Céline's fascination with dance, which will be analysed more fully later. In the context of *Mort à crédit* it is enough to stress that the novel is full of formal patterns. Ferdinand always sees beauty in terms of rhythm: the shifting light from the church window on Nora's face, the changing moods of the sea – 'the dancing water with all the reflections, headlights winking, approaching, crossing'. *Mort à crédit* provides the kind of pleasure one gets from modern dance: the revelation of a new kind of symmetry. The style of the novel is extremely rhythmic, because Céline has broken down the heavy, traditional sentence into little phrases that permit abrupt twists and juxtapositions.

Yet the dance is always the *danse macabre* and things disintegrate because death strikes them. The harmonies that the visionary Ferdinand loves are inseparable from violence. He describes how the inventors smash up Courtial's shop with their diving-bell: 'Everything shattered to smithereens. The woodwork ripped and splintered and broke – everything went! There was a shower of falling glass . . . as the colossus lunged, drove, toppled, vacillated, scrunched through'. The verbs that convey motion describe destruction too. Ferdinand expands his description for its own sake – for the sheer joy of movement. But he does not forget the horror. He knows that the crowds he likes to watch can quickly become bloodthirsty. He is aware too that another kind of dehumanization has taken place. People are reduced to blobs on a street, their individuality sacrificed to their role in the dance. Only then do they become part of the universal harmony. Céline knows, as Baudelaire knew too, that rhythm is dearly bought.

Even more dearly bought is style, the glittering flood of language that rolls across the gloomy world of Paris. In *Mort à crédit* Céline has created a new language precisely to express Ferdinand's hell. He has twisted traditional French prose to give form to his despair. In doing so he makes us so conscious of the possibilities of language that the despair is lightened. He builds stylistic castles in his wasteland.

Between *Voyage* and *Mort à crédit* lies a stylistic revolution that revolves around the problem of immediacy.* *Voyage* is written in the

---

* The English edition of *Mort à Crédit* gives little idea of Céline's style. Some of the more obscene passages have been cut and the crudeness has been

style of a traditional novel: it has sentences and grammar and its vocabulary is accessible to readers of Proust and Gide. In *Mort à crédit* the sentence has been broken down into a series of phrases separated by exclamation marks and ellipses. A page of the second book is even visually different:

> Under the lamp I counted my dough. There was still thirty-five francs left, and I'd paid both my fare and padre's. I shelled the egg at the counter. I took a bite. I spat it straight out. I couldn't swallow ... Hell! It didn't get any better ... ! 'Oh, hell, I'm ill,' I realized. I felt seasick. I stepped back into the street – everything rocked ... the sidewalk, the gas-lamp, the shop.

The breakdown of well-ordered style was clearly the next step in Céline's evolution. How was he to write about absurdity in logical language? The dislocation of his sentences reflects the lack of moral and social values. But the innovations of *Mort à crédit* have a positive side: Céline creates a new style to capture the horror he describes.

Ferdinand's passage should be compared with any passage from *Voyage* – like the description of how Bardamu watches over the dying Robinson:

> He must have been looking for some other Ferdinand, one of course much greater than me, so as to die, or rather, for me to help him to die, more quietly. He made efforts to discover whether there hadn't been perhaps some improvement in the world. He was going over it all, poor wretch, in his mind wondering whether men hadn't changed just a bit for the better while he had been alive.

Even in translation the tone is quite different: *Voyage* is reflective where *Mort à crédit* is emotional. Bardamu, who is trying to piece together his experiences, wonders about Robinson. He stands outside the event – his friend's death – and tries to understand it, hence the 'or rather' and the 'perhaps'. Not so in *Mort à crédit*. In general Ferdinand describes things from within and his aim is to express his immediate horror. An internal narrator, he tells his story like a monologue. And he has a new vocabulary – *argot*.

watered down. More important, the translator has frequently used full stops instead of the three points ellipsis Céline loves. This alters the visual effect, which is itself quite important. It also makes the book more static and spoils its rapid staccato rhythm. In the translation the style seems uniform and grey, whereas the French has many hues. Ralph Manheim's translation is better.

Céline

Mort à crédit is full of slang: *grolles* for feet, *thunes* for money, *gueule* for face, and the like. Céline uses many words that do not appear in the literary language: *se dépiauter, crounir, faire vinaigre, moujingue, rataplan, mouscaille, gogs, rombière*, the list is endless. Whole pages are unintelligible to readers not acquainted with the slang of the Paris backstreets. At first sight this looks like a realistic device: Céline is using the language of the poor to get closer to their lives. Zola had done this with the mineworkers of *Germinal* and so had Maupassant in his stories about Normandy peasants. But Céline has different aims. His language is not realistic, because all the characters use the same kind of vocabulary despite their social and personal differences. One would not have expected Ferdinand's father, a respectable white-collar worker, to talk like one of his son's urchin friends. Why does the adult Ferdinand use the same vocabulary as the child? Nuances are needed if language is to delineate social reality. The flood of slang – a slang which is now quite out of date – creates in *Mort à crédit* an effect too unvaried to be realistic.

It does create emotional intensity. Later Céline explained that he was using slang because it was the language of hatred.[9] Rich in crude terms, it expressed the resentment of the poor against their lot. Céline's slang is a huge cry of despair rather than an exact speech. His aim is to introduce 'emotion into the written language'.[10] No longer will the writer stand outside his subject and discuss it in polished, abstract French. The child Ferdinand screams his reaction to the world in virulent tones. This is how he attacks his father: 'I snatch up his machine ... I give it him full in the phizz. He hasn't time to ward it off. He goes arse-over-tip like a ninepin ... I'll have to finish the bastard off ... Whack! He's down on the floor again ... I'm going to shut his trap for him'.

Such direct expression of emotion is lyrical and Céline once described his writing as 'black lyricism'.[11] The same is true of the crudities that litter the book. There are endless descriptions of excretion. This is how Ferdinand's grandmother cleans out the lavatories in her tenants' houses: 'Caroline would start prodding into the bowl. She jabbed about resolutely, raking through the muck. All the tenants crowded round with their young to see if we could dislodge their own filth.' Céline is not making a sociological point about poverty. He is showing the depths to which people of various social classes will descend. Such descriptions serve the same purpose as the sordid account of Madame Gorloge's love-making. The torrent of obscenities is the most vivid way of expressing man's fallen nature.

The question of realism is a red herring. Céline does say that he wishes to introduce spoken French into the literary tongue; but this is because 'emotion can only be seized and transmitted through the spoken language'.[12] He breaks down formal grammar to create immediacy, but he does not fall into the opposite trap. Ordinary speech is full of imprecise terms, it contains hesitations and repetitions. All of these detract from the emotional impact. Céline refines everyday language to make it concise. He introduces abrupt transitions leaping from person to person, thought to thought. His style is telegrammatic or, to use the term he preferred, impressionistic.[13] Like the Impressionist painters, Céline felt he seized the effect rather than the object. Ferdinand, whose monologue is frequently obscene but seldom ordinary, notes a fact, reacts to it, jumps to something else. In the description of the father helping the child with his homework the confusion of the one and the hostility of the other are more immediate than in any conventional narrative. The juxtaposed personal pronouns seem themselves to be at war: 'He always made me go over my sums with him ... I was then entirely stumped, my mind became an absolute blank, with him getting into such a devil of a tangle in the thick of his own explanations ... I got hold of everything the wrong way round ... He considered my case more than hopeless. I thought him as crazy as a coot'.

Although it is hard to convey this in translation, Céline's style is closer to poetry than to traditional prose. It is a refined style, chiselled and polished to achieve its naked, emotional impact. The easy flood of slang is the result of hard writing. Céline is quite aware that he is a very 'literary' writer and he is proud of it. He liked to compare himself with musicians. His books, he said, were 'songs not prose', his language had 'internal rhythm'.[14] Like a poet, he considered that style has independent value. Language does not describe an object, it is the object. In *Mort à crédit* language has an existence of its own. Céline uses different kinds of vocabulary and invents new words in order to show the artist's creative power.

When he describes Metitpois's death Ferdinand uses medical jargon to explain the heart-attack: 'encephalon, arteriole, neoplasm, angina pectoris, Rolandic fissure'. This is perfectly appropriate since Ferdinand is a doctor; but he juxtaposes these terms with naturalistic comments such as 'he screamed like a pig having its throat slit'. The mixture of two different kinds of speech is important because it shows Ferdinand's power as a writer. He can change the subject he is writing about by his choice of words. He can alter the reader's reactions. Ferdinand cannot conquer death but he can play with it.

This is why style is an independent entity. Ferdinand is free to explore language. He creates neologisms like *crassouillant*, formed out of *crasseux* and *souillant*, *tintamarrante*, the adjective from *tintamarre*, *pourrisseur*, the noun from *pourri* and many others. In the English section of the book he throws in English phrases like 'don't worry' and 'hello there'. These are used out of context for their value as foreign sounds, rather than for their meaning. The Krogold episodes provide Ferdinand with the opportunity to write in an entirely new style. He plunges into sentences full of 'knights, pages and squires', 'waggons of the baggage-train' and of 'crenellated ramparts surmounting deep and loathsome dungeons'. This constant invention of language is more reminiscent of Rabelais than of Zola. Céline enjoys words and makes them into living things.

In many chapters of *Mort à crédit* the language is all there is – except again for comedy and movement. Take, for example, the trip the family makes to England. This is a verbal epic, where a trivial subject is inflated to colossal proportions. The sea-sickness becomes a plague infesting the ship and smothering the passengers with filth: 'The winds tore Mother's veil away – it flapped in the face of a woman at the other end of the ship, dead with retching. All control was lost! Sweets, salad, a meringue, coffee, the whole menu – it all came up with a rush.' Naturally the passengers howl and fight, they go wild with agony. When Ferdinand and his parents arrive, their walk through the English countryside becomes a huge battle with the rain – 'rain in England's like an ocean in mid-air: it can drown you by degrees'. They stagger up and down cliffs, the mother is trapped in a ditch, they return ignominiously to the harbour. The episode is a parody of an adventure story. Ferdinand's father is the hero, an intrepid warrior – 'Father was always in front'. But the family is vanquished, its suitcase is stolen and it retreats in disarray. Another setback, another small misery, nothing more. What is great is the language: the flamboyant exaggeration that transforms a banal outing into a mock-epic of defeat. Céline rams home this point by letting Ferdinand's father describe their trip to the neighbours: it becomes a saga of 'unguessed, fantastic, miraculous things'. Great is the power of the word.

This language-game is extremely serious because it enables Céline to cope with death. At will he makes it comic, disgusting or scientific. His extravagant language rises above his terrible subject. In his slangy, telegrammatic phrases he is able both to pin down the truth and to make it beautiful. By his conscious creation of language he affirms himself as a man. This accounts for the gaiety of *Mort à crédit*. How can such a terrible book be gay? It is because Ferdinand mocks death through style.

The Rabelaisian style, realistic and refined, full of obscenity and of poetry, is Céline's great contribution to the technique of novel-writing. It sets him apart from all other modern French writers and in looking for parallels one turns inevitably to Joyce. Both men have faith in language and believe it can express anything. Both use it in its own right as a triumphant, independent entity. The creation of a new style that Céline carries out in *Mort à crédit* is the task Joyce undertook in *Finnegans Wake*. Of course there are great differences between the two. Céline's aim is to make language more emotional, whereas *Finnegans Wake* is very much an intellectual exercise. Shades of meaning and origins of words are more important than in *Mort à crédit* and the impact of the innovations comes more slowly. Céline denied owing anything to Joyce and there is no evidence that Joyce ever read Céline. But in an age when writers doubt language and criticize the spurious magic of metaphors, these two hold fast to their belief in the word.

To Céline style is more than a contribution to the art of novel-writing. It is the form of beauty accessible to the writer, hence it is the creed by which he must live. In *Mort à crédit* beauty is life's highest aim and yet it is the flower of death. It can be discovered only by those who have penetrated the nightmare, who have given up pretending because they know they are dying.

Céline's aesthetic is a strange one and it is all too easy to reduce it to what it is not. It is not a *fin-de-siècle* preoccupation with the macabre. When Des Esseintes in Huysmans' *Against Nature* gives his elegant dinner in a black-draped hall with funeral announcements as invitation cards, he is playing with horror. To his jaded aesthete's palate death is a perverse stimulant, a new trinket for the jewel of beauty. His interest in both death and beauty is a petty affair, for he encloses them in his decadent, artificial world. In *Mort à crédit* Céline sees death as horrifying and he sees beauty in real rather than in paper flowers and in genuine not artificial landscapes. He is not running from reality into an aesthete's hothouse.

In retrospect, the introduction of the narrator into the book seems to have been inevitable. As Céline's fictional selves are close to him, one of them will become a novelist. As he explores his nightmare through his writing, the exploration itself becomes part of the writing. He will create a self who is hypnotized with visions of beauty and squalor. The novelist Ferdinand should not be confused with the novelist Céline. He has not lived through the years of refined labour that have been lavished on *Mort à crédit*. Ferdinand is a narrower and more striking figure, because he represents only the extreme elements in Céline's artist's personality. Beauty is Ferdinand's reward for his agony in the Passage and the nightmare of his hallucinations. Céline can laugh at people who say that he describes only the ugly side of life, because he knows that he is affirming the aesthetic. All people can participate in artistic creation so Céline is not seeking a special dispensation for the writer. On the contrary, he is insisting that beauty is man's vital response to the world. This is both the step forward from *Voyage* and the last word of *Mort à crédit*.

[4]

Novels and Politics
(1932–40)

As the controversy over *Voyage* died down in 1933, Céline continued
working at his clinic and at *Mort à crédit*. Denoël, anxious to capitalize
on *Voyage*'s success, brought out *L'Église* which Céline considered
'the prototype of the failed play'.[1] It was performed once by a group
of amateurs in Lyon and then forgotten. Céline and Denoël did not
always see eye to eye. Denoël kept trying to promote his discovery by
publishing anything of Céline's that he could lay his hands on. In
1937 he published the thesis on Semmelweis which had been lying in a
drawer for thirteen years. Denoël wanted Céline to give interviews
and get publicity, which Céline hated. By contrast the reluctant author
was very prickly about his royalties. He was certain that Denoël had
cheated him over *Voyage*. In June 1933 he writes that they are 'on very
bad terms for reasons that are easy to guess'.[2] A friend of his, Eveline
Pollet, had submitted a novel to Denoël and, although Céline was
trying to help her, he was not surprised when it was refused: 'I was
afraid of this for I have no influence, alas, on his verdict – and for lots
of reasons.'[3] Céline felt that Denoël did not care about the value of
his writing – he 'never understood a thing about it'[4] – and that the
publisher was just out to make money. When Céline was finishing
Mort à crédit early in 1936, he was enraged at Denoël's attempts to
hurry him up so that the book could appear before the summer
holidays. He retaliated by demanding more money. Mahé describes
a noisy quarrel where Céline threatened to throw the manuscript of
Mort à crédit down the lavatory unless his royalties were increased.[5]
On the question of money Céline may have been right, but it is clear
that he wanted to complain. Some of his criticisms were unjustified.
Denoël was a good judge of writing and he had appreciated Dr
Destouches's originality before anyone else. Céline did not want to see
this. He wanted to feel persecuted: 'I don't trust that zebra an inch,'
he told his secretary.[6]

The disputes about money were characteristic. Poulet, Mahé and all his friends testify to Céline's preoccupation with money. Mahé suffered from it because he asked Céline to write the introduction to his book of sketches, *31, Cité d'Antin*. He thought that Céline would do it for nothing, as a gesture of friendship. Not so. The request came not long after the publication of *Voyage* and the new celebrity was alive to the huge sums he could earn: 'Warned by forty years of living like a turd I now want the mugs to pay a high price for anything I deign to sell them.'[7] First he demanded 10,000 francs and then 25,000 francs. While the publishers hesitated Céline wrote the preface – an erotic piece about a newly-wed couple going to a brothel – for nothing.[8] By this time the project had collapsed and Mahé was left fulminating against his difficult friend. His annoyance did not last long. He understood that Céline was a creature of contradictions: trying to grab all he could from publishers, but generous to people in need; saving frantically one minute, and pouring out money the next. Céline was more than disinterested in dealing with his Clichy patients, he was generous to Erika Landry and he spent money freely on his travels. He was erratic about his finances and he had no head for business. But he needed to save. When he was paid his royalties from *Voyage* he looked around for a safe place to store them. After examining the different countries of Europe, he decided that Denmark was the most peaceful, so he began making trips to Copenhagen. The money he deposited there was a nest-egg for the trouble he saw ahead. He saved partly because his parents had taught him to and partly because he distrusted the future: 'I have always been terribly afraid of the future.'[9]

One of the ways he tried to make money was through the cinema. Céline loved the cinema. It was a popular amusement, drawing its clientele from the streets. It was an easy fountain of exotic dreams about gangsters and beautiful girls. He also hoped to make money writing for the cinema and having *Voyage* filmed. He talked at length about these plans to Mahé – mixing them up with schemes for making a fortune by writing popular songs on the lines of 'Long live the harlot Katinka'.[10] His negotiations about *Voyage* were unsuccessful. He disliked the ideas that film directors proposed and he decided, inevitably, that they were trying to cheat him. During his 1934 visit to Los Angeles he had discussions with Hollywood directors, but nothing came of them. 'All they allow here is chastity and gaiety,' he grumbled.[11] Eventually he sold the film rights of his book, but he went on with his other plans. He was a friend of Abel Gance, but Gance had financial difficulties of his own. Then there was Mahé, who was trying to become a director. The two planned a gangster film, for which Céline would write the script. But this again came to nothing.[12]

Céline's fascination with the cinema was as real as it was frustrated. In 1936 he published a film-script, *Secrets dans l'île*.[13] It is a heady brew of religious superstition, hatred and cruelty. Once again the main character is a victim. Erika, the mysterious American film-star, comes to live on a remote Brittany island. The magic of her beauty, her lesbianism and her fine clothes trouble the islanders who are backward and brutal. The sorcerer Kralik, jealous of Erika's new magic, incites a mob of women, led by an abandoned fiancée Yvonnik, to kill Erika. The men return from a fishing trip. Many of them are dead. The rest accept what has happened. Erika has been destroyed by hatred and by her own mysterious charm. 'You come from the devil,' Yvonnik said to her.[14] Perhaps this is true.

Secrets dans l'île has never been filmed. Céline had no more success in writing for the cinema than in writing for the ballet. His failure embittered him a little and he looked for reasons. In particular he looked at an acquaintance, Jacques Deval: 'The Jew Deval is having a great time in Hollywood,' he wrote caustically to Mahé.[15] Mahé paraphrases Céline's 1934 attitude towards Jews: 'No! we are not anti-semitic . . . But unlike the rest of the Goys we can distinguish a Jew from a Goy. So we are perfectly well aware of the great Jewish international solidarity.'[16] Deval was a friend with whom Céline stayed while he was in Los Angeles. He remained a friend even after World War Two. This did not prevent Céline from thinking that Deval's success in the cinema was part of a Jewish plot to exclude Aryans like himself. He associates this with Deval's success as a womanizer. Writing later he describes his stay in Hollywood: 'We lived together for several months, he, myself and *His* women – for he lives like a nabob.'[17] A familiar theme of anti-semitism is present here: the Jew preying on Aryan women. In Céline's mind the Jews who run the cinema are using their position to take advantage of Aryan girls who want to become stars. 'The Hollywood Jews . . . know what a pretty girl is,' he notes later.[18] 'Ah Goldwyn Mayer! I would have given ten years of my life to sit for one moment in their armchairs. All those goddesses at my mercy.'[19] This is not to be taken seriously; Céline enjoys playing

games. But the association of ideas, even in jest, is clear: Hollywood=
sex and money=Jews who exclude Aryans.

In the middle of his film projects, Céline took part in another
cultural activity much less to his taste. In October 1933 he gave the
address at the annual reunion of the Zola society. He was not all
flattered: 'Last Sunday to please Descaves I had to go and chat about
Zola at Meudon. I always hate these occasions.'[20] Lucien Descaves was
the guardian of the Naturalist heritage and Céline was making the
pilgrimage to Zola's home at Meudon in order to show his gratitude
for Descaves's support in the Goncourt decision. After *Voyage*,
Céline was considered a realistic novelist and a left-winger, so it seemed
appropriate that he should make the address. This was a misconception.
'Good heavens, I don't like Zola at all,' Céline lamented.[21] He disliked
literary gatherings even more.

His speech must have surprised the guests, who were expecting a
discussion of Zola's work. Céline said little about the Rougon-Macquart
saga, except that it was no longer relevant. Zola's optimism separated
him from a period dominated by 'the death instinct'.[22] Céline went on
to deliver a diatribe against contemporary life: the 'terrible poverty',
the 'headlong rush to extreme nationalisms' and, in the background,
'an incurable martial psychosis'.[23] Out of the economic depression
would come a European war that would be the end of Western
civilization.

After this startling speech the guests were invited to the home of
Maurice Maeterlinck, the old Symbolist master who had a mansion
near Meudon. There was a refined reception which Céline watched
with huge amusement. Years later he related how Maeterlinck's mistress
welcomed the group in a lilting voice, as if she were singing the music
of *Pelléas et Mélisande*. In Debussy's cadences she offered them
refreshments. They sat and chatted in the elegant drawing-room which
had a fountain in the middle. Whenever a door was opened, the draught
sprayed water on one of the guests. This was no milieu for Dr Destouches.[24]

The experience was a lesson to him: he went to no more literary
evenings. But in his own way he was a writer to his fingertips. He
went doggedly on with *Mort à crédit*. His work-habits were secretive
and strange. In his little study he covered hundreds of pages with his
tiny hand-writing. He pinned the pages together with clothes-pegs and

tossed them into a basket or hung them on a clothes-line. When visitors came they saw the sheets but could not lure Céline into talking about them. He would work and re-work these first drafts, changing a name, crossing out a sentence, starting a page over again. His manuscripts bear witness to an agonizing search for the *mot juste*. He was dominated by 'the violent passion to perfect, death's cousin'.[25] When he worked he immersed himself in his writing. Like Balzac, he could surprise his friends who did not understand that he was miles away from them, living in his other world. 'You know that I killed my father?' he said one day to Marie Canavaggia[26] who did not realize at first that he was talking about *Mort à crédit*. It was style that preoccupied him most. He tortured himself to find the word that had the melody and the impact he wanted, as well as the meaning. He corrected his final drafts, labouring over commas and ellipses. No amount of trouble was too great for a writer who consciously sacrificed himself to his art.

During these years Céline went on travelling. Whenever he could escape from his work he set out: 'A little cash in his pocket and off – Vienna! London! Africa!'[27] He was still looking for incident – 'life in the United States is a boundless adventure',[28] he writes from Chicago in 1934. Restless as ever, he could not resist ships that set out for new lands. He was alert to the fresh knowledge he could gain: 'The journey in Central Europe was exhausting, there were so many things I had to learn,' he wrote in 1933.[29]

The truth he was looking for was always grim. On his return from his 1932 trip to Germany he wrote an article about unemployment. He described the general poverty: 'the monthly allowance of about 250 francs condemns the unemployed man in practice to die slowly of hunger'.[30] Yet there was enough food in the country for everyone to eat. What could be done? As in his article on social hygiene he insisted that man could do little to change the economic laws: it was foolish to talk about revolution. What the German government could do was distribute the available food fairly. But Céline had no hope that the new Hitler government would do this – 'fraternity is a nuisance to everyone'.[31]

Dr Destouches was a strange traveller. Where did he go and what interested him? French writers are traditionally attracted to southern or northern Europe: to Italian sunshine or the mists of the Baltic. Gide felt the lure of the Mediterranean and of winds that blew southward. Jules Laforgue's travels took him to long German winters. Céline followed in Laforgue's footsteps: 'I have trouble not going completely overboard for the north.'[32] In 1933 he went to Antwerp where he strolled with Eveline Pollet around museums full of Flemish paintings. A month later he went through Germany to Vienna and on to the Balkans – this was the trip he found so exhausting. Much of 1934 was spent in the United States, on an immense journey that took him from New York to Los Angeles and back to Chicago. In the same year he found time to visit Erika Irrgang in Berlin. No mention of Italy, Spain and Portugal. Céline rejected the Latin heritage. In 1935 he went back to London to revisit his old Soho haunts along with Paulette Ladoux. He continued making his trips to Denmark, where he was storing the fairy gold from *Voyage*.

'On Thursday I am leaving for Copenhagen to see Karen and from there on to Finland to see the last long-distance sailing ships.'[33] Two of Céline's great enthusiasms are expressed here. Karen Jensen, to whom *L'Église* is dedicated, was a Danish dancer whom he never failed to visit in Copenhagen. Most of his travels involve women: he went to see Eveline Pollet in Belgium, Erika Landry in Germany. Whenever he found Paris too exhausting he fled, anxious to be consoled. As well as the need for novelty his travels reveal his search for a refuge. This was the other pole of his restless temperament. He wanted to run miles from his patients' troubles and his literary fame. 'I would like to have a little farm in Belgium – near the sea,' he tells Eveline Pollet.[34] Another time he remarks: 'If I were rich I would change my name, my country, everything.'[35] He could not vanish completely but his travels were the next best thing.

But they brought no real respite. Whatever the charms of Karen and Erika, whatever the interest of Belgian art galleries and German politics, Céline went on looking for the worst. Capable of brilliant insights into the English or Danish character, he was still the most subjective of travellers. He imposed his own vision on every country he visited. His 1933 trip to Central Europe was a peculiarly Célinian revelation. There is no word in his letters about the beauties of the countryside or the culture of capitals. Instead he saw 'entire nations starving and masochistic'.[36] His visits to Germany left him unimpressed. He warned against the dangers of reviving nationalism, but his antipathy went deeper. Nothing pleased him, not even Breslau which he explored in 1932 with Erika Irrgang and which he dismisses as a 'poor town'.[37] His trip to Berlin did not make him change his mind. When Erika left Germany in 1936, he summed up his impressions of her country: 'what madness! what dirty disgusting horror'.[38] But this was what he wanted. He might say that American life was a 'boundless adventure'; what really fascinated him was the way the individual floundered in the wave of urban life, hence his comment to Eugène Dabit about the 'humiliation' of New York.[39] When he returned to England in 1935 and in 1936, he asked Mahé to find him someone who could show him the seamy side of London. Mahé found Jean Cive, a pimp with vast experience of Soho brothels. Céline was delighted and wrote to thank Mahé. Jean Cive had 'piloted him around Soho', and he had seen what he wanted to see.[40] Starving German workers, lonely New Yorkers, London prostitutes, such were the images Céline retained from his travels. They reinforced his belief that the Western world was collapsing and that another war was inevitable. They also taught him that human misery lay deeper than political creeds. Nazi Germany was bad, but was it worse than democratic America? Céline did not think so.

The 1934 trip to the United States had a deeply personal motive. The previous year Elisabeth Craig's father had died and she had returned home. There she discovered the worst: 'Her father has behaved as usual like a real swine.' He had disinherited his errant daughter.[41] Elisabeth fought back. She found a lawyer and went to court. The case dragged on: 'News grew less frequent . . . Laconic.'[42] The impatient Céline could wait no longer and he set out for the United States on the steamer *Champlain*. He was afraid the Americans would consider the author of *Voyage* a Communist and dispatch him to Ellis Island. But nothing of the kind took place. At New York he heard rumours in the backstage of dance-theatres that all was not well with Elisabeth. He rushed off to California to discover 'an atrocious drama, so low, so disgusting, so degrading that even I . . .'[43]

What had happened seemed to Mahé to be simple enough. Elisabeth had decided to marry one of her lawyers and settle in Los Angeles. The bohemian years in Paris were over. A French doctor with a taste for low life could not, however great his literary talents, compete with an American lawyer. As Mahé puts it, it was a case of 'cash and wedding ring on finger.'[44] He is certainly being too cynical. His explanation ignores the complicated relationship between Céline and Elisabeth and the almost impossible situation he had put her in, while he was finishing *Voyage*. She doubtless felt that she had to escape. She had to leave him and begin a new life. Once she had made up her mind she was adamant: she was not coming back to him. Céline rejected both of these explanations. When he arrived in Los Angeles he found Elisabeth living 'in a cloud of alcohol, tobacco, police and cheap gangsters'.[45] He tried to persuade her to change her mind. He pleaded – to no avail. 'Elisabeth has given herself to gangsters,' he repeats.[46] He refused to see that she had rejected him. In his eyes he was fighting powerful and evil enemies. He was the victim of mysterious underworld forces. One more ingredient was needed to make the conspiracy complete. Elisabeth had been seduced by the Jews: 'a "Jewish judge" had "swiped" her from him.'[47] The lovely red-haired dancer had fallen victim to the international conspiracy. Once again Céline was inventing enemies instead of analysing the situation. Mahé notes that the loss of Elisabeth was an important milestone on his road to anti-semitism.[48]

Disconsolately he made his way back from Los Angeles. At Chicago he stopped in the New Lawrence Hotel to take stock of things: 'In the last month such fantastic things have happened to me that I am still a bit delirious.'[49] His nervous temperament made him distort and exaggerate what had taken place. Fortunately Karen Jensen was on tour in Chicago and she tried to console him. But when he returned to France he was in a state of despair: 'I have lived through ... an atrocious adventure,' he told Erika Irrgang.[50] He never saw Elisabeth again.*

Back in France public events forced themselves on his attention. Until 1934 Céline had made few political pronouncements. In the Zola lecture he had warned against 'extreme nationalisms'.[51] He had declared that France was 'surrounded by whole nations of anaphylaxic fools'. Hitler was an 'epileptic' and Fascism a menace. But Céline refused to enter politics. 'Desertion for the artist means abandoning

---

* On the one hand Céline was deeply and lastingly hurt by Elisabeth's decision, on the other hand he consoled himself quickly on the sexual level with Karen Jensen, Eveline Pollet and many others. As already stated, his emotional and sexual needs were not clear-cut and he himself did not fully understand them. Certainly they were more complex than the ageing Céline would have us believe.

the concrete.'[52] His role as a writer was to work on *Mort à crédit*, where he would expose the fundamental evil of human nature.

Now political agitation was rampant in France. In the previous February Paris had seen bitter rioting. Outraged by the Stavisky scandal, the right-wing leagues unleashed their followers on the streets. The Republic tottered and then rallied. Gaston Doumergue was brought in as a rather weak strong-man and the leagues failed to pass from rhetoric to action. But the February riots were another step in the Third Republic's disintegration. To contemporaries they were a warning of the growing threat from the right. The Communist Party began slowly to discard its view that the first enemy were the socialists, traitors to the working class. Cries went up for a Popular Front. In intellectual circles commitment became the slogan of the day. Céline discussed politics with another admirer of *Voyage*, the art historian Elie Faure.

Faure was in favour of prompt political action to combat the threat from the right. In his eyes there was a simple issue: 'There is fighting in the streets. I look to see which side the police are on and which side the poor devils.'[53] Céline rejects the notion that the working classes have right on their side: 'there is no "people" in the sentimental sense you are using, there are only exploiters and exploited, and the exploited are all trying to become exploiters'.[54] When he wrote about politics, Céline showed none of the pity he practised in his daily life. He could not admit that one section of society was better than another, because he was certain that human nature was flawed. The pessimism that he had learned on the battlefields, at the Ford factory and throughout his travels had convinced him that politics was useless. 'Our society is rotten, dying,' he writes, 'we are going, flying towards Fascism.'[55] He was not at all pro-Fascist. He was sure that it would triumph because it was the ultimate evil.

What position was he taking himself? 'I refuse completely, absolutely, to take one stance or another. I am an anarchist through and through, I have always been one and I shall never be anything else.'[56] This was quite true. A man so insistent on his independence could be nothing else. But an anarchist can enter politics; Céline would not. His point of view was religious rather than political: 'There is no more contrition,' he writes, 'there are only cries of revolt and hope. Hope for what? That the shit will start to smell good.'[57]

Throughout the discussion he was attacking the left. Elie Faure was trying to win him over to left-wing commitment and Céline would not allow him. More is involved than the dialectic of the argument. Céline rejected left-wing optimism – the call for revolution, the belief that a new society could be built. The left places its faith in the future; for Céline there was no future but the cemetery. There is a clue here to his political evolution. In his eyes the left was more guilty than anyone of the fault of abstraction. It talked about changes that were never made and it used utopian slogans that had no meaning. Later when Céline took a political position, it was based on a denial of left-wing optimism.

For the moment he stood firm: a plague on all your houses. Elie Faure rebuked him: 'Your transcendental realism, as you well know ... leads exclusively to death.'[58] 'What else is there?' Céline might have replied. Neither protagonist convinced the other. Faure continued on the path of commitment. In 1935 he joined the Committee for the Defence of the Asturian Miners and he supported the Republicans in the Spanish Civil War.[59] Céline stood aside from politics and uttered occasional, warning cries. 'We are going towards violence. It is very close,' he wrote to Eugène Dabit.[60] Over the next few years he watched as Hitler took back the Saar and started to re-arm. To his friends he prophesied disaster. It was his temperament that governed his views. He was a Cassandra who would have predicted catastrophes in Eldorado itself. But he was in harmony with his age. His sensitive antennae had picked up the danger-signals in the troubled 1930s.

While the Italians invaded Abyssinia in 1935 and while the French Parliament fell into sterile debates about sanctions, Céline went on writing *Mort à crédit*. His mood was sombre and in his letters he pours out his pessimism: 'We are condemned to misery,' he writes, 'our life is nothing more than a death.'[61] He was no stoic. Every day he uncovered fresh terrors. His own death appeared before him in a million different disguises. 'I fell rather ill in Vienna. My heart is affected. I haven't got long to go,' he wrote to Mahé.[62] Another time he was convinced he was dying of cancer. He worried about everything – money, wars, the future. He was sure Denoël was cheating him; certain the Clichy authorities were trying to get rid of him. Seeing war ahead, he trembled for himself: 'The Nazis hate me as much as the Socialists,' he had told Elie Faure.[63] Death obsessed him. Mahé relates how Céline obtained a ticket for the execution of a criminal. When he returned, he regaled his friends with a gory description of how the dead man's head had jumped off the guillotine and fallen a few feet from where he was standing.[64]

There was more to his character than a frenetic pessimism. He was a Jekyll and Hyde figure who continued to enjoy himself. His circle of friends was widening. There was fellow-Montmartrian Marcel Aymé, another writer who liked to forget his work the moment he put down his pen. Céline admired Aymé's facility, while recognizing that it was the antithesis of his own talent. Like Céline, Aymé enjoyed observing people and he would sit quietly in a corner while the noisy group of friends argued and told stories. Then there was Robert le Vigan, a man of strange moods, given to wild outbursts of laughter and Mephistophelian poses. Le Vigan was a film actor hated, according to Mahé, by stars because he could steal the glory even in a minor role.[65] Off the set he went on acting, 'playing for you successively ... an English ex-India colonel, a homosexual seminarian, a jockey'.[66] In particular le Vigan could never forget that he had played the part of Christ and he used to adopt messianic gestures. He was a constant source of amusement to Céline, who also felt that beneath the changing moods was a man of real sensibility: 'Very heart on sleeve, and poet and everything.'[67] When the Mafia assembled, le Vigan would read long passages from plays, acting out the different roles.

One of Aymé's stories describes the group of friends congregated to make fun of a pretentious poet.[68] There is Gen Paul, his studio a chaotic mess of easels and furniture with a big hole in the middle, Daragnès the engraver, Ralph Soupault the cartoonist, Pierre Mac Orlan, who was married to Max Revol's daughter, and others. The problem is that the young heroine Adélaïde has fallen in love with a bearded, sophisticated poet, Eutrope, and is ignoring her sincere suitor Boquillard. Céline arrives on his motorcycle wrapped up in raincoat, scarves and gloves. Speaking in *argot* he pours out ribald medical jokes and insults. He prophesies 'for the end of the summer catastrophes, stinking wars, famines'.[69] He dislikes Eutrope on sight. Eutrope reads one of his ethereal, complicated poems. The group bursts out laughing and Céline starts to tear Eutrope apart, like a giant dismembering a baby. Adélaïde realizes that she has made a mistake and she is actually in love with Boquillard. All ends happily.

A fictitious tale, but one that captures Céline as his friends saw him:

prophetic, boisterous, goodhearted and athletic. Historian René Héron de Villefosse, who met him for the first time on Mahé's boat, was impressed: 'he talked with the rhythms of a bard, with the sureness of a preacher, a man inspired'.[70] Céline could listen too. When they lunched together at a Breton restaurant on the rue Vandamme, Héron de Villefosse lectured him on the Charlemagne period and the Treaty of Verdun. This early history seemed to Céline a kind of legend. He was not interested in documents and ruins, but in the mythical figures his friend evoked for him. Perhaps he was thinking of his own Krogold legend, as he listened. Héron de Villefosse remembers him as polite and enthusiastic. Céline had a wide range of interests: he talked to Dr Camus about modern physics and to Mahé about Dutch painting. He was still anxious to help his friends. When Mahé applied for the Prix Blumenthal in 1934, Céline tried hard to get it for him. He intervened with people he knew and called on Lucien Descaves to make the rounds of the jury.[71] Mahé remained a particularly close friend because he encouraged the athletic side of Céline's nature. The two continued to spend happy hours sailing.

Mahé encouraged Céline in his love of Brittany. Céline spent his summers there, descending on the Hôtel Frascati at Le Havre or on the Maison Francklin at Saint-Malo. The Maison Francklin belonged to Maria Lebannier, his father-in-law's former mistress. She was a friend of his and she had a charming adopted daughter, a child Sergine whom Mahé admired.[72] Céline and Maria used to walk and cycle around the Brittany countryside. He also used to spend hours in the Saint-Malo harbour watching the ships: the liners, tugs and fishing-boats. The movement of ships fascinated him as much as the rhythms of dance. Céline grew more and more interested in Brittany – in its folklore and Druids. He became conscious of his Breton roots and attributed to them his mania for prophesying and haranguing.[73] Most of all, Brittany was a refuge. For a few days he could realize his dream of peace, of an existence undisturbed by wars and publishers. 'This Brittany is a heavenly country,' he wrote to Mahé, 'I would like to end up there . . . in a house at Le Conquet, on the rainy headland, in the middle of a little garden where nothing grows any more'.[74]

Maria Lebannier was an excellent companion – 'intelligent, educated . . . and clever in bed'.[75] This suited Céline well, especially since Elisabeth's departure. Mahé remembers the flood of young girls he brought to the *Enez Glaz*. There was Ma Joncque, 'a tall beautiful Chinese girl, and a virgin too. That did not matter, the back is as good as the front.'[76] There was an even stranger girl, whom Céline met on one of his travels and whom he describes as 'a psychoanalyst who talks like a superprostitute'.[77] Paulette Ladoux, whom he took to London, was another companion who was willing to indulge his liking for voyeurism. These brief sexual encounters continue the pattern that he had established during the years before *Voyage*. There were rather more serious affairs; with Karen Jensen, who seems to have wanted no more than he could give; with Erika Irrgang, who was also content with their relationship; and with Eveline Pollet, who was not.[78] Distance played a significant role in these affairs: all three women were far enough away not to be a threat. Friendship was important too. Karen Jensen remained a friend long after Céline remarried; with Eveline Pollet one senses that he was using the weapon of friendship to avoid greater intimacy. In all his relationships with women he was asking to be sexually pleased, to be protected against loneliness, to receive affection without being tied down. His enjoyment of women's beauty included an appreciation of their femininity. Their instinct to live was strong and it comforted him.

This was especially the case with Lucette Almanzor. Céline met her in 1935 on a visit to Madame d'Allessandri's dance-class. Lucette was a dancer at the Opéra Comique. She was interested in classical and Eastern ballet and she once toured Europe with an Oriental troupe. When she left the Opéra Comique, she became a teacher of ballet and she gave lessons at the Studio Wacker, near the Place Clichy. She fitted Céline's ideal of womanhood almost as well as Elisabeth had done. She was young, her body was supple and strong and she radiated health. Rebatet remembers her as 'young, well-built, nice, discreet and gay'.[79] The word 'discreet' is important because Céline's distrust of other people made him suspicious of women who might get him into trouble. He later describes Lucette as 'a very, very pleasant creature, the nicest soul in the world – oh, I don't like saints. My saints have to dance and, in God's name, they have to be sexy and amusing, pagan.'[80] Initially this affair was no different from any of his others. He saw Lucette frequently, went for long periods without seeing her and had other women friends. It seems likely that, to prevent her from becoming a sexual burden, he tried to encourage her towards lesbianism.[81]

But sexual and perhaps even emotional considerations were giving way to something else. Céline's desire to be protected against death increased as he grew older. It became particularly strong in the late 1930s when his life was becoming dangerous. More than ever he needed a woman's instinctive devotion. This Lucette was prepared to offer. She did not question, she did not interfere in his work. When his friends came to visit she hovered in the background. At all times she followed him and, by her physical presence, she strengthened him. Their relationship deepened as the danger grew more pressing. They began to live together under the Occupation and they were married in 1943.

Céline never gave way to his black moods. His letters are marked by abrupt switches of humour and the determination to struggle on. He could truthfully say that he was on the side of life. In the flood of letters that he wrote to Erika Irrgang, the recurrent theme is that she must work hard to avoid misery. 'I see that you are continuing to struggle bravely against life, that's a very good thing,' he writes in 1933.[82] In the background lies his belief that the world is desperately hard and that people must battle to survive. His years in jewellers' shops have left their mark: 'I was very poor too and I had to fight my way out of terrible ordeals.'[83] He repeats the message: 'ambition, Erika, no Slavism'.[84] Frequently he discusses money: 'Be careful with money, *very careful*.'[85] On sexual matters he offers his own brand of realism: 'Be very depraved,' he writes before one of his visits, 'we will see to that together.'[86] But she must take care: not get herself pregnant, not catch venereal disease, watch out for men who will exploit her.

Céline took a similar stance in his letters to Eveline Pollet. Even more than with Erika, his robust friendship was not unambiguous. Yet there is no reason to dismiss it as a mere stratagem. This tenacious strength, with its concomitant weakness, was something he offered to all his friends, both male and female. It was one reason that women were attracted to him. In any case he seems to be trying to convince himself as much as her. He lectures her: 'You must not get disgusted with your life, nor with anything and certainly not with yourself,'[87] he writes. He kept trying to cheer her up. He told her about his travels, sent her novels to read, tried to persuade Denoël to publish her book. Although he is often depressed he is always firm in his tone and, at the end of one very melancholic epistle, he promises another 'more frivolous' letter.[88] Again and again he tries to make some sense of existence and he comes up with the same notion: 'To croak quite free, that at least is Man's work.'[89] Later he elaborates: 'As we get closer to the cemetery we must lighten ourselves of all these things, so that we arrive there as little burdened with stupidities as possible. That's our task.'[90]

In 1936 Céline finally finished *Mort à crédit*. It was a tremendous labour and it left him exhausted. By this time he was finding his Paris routine too tiring, and he used to escape to a hotel in the suburb of Saint-Germain. This was not successful either, because his visitors, notably Mahé, made too much noise and the other residents complained. He was in bad health – the result of over-work – and had to be looked after by his doctor, Dr Gozlan. 'I am worn out,' he wrote to Mahé.[91] He had all kinds of troubles – disputes with Denoël and disputes at his clinic. In April he went off to finish the book at his 'Brittany retreat' the Hôtel Frascati. There he did the final revisions and *Mort à crédit* appeared in the bookshops on 12 May. As soon as he had finished Céline set out again on his travels. He visited Eveline Pollet at Antwerp and then went to England. Erika Irrgang had married and was living at Cambridge, where Céline went to see her. 'I am extremely tired,' he wrote to her from London.[92] When they met they had little to say to each other and the reunion marks the end of their friendship. She found him 'overwhelmed with a terrible anxiety'.[93] It was partly the weariness of *Mort à crédit*, but he may also have known that a crisis was approaching.

In August Céline set out on a most important journey: to Russia. The Aragon–Triolet translation of *Voyage* had been published – with changes, according to Céline, that made it more suitable for a Marxist public.[94] As the royalties could not be taken out of the country he was invited to come and spend them in Russia. He packed his bags and set out. Like so many writers of the day, he made the pilgrimage to the new Jerusalem. Did the Russians know what they were doing? They were deceived by the supposedly left-wing tendencies of *Voyage* and they hoped to win over another recruit. One can only pity them, faced with such a guest. Was the enemy of utopias to become the admirer of the Marxist paradise? Was Elie Faure's opponent to be won over by Stalin? Céline was treated in the Soviet Union with the highest honours. He was escorted around Moscow and Leningrad. He visited factories thronged with happy workers and hospitals staffed by enthusiastic doctors. He was entranced by the ballet but, unfortunately for his hosts, by nothing else.

'I have just come back by sea from Russia. What a journey!', he wrote to Lucien Descaves on 25 September.[95] He had cut short his visit. On his return to Paris he explained why. The noisy group in Gen Paul's studio listened, fascinated, to his stories. As one of them said, it was 'Karl Marx pulverized, ridiculed'. The conclusion of his hilarious anecdotes was always the same: 'three things, only three things work well in the Soviet Union: army, police, propaganda'. This was not what the Russians had hoped for. A Monsieur Braun from the Soviet embassy came to call on Céline. He reminded him that Russia was a vast country with millions of potential readers. *Voyage* had sold well, there was no reason why *Mort à crédit* should not be translated with equal success. In the meantime Céline's admirers were waiting to see 'the fine pages he would surely not fail to write about Soviet Russia'.[96] They did not have long to wait.

On his return Céline found France more divided than ever. The May 1936 elections returned to power the Popular Front. For the first time France had a Socialist Prime Minister – Léon Blum, who was to become one of the villains of *Bagatelles*. The summer brought huge sit-down strikes, which were settled by the Matignon agreements. In retrospect Blum was far from revolutionary and the workers demands were modest. To contemporaries a Marxist, Jewish Prime Minister seemed the ultimate evil. The revelation of the workers' power shocked the middle classes and fears of a red terror grew hysterical. The right-wing press thundered against Blum and drove one of his ministers, Roger Salengro, to suicide. The rifts in society seemed beyond repair. Abroad Hitler remilitarized the Rhineland, while the sanctions against Italy, although unsuccessful, had alienated her from France. In Spain the civil war appeared to many, including Céline, the first sign of a conflict that would engulf Europe.

Faced with this chaos Céline threw himself into politics. After finishing *Mort à crédit* he began work on another novel, *Casse-pipe*, and he had started to think already about a novel set in England – the future *Guignol's Band*.[97] But he switched direction. In 1937 he published *Mea Culpa*, the denunciation of Soviet Russia, and *Bagatelles*, the first anti-semitic pamphlet. The novelist gave way to the polemist. Céline abandoned *Casse-pipe* after a few chapters and he did not publish a work of fiction until *Guignol's Band* (1944). The pamphlet is less a book than an act: it attempts to influence opinion. Céline had entered the arena. He ceased simply to cry out that Europe would be destroyed. He explained what was wrong and he proposed solutions. Once started down this road, he went further. After the Munich crisis he published *L'École des cadavres*, which reiterates the anti-semitic theme. In 1941 he wrote *Les Beaux Draps* which draws lessons from the defeat of France.

Céline's political thought will be analysed in the next chapter; here it will be looked at in the context of his life. Why did he enter politics after rejecting Elie Faure's arguments? What happened between 1934 and 1937? The answer is simple: the political situation grew worse. With disorder at home and threats abroad, Céline decided he could no longer stand aside. His trip to Russia acted as a catalyst. Not that he had expected a utopia. But he discovered a society as materialistic as the West, worse in fact because materialism was its avowed philosophy. Meanwhile the danger of war was increasing and no one was paying attention to his warnings. There was another reason: Céline's personal life had taken a turn for the worse: he had increasing problems at his clinic, *Mort à crédit* had been badly received and his weariness was mounting. He could no longer suffer in silence. So he poured forth his hatreds in the pamphlets. He castigated contemporary society, he preached appeasement, he fixed the blame for the world's ills on the Jew.

The pamphlets trace out Céline's evolution. *Mea Culpa* does not go much beyond the 1934 nihilism. It excoriates Soviet Russia as morally bankrupt. *Bagatelles* attacks the West in the same language, but it points out the culprit – the Jew – and advocates a policy – anti-semitism. *L'École des cadavres* is even more specific. It deals with the threat of war. Céline cuts through idealistic rubbish about defence of democracy and crusades against Fascism. The only course for a bankrupt society is appeasement, combined with strong measures against the warmongering Jews. *Les Beaux Draps* fits this thesis to the new world of the Occupation.

The distance from nihilism to appeasement and anti-semitism was not great. Céline's frantic despair – the special mark of his temperament – echoes through the pamphlets. Page after page expresses his hatred for contemporary life: for factories, standardization and international-ism. His pessimism shaped his politics. In the current European situation appeasement was the only course. A country as rotten as France could not survive, much less win a war. In any case it was ridiculous to talk about freedom and honour; an appalling creature like Man was capable of neither. Survival was all he could aim for. Anti-semitism was a consequence – although a perversion – of Céline's belief in evil. If life was a chamber of horrors, there had to be a master-torturer: the Jew. And running through the pamphlets is the certainty that Céline would fail to alter the course of events, that no one would listen to him, that war was inevitable.

The policies he advocated grew out of his life. To explain his pacifism one need look no further than his experiences in Flanders. His headaches reminded him of past wars and inspired him with a dread of violence. He saw new holocausts behind every newspaper headline and he was willing to do anything to avoid them. Obsessed with his own death, he had nightmares of general slaughter. What of the other side of the coin: anti-semitism? After the war Céline found an explanation: he was simply attacking the Jewish groups that were pushing France into an anti-German crusade.[98] This is nonsense. It is historically false and too neat. Anti-semitism is no such rational pheno-menon. Céline attacked the Jews because he hated them, not because they were warmongering. The steps leading to his anti-semitism have been discussed: the childhood in the Passage, the experiences at the League of Nations, the disappointment of the cinema projects, the loss of Elisabeth Craig. But the matter is not that simple. These events did not lead Céline to anti-semitism; he interpreted them in an anti-semitic light. As Sartre has pointed out, a man 'chooses' to become an anti-semite. Céline refused to accept his own principle that life is fundamentally flawed. He did not attribute his misfortunes to the ubiquitous human malice he talks of so often. He blamed everything on the Jews. Needing a target, he found the most convenient one for a man of his generation and background. In 1937 he shrank from the truth he had been seeking and preaching. He could not accept that war was inevitable. There had to be some escape-hatch and the Jew provided it. Like one of his minor characters, Céline sought refuge in hatred. Then too he was misled by his need to be a victim. He personi-fied his persecutors in the figure of the Jew.

In one sense Céline was genuine enough: by writing the pamphlets he was putting himself in a dangerous position. He was setting out to alienate all shades of opinion: from Mussolini to Blum, from Roosevelt to Stalin. His left-wing admirers were horrified. *Mea Culpa* cost him his Communist friends and *Bagatelles* revolted non-Communists like George Altman. Driven by the pessimism that separated him from Elie Faure, Céline seemed to have found a home on the right. This is a deceptive view. The orthodox conservatives had no use for anyone who advocated total pacifism or who denounced England in such vitriolic terms. Even the extra-parliamentary Action Française rejected such a defeatist stance. The only group that supported Céline was the tiny band of men on the Fascist fringe. In the milieu of *Je suis partout*, Rebatet and his friends welcomed *Bagatelles* with 'an enthusiasm allowing for no reserve'.[99] But they had little influence outside a few restricted, Parisian circles. Céline remained a lone voice, belonging to neither the right nor the left. If labels must be attached, he was an anarchist in the tradition of the French pamphleteers – the descendant of Bloy, Vallès and Péguy. In the context of contemporary France he was almost completely isolated. This pleased him: 'I do not want to be assisted, helped, or defended. *Once and for all*,' he wrote to Eveline Pollet, when she supported him in the Belgian press.[100] He revelled in the danger. At the head of *Mea Culpa* he affirms: 'There are still a few hatreds that I lack. I am sure that they exist.'[101]

There is a distinction between what Céline says and what he does. His political theory is more extreme than his practice. He called for terrible persecution of the Jews, but he did nothing to promote it. Later he was able to say that 'the Jews ought to erect a statue to me for all the harm I could have done them but did not'.[102] He belonged to no anti-semitic organizations and he had Jewish friends like Dr Gozlan and Jacques Deval. This is not meant to excuse him, but to stress the difference between the extremism of his writing and the complexity of his life. Despite his furious criticism of the French, he retained a good dose of old-fashioned, 1914-style patriotism and, when the war broke out, he rushed to volunteer. Nor was he willing to play out his self-imposed role of victim. In 1944 he gave his enemies the slip.

In the years before the war his personal life grew more chaotic. He went on commuting between Saint-Germain and the rue Lepic, until in June 1937 he gave up the flat. It was too expensive, he said.[103] In 1939 he moved again – to his mother's flat in the rue Marsollier. He now had no settled home.

By this time he had resigned from the Clichy clinic. He had clashed with the municipal authorities and particularly with the director Dr Idouc. Idouc is another of the strange characters who keep turning up in Céline's life. According to Céline he was nothing more than 'Moscow's eye', a spy for the International who had been put in charge of the clinic by the Communist local authority.[104] Idouc's fate in 1939 would support this. Summoned to appear before General Héring, the military governor of Paris, he committed suicide in mysterious circumstances.[105] From 1935 on, he had disputes with Céline. Mahé mentions a medical report written by Céline and altered by Idouc.[106] Relations between the two grew worse. Céline began to spend less time in the clinic and in December 1937 he resigned.

It is hard to discover exactly what happened. Céline's interpretation was simple: 'I have been thrown out of Clichy like a piece of dung.'[107] It was another Jewish plot: Idouc 'undertook to throw out everyone who was not Jewish'.[108] Around this time an old doctor friend wrote to ask about finding a job in Paris. Céline's reply was prompt: 'My dear friend – no chance, all Jews and Freemasons here.'[109]

Céline now had no regular medical work. In the summer he went to Brittany to replace doctors who were on holiday. He made an abortive attempt to open a clinic of his own at Saint-Germain but it failed – decidedly he was not made for private practice. In 1937 he went as ship's doctor on a boat bound for Newfoundland. The trip fascinated him. He pored over maps of old sea-routes and studied the life of explorer Jacques Cartier. In particular he stared at the atlas at the tiny French islands of Saint-Pierre and Miquelon.[110] They were a long way from Europe. Perhaps they could be a haven in the holocaust to come.

His search for a refuge was leading him into mishaps. On his return from Newfoundland he made a visit to the Channel Islands. He arrived in Jersey to 'look for a possible shelter'.[111] Unfortunately it was the moment of George VI's coronation. Special police precautions were being taken and Céline was arrested on charges of plotting against the king's life. The French consul intervened, to no avail. Céline was held while the police hunted for his accomplices. Finally he was released,

convinced that Jersey was no refuge. The 'Jew-British'[112] were persecutors like all the rest.

Throughout 1938 he worked on *L'École des cadavres*. In January he
went to visit Eveline Pollet and on his return he wrote: 'I came back to
Paris which is still in a perilous and hateful state.'[113] By now he was
obsessed with the war. 'We just about escaped,' he noted after the
Munich meeting.[114] He was not among the cheering crowds which
greeted Daladier, and he did not believe there would be peace in our
time. 'The worst is being prepared, the Apocalypse,' he wrote in
February 1939.[115] In June he suffered another blow. He and Denoël
were sued for slander by Dr Rouquès, who is attacked as a Jewish
intriguer in the closing pages of *L'École des cadavres*. Rouquès won
the suit, Céline was fined and *L'École* banned – it did not appear again
until 1943.[116] Céline poured out his grievances to Eveline Pollet: 'Two
cases in court with 100,000 francs damages . . . Denoël in bad faith and
bankrupt – he isn't paying me any more – books banned by decree . . .
A cascade. Medicine impossible . . . Jobs lost.'[117]

On 3 September 1939 Céline was at Saint-Malo. Mahé was out
sailing with some friends. When they came back, Céline was standing
in the harbour. Long before they had docked he was bellowing at them:
'Scrape out your entrails, my heroes! Come and have your breasts
stuffed, my brave ones! . . . All to the scrap heap, guts everywhere.
The debraining is going to start.'[118]

Céline was delighted: the danger he secretly coveted was at hand. A
pacifist, he knew he was born for battlefields. While his compatriots
had to be dragged kicking and screaming into war and while French
generals thought about avoiding defeat but never about victory, Céline
threw himself into the nightmare. He volunteered for active service
but was rejected on medical grounds. He became a ship's doctor and
was posted to the *Shella*, an armoured merchant vessel making runs
from Marseilles to Casablanca. He was pleased with this assignment.
'Unnecessary to tell you . . . that the commandant is satisfied on every
point with my services,' he wrote proudly to Dr Camus.[119] With such
a man on board, however, there was no hope for the *Shella*. It collided
with an English ship near Gibraltar. Céline describes what happened:
'We were badly damaged and in distress all night. It is not necessary
to tell you that your friend, in the course of this most tragic night,
amidst corpses, drownings and wounded, did honour to those who

taught him the science of warfare.' The English ship went down and the *Shella* limped back to Marseilles, where it put in for extensive repairs. Céline hoped that he would be given another medal and that he would be posted to a new ship. Neither event took place and he returned to Paris, his naval career terminated. But he was happy: 'I have never had such a good time,' he noted.

Céline went back to the Paris suburbs. He was sent to the Sartrouville clinic to replace a doctor who had been called up. He was still there in May 1940, when the German armies hurled themselves on the supposedly impregnable French lines. Disaster followed disaster. On 13 May the front was broken, at the end of the month the British forces were evacuated from Dunkirk, on 10 June the French government fled, leaving Paris to the Germans. Before the Nazis arrived Céline left: he carried two newborn babies to safety in an ambulance. Accompanied by Lucette he set out along roads crowded with refugees. German planes controlled the air and traffic jams were immense. After a hazardous journey he reached La Rochelle, where he deposited the babies and went to work as the doctor in a refugee camp.[120]

Events moved swiftly. On 16 June Paul Reynaud resigned and was succeeded by Pétain who began negotiations for an armistice. On 18 June de Gaulle's now famous appeal for continued resistance fell upon deaf ears. On 22 June the armistice was concluded. Céline's prophecy had come true: the French people were faced with defeat. Ill-prepared for war, they were no match for the armies of the Reich. In July Pétain established his government at Vichy and tried to make the best of an impossible situation. The war seemed virtually over and irrevocably lost.

[5]

Céline the Pamphleteer

However chaotic Céline's life may have been, it was mild compared with the frenzy of the pamphlets. *Bagatelles* exaggerates his feelings to the point where the reader scarcely knows if he is supposed to take them seriously. The question of whether they are sincere is perhaps simplistic. What does sincerity mean to a chameleon like Céline? In the late 1930s he worked himself up into a paroxysm of anti-semitism. It was part of his being, along with his love of dance and his quarrels with Denoël. The pamphlets, with their deliberate exaggerations and their irony, are another mask that he adopts. They are the third and most extreme way of coping with his catastrophic pessimism. In his life he wrestled with his despair, using the Jekyll side of his character against the Hyde. In his novels he faced the night intrepidly. Now the pamphlets set out to examine the appalling political reality of the late 1930s. They see the Depression and the Munich crisis in terms of Jewish plots, Eastern hordes – and ballet. Their narrator is another of Dr Destouches's many selves. He is Cassandra-Céline, obsessed with his vision of massacres and corpses. To be more precise, there are several narrators: there is Ferdinand the anti-semite, Ferdinand, the clown, and Ferdinand, the writer of ballets. Each has his own picture of contemporary Europe.

All this is very Célinian. Certainly the pamphlets cannot be severed from the rest of his work. The publishing house of Gallimard has tried to do this. They have refused to include them – except for *Mea Culpa* – in the *Oeuvres complètes*. This is understandable, but it will not work. The pamphlets are close to the novels: Princhard's diatribe against patriotism could fit into *Bagatelles* as easily as into *Voyage*. In a deeper sense they stand close to the centre of Céline's thought. The theme of the victim recurs here, so does hatred and so does the pursuit of beauty. The pamphlets are not outbursts of lunacy: they make sense. One must look beyond the wilful intellectual confusion and the emotional extremism in order to understand what Céline is doing.

One may begin by setting them in a tradition. To the French reader of the 1930s *Bagatelles* was not a complete novelty. It belonged to an established genre. During the last century there has been a line of French pamphleteers. It runs from Drumont, Vallès and Bloy through Péguy, Daudet and Maurras to Bernanos and Béraud. The pre-war years produced a goodly crop of pamphlets, of which Béraud's *Faut-il réduire l'Angleterre en esclavage?* (1935), and Bernanos's *Les Grands Cimetières sous la lune* (1937), are only the most famous. The audience that greeted *Bagatelles* was prepared for violent rhetoric, as Céline well knew. His pamphlets may be read as part of a distinguished, yet troubling tradition.*

France has always mixed politics with literature, and many great writers have been polemists – Rabelais, Pascal and Voltaire are three names that come to mind. But the modern pamphleteers are a special breed. They emerge at times of crisis: Vallès at the Commune, Daudet and Maurras in the aftermath of the Dreyfus case, Céline in the late 1930s. At bottom they are fighting the battle of modernity, a battle waged all the more fiercely in France's 'stalemate society'.[1] Péguy defends the Catholicism of Joan of Arc against Combes's campaign to separate church and state. Maurras is fighting for the monarchy, Céline denounces industrialization. The struggle takes many forms, but it does not really change. France is being menaced by a new barbarism. For Drumont it is the Jew, for Maurras the Third Republic. The pamphleteers flaunt their allegiance to traditional segments of French society. Péguy exalts the peasantry while Céline is proud of coming from the lesser bourgeoisie – France's 'serious class'.[2]

As they are fighting a rearguard action, the pamphleteers are deeply pessimistic. They are conscious of their defeats: the Commune's collapse, Dreyfus's acquittal. Their enemies are growing in strength, while they remain voices crying out in the wilderness. Maurras strove for forty years to restore the monarchy to a country that had twice rejected it. Even more important, the pamphleteers know they cannot win, because their deals cannot be reached by political change. Péguy's medieval Catholic France is as remote from reality as Vallès's romantic

---

* The point of setting Céline's pamphlets in the context of this tradition is to show that they do make sense. Some of their exaggerations are no more than a standard trait of the genre.

revolutionary proletariat. They turn their hatred against the present, blackening it as Céline blackens the France of the 1930s.

His apocalyptic vision belongs in their tradition. Bloy is waiting for the Cossacks, who will ravage a godless universe, while at the end of *Les Grands Cimetières* Bernanos sees Christendom destroyed by Hitler. The pamphleteers scorn moderation. Bernanos despises bourgeois Catholicism and Vallès reserves his sharpest criticism for the moderate leftist Gambetta. Like Céline they will not settle for easy solutions. He is one of them when he rejects an alliance with Fascist Italy in favour of collaboration with Nazi Germany. As the modern world is rotten it must be destroyed before it can be rebuilt on new foundations. Maurras, sworn enemy of Germany, welcomes the 1940 defeat because it puts an end to the despised Republic and permits the Vichy experiment. For the Catholic pamphleteers the world's end comes before the establishment of God's kingdom. Beyond the anti-Christ Hitler, Bernanos sees a great Christian upsurge.

In this gigantic struggle there is small place for reason. The pamphleteers fear it, feeling it will destroy revealed truths. Long before Céline denounces those 'who will only "think" life . . . and not "feel" it',[3] Péguy launched his attack on the Sorbonne. Although some pamphleteers are capable of subtle dialectic – witness Maurras – most rely on emotion. They bury opponents rather than refute them. Their tactic is to find targets and overwhelm them with rhetoric. In *Faut-il réduire l'Angleterre en esclavage?* Béraud does not analyse the Abyssinian crisis. He labels England as the villain and paints the picture of a country dominated by evil bankers and a mysterious Intelligence Service. He proclaims, on no evidence, that England's aim is to drag France into war with Italy in order to keep open the sea route to India. His pamphlet, which drew a sharp protest from the British embassy in Paris, is a good example of the rhetorical method. The pamphleteers do not wish to understand the complex economic and social forces that create the modern world. Analysis is too difficult, it is easier and more dramatic to pick on scapegoats. Drumont blames the 1870 defeat on the Jew, Bernanos ascribes the corruption of French life to capitalism. The same scapegoat may be used over and again. Foreigners, Freemasons, Jews and capitalists are all fair game. Whey then should Céline not blame the Jew for the coming war?

The pamphleteers' style reflects their emotion. Péguy goes to extremes of virulence as he assaults his enemies. Some, like Bloy and Daudet, have picked up the coarse vocabulary of the Naturalists and put it to a new use. But most are conservative stylists who use long periods and grandiose metaphors. They do not dismember the language like Céline. Still, the writing in *Bagatelles* is different from *Mort à crédit* and the influence of the pamphlet genre is evident. Céline still uses the three-point ellipsis but the movement of the paragraph is not as rapid. Instead of jumping from thought to thought he hammers away at the same things. In *L'École des cadavres* the style is even more static because the three points have been replaced by exclamation marks and capital letters. Each phrase follows the preceding one, like a regular series of blows. Céline has developed his own rhetoric, breaking down the sentence as in *Mort à crédit*, but with fewer syntactical surprises.

Such writing expresses an emotion that is not merely literary. The pamphleteers live in a world dangerous for themselves and their opponents. Céline's destiny is not exceptional. Daudet and Maurras both served jail sentences. Péguy's campaign against Jaurès helped cause his assassination. Béraud's newspaper *Gringoire* certainly drove Popular Front minister Roger Salengro to suicide. Vallès was condemned to death after the Commune and fled to England. Like Céline, these men faced greater danger than practical politicians. Violence flooded over from their books into their lives.

For them the stakes are high. Politics is a matter of morality and religion, never of statecraft. Béraud rebukes England for its *realpolitik* view of foreign affairs. For Maurras politics is partly an aesthetic problem: the monarchy and Classicism are inseparable. This explains why the pamphleteers adopt their curiously unpolitical stance. Bloy attacks capitalism in the outraged tones of Christ driving the money-lenders from the temple. Daudet castigates the Republic in moral terms as a harlot. Céline does the same. His argument with Moscow in *Mea Culpa* has less to do with Marxism than with original sin.

How can one define these strange creatures in political terms? To what party do they belong? They are mostly men of the right – Vallès being the exception. Their preference for emotion over reason, their nationalism and their resistance to modernity mark them as rightwingers. But they are no orthodox conservatives. A strain of anticapitalism runs through their thinking from Drumont on, and the Action Française never succeeded in winning over the leading financial circles. They are too extreme for most conservatives, who might agree that sanctions should not be imposed on Italy but would not join in Béraud's anti-England crusade. Moreover the pamphleteers shift their positions with disconcerting rapidity. Péguy began as Dreyfus's supporter and Jaurès' friend; he died a mortal enemy of socialism. And where is one to class Bernanos, Drumont's anti-semitic disciple, who became the darling of the left with his attacks on Franco and his wartime support of de Gaulle, but who survived long enough to denounce the Liberation? Céline went the other way: the supposedly left-wing author of *Voyage* became the raving anti-semite of *Bagatelles*. He is no more inconsistent than the others. Maurras has a clearly defined position to which he adhered all his life; but most pamphleteers react to an issue without a thought of logic. They are too emotional to follow any party line. Like Céline they are best viewed as anarchists.

This is the army Céline was joining when he published *Mea Culpa* and *Bagatelles*. His opinions – his anti-semitism, his anglophobia and his dislike of industrialization – were theirs. More important, his temperament was the same. Hatred and despair are the driving forces behind most pamphleteers. Yet there are great differences. There is a game-playing in *Bagatelles* that was new. Game-playing is not uncommon among men who are trying consciously to whip up a frenzy – the insults Bernanos hurls at the reader in the opening pages of *Les Grands Cimetières* are one example. But Céline goes much further. In *Bagatelles* he exaggerates to the point of creating disbelief. Léon Blum is Jewish, he tells us correctly; Masaryk and Benes are also Jewish, so are Gide, Maurras and the Pope; the entire English nation is Jewish. At this point one stops: clearly Céline does not want to be believed. He himself dismisses the narrator Ferdinand as a 'poor imbecile'[4] whose Jewish friend Gutman makes fun of him. Céline is criticizing his own anti-semitism. It is one way of dealing with the hopeless political situation, but he is not quite ready to embrace it.

Bagatelles begins and ends with ballet. The narrator is trying to turn reality into dance. Having read *Mort à crédit* he knows that man needs, more than anything else, to create beauty. (This is the test and the self-laid trap of the pamphlets: do they offer a convincing aesthetic transformation of the late 1930s?) The Jew, Céline tells us, is uncreative. Once he is destroyed, the world may become ballet. Yet Céline is not certain of this – he hesitates once again. Either way his aesthetic preoccupations separate him from the other pamphleteers. Maurras has integrated a literary creed into his political doctrine. But he could not imagine a society based on dance, as Céline does in *Les Beaux Draps*.

In discussing Céline's pamphlets, analysis of themes is not the most difficult task. He flaunts his rejection of reason: 'I am really one of the most complete idiots in the world.'[5] His arguments have no intellectual merit, but then he has said that 'opinions don't count'.[6] Hostile critics like Emmanuel Mounier and Maurice Vanino have no trouble proving that he drew his anti-semitic statistics from gutter sources like *La Prochaine Révolution des travailleurs* and *Le Règne des juifs*.[7] Not content with that, he inflated his figures at will. No attention need be paid to such 'proofs'. Céline enjoys being absurd. But the pamphlets are important as the expression of an emotional reaction which is caught up with an aesthetic vision.

Mea Culpa is the fruit of Céline's Russian journey.[8] It seems to be one more book about communism, part of the debate that raged in the intellectual circles of the 1930s, but it contains little information about Russia. Céline does not analyse the economic system nor the role of the Communist Party. He engages in his familiar debate about truth. The fascination of the Soviet Union is that it presents an un-oppressed society. Freed from capitalist exploitation man is revealed for what he really is.

Immediately Céline makes his onslaught. The Russian people are poverty-stricken and brutish, a living proof that man in his fallen state is appalling. The proletariat has a 'devilish nature' which leads him to 'false values'. He is materialistic, he 'apes' the bourgeoisie and he is 'corrupt'. The only course left open is to admit man's condition in all humility. As the Russians will not do this their new society is futile. 'The true Revolution will be the Revolution of Confession,' says Céline. His title repeats the theme: the Russians should accept their guilt, as Bardamu did in *Voyage*.

Instead they insist that man is good. Having accepted the Marxist critique of capitalism, they have concluded that in a classless society virtue will reign supreme. Such optimism is anathema to Céline who delights in pointing out the cruelty and poverty he saw in Russia. He mocks the communists and contrasts them with Christians: 'the practical superiority of the great Christian religions is that they did not sweeten the pill'. Instead of promising paradise on this earth they insisted on original sin. In tones reminiscent of Bloy, Céline sides with this harsh view. He is returning to the theme of the Elie Faure letters: there can be no innocent working class because humanity as a whole is flawed. He redefines his opposition to communism in moral terms. Christianity keeps man in a state of 'perfect humility' while the Russians unleash in him 'the most vile and destructive arrogance'.

Their optimism causes them two kinds of problems. Firstly they have to explain away the flaws in their society, which, according to Marx, should have vanished with capitalism. One of their methods is to pick on scapegoats. An expert on this subject, Céline points to the Moscow trials as an attempt to blame the country's ills on a small group of traitors. Then too there is a huge police force – 'the most numerous, the most suspicious, the most disgusting, the most sadistic on earth'. Its role is to repress discontent and preserve the illusion of utopia. The second problem is even greater. The Russians are giving free rein to human nature, which means, for Céline, that they are encouraging evil. In flattering man's pride and telling him that his inclinations are good – this must be the most peculiar criticism ever made of Stalin's Russia – they are driving him to materialism and murder.

The issue of materialism provokes Céline's fury. Instead of condemning it the communists have made it an official creed. Céline rails against the glorification of industry: 'To tell the truth the machine defiles, ruins and destroys everything it touches.' His disgust for the flesh makes him loathe the production and consumption of material goods. Industrialization is the 'ultimate defeat'. In characteristic manner Céline shows how materialism leads to violence. Prosperity is nothing but a *divertissement* and Pascalian man will not be content with cars and radios. When he becomes dissatisfied he will turn to the mirage of revolution. 'Since the Flood all wars have been fought to cries of optimism,' says Céline. He ends with a prophecy of disaster: as the Russians discover that they have not built a utopia, they will be driven on to purges, new revolutions and foreign wars. Rather than face the 'impossible confession, the pill that cannot be swallowed ...

that Man is the worst of all species', they will resort to endless, sense-less massacres.

This is the grim picture Céline paints of the Soviet Union. But he does not damn Russia in order to praise the West. 'All Fords are the same,' he says, 'Soviet or otherwise.' The dream of a socialist revolution is just a particular form of the heresy that plagues the Western world: the belief that political change can improve humanity. 'Politics has ruined man,' says Céline, meaning France as well as Russia. The Soviet Union has simply gone further down the same path.

Céline does not trouble himself with logic. He describes the Russians as free and as police-ridden. He criticizes them because they have not solved the problem of poverty, and he criticizes them for making prosperity a goal. Inconsistency is the pamphleteer's prerogative. But *Mea Culpa* is not a fully-fledged pamphlet. Stylistically it is uncertain, because Céline hesitates between argument and invective. He outlines the Russian creed, knocks it down and proceeds with his harangue. But he does not pile up page upon page of rhetoric, as he will do in *Bagatelles*. In content *Mea Culpa* is a starting-point. Céline condemns Western society, but he does not elaborate. If the Soviet Union is the particular form of a general disease, Céline may choose to treat the disease. In doing so he will be driven to offer solutions, which he does not do in *Mea Culpa*. The author of this first pamphlet speaks with the voice of *Voyage* and *Mort à crédit*. An ascetic moralist, he affirms that man is evil and that he must face this. His next pamphlet will offer a solution: entry into the dream world of anti-semitism.

Bagatelles is the hallucinating picture of a country in its death throes. In a memorable paragraph Céline writes: 'Always there, present, hidden, the instinct that cannot be avoided or deceived, the Death instinct, buried in the hearts of men ... and races that will disappear, the instinct that is never talked about and never talks, the most tenacious, solid and perfect, the silent instinct'. Materialism is one face of death: factories stifle human lives. The abstraction of con-temporary culture is another: it kills emotion. 'The French have no soul any more,' Céline complains, 'a cancer has gobbled up their souls.' His examples of French decadence range from the *apéritif* to the Popular Front government. Lurking in the background is the demon of violence: France is too weak to stop herself being lured into war with Germany. Everything he sees leads Céline back to death: Paris is one huge Père Lachaise. 'People drag themselves around in Paris,' writes Céline, 'they don't live any more. They always seem to be struggling in a general suicide!'

The onslaught on materialism elaborates on the views of *Mea Culpa*. 'What do the mob want nowadays? They want to go down on their knees and worship gold.' The highest goal is industrialization, although it is creating a 'robot world'. 'Modern civilization means total standardization,' says Céline, who attacks cinema and radio because they destroy the mind. Meanwhile the French are ruining their bodies by eating and drinking. Like a prohibitionist, Céline denounces 'wine, the national poison'. He criticizes the Popular Front which, by introducing the forty-hour week, increased the time Frenchmen could spend in cafés.

Faced with such decadence he is tempted to hark back – like Péguy or Maurras – to a golden age: 'In 1914 the world was much simpler, more natural, more sincere, much less underhand, less depraved than today!' The era he condemned in *Mort à crédit* has become the pre-industrial, pre-Jewish age. 'We were quiet then ... We lived without harming one another,' sighs the narrator's friend Gustin. This is more a matter of rhetoric than conviction. Any polemist feels an urge to point out examples of his ideal and 'We, the pre-1914 Frenchmen' provide a happy alternative to the despised 1930s. Several times in his pamphlets Céline is driven to defend certain groups – in *L'École des cadavres* he praises the Nazis – but it is as the lesser evil, or as a stick to beat his opponents.

While attacking the *apéritif* Céline turns to the other side of the coin: abstraction. He returns to the United Nations and to Yudenzweck, now renamed Yubelblat: 'Endless Congresses for Peace, for eternal Peace, for progress, enlightenment, the advancement of knowledge and mankind'. Like Péguy, Céline condemns the intellectualism of his age. 'He talks all of the time,' he says of the Frenchman: 'He intoxicates himself with his arguments, his own words. He is conceited, he thinks he is a critic.' Verbal reasoning divorces man from the horrible reality of his situation. Céline's peculiar positivism comes into play here. Although he condemns the flesh, he insists it is the only reality. He demands sensations as opposed to 'Gidisms and hypotheses'.

Gide is a favourite target in *Bagatelles*, but he is in good company. Claudel, Maurois, Alain, 'Prout-Proust' and the Surrealists also incur Céline's wrath. In a decadent society how can literature be good? French writing is 'more dead than death itself'. It has no lyricism, it is analytical, psychological and complicated. 'All bourgeois writers are impostors at heart! They fake experience and emotions.' The term 'bourgeois' is important because Céline is making a political as well as an aesthetic protest. He is claiming that France's hierarchical social system produces an élite divorced from real people. It is a short step to attacking the *lycée* – Céline's personal background is evident here – and the 'stupid educational system'. French artists cannot write because they have been 'castrated' by their education. 'A style is first and foremost an emotion,' says Céline, remembering the innovations of *Mort à crédit*. Most authors use 'a French that is disgustingly elegant, moulded, oriental, oily, slippery like shit'. This is genuine pamphleteer stuff: Maurras' disciple, Henri Massis, had attacked the *Nouvelle Revue française* in similar terms a decade before. But Céline devotes many pages to the problem, because to him style is the fundamental issue. The French are dying because they cannot create beauty, because they have forgotten how to dance.

Céline is obsessed with French decadence. He is acutely aware of the 1914 bloodletting and the declining birthrate. He reserves his sharpest sarcasm for nationalists like Pétain, who were appealing for a revival of grandeur. 'Ours is actually a poor country,' he says, 'a country with scanty resources and wealth, a naturally stingy country.' A good deal of twentieth-century French thought has revolved around the theme of greatness. France's decline as a military power coupled with her continued cultural prestige, the paradox of a land seemingly rich but economically backward, have prompted a debate about her destiny. In this argument de Gaulle, for whom 'France . . . cannot be France without greatness' and who calls her 'the Princess in a fairytale or the Madonna of the Frescoes',[9] stands at one end of the spectrum, Céline at the other. Later Céline will turn on de Gaulle, but in *Bagatelles* it is, ironically enough, Pétain who is attacked as the advocate of false grandeur.

In a dying country politics is almost irrelevant. Aside from the 'Revolution of Confession', which no one is willing to make, it scarcely matters which line one follows. 'I have never voted in my life,' boasts Céline. 'I have always known and understood that the idiots are in a majority so it's certain they will win.' He satirizes all sides. The Communists have nothing to offer but 'the complete enslavement of the proletariat'. Russia is dismissed in a sentence: 'Russian poverty, as I could see, is unimaginable, Asiatic, like something out of Dostoyevsky.' The right is no better: 'Our Aryan bourgeoisie is debased, they wail like babies, they are a thousand times worse than the most stinking Yids.' Bernanos himself could not do a better job of ridiculing both camps. Céline does spend time attacking the Popular Front; but, if Blum is bad, Pétain and Reynaud are no better.

The only genuine political problem is the threat of war. The French are allowing themselves to be dragged into an anti-Fascist crusade. To Céline this is simply suicidal, another example of Popular Front optimism, another delusion of grandeur. He advocates pacifism at any price. Peace with or without honour is the goal set out in *Bagatelles*. He goes to work on France's allies because without them she could not go to war. The Russians, the traditional Eastern friend, have been disposed of. England, perfidious Albion, is the main target. Like Béraud, Céline is sure Britain will encourage France to fight and then desert her: 'The English our allies? Balls! Another great swindle! They'll go easy this time, I can tell you. We'll all be maggots by the time the first Oxford queers disembark in Flanders'.

Céline's pacifism leads him to support Germany. 'I would prefer twelve Hitlers to one Blum,' he says, knowing that many Frenchmen were weighing the same choice. Admiration for the Nazis is a minor theme of *Bagatelles* and Céline is forced into it by the dialectic of his argument. If war is the ultimate evil, Hitler is a lesser evil. If the Jew is the agent of death, the Nazis must be on Céline's side. 'Hitler doesn't like the Jews, neither do I,' is how he puts it. Rebatet advocates pacifism because he admires the Nazis, Céline does the reverse.

This viewpoint, although pushed to extremes in *Bagatelles*, was not exceptional in the France of the late 1930s. Only the tiny Fascist groups followed Rebatet's line, but many people wanted to conciliate Germany.* A revolution was taking place in foreign policy. The nationalist

---

* The terms 'anti-semite', 'collaborator' and 'Fascist' are often used rather loosely. Here an attempt has been made to define them and to keep them separate. For 'anti-semite' Sartre's definition has been accepted. In Chapter Six 'collaboration' is used in two ways: firstly the broad sense of one whose thought was

right, which had been traditionally hostile to the Lutheran hordes from across the Rhine, was becoming more pacifist, while the governments of the left accepted rearmament.

Ideology accounts for much of this. The right was disturbed by the spectre of communism. It feared the Soviet alliance and the red flag flying over Madrid. It was horrified by the growing strength of the domestic Communist Party and its participation in the Popular Front. Trapped between dislike of Germany and terror of a red take-over, Maurras was unable to play the role he had played before the 1914 war. After the defeat Weygand would plead for an armistice, so that the army might be used to put down the expected communist uprising.

The left was going through the opposite evolution. The Parti Communiste, determined to defend Russia, had accepted rearmament and was using its influence to strengthen the moribund Franco-Soviet alliance. The socialists were being lured away from their pacifism by their opposition to Fascism. With much hesitation the left was moving to fill the anti-German role vacated by the right.

On both sides there was confusion. The communists were thrown into complete disarray by the Nazi-Soviet pact, which left them without a policy and exposed them to Daladier's vengeance. The socialists split over the rearmament issue and the pacifist wing refused to follow Léon Blum. On the right, moderate nationalists and Action Française supporters tried to have their cake and eat it. They placed their faith in an alliance with their latin sister Italy or they looked for support to conservative England. They pondered on the choice between Blum and Hitler but they could not bring themselves to make it. Without welcoming the hysteria of *Bagatelles*, they could share some of Céline's fears.

He also found echoes in the country as a whole. Like Céline, France had not recovered from the 1914 war. The crowds who welcomed Daladier on his return from Munich were expressing their desire for peace, and the feeble resistance of 1940 showed how reluctant the

---

in harmony with the Nazi view of things, secondly the more restricted, legal definition given by the Liberation law-courts. The term 'fascist' is used for writers who admired and actively supported the Italian and German governments and who believed in the positive values of a Fascist revolution. By this yardstick Drieu, Brasillach and Rebatet were fascists, Céline was not. But the question of whether there are Fascist elements in Céline's writing is discussed in Chapter Ten and again in the Conclusion.

French had been to take up arms again. This defeatist strain is voiced in *Bagatelles*. Céline exaggerates it until it is almost unrecognizable, but he has picked on a very real sentiment.

This is not true of his other great theme: anti-semitism. In *Bagatelles* all ills are blamed on the Jew who is capitalist and communist, Catholic and Freemason. 'The world doesn't keep going on its own,' Céline insists. 'The Jews run things.' Bardamu had analysed the mechanism of hatred and wars; but the author of *Bagatelles* runs straight into the trap he had described.

In the nature of his anti-semitism Céline follows the pamphleteer tradition. French anti-semitism is usually cultural and not pseudo-scientific in the Nazi manner. Drumont sees the Jew under various stereotypes: as the social climber (Arthur Meyer), or the foreign spy (La Païva). He, Bloy and Bernanos condemn the Jew as usurer. They do not consider the Jewish race to be flawed *per se*. Bloy even admires the Jews as God's chosen people. The hostility and admiration that run together in his writing show that his anti-semitism is based on what certain Jewish people supposedly chose to become, rather than on what all of them inevitably were. In *Bagatelles* the pseudo-scientific view is present, but it is not stressed. Céline talks of the Aryan's 'biological superiority' and dismisses the Jewish nervous system as barren – one is reminded of the Volkish notion that the Germans are a forest people and the Jews a desert people. Céline associates sensibility with race, speaking of the 'racial or lyrical tone'. He declares that the Jew's biological inferiority makes him spiritually inferior.

Racism of this kind has some attraction for him. It appeals to his positivism. To be sure the body is appalling, but where it can be mastered, it offers flashes of beauty. These Céline reserves for Aryans. But this line of thought, which drew him an approving nod from the Nazi review *Stürmer*,[10] was too optimistic to please him. If one race is inferior the other must be superior. How is the drink-sodden, cinema-loving Aryan to be considered superior? Céline is not the man to wax eloquent on sturdy peasants and flaxen-haired children. *Stürmer*'s praise was not unqualified: it lamented his frantic despair.

His anti-semitism is supposedly cultural. Everything he hates in the modern world is ascribed to the Jew. 'For me Jews and communists are the same thing,' he says, expressing a view common among anti-semites. Equally common is the complementary prejudice: the Jew as wicked capitalist. Céline combines the two when he explains how the Russian revolution was financed by American-Jewish bankers. French politics is riddled with semitic intrigues. Blum is the chief villain and the Popular Front part of the international conspiracy. England is no different: 'a Jew or an Englishman, same thing,' says Céline.

He is a true pamphleteer. Daudet, too, attributes all France's ills to the Jew who is both the Republic's guiding spirit and the Germans' fifth column. Céline blames the Jew for the fundamental lack of lyricism: they 'have absolutely no direct or spontaneous emotion. They talk instead of feeling ... They reason before they react ... Strictly speaking they don't feel anything.' Modernity itself has been invented by the Jews, symbols of rootlessness: 'they never stop moving around the world all the time, they are always travelling'. In particular they are responsible for the past war: 'The Yids emerged victorious from the last piece of bourgeois folly 1914–18.' Now they are plotting a holy war against Fascism: 'It's the Jews and only the Jews who are thrusting us up against the machine-guns.' The spurious argument is now complete: appeasement and anti-semitism go together.

Over and above his role as warmonger the Jew is the incarnation of evil ('the necessary "infamous, unworthy wretch"' that Bardamu had talked about). Céline makes him personify the fears that lurk in man's subconscious. He is the foreign invader, the disgusting ghetto-dweller, the Asiatic peril, the half-black, half-yellow mongrel, the despoiler of Aryan woman, herself a 'traitorous bitch'. The Jew is synonymous with the death instinct: 'The kind of grimace you find on Jewish mugs ... rises up from the depths of the ages to terrify us, out of the confusions of cross-breeding, out of bloody, talmudic mires, the whole Apocalypse is there'.

At such moments Céline comes near answering a question he usually avoids: why is he anti-semitic? The reasons he offers are merely the hackneyed themes of anti-semitism, updated to the 1930s. The answer lies, as with all pamphleteers, in the violent irrationality of his arguments. The best guide to *Bagatelles*' hysteria is Sartre's *Réflexions sur la question juive*, written with Céline in mind.[11]

For Sartre, the anti-semite is the man who avoids the human condition: 'what he flees even more than Reason is his intimate awareness of himself'. Fearing that he is trapped in an absurd universe, the anti-semite escapes rather than face reality. He takes refuge in the fiction that the Jew has ruined everything. Sartre criticizes him for shunning the liberty that results from knowing absurdity: 'Authentic liberty comes from assuming responsibilities and the liberty of the anti-semite comes from the fact that he escapes all of his.' He is free only to hate. Sartre says that 'hatred is a faith' which enables him to avoid the confrontation with himself. In all of this the real Jew, as individual or race, is unimportant: 'if the Jew did not exist, the anti-semite would invent him'.

This argument fits Céline well. Unable to face the terrible fact that France is blundering into a war with a strong, rapacious neighbour, he seizes on the fiction that the Jew is a warmonger. Sartre goes further: two features mark the anti-semite's temperament – passionate emotion and pessimism. Both are abundantly present in *Bagatelles*. Sartre makes a distinction between anti-semites like Maurras, who maintains that after a long struggle the Aryan will triumph, and Céline. In a striking passage he adds: 'Look at Céline, his vision of the universe is catas-trophic. The Jew is everywhere, the earth is lost, it is up to the Aryan not to compromise, never to make peace. Yet he must be on his guard; if he breathes he has already lost his purity.' For Céline, Sartre con-cludes, 'there is no solution except collective suicide, non-reproduction, death'.[12]

In what sense can such anti-semitism be the 'escape-hatch' men-tioned in the last chapter? The Jew is man himself revealed in all his horror. But escape lies in the creation of an executioner. By depicting a tyrant Céline can objectivize his fears and plunge into a nightmare of hatred. He will be destroyed; but such a suicide is preferable to the lucid agony that Bardamu undergoes, or the constant struggle that is Dr Destouches's existence. Death is a solution to the fears of life.

Not surprisingly, *Bagatelles* is riddled with self-hatred. The refusal to hide any prejudice and the determination to alienate all political groups are only two of its manifestations. Céline persists in seeing himself as a victim: an Aryan, he is exploited by the Jew; a French-man, by the English; an artist, by the critic. Paradoxically he is drawn closer to the Jew, the traditional victim.

At this point one may leave Sartre's analysis. One question that he does not ask is: why the Jew? If it were asked, he might reply that the anti-semite is looking for a powerless enemy or that the Jew is the traditional target of Western–Christian culture. But this is not enough.

It does not explain the obsessive hatred of *Bagatelles*. It is clear that the anti-semite considers the Jew a rival, considers that they have much in common. The Nazis *had* to eliminate the Jews in order to show that the Germans were the chosen people. The Jews, with their history, their sacred traditions and their sense of Israel, were a threat. Here was another, perhaps more authentic, version of the Nazi creed of the holy German soil and Aryan supremacy. One has the same sense with Bloy: his ambivalent view of the Jews comes from a feeling that Judaism was competing with his brand of Catholicism. Céline too feels that the Jew is brother and enemy. He is a rival claimant for Céline's particular kind of sacredness: his sense of being a creature of the night, burdened with exceptional suffering and rewarded with mystical insight. Why does the Jew come 'from the depths of the ages to terrify us'? It is because he is Western man's bad conscience, the victim of his brutality, the reminder of death. Why does the Ferdinand of *Féerie*, the monster of Montmartre, disturb the other Parisians? It is because he has been condemned to death by the Resistance. The Jew and Céline are sacred vessels singled out for a special fate. There is a story, which may or may not be true, that after the war Céline met a Lithuanian Jew on the streets of Copenhagen. Céline had just come out of prison, the Jew had survived the holocaust. Both men shrank from the crowds of ordinary, happy people. They sought each other out. 'I am a Jew,' whispered the man, 'I am Céline,' was the reply. They stood for a moment together.[13]

There are remarks in *Bagatelles* that reveal the link. Ferdinand recognizes that he and the Jew have much in common. 'You are boasting like a Jew,' says Gutman to Ferdinand. Ferdinand admits that Jewish readers like him because he has the same temperament as they. His 'lyricism ... both vociferous and full of anathemas' pleases them. He is 'quite Jewish in some ways'. He discusses Jewish prophecy and mysticism and warns his sceptical readers not to ignore them. But he resents the Jew's incursion on his role. He repeats his aversion for Charlie Chaplin – the personification of 'good old Jewish snivelling'. Chaplin evokes a pity that is mere 'blackmail'. It leads Ferdinand to conclude that 'the trick of the Jew who is "hunted" and "martyred" never fails to work on the stupid cuckold of an Aryan'. The true victim is Ferdinand: 'It is they who are persecuting us ... We are the martyrs' victims.'

In calling for the Jew's destruction Céline is getting rid of his most dangerous rival. Once more self-destruction and murder run together. Throughout Céline's writing victim and executioner switch roles: the reader persecutes the author who terrifies the reader; lover and mistress torture one another. Here Céline is committing suicide. The Jew is himself, Cassandra-Céline who must at all costs be silenced. But there is also an element of revenge. Céline will not have a rival who is better than he. Despite the persecution mounted against him, the Jew affirms his faith in mankind by his left-wing political stance and his belief in culture. Such goodness is anathema to Céline who resents his scapegoat's role, who is – as Sartre says – afraid. He reserves his sharpest criticism for the Jew's 'oracular socialistic–communistic jargon'. There is more involved than the usual attack on optimism. Céline cannot tolerate the notion that the Jew is not afraid. It might mean that the Jew has gone further into the night than he . . .

Céline did not himself see the matter in this light. Ferdinand is obsessed with his own role as sacrificial offering. He is putting his head on the block so that Europe may be saved. He calls for the Jew to kill him so that the Germans may not slaughter the French. He is placating the gods of war. Like so much in Céline's work this attitude is only explicable in terms of primitive religion. Every mythology has its own versions of the Christ legend; Celtic mythology is particularly rich in them.* But this does not really explain the wildly destructive element in *Bagatelles*. In any case there is a kind of cheating here. Locked in a deadly embrace both protagonists will die – Ferdinand the anti-semite and the Jew. Since Céline is risking all for himself – so the argument runs – he has the right to risk all for the Jew. But the two are not on the same plane. Firstly the Jew has not asked to join in the game; he has been dragooned into playing and his role has been defined for him by the anti-semite. Even more important: for the Jew everything is at stake, whereas Céline is sacrificing only one of his many selves. Ferdinand the anti-semite will be condemned, but Dr Destouches will go on practising and the author of *Mort à crédit* will write another novel. Hydra-Céline is putting only

---

* They exert much influence on modern Ireland. The leaders of the Easter Rebellion, like the present-day I.R.A., were imbued with sacrificial mania. But Padraig Pearse was not as virulently aggressive as the author of *Bagatelles*. This is another reason for disputing the simple 'victim' explanation.

one of his heads on the block. He is still evading, still showing fear.[14]

He has fallen into a *délire*, just like one of the minor characters in his novels. The *délire* may be defined as the other, separate world that the maniacs and exiles invent when the normal world becomes impossible.* It is passionate, full of dislikes and haunted by death, exactly Sartre's description of anti-semitism. Most of *Bagatelles* is made up of this *délire*, but not all of it. Céline makes fun of his own fiction.

The comedy in the book was picked up by the earliest readers. André Gide says that Céline 'did everything he could to warn people that his whole argument was no more serious than Don Quixote's ride in the heavens'.[15] He does this by punctuating his harangues with humour. He strings out the outbursts along a series of haphazard meetings and newspaper reports. A conversation with Gen Paul is the starting-point for a diatribe against Jewish domination of the arts; a mention of Ferdinand's work at the League of Nations provokes a speech about the Jew and modernity. Céline creates an impression of arbitrariness, rather like a Molière farce. One chapter does not lead to another, each has its own pet mania. There is much repetition and many blind alleys. The book could end at any time depending on the author's whim: 'I am going to add on a few chapters,' he says.

The narrator Ferdinand is a clown, a 'poor imbecile obsessed with unnecessary vulgarity'. Small wonder that he exaggerates his stories. London docks, he claims, are crawling with Jewish plotters, the Consistory is behind every political event from the Russian revolution to the Abyssinian invasion. Gutman just laughs at him: 'You are delirious, Ferdinand,' he says. 'You will have the whole world against you,' says another friend. Ferdinand knows his task is hopeless because the Aryans will not listen to a buffoon like him. He becomes precisely the kind of Charlie Chaplin figure he attacks. 'Always he has struggled, battled for his life, Ferdinand,' he says in an orgy of self-pity. 'I had to steal my life . . . and yet I have never been free.' He is the eternal little man, inflated with dreams of ballet and anti-semitic crusades, but forced back on his own futility.

This is another of Céline's attempts to deal with the 1930s. In a

---

* The term *délire* is much used both by Céline and his critics. Good use is made of the concept by Michel Beaujour in 'La Quête du délire', *L'Herne*, 3, pp. 279–88. Here the word is used in another sense: to denote the world of the mad, as described in Chapter Three.

world growing absurd he will become a clown. Perhaps, he is saying, the problem is not a menacing Germany versus a weak France but the delirium of ridiculous Ferdinand. Such comedy serves several purposes. It is another way of destroying Cassandra-Céline: his prophecies are not to be taken seriously. It is an insurance policy against hostility: how could Céline be considered anti-semitic? Surely he was only making fun.* More than anything, this is another role and the mere shifting of roles is a comfort to Céline.

He dons a third mask: Ferdinand is also a failed writer of ballets. He describes two ballets he has written – *La Naissance d'une fée* and *Paul et Virginie*. Like the Krogold legend, they are enchanting but menacing. In the first, the heroine, Eveline, is murdered by an evil witch, Karalik, who is jealous of her ballerina's talent. In the second Virginia is killed by a rival, Mireille, in the middle of a wild dance. Yet both ballets end with a kind of victory. Through suffering at her loss the poet will learn to express Eveline's beauty; after Virginie's death the dance continues triumphant, until the troupe is carried off on the Fulmicoach. The ballets remain unperformed, as the Krogold legend remained unwritten. Later Céline published these dances on their own in a book called *Ballets sans musique, sans personne, sans rien*, a Beckettian title which reverses their significance in *Bagatelles*. Here the message is clear: dance is not possible because the world is not right. Jewish musicians refuse to set Ferdinand's ballets to music, the Jewish organizers of the 1937 Exhibition turn them down. The Jew is the enemy of the aesthetic. He has already ruined French writing, which is dying for lack of Aryan substance. Now he is preventing ballet. Ferdinand, the lover of beauty, must turn to anti-semitism. He starts out on his three hundred pages of hatred.

But at the end he hesitates again. In a part of the book that he has consciously set apart from the rest he looks back to *Mea Culpa* and his Russian experience. He describes Leningrad, capital of ballet, 'its great Northern sky blue-green, more transparent than the immense river'. He paints a truer picture of human misery – the snow, the poverty, the old lady who has nothing to live for. He tells the anecdote

---

* This worked. At Céline's trial in 1950 extracts from *Les Beaux Draps* were read and the courtroom rocked with laughter. This may have influenced the court's decision to impose a light sentence. The comedy does not, one feels, make the anti-semitism harmless. But it does enable Céline to have his cake and eat it.

of Borokrom the anarchist, whose dream is to become a brutal king so that he can offer his subjects a target for their bitterness: 'I would have centralized, magnetized, fanaticized all the hatreds in my kingdom.' Such an understanding of the way hatred works acts as an ironic commentary on *Bagatelles*' anti-semitism. Céline talks of suffering, of the Russian prince he knew at Nice who was killed in the revolution, of Nathalie his interpreter who has been ill, of Elisabeth Craig the empress he has lost.

The misery of man's lot is the real explanation of the political crisis. It is also, according to *Mort à crédit*, the starting-point of the aesthetic transformation. Not surprisingly, the old lady is a pianist, Elisabeth, a dancer. Céline finishes with another ballet: the tale of Van Bagaden, a rich industrialist who oppresses his workers and fights to stop the gaiety of the Antwerp crowd. He cannot do this and he dies while they, although poor and miserable, assert the beauty of life in their dance. Céline ends with 'all this joy, this madness . . . this huge farandola'.

But the ending is ambivalent. Ferdinand's ballets are turned down by Leningrad because the Jewish communists decide he is not 'sozial' enough. Back to anti-semitism. And how do the Russian pages fit in with the rest of the book? How is the inescapable human misery to be reconciled with the international Jewish conspiracy? Is it the Leningrad streets that are the material of ballet or the future Jewless world?

The final question is whether Céline has succeeded where Ferdinand failed: has he transformed reality into art? In his own terms – no others are needed – the answer is no. As a book, *Bagatelles* is a failure. Emmanuel Mounier has pointed out why: 'the Célinian character sits now with the masters; his world is active apart from him and clearly beneath him'.[16] Because he is not a part of the political chaos he describes, Céline's creatures are dehumanized. Jews, English and communists become puppets who could be eliminated without guilt – it is in this sense that *Bagatelles* is a defence of genocide – but who could not possibly provoke wars. For this reason the book is boring. Hundreds of pages are devoted to supposed Jewish crimes; but the agony that is so vividly portrayed in the novels is absent. Céline has fled into hatred and self-destruction, leaving behind him a vacuum that nothing can fill. He has forgotten the main tenet of his aesthetic creed: the need for moral integrity. Only by facing the Passage Choiseul can the narrator of *Mort à crédit* recover the beauty of the Krogold legend. No such effort is made in *Bagatelles* where the *délire* is substituted for reality. Céline's flight has ruined his book. It is the anti-semite, not the Jew, who is beauty's enemy.

The only successful part of *Bagatelles* is the questioning of the *délire*. The comedy and the Leningrad section reveal a man engaged in a genuine struggle against an obsession. After *Bagatelles* two choices were open to Céline. He could give up the quest to explain and dissolve the political crisis, or he could go further down the road of anti-semitism and try to make the *délire* complete. Like a real pamphleteer he chose the second course.

Despite its Molièresque title *L'École des cadavres* contains less comedy and no ballet. Although Céline still mocks the confused Ferdinand, almost all of the book is given up to his tirades. These have a sharper focus and are more extreme. The Munich crisis had shown that the threat of war was imminent, so Céline spends less time talking about materialism and concentrates on appeasement. He adopts a strongly pro-German line, driven on once again by the force of his argument. *L'École* is a different kind of book from *Bagatelles* – the substitution of exclamation marks for ellipses changes even the visual impact. It is much more of a traditional pamphlet. Doubt has given way to faith, to the urgent, emotional certainty of the pamphleteer.

It begins where *Bagatelles* stopped. Walking through the Paris suburbs along the Seine, Ferdinand meets the Sirène, his muse. Both of them have gone down in the world – 'life is not always amusing', says Ferdinand wrily. The Sirène's 'decline' marks the failure of the aesthetic dream. The hope of ballet, flung out so ambiguously during the Leningrad episode, is dashed. Ferdinand realizes that he is an author cast adrift in Paris, just as the Sirène flounders in the Seine's polluted waters. He turns on the agent of all misfortunes – the Jew.

The culture criticism of *Bagatelles* is repeated in strident tones. France is laid low by materialism: 'material things have besotted, debased, trivialized, bewildered, dulled, enslaved us'. 'When man makes matter into a God he destroys himself,' Céline warns in Jansenist tones. All sections of French society are equally rotten, he can admit of no preference. 'The bourgeois shits and he is hungry, that's all.' 'The worker's ideal is to have twice as many bourgeois pleasures just for himself.' Only one exception is made – the lower middle class;

but Céline does not pursue this theme. He does spend long pages denouncing an old target: left-wing optimism. 'Class-consciousness is rubbish,' he concludes.

But his main theme is war. The French, whose 'vocation is to end up in the slaughter-house', are being driven back to the trenches by the Jew. Pamphleteers do not shrink from repetition – Maurras spend his life saying the same few things – and Céline piles up examples of the Jewish conspiracy.

France's allies are leading it. Céline runs over his usual targets – England which is 'governed by Jews' and Russia where 'Jewish arrogance reigns supreme'. He talks more of the United States: America is 'completely Jewish', dominated by 'that spoilt darling Samuel Cohen of Brooklyn'. Céline seizes the opportunity to link the Jews with the Blacks, calling the United States 'the most negroized, judaized democracy on the face of the earth'. He also associates the Jews with sexual debauchery by describing the orgies portrayed in the cinemas of Times Square, New York. This kind of reasoning, which is the stock-in-trade of anti-semitism, provides the background for the real attack. Céline affirms, on no evidence, that the Americans need a war to pull their industry out of the Depression. Their leaders, whether populists like La Guardia or bankers like Warburg, are baying for blood. President 'Roosevelt-Rosenfeld' is shouting louder than anyone. American industry, 'stagnant and weary for twenty years', is awaiting the 'fantastic, providential orders' that will result from war. New York, 'the raving ghetto', is the headquarters of the international conspiracy. The three countries that fought with France in the First World War are bent on destroying her.

For Céline, as for Drumont, the Jew is the *provocateur* who deals in bloodshed. The Sudeten crisis is treated as part of the plot. Benes is a 'little, talmudic piece of shit' and Czechoslovakia another false victim – 'Miss Martyr 38'. Céline is not impressed by the Munich settlement – 'It didn't work out but Spain will go better'. The communist-dominated International Brigades will precipitate the war that Benès could not arrange.

Céline is ambivalent when he explains what the Jews hope to gain from the war. Sometimes he says their dream is to crush Hitler: 'This Aryan pseudo-revolt must be smashed, flattened, squashed, wiped out completely!' But this would entail a French victory, which contradicts his argument. He repeats that 'for us, war . . . is suicide' and that the 'French, from the first day . . . from the Gare de L'Est on, will literally fall apart'. Even to strengthen his theme of a Jewish plot, he is reluctant to admit that France might be triumphant. He has another explanation: even a French defeat will please the Jews whose aim is to weaken the white race. Franco-German rivalry is a mask for the real conflict: 'An implacable battle of the species . . . Negrified Jews against Whites. No more, no less.'

The *délire* is more complete than in *Bagatelles*. Céline has turned the German threat into an American–Russian–British conspiracy and, by inventing the Aryan–Jew war, he has substituted a feeble enemy for a strong one. He goes further when he throws his weight behind the German side. In *Bagatelles* he was reluctant to believe the Aryans were any better than the Jews. Here he praises that great Aryan bulwark, the Reich.

There is more pseudo-scientific anti-semitism in *L'École*. Céline speaks of the Jews as 'gangrenous bastards'. 'We are not moving towards a melting pot of races,' he declares. 'On the contrary we are heading for the exaltation of race, a biological exaltation, very natural.' He praises racial selection, showing his pessimism when he affirms that it must be done 'a hundred thousand times over' because the Aryans are so rotten. Force will be needed: 'It's the stick we need,' he keeps repeating. He shows an uncharacteristic admiration for dictators – Stalin, Mussolini and especially Hitler. This is logical because, if one believes that society is corrupt, a brutal dictatorship may seem the only way to improve it. But Céline is usually too much of an anarchist to admire dictators and too sceptical of human nature to believe they are altruistic. Here he stresses that a tough leader like Hitler is needed to combat the Jews.

It may be a choice between bad and worse, but 'at the present time, in such tragic circumstances, indifference is no answer. We must decide, we must choose one kind of perversion . . . we must have a terrible faith, a frightening intolerance.' Céline, one feels, is delighted to find himself in a crisis that demands extreme measures. He enjoys his own audacity in praising Hitler: 'Hitler is a good breeder of peoples . . . he cares about the lives of peoples and even about ours. He is an Aryan'.

So Céline calls for a treaty with the Nazis: 'As for me I want an alliance with Germany, at once.' He makes fun of the Italian link and mocks Maurras' admiration for Classical Italy: 'the idea of a latin bond comes straight out of the classroom'. He rebukes Mussolini's half-hearted anti-semitism, riddled with 'liberal scruples'. The Reich is the model for France. Céline calls for a Franco-German army which will be truly strong. Anticipating his 1942 letter to *Je suis partout*, he claims that 'the solid, non-speechifying part of France has always been the Celtic and Germanic part' – the two are presumably the same! Northern France is the embodiment of the Nordic state, ready to stand beside the Reich in a 'Confederation of the Aryan States of Europe'. Much is to be feared from the Arab–Jewish Southerners as well as from the City of London; but in the union of a Germanic France and Nazi Germany Céline sees grounds for hope.

The *délire* can go no further. The lines have been drawn and the stage is set for a pogrom. Céline has moved closer to orthodox anti-semitism and he has left behind his nihilism. All is not lost if the German alliance is formed, the Aryan may yet conquer the Jew. In *L'École* anti-semitism does provide an easy escape-hatch, although it is hard to tell how far Céline believes in his own optimism. The closing pages contradict the rest of the book. The solid Franco-Nazi block will surely be destroyed by the American–Russian–British Jews. And *L'École* is still full of self-hatred. Céline begins to write because the animosity *Bagatelles* aroused was lukewarm. He calls on all camps to persecute him – Doriot and Pétain as well as Thorez and Blum. 'They would like to kill me,' he keeps saying, 'my rivals, even my little disciples.' His confidence in the Nazis grows as he goes along, because he is convinced by his own rhetoric. As with his wartime journalism one feels that the positive things he says are fragile and that they are only pretexts for his rejection of the other side. He does not really believe the Nazis will win. He is simply filling in the gaps in the *délire*.

L'École's structure reflects this. After the meeting with the Sirène Ferdinand introduces the topic of anti-semitism and never really leaves it. As in *Bagatelles* he pours out his views in short chapters, using anecdotes as a starting-point. But the line of argument is simpler because he is so obsessed with the war. There is still exaggeration: the Pope is Jewish and his name is Isaac Ratisch; Céline will not fight for Belgium because he dislikes Huysmans' novels; the Jews are responsible for the 843 treaty of Verdun which separated France from Germany.

Céline continues to play with the author–reader relationship and to laugh at his role as victim. 'Perhaps you are going to consider me disgusting,' he says knowingly. He makes fun of narrator Ferdinand, who is writing for no reason and no public: 'Now look here, Ferdinand, aren't you going to stop being so pretentious?' But there is less of this than in *Bagatelles* and the self-criticism is replaced by a furious desire to proselytize. The endings of the two books are quite different. *Bagatelles*' Leningrad section is ambivalent; but *L'École* finishes with rambling diatribes against Popular Front minister Jean Zay and against the vengeful Dr Rouquès. There is no note of doubt here.

To the reader the second pamphlet is even less interesting than the first, precisely because the *délire* is more complete. Céline has dehumanized all instead of most of his book. As he himself admitted, he had exhausted the Jewish question. He had nothing left to say.

Les Beaux Draps is an appendage to *Bagatelles* and *L'École*. It was written to drive home the same lesson in a different political situation and to propose a constructive programme.* Like *Bagatelles*, its main thrust is aesthetic. It is exceptional in the history of the pamphlet because its author was now on the winning side. Pamphleteers do not often win and, when they do, they rarely write about it. One cannot imagine Jules Vallès writing a pamphlet about the innovations he made as the Commune's Minister of Education. Even Céline could not whip up a frenzy after the German victory.

Not surprisingly *Les Beaux Draps* is partly a rehash. Céline talks about the international conspiracy: 'Lenin, Warburg, Trotsky, Rothschild all have the same opinions.' He has not forgotten Léon Blum: 'Do you remember the pisspool of 36! We are still drinking it, the Popular Front! The Yid's potion!' He repeats that the Jew is the ultimate, hidden evil – 'he is mysterious, he has weird habits'. The style, however, has changed. It is more conversational and less virulent. The concise rhetoric of *L'École* is replaced by an anecdotal tone, which is more relaxed than in *Mea Culpa*. Céline uses the Paris *argot* and the familiar syntax of a conversation on the streets. He is trying to persuade, not to menace.

But he begins, in his usual manner, as teller of evil tales that happen

* *Les Beaux Draps* was published in 1941. Céline's situation at the time he was writing it is discussed in the next chapter.

to be true. 'No one wants to know about truth,' he says. His aim, as in his journalism, is to cut through the consoling myths which purport to explain the 1940 disaster. He will sweep aside the Vichy line that corrupt politicians were responsible and that France can easily be revived. He will describe the defeat as it really happened. In *Mea Culpa* his antagonist was the Russian commissar; here it is the Vichy youth leader, but his role has not changed. He makes a remark that is another paradoxical comment on his anti-semitism: 'Men seem to feel a huge, absolutely unbearable terror that they will find themselves one fine day alone, quite alone, faced with nothingness.' Céline will compel them to face this 'nothingness'. He mocks the facile Vichy notion of 'redemption'. Is Céline to be redeemed? 'I don't know where to hide,' he jokes.

His account of the defeat is vintage Céline. As in his *Pays libre* article, he refuses to exonerate the French army, 'champions of the world at bragging'. He describes his own flight from Paris: 'we could not possibly go any faster, we tried all we could to catch up with the French army, road after road, bends and curves . . . we could never catch up with the French army'. Céline blames the entire country for the defeat, reiterating his charges of decadence. He has not changed his mind about the French: 'they don't have a single idea in common, except a gloomy dislike for one another, cheap anarchists, cheating, shabby and insipid'. Ironically enough, this recalls de Gaulle's comment about the 'disrupting ferment' the French carried within themselves, which helped account for the 1940 defeat.[17] In these pages of *Les Beaux Draps* Céline hammers home the lesson that the French had fared as badly as he had said they would.

He also has his programme of reform and it alone, not Vichy's National Revolution nor the Resistance's pseudo-heroism, can overcome the disaster. He advocates changes in education, a new salary policy and his own brand of Labiche Communism.* This is an unfamiliar role for Cassandra-Céline and he has doubts about it. He calls for 'a perpetual struggle, an eternal effort of recovery'. He does not sound very confident. But 1941 is Céline's so-called optimistic period and he pushes ahead with his scheme.

* Labiche is the popular nineteenth-century dramatist who held rather naïve, utopian political views. The term 'Labiche Communism' was applied to Céline by Rebatet.

As a piece of political writing his Labiche Communism is an absurdity. It proposes a 'middle of the road revolution' where a man will receive a salary of 100 francs a day in the context of a nationalized economy and government-run social welfare. This will satisfy everyone and will create no excess. Céline claims that the Frenchman 'cherishes his little comforts' too much to be capable of 'great communism', but he will accept this 'lower-middle-class communism' – as dreamed up by the child of the Passage. These pages, like the pamphlets in general, are explicable only in Céline's own terms. He is still trying to destroy materialism, this is the difference between his and Russian communism. He repeats his dislike of industrialization: 'the factory is an evil, like the shit-house'. Ridiculing the Vichy slogan of work he writes: 'wherever you blind man and make him subservient to matter and make him exhaust himself for the sake of profit, straightaway hell breaks out'. Céline's plan is founded on asceticism: by satisfying man's minimal wants you encourage him to forget about riches. Equality of salaries will be 'the radical treatment for jealousy'. No longer will each class hate the one above and fear the one below. Society will be purged.

The point of view switches from the moral to the aesthetic. Having abolished selfishness Céline thinks that 'all one's little hopes are possible'. 'Only the gratuitous is divine,' he repeats. In what does it consist? Instead of battling towards an illusory prosperity, man will respond to the world freely, that is aesthetically. 'We must learn to dance. France was happy up to the time of the rigadoon.' The emotion, praised in *Bagatelles* but lost in a welter of standardization and abstraction, will be liberated and style will be restored to literature. 'We are croaking because we have no legends, no mysteries, no greatness,' says Céline. 'Without incessant artistic creation by everyone, there can be no lasting society.' He demands a reform of the educational system because 'children lose their taste, enthusiasms, passions'. All men must become dancers whose vanquished bodies and purified minds will be able to create harmony. As he describes the utopia of ballet Céline changes his style and becomes lyrical. Sentences are shortened, medieval turns of phrase recur and words like 'gaiety, music, magic' are everywhere. Political argument takes second place to the vision of 'the little rigadoon of dream', where the universe is deluged in 'song and dance'.

This is a new version of *Bagatelles'* message: once the Jew is destroyed the world will become ballet. Céline reminds us that 'art is only race and country' and anti-semitism is a prerequisite for his utopia. Needless to say the reader cannot help seeing this Aryan dream-world as another flight from the reality of the Nazi occupation into a realm without executioners or victims. But there is a second problem. Céline has forgotten that, according to *Mort à crédit*, the gold of art is shaped out of the mud of man's condition. Once evil is abolished, there can be no more beauty. He himself proves this in *Les Beaux Draps*, which is a boring book because the raw humanity of the novels is absent. Labichian man with his 100 francs a day and his unjealous nature is not a promising character.

Céline suspects this himself and, like *Bagatelles*, *Les Beaux Draps* has an ambiguous ending. It is the winter of 1940 and the cold is terrible; Paris is a prey to sickness and hunger. 'There are problems that go beyond man . . . there are fatalities that are rigorous and awful' – Céline shifts back to his novelist's view of the world. He is going to see a patient, an old woman with no one to look after her. But she has danced off into the night: 'the moment that her music comes back to her she is off!'. She has gone to her death, but at least it is beautiful because she meets it with courage and gaiety. Whereas most people die like 'calamitous rats', dancers vanish in 'ethereal rigadoons'. Here the concept of the aesthetic has changed: the old lady's sufferings in stricken Paris are the price of her dance. This is why the book can end convincingly with a ballet: 'all weight is dissolved! should fly away! joyful souls . . . ! Let everything vanish, charm, fly away!'

The ambiguity remains: how does this Paris fit in with the new utopia? It seems to be a criticism of it, because Céline is admitting that his reforms are a delusion. He is hesitating, unable to believe in the new Nazi order or his lower-middle-class communism, unable to make his anti-semitic *délire* quite real. In *L'École* he could convince himself but here he cannot.

All three pamphlets must be considered failures. Céline has not grasped the political reality of his age, has not explained it honestly, has not made it into interesting writing. He has cut himself off from the reader, who cannot share his vision. In his novels he talks of the break-down of the author–reader relationship, but no one has any trouble participating in *Voyage*. In his pamphlets he falls into the solipsism he has condemned. Perhaps all the pamphleteers are failures. Péguy does not really capture the spirit of the Sorbonne any more than Béraud understands English foreign policy. Like them, Céline is writing for himself.

In all probability he had no influence.[18] Most of *Voyage*'s readers did not bother with *Bagatelles*. Their reasons were not political. They simply did not want to read three hundred pages about Jews. The pamphleteer's audience was smaller. Those who did read him had already made up their minds, one way or the other. In any case Céline's blend of comedy, ballet and hysteria made it difficult for him to have any influence on real-life attitudes. He did not persist after *Les Beaux Draps*. He turned to buying butter on the black market and working on *Guignol's Band*. But the damage was already done. For the rest of his life and after his death he would be as much the author of *Bagatelles* as of *Voyage*. The pamphlets account in large part for his lonely place in modern literature. In post-war France he was shunned. Gaëtan Picon scarcely mentions him in his *Panorama de la nouvelle littérature française*, which reflects the Liberation viewpoint on modern French literature. Picon admits that *Voyage* was a major influence on young writers of the 1930s and then he hurries on to more congenial subjects. After his return to France in 1951 Céline had to face a mixture of hostility and neglect.* In the last years of his life the tide started to turn. But it was not until after his death, not until the mid-1960s when a generation grew up that remembered little of the war, that he began to be treated as an important writer. The two *Cahiers de L'Herne* – 1963 and 1965 – were a major impetus. In recent years Fascism and collaboration have been viewed more dispassionately and Céline, along with other compromised writers like Drieu and Brasillach, is being re-read.

But the pamphlets remain, rightly, a problem. How can one deal with them? Roughly there have been two lines of approach. The first is represented by Sartre. Sartre has simply read out of French literature the writers he considers Fascist. When Lucien Rebatet published *Les Deux Étendards*, Sartre did not want to review it in *Les Temps modernes*. When Dominique de Roux was collecting the material for *L'Herne*, Sartre went on record as opposing the project.[19] The reasons for this view may be found in the *Portrait d'un anti-sémite*. For Sartre,

* This is discussed in Chapter Nine.

anti-semitism is a commitment which engages the whole man vis-à-vis the entire universe. Céline was putting *Voyage* on the line as well as *Bagatelles*. He must suffer the consequences. Sartre has excommunicated the novelist as well as the pamphleteer. Céline's shrill attacks on him – in *À l'agité du bocal*, in *Féerie* and in *D'un château l'autre* – failed to provoke any reply. For Sartre, Céline no longer existed.* What then of the case for the defence? It is not very convincing. Hanrez, Vandromme and others, drawing on the master himself, repeat the same arguments. They claim that the man Céline did no harm to the Jews, which misses the point. They say that the real aim of the pamphlets is to promote pacifism, which is a strange interpretation. Either way they – like the publishing house of Gallimard – are trying to whitewash Céline: to minimize or ignore his anti-semitism, to make him respectable.

The truth is harder. Firstly the pamphlets are overwhelmingly anti-semitic, full of a hatred that pacifism cannot by itself inspire. Even worse, this hatred has its roots in the core of Céline's literary inspiration, in his agonized vision of catastrophe. *Bagatelles* is his moment of fear, it expresses the wild, destructive urge of a frightened man. It is one of this book's main themes to show that the novels are different from the pamphlets. They possess a moral courage and a human pity that are absent from *Bagatelles*. Yet all of Céline's roles overlap because they are ways of approaching the same problem. One may separate them in order to examine them. But one may not select some and discard others. On this point Sartre is right. Yet it may still be possible to distinguish without discarding. One may say that some of Céline's efforts to confront his truth were bad and that others were good. Sartre's idea of total commitment seems rather romantic. One wonders whether he himself still adheres to it. In recent years he has modified his concept of freedom. He now thinks that liberty is a narrow margin that the individual preserves in a complex world, rather than a new existence that is won or lost by a single act. Taking this more nuanced view one may say that Céline made a series of choices, that there is good and bad, responsibility and abdication of responsibility, in his life and in his writing. What one may not do is to forget

* Andrew Sinclair goes part of the way with Sartre. In the introduction to the Panther translation of *Mort à crédit* he states that only the works written before *Bagatelles* may be considered as part of French literature.

the bad, or to ignore the integral connection between the anathemas of *Bagatelle* and the pity of *Voyage*. Who knows whether Céline could have survived the war and written his later novels, if he had not had a cathartic outpouring of anger in *Bagatelles*? He needed to be a pamphleteer.

[6]

Occupation and Exile
1940-51

Céline remained in the Saint-Jean d'Angély camp until October 1940.
In July Laval became Prime Minister; the same month the British navy
attacked and destroyed the French fleet at Mers-el-Kebir; in September
de Gaulle's attempt to take Dakar failed. Despite his prophecies Céline
was shocked by what had happened. The 'defeat of 1940 was a humiliation for him . . . he felt it like a personal affront,' notes Marcel Aymé.[1]
He even thought, so he says, about fleeing to England.[2] Instead he
returned to Paris, bringing back the ambulance he had borrowed. Gen
Paul found him a flat on the rue Girardon, a stone's throw from the
Sacré-Coeur and opposite the Moulin de la Galette. Céline moved in
with Lucette. He decorated the flat in his usual bare style and he was
particularly pleased with the view from his window: he could see
right across the Paris roof-tops. He was posted to the municipal clinic
in yet another suburb – Bezons.

'A whole world has collapsed,' he wrote a few months later.[3] He
explained how he felt: 'Fate towers so high above us, the squall carries
us off like fleas in the water.'[4] He had grasped the mood of the Parisians, as they crept back to the city in the autumn of 1940. They were
bewildered. Nazi soldiers patrolled the streets and thronged the cafés of
the Champs Elysées. Food was rationed and the old newspapers had
vanished from the stands. As there was little petrol, the *métro* was
crowded and a flood of bicycles appeared. There was nothing terrifying
in this transformed Paris. The German soldiers were well behaved.
Slowly the cinemas and theatres re-opened. There was a splurge of
military concerts.

A new élite had appeared: German officers and French collaborators
wined and dined in expensive restaurants. 'Horizontal collaboration'
brought easy money to willing girls. Most people did not find life so
pleasant. The winter was desperately hard. Fuel was in short supply.
Long queues formed outside the foodshops and hatred of the grocer

became a national characteristic. The black market grew to huge proportions: shrewd men made fortunes, everyone had some pet scheme. In the *Quartier latin* the general austerity provoked an outburst of dandyism. Young men called 'zazous' appeared on the streets looking for gaiety. There was little enough to be found. Few Parisians took the trouble to read the new newspapers that had replaced the old. Some listened to the briefings of the *Propaganda-Staffel*, but most did not. They had assumed that the war was over, but Germany's defeat in the Battle of Britain made them wonder. They had been through too much to be hopeful but they had doubts and they were disenchanted. They expressed their grumbling resentment by listening to the B.B.C.[5]

Meanwhile Céline had returned seemingly like a prophet into his kingdom. Had he not warned of the war and the defeat? He had foretold the bankruptcy of the Third Republic and demanded an alliance with Germany. Now his anti-semitism was official policy and the Paris radio echoed his anti-English tirades. He was 'the god of the anti-semites, the messiah of the new order . . . the "prophet", the "gospel".'[6] In the restarted *Nouvelle Revue française* Drieu la Rochelle praised him as one of the few great writers of the age;[7] Lucien Rebatet imitated him in the collaborationist classic *Les Décombres*. To Céline the pro-German press opened wide its pages. It published his letters under huge headlines, it quoted his slightest comments. It was after all Céline 'who had been the first . . . to sound the alarm on the Jewish–Masonic peril,' said *La Gerbe*.[8] When *Les Beaux Draps* appeared in 1941, it was greeted with shouts of approval. 'This explosive work stops a certain number of the valets of the Jews and the Masons from sleeping,' gloated *Au pilori*.[9] The Gaullists, few in number and mostly in exile, agreed with their enemies' judgement. Yet the truth was more complex. 'Certainly, one might have thought, given my books,' admitted Céline, 'that I was going to become the Germans' most fanatical collaborator.'[10] But he did not. He wrote little and did less. When he spoke out he did not always follow the orthodox pro-German line. Sometimes he turned the other way and was quietly helpful to the Resistance. He remained the brooding, pessimistic anarchist of the pre-war years.

To understand Céline's wartime role one must look at the personalities and politics of the Occupation. A world, as he had said, had collapsed. A new breed of men had replaced the discredited leaders of the Third Republic. What was the new order? One must examine the politicians who praised Céline and the newspapers that published his letters.

Frenchmen had put their trust in Pétain, victor of Verdun. By the terms of the armistice France was divided into two parts: the southern half was to be administered by the Vichy government, the north was to remain under the control of the Germans until the imminent defeat of England. Pétain's government was conservative and authoritarian, but it was not fascist. Its philosophy was one part hero-worship of Pétain, one part subservience to big business and one part Action Française monarchism. It harked back to a France of smiling peasants and benign aristocrats. The men of Vichy did not welcome German hegemony but they accepted it – at least for the time being. Laval, the prime minister, like Céline a pacifist and a defeatist, sought, by juggling, to please the Reich while retaining some independence.

While the cult of Pétain ran high in the Vichy hotels and Charles Maurras became the philosopher of the National Revolution, a different breed of men reigned in Paris. Their doctrine was French-style National Socialism. It called for nothing less than the building of a fascist France. Anti-semitism was the main plank in the platform: an end to the class war and the uniting of all Aryan Frenchmen. As for foreign policy, the Fascists demanded collaboration with the Germans and entry into the war on Hitler's side. Thus would France take her place in the new Europe. This doctrine was very vague. The fascist clans never banded together in a solid organization, although the *parti unique* was a recurrent dream. They were united by a deep hatred for the Third Republic and a feeling that the radical right – the Action Française and the Ligues – had not gone far enough. For the rest they squabbled over doctrinal trifles, competed for German patronage and flaunted slogans like socialism and revolution.

The two main leaders were Doriot and Déat, both of whom tried to enlist Céline's support. Jacques Doriot, 'the black-haired Danton', began as a worker, joined the Communist Party and rose to become mayor of the red bastion, Saint-Denis. In 1934 it was he who organized the counter-riots of 9 February to demonstrate against the Ligues. Afterwards he called for something like a Popular Front, but the official communist leadership under Maurice Thorez was not yet ready to move: Thorez was still following the doctrine that the socialists were the number one enemy. Doriot was expelled from the party and over the next few years he drifted rapidly to the right, inspired by Hitler's success. He became an ardent anti-Communist and an expert in denouncing his old comrades. In 1936 he founded the Parti Populaire Français, a fascist-type organization with its newspaper *L'Emancipation nationale* and its hired thugs from Marseilles. In 1939 Doriot had been defeatist, now he hoped to reap his reward. His great rival was Marcel Déat, a former socialist and professor of sociology. In the 1933 Socialist congress Déat clashed with Léon Blum, when he proposed that the party abandon its internationalism in an age of resurgent nationalism. He attacked Blum's 'byzantinism' and called for a dynamic, authoritarian line. Like Doriot, Déat was attracted to strong action, like Doriot he was drawn to Hitler. In 1939 Déat denounced the Anglo-French guarantees to Poland in a famous article entitled 'Die for Dantzig?'. After the defeat he founded the Rassemblement National Populaire, where he assembled the former pacifists and syndicalists who had found their way to collaboration.

Doriot led the right wing, Déat the left; but ideological differences counted for little. Personal rivalry kept the two men apart. To their ranks flocked politicians and journalists, some sinister, others merely eccentric, all anxious to grab the spoils of the new order. There was Fernand de Brinon, the Vichy government's 'ambassador' to Paris and a long-standing supporter of Franco-German cooperation. He was being rewarded for years of organizing youth congresses and cultural contacts. There was Laval's friend, Jean Luchaire, the golden boy of the Occupation, whose daughter Corinne was a film-star. Luchaire's dinner-parties at the Tour d'Argent drew the celebrities of the collaborationist camp but never Céline. A stranger figure was Eugène Deloncle, at first a supporter of Déat who quarrelled with him and sold his soul many times over. His shadowy career ended in 1943 when he was executed by the Gestapo for plotting with anti-Hitler elements in the Wehrmacht.

The politicians had their battalions of intellectuals. If many leading French writers were in opposition – Malraux, Mauriac, Aragon and younger men like Camus and Sartre – many were not. Montherlant and Giono were prepared to be sympathetic to the new order, Béraud continued his anti-English tirades, Drieu was an avowed fascist and the young team of *Je suis partout* cried hysterically for collaboration.

There were great differences among these writers and, in particular, there was a gulf between the most clearly fascist of them and Céline.

Robert Brasillach describes his evolution to fascism in his auto-biographical work *Notre avant-guerre* (1941). As a schoolboy at Louis-le-Grand and a student at the École Normale he absorbed Charles Maurras' heady doctrines. Disliking the tepid politics of the cautious Third Republic he turned to the nationalism, the monarchism and, most important perhaps, the strong dose of anarchism in the Action Française. But, as he grew older, he felt that Maurras was out of date and this his anti-German stance was sterile. Brasillach was attracted to the new Nazi Germany. On his visit to Berlin he was impressed: 'One cannot judge Hitler like an ordinary head of state,' he writes, 'he is called to a mission which he believes to be divine.'[11] Brasillach became a fascist. He supported Mussolini in Ethiopia and the Nationalists in Spain. In fascism he saw a great new dawn: 'the universe was ablaze, the universe sang and mustered itself, the universe toiled'.[12] For him the war was a tragedy and the defeat a blessing in disguise. Now that the despised Republic was overthrown, a rebuilt France could stand alongside Nazi Germany. 'Only a French fascism can collaborate with the new world,' writes the innocent Brasillach.[13]

He greatly admired Céline: 'Instinctive anti-semitism found its prophet in Louis-Ferdinand Céline.'[14] But the two men have little in common. For Brasillach fascism was a glorious struggle. Not so for Céline who picked up the negative side – anti-semitism – but had no faith in the new fascist dawn. Whereas Brasillach supported the Germans out of idealism, Céline did so out of the starkest realism – because France had no other choice.

The same question of romanticism separates Céline from Rebatet, another fiery young idealist. He too despised the Third Republic and came to Fascism via Maurras' monarchism. Rebatet hated the leftward drift of the 1930s, and *Les Décombres* heaps anathema on Blum, the Popular Front and its intellectuals like André Malraux. Rebatet was drawn to the pageantry of Nazi Germany. He describes the solemnity of Hindenburg's funeral, the torchlight procession across the Prussian plain, the tomb at Tannenburg. Rebatet was wildly emotional. He loved the French army: 'I am an admirer of the sabre, I would have welcomed its reign with joy.'[15] He hated Jews. The Stavisky scandal and the flood of Jewish refugees from Eastern Europe made him furious. For him, as for Brasillach, collaboration offered the opportunity to create a new world. 'We are in the act of living one of the greatest chapters of human history,' he writes.[16]

Such romanticism was quite alien to Céline, child of the Passage. Drieu la Rochelle was closer to him in age and he too remembered the battlefields of Flanders. In *Voyage* Drieu saw his own vision of the post-war world – grim and meaningless. Both writers have a deep sense of decadence and see death everywhere around them. But there the resemblance stops. Drieu insists that 'the hands of deep despair in probing death soon feel the secrets of new life palpitating within'.[17] Certainly decadence reigned in the France of the Popular Front; but then 'suddenly there was Fascism. Everything was once more possible, o' my heart.'[18] Drieu had the Célinian sense of despair – which Brasillach and Rebatet did not – but he was able to transcend it.

The difference between Céline and his admirers emerges clearly in a conversation he had with Rebatet in the winter of 1940. Rebatet had just returned from Vichy, where he had spent 'two stupidly debilitating months' witnessing 'bar-room chatter, plots in hotel corridors'.[19] Exasperated by this new version of Third Republic parliamentarianism, he left Vichy to look for a stronger line in Paris. He came at once to visit Céline, newly established on the rue Girardon. Like other visitors he was struck by the furnishings: 'rustic Breton style, the sort of thing an office clerk would have chosen if he had been left some money'. After paying his repects to Lucette, Rebatet was admitted into the little study where Céline sat in his old dressing-gown, surrounded by the heaps of paper that were the first draft of *Les Beaux Draps*. Rebatet was struck by 'Céline's blue, Gallic eyes, gay and malicious, with frankness and despair in the background'. The two discussed politics. Rebatet talked about the opportunity the defeat offered, the mistakes of Vichy, the hopes of Paris. Céline interrupted: 'The only true thing is that the Fritz have lost the war.' Rebatet was astounded – even Churchill would not have claimed that. The German armies had swept across Europe. A Nazi victory seemed certain and with it the new Fascist order Rebatet had come to discuss. But Céline would not budge. Rebatet left him and went off to the offices of *Je suis partout*, where he declared that the author of *Bagatelles* had gone mad. That was not the reason. The pessimism that separated Céline from the left in the 1930s, was now to alienate him from collaborators.

It was only a partial alienation. Céline wrote in the Paris press. He attacked Germany's enemies and called for anti-semitism. But he had no time for the supposed triumphs of collaboration. He stood out against the optimism of the editorials.

The press in which he wrote was a strange one. In 1940 the bewildered Parisian saw a galaxy of newspapers appear with German permission and backed by German money. There was Doriot's *L'Emancipation nationale*, *Au pilori*, which styled itself an organ of 'struggle against Jews and Freemasons', *L'Appel*, edited by the pro-Doriot Constantini, who was declared insane at the Liberation. Some of the papers were new, others had been banned by Daladier under the plenary powers voted him in March 1939. All of them took much the same line. There was *La Gerbe*, in which Céline published his first article. This was edited by Alphonse de Chateaubriand, the admirer of Nordic nature who was ready to fall on his knees before the smallest Black Forest pine. There was the eclectic *Pays libre*, and *Révolution nationale* founded by Deloncle and edited by Lucien Combelle, another of Céline's admirers who wrote a glowing review of *Les Beaux Draps*.[20] *Je suis partout* returned to the stands and the prestigious *Nouvelle Revue française* reappeared, without its former editor Jean Paulhan.

The great theme of the collaborationist press was grandeur: 'We are a brave people ... We are a courageous people ... We are a strong people,' hymns Bernard Faÿ, an intelligent literary critic who ought to have known better.[21] References to the great figures of French history abound: to Charlemagne, to Napoleon, even to Jaurès. A contributor to *La Gerbe* talks of France's 'intimate need for grandeur'.[22] The aim is clear: like Pétain with his National Revolution, like de Gaulle in his own very different way and quite unlike Céline, the collaborators wanted to offer the French a way of recovering their traditional greatness. The 1940 defeat had been a plunge into the depths of tragedy, but now France could rise again. This is precisely what de Gaulle was saying. His famous declaration in June 1940 that 'France has lost a battle but she has not lost the war' is echoed by Pierre Clémenti's article in *Pays libre* entitled 'We can win the war'.[23] The Paris press repeated its simple thesis: France was a great country that had been betrayed by the Third Republic politicians. Pariahs like the Freemason Daladier and the Jew Blum were responsible for defeat, and they must be convicted and condemned. France must be revitalized through a National Socialist revolution. Thus Drieu could claim that in collaboration there was 'glory'.[24] France would once more stand among the major European powers. Naturally this privilege must be bought: France must fight on Germany's side. 'The stark reality is that we must know how to die for the honour of being called French,' writes *L'Appel*.[25]

'Reactionaries no, Revolutionaries yes', runs another headline.[26] There could be no question of looking back like Vichy. Grandeur could be attained only by a transformation of the social structure. The working classes, freed of the disease of communism, were the 'hope of the nation'. Manual labour, whether in the factory or on the land, was praised in grandiloquent terms. *La Gerbe* waxes lyrical over 'the nobility of manual work, the superhuman power of fraternity'.[27] Management must also be purified: cartoons of wicked capitalists and blackmarketeers appear everywhere. Imbued with selfless patriotism, the owners must cooperate with the workers to restore the national economy.

The snake in this Garden of Eden is the Jew. 'The Jews must be exterminated' runs a headline in *Pays libre*.[28] Every issue contains caricatures of Jewish bankers with deformed faces and huge stomachs. Instructions are given to readers on how to recognize Jews in the streets by their racial characteristics. When the Germans began to strengthen the anti-semitic ordinances in the zone the press was exultant. *L'Appel* advocated on its front page that 'the Jews be expelled from Europe or sent to work-camps'[29] and Rebatet called them 'a race for whom the only just punishment is collective punishment'.[30] Xavier Vallat, head of the Commissariat Général aux Questions Juives, was frequently criticized as too lax. The press insisted that 'those hateful, clamorous Jews' were still dominant in France.[31] This was a useful line to take, both because it justified further anti-semitism and because it helped explain the hardships of life under the new Fascist order. It was nothing more than the age-old *raison d'être* of anti-semitism: the Jews could be held responsible for any and every evil.

When the collaborators looked outside of France they discovered that foreign policy was a simple matter. 'We are profoundly European,' claims *Révolution nationale*.[32] The model for Europe's future is Germany and the old allies, England and Russia, are anathema. 'We are witnessing the last convulsions of the last potentates of British, Masonic and Jewish tyranny,' exults *L'Appel*.[33] The attack runs along two lines: England as the centre of Jewish capitalism, England as the betrayer of France. 'How England controlled the world' is the title of an article about the City of London and its 10,000 profiteers. The City's main weapon is the Intelligence Service: a secret society that manipulates governments and that had exerted a sinister influence in France.[34] The theme of betrayal is discussed by Abel Bonnard, a minister in the Vichy government, who puts the blame for the defeat on to England.[35] Dunkirk and Mers-el-Kebir are names that recur. The collaborators also delve deep into French history for anti-English heroes: Napoleon is one, creator of a united continental Europe that stood firm against Albion; Joan of Arc is another, victim of English treachery. This fictitious England fits in well with the international Jewish conspiracy, and it explains the defeat in a way that leaves French honour intact. The whole argument is an updated version of the anti-English line taken by Céline and Béraud in their pamphlets. The collaborators inherited a rich harvest of hatred that had been sown before the war. Now, however, they are triumphant because the German invasion of Britain will be their revenge. Since 'Albion no longer has the shield of our breasts' it will fall.[36]

Dislike of Britain was tepid compared with phobia about the Soviet Union. There was a problem here, because Russia was Germany's ally. The press remained silent until the June 1941 invasion released the pent-up flood of anti-communism. The Reich had, in Brasillach's words, 'taken up arms to defend the whole of European civilization'.[37] Now the lines were clearly drawn. The press saw the German–Russian struggle not as the clash of two nations but as a fundamental racial battle: white, European, civilized Germans against the yellow, Asiatic, barbaric hordes. Rebatet, drawing on his conversation with Céline, paints a frightening picture of Europe invaded by Mongol hordes laying waste to the countryside and interbreeding with white women.[38] The press called more loudly than ever for France to enter the war. It applauded the Legion of French Volunteers, formed to fight on the Eastern front. The Legion was blessed by Pétain and the ubiquitous Deloncle became its president. *L'Emancipation nationale* was particularly fervent in the anti-Russian campaign, because Doriot could play the role he had enjoyed during the Popular Front, namely, denouncing his old comrades. He made a tour of the Eastern battlefields that was lavishly reported in *L'Emancipation nationale*. The report was accompanied by photographs of the 'black-haired Danton' urging on French soldiers.[39] *L'Appel* defines the Legion's role as 'to defend order against Asiatic disorder'.[40] Its soldiers were the descendants of Charlemagne's men who had stood firm against the heathen Moors.

In the rosy collaborationist world of 1941 there was one black spot – Vichy. In October of the previous year the press had lavish praise for the Montoire meeting, which was in reality inconclusive but which launched the slogan of collaboration. But already the virulent *Au pilori* had warned Pétain that it expected him to take a hard line – on England, on Jews, on anything.[41] Pétain did not seem to want to do this. Criticism mounted, after Laval, who was counted as pro-German, was dismissed in December. *Révolution nationale* complained that Pétain's foreign policy was weak: he was sitting on the fence, perhaps even hoping for an English victory. When he backed the Legion of Volunteers Pétain rose briefly in the press's estimation, but soon there were fresh grumbles. Rebatet's satire of politicians plotting in bars made Vichy seem an effete régime, without the dynamism to build a fascist France. In 1942 came two more disputes, one tiny but symptomatic, the other major. The first was the banning of *Les Beaux Draps*. Fourteen copies were seized in Toulouse in March and the book was banned along with *Les Décombres*. The most plausible reasons are that Céline was known to be anti-Pétain and that his book attributes the defeat not to corrupt parliamentarians but to the cowardice of the French army. Céline, delighted by this new persecution, weighed in against Pétain with incredible violence. The Paris press supported him, and *Au pilori* published a cartoon satirizing the Vichy authorities for seizing *Les Beaux Draps* in the name of the National Revolution.[42] The action was another proof that Vichy was unreliable – why should it ban the prophet Céline? More important were the Riom trials which spluttered and collapsed. The plan had been to convict Blum, Daladier and Reynaud of leading France to defeat. The Paris press was wildly enthusiastic and, on the front page of *L'Appel*, a raving Constantini described his dream of seeing Blum executed in public.[43] But the despised politicians showed great flair in defending themselves. No legal grounds could be found for convicting them and the trials were abandoned. This was another proof of Vichy's folly, perhaps even complicity. There are several reasons for the press's onslaughts against Pétain. The Germans were using it as a threat to keep Vichy in line and Laval was using it to try and regain power. But there was a real difference between hard-line collaboration and Pétain's waiting-game.

The press's style was as important as its content. The virulent writing that had been the pamphleteers' prerogative had been vulgarized. Many of the articles read like third-rate Céline. There was no question of logic: the collaborators did not attempt to analyse the economic situation or to report the war accurately. Instead they went target-hunting as Daudet, Céline and Béraud had taught them. They overwhelmed their readers with tirades of rhetoric. Their language was extravagant: sensational headlines jockeyed with sick cartoons. *Au pilori* gives accounts of Jewish crimes that no sane reader could possibly believe. Its front page is invariably a jumble of slogans about Europeanism, revolutions and purges. Each paper tried to outdo the others in invective. Constantini accused Deloncle of being soft on Jews, Doriot tried to prove he was more anti-communist than Déat.*

What was Céline's role in this press? He wrote nothing until February 1941. The collaborators wondered at his silence: eight months had gone by since the defeat.[44] Céline was working on *Les Beaux Draps*, which appeared in March, and he had as little love as ever for journalism. Still, from February 1941 to April 1942 he published about ten short articles, usually in the form of letters to the editor.† His aim was to ram home the lessons he had been teaching in the pamphlets: to wean the French away from heroism and to attack the Jews. For a short time he seemed to toy with the peculiar notion that the Nazi new order might work. Such optimism was both alien and

---

* One thing the press did not learn from Céline was humour. Despite their follies these newspapers show no trace of the comic spirit.

† A not quite accurate list of Céline's articles is given in *Essai de bibliographie complète* in *L'Herne*, 3, pp. 15–39. One might wonder why Céline, who loathed journalists, wrote anything at all for the press. The answer is that he was playing out his role as pamphleteer. His style and themes are the same as in *Bagatelles*. The difference, noted in Chapter Four, between his writings and his life, persists throughout the war. But, although that is stressed again in this chapter, the journalist and the man are considered together. Céline was a public figure, whose words and actions were watched by collaborators and Gaullists alike. In any case, as pointed out in the Introduction and in Chapter Five, all his roles overlap. During the war, the pamphleteer and the private citizen, Dr Destouches, were completely interwoven.

fleeting. The pessimistic views he had expressed to Rebatet were closer to the real Céline. In 1942 the banning of *Les Beaux Draps* produced three hate-filled articles, and then Céline withdrew altogether. He published nothing more until April 1944. He was convinced that collaboration was a worthless enterprise and that he had been right when he had prophesied the Reich's defeat.

His moment of optimism shows itself twice in his articles. In December 1941 he took part in a discussion organized by *Au pilori* to promote the *parti unique*. There are two descriptions of conversations with Céline. On 11 December the newspaper reports him lamenting 'the lack of liaison among the French who have the formidable mission of enlightening public opinion and directing the political parties'.[45] Using Céline's name, *Au pilori* calls for unity. On 25 December it describes a meeting that has taken place in its offices. Among those present were Déat, Deloncle, Constantini, P.-A. Cousteau, the third member of the *Je suis partout* team, and Céline. They agreed on a common programme based on racism: the Jew was to be eliminated from French life, the Catholic Church was to declare itself racist, there was to be a minimum wage of 2,500 francs. This programme was summed up by Céline 'in concise, striking phrases'.[46] Naturally enough nothing came of it. It is clear that Céline's role was slight. *Au pilori* was using his name to attract support, but he gave little time to the project.

Before encouraging Déat, he had turned a helping hand to Doriot. In November 1941 he gave an interview in *L'Emancipation nationale*.[47] The reporter was Maurice-Ivan Sicard, an old admirer of *Voyage* and a member of the Parti Populaire Français since 1936. The delighted Sicard heard Céline utter the words that would be remembered at the Liberation: 'We must work and struggle with Doriot.' The statement must be understood in the context of the discussion. The two were talking about the Russian campaign and Céline had a kind word for the Legion – 'It's very good, the Legion, it's the best thing around.' He was inspired, not by any great confidence in Doriot or the Legion, but by his fear of the Russians. The remark about Doriot stands as possible evidence of collaboration, but it cannot be used to argue that Céline had any lasting faith in the P.P.F.

The moment of optimism did not last. In April 1942 Céline took back his praise for the Legion, dismissing it as 'entirely Jewish'.[48]

In the same month he attacked the inconclusive ending of the Riom trials. He makes two kinds of criticism. He condemns the revelation during the trials of Third Republic behaviour – 'the legal demonstration of our complete, utter and unchallengeable rottenness'. He goes on to castigate Vichy for suspending the hearings: 'To the true patriot – how suspicious this attitude is.'[49] The Riom trials and the banning of *Les Beaux Draps* – as well as the Germain failure to defeat England – wrote *finis* to any optimism. But Céline had never hoped for much. In February 1941 he published his 'act of faith' in *La Gerbe* and called for 'two weeks, no more, to start France moving, two weeks if we know what we want'.[50] The next month he wrote to a friend that '*La Gerbe* seems to me more Jewish than ever'.[51]

Céline picked on the negative side of collaboration: anti-semitism and anti-communism. In December 1941, when the Occupation authorities had begun to deport Jews, he lamented the popular indifference to anti-semitism. He compared it with the German attitude: 'At bottom Chancellor Hitler is the only one who is talking about Jews.' Céline adds the damning sentence: 'It is the side of Hitler that most people like the least ... it is the side I like the most'.[52] Along with other collaborators he affirmed that the Jews were still a mighty force in the land – he too still needed a target. In October 1941 he wrote a satirical piece in *Au pilori* entitled 'Long live the Jews'.[53] He puzzled over the strange and incurable love the French felt for Jews. The country needed to be 'rebuilt entirely on a racist–communal basis'. Not that there was any chance of this happening, he hastens to add.

On the Russian question he was equally predictable. The Nazi–Soviet fighting was the real struggle of the war: 'Comrade Stalin's Asiatics are massacring white Soldiers ... We are not sufficiently aware of the need to protect the white race.'[54] To Céline the Russians were not an actual people but a mysterious menace, the contemporary manifestation of the Asian hordes. Like the Jews they had become dehumanized incarnations of evil. Still, he knew that the fighting on the Eastern front was real enough and he was ready to join in. 'I would have liked to go off on a boat and settle things with the Russians,' he tells Sicard. Once again the prophet of peace was anxious to go to war. Céline explained to Robert Chamfleury, a friend in the opposite camp, that the fear of Russia was the pivot of his political views: 'I am resigned to supporting them [the Germans] because they are removing a worse danger.'[55] This cannot be accepted at its face value, but it does indicate the terror that filled Céline's mind since his 1936 trip to Moscow.

In his negative opinions Céline was an orthodox hard-line collaborator; differences arose when he discussed the theme of grandeur. In April 1941, during his so-called optimistic period, he engaged in a controversy in *Pays libre*. A woman journalist, Maryse Desneiges, attacked him for portraying the French army in *Les Beaux Draps* as a cowardly rabble.[56] She pointed out the heroism of individual men and took the usual line in blaming the defeat on the politicians. Céline would have none of it. This seemed to him a new phase of his pre-war battle: he had to convince the French that they should never go to war. The defeat should have been proof enough, but here was Maryse Desneiges praising the army and claiming, by implication, that it could conquer. More is at stake than Céline's attack on a romantic woman journalist. Orthodox collaborators should have been on Maryse Desneiges' side. They wanted the French to fight for Germany – Pierre Clémenti states this explicitly in the same issue of *Pays libre* as Céline's article.[57] Her interpretation of the defeat suits them well and, although they do not realize it, Céline is their enemy.

Faced with a revival of the sickness he had diagnosed in *Bagatelles*, Céline delivers a broadside: 'Cornelian hamming never fails to fill the theatre in France.'[58] The adjective 'Cornelian' is significant, because the collaborators are appealing to precisely this current of French history. To Céline Cornelianism is 'a tradition from which we deserve to die, all of us, I hope, and once and for all'. Talk of France's military glory, of Napoleon and of the new Europe, amounted to one thing: another cataclysm. 'It is with great strokes of bravery that slaughter-houses are replenished,' Céline warns.

Céline's place in the pro-German ranks was a lonely one: he was always destructive. Another controversy in *L'Appel* about Péguy reveals this. The collaborators had undertaken to rewrite the whole of French literature. Gide was excommunicated, on the grounds that his subtle moralizing had undermined French youth. Left-wingers like Malraux and Aragon were anathema. Proust was very suspect, although Brasillach tried hard to save him. In place of these writers the collaborators exalted Barrès, the true nationalist, and Péguy. But Péguy presented a problem because he had been a Dreyfusard as well as a nationalist, a friend as well as an enemy of Jaurès. With his son's cooperation, a Péguy suitable to the needs of 1941 was worked out. Then Céline intervened. In a thunderous letter to *L'Appel* he demolished the simple view of Péguy, servant of Joan of Arc and the Virgin Mary. He replaced it with a confused Péguy 'at one and the same time Dreyfusard, monarchist and third-rate ham'.[59] In a private letter to Lucien Combelle, Céline performed the same hatchet-job on Brasillach's Proust. Proust was nothing but a Jew whose novel was constructed like the Talmud. It was 'tortuous, arabesque, a disordered mosaic', quite the reverse of what the collaborators should be looking for.[60]

Céline repeats again and again that the whole enterprise of collaboration is doomed. The Vichy government is beyond contempt and Pétain merely the 'man who is at this moment deputizing in Vichy for the Rothschilds'.[61] This is a standard collaborationist line, although rarely expressed with such violence. But Céline turns on the Paris leaders too. In a letter to Lucien Combelle he is quite frank: 'And then what can one say to the French. Except long live Stalin and long live de Gaulle? ... Radio London is making all your efforts perfectly and grotesquely useless.'[62] In his articles Céline repeated this view. One of his favourite techniques was to demand a course of action, while insisting on its futility: anti-semitism is essential but the French love Jews, the German alliance must be strengthened but Vichy is London's tool. Céline was playing his Cassandra role. Once again he had a grasp of his age. He understood that the mass of the French people ignored the Paris press and that they hated the Occupation forces. He understood as few did – except de Gaulle – that the fall of France did not mean the end of the war, and that the Russian invasion was more of a problem than a victory. Most of all Céline knew that he himself was not made for victory parades. His side had to lose.

The real significance of his writings lies in his determination to alienate all parties. In an amazing passage, that equals Constantini's hysteria, he demands the heads of Pétain's ministers: 'Let them all be hanged ... I will watch them swing.'[63] His 'act of faith' consists chiefly of onslaughts on the collaborators. He dismisses them as 'a bunch of screaming supernationalists' who have jumped on the bandwagon.[64] Under Blum they were Popular Fronters, now they are collaborators. This attitude was not at all unique. The collaborators spent their time quarrelling, as they scrabbled for power. But no one goes as far as Céline when he condemns the whole movement as 'chatter' and 'hypocrisy'.

In his *Pays libre* article he defines his own contribution as a 'work of truth' and a 'national de-intoxication'.[65] This is true, although only up to a point. Truth still means for Céline the worst and, in particular, the worst for him personally. While attacking the collaborators he keeps demanding a harder and harder line. 'Let us compromise ourselves,' he cries. 'Freely, of course, spontaneously.'[66] He concentrates on the toughest issues: 'A hundred thousand cries of "Long live Pétain" do not equal a little "Kick out the Jews" in practice.' He is determined to be the target of the other camp. This explains two of his rare sorties into journalism after mid-1942. Rebatet relates how Céline sent an article to *Je suis partout*, after the Allied landings in North Africa and the subsequent German occupation of Vichy France. The article regrets that there is now no demarcation line between the true Frenchmen of the North and the 'Mediterranean bastards', the 'degenerate, arab, negro South'.[67] *Je suis partout* greeted the letter with huge amusement and refused to publish it on the grounds that it was 'deliriously racist'. Rebatet concludes that Céline wanted to be censured by the most Nazi of the collaborationist groups. Perhaps, but there is more. To be sure, the refusal implied that the pro-German faction was rejecting Céline, but if the article had been published it would have aroused animosity among the Gaullists. Either way it suited Céline's purpose. A sacrificial mania is the only explanation of a letter he wrote to *Germinal* in April 1944. At a time when it was obvious the Allies were going to win the war and when the *maquisards* were rising in full strength, he denounced the 'gigantic hypocrisy' of the Resistance.[68] He was trying to remain 'if not the richest man in France at least the most unpopular'.[69] He did not care whom he attacked. Vichy, the collaborators, the Resistance, all were incarnations of evil. The Jews or the P.P.F., it scarcely mattered as long as Céline had a target. And the self-hatred was greater than the hatred: he was surrounding himself with executioners.*

* This sacrificial mania is more convincing as an explanation of the *Germinal* article than of *Bagatelles*. By now Céline was putting himself in dreadful danger. Yet, as stated in Chapter Five, he was sacrificing only one of his selves. He could, and did, demand a few years later to be viewed as the First World War hero or as the kindly Dr Destouches.

One must – at risk of repetition – distinguish between invention and fact. After the war Céline claimed that he had been hated by all factions: 'As for Laval, as for Pétain, I was their *bête noire*, all they could think about was having me locked up.'[70] This is not true, if only because Vichy had bigger worries than *Les Beaux Draps*. Céline liked to maintain that the collaborators resented his attacks and were trying to 'have [him] arrested as a defeatist and a saboteur'.[71] But he remained, until 1945 and after, the idol of the pro-German camp, the great writer whose deviations from the official line were tolerated. He was able to claim, after the refusal of his letter, that he was 'detested' by *Je suis partout*.[72] But Rebatet remained his most loyal supporter right up to the end. The Gaullist faction was less tolerant; here Céline was not exaggerating.

For the collaborators he remained the prophet of *Bagatelles*. They liked to invoke his name, even if they had to select from his writings what suited them. They could not make much use of him, because his defeatist strain was unacceptable. Saint-Paulien, who is Maurice-Ivan Sicard under a new name, says that Céline was difficult to publish.[73] There was a wild delirium in his writings that could not be channelled along orthodox lines. He would keep crying out that death was everywhere, when the press was talking about building a new France. He was 'unusable'.[74] He was neither a journalist of day-to-day issues like Cousteau, nor a hopeful dreamer like Drieu. He was a phenomenon that Sicard admired with trepidation.

Small wonder that Céline played little active part in collaborationist politics. He was a member of no organized groups. He met Doriot,[75] he claims, only three times during the Occupation and he knew Déat very slightly. Otto Abetz, the Reich's ambassador, proposed Céline's name for an important post in the anti-semitic campaign, but nothing came of it.[76] Rebatet remembers seeing Céline once in a meeting of the Institut des Questions Juives. While incompetent speakers droned on about 'Jewish–Marxist tyranny', Céline, seated by himself, interrupted with stage whispers about 'Aryan stupidity'. The audience grew restive – there must be a Jewish spy in the hall. Fighting broke out and the meeting was abandoned. To the disappointed Germans it was another proof of French frivolity.[77]

Such action as Céline did take was on a strictly individual basis. In 1942 he signed a petition to protest against the Allied bombing of

Billancourt.[78] He also wrote to the organizers of an anti-semitic exhibition, complaining that 'in visiting your exhibition I was surprised and a little hurt to see that in the bookshop neither *Bagatelles* nor *L'École* was on display'. Such negligence was another proof of 'the frightening lack of . . . Aryan intelligence and solidarity'.[79] Céline's name might be used for group projects – *Au pilori* wrote to Xavier Vallat telling him that Céline wanted him to attend the *parti unique* discussions – but he took small part in them.[80] He was still an anarchist.

He had some contact with the wartime authorities, both German and French. Karl Epting, head of the Institut Allemand, set up to encourage cultural contacts, became a friend of Céline's. He remembers that Céline asked for paper – which was very scarce – to publish his books and that he made similar demands for friends.[81] As a doctor Céline dealt with Dr Knapp, an official in the Reich's public-health programme, who was in charge of Franco-German cooperation. Céline made demands on behalf of his patients: he asked for extra ration cards, special drugs or exemptions from the Service du Travail Obligatoire. On certain matters he had to go to Fernand de Brinon's office and the secretary, Simone Mittre, recalls that he never asked for anything for himself.[82] It was always a patient who needed to go to the South of France or who had to be given a pension. And whenever he was leaving Simone Mittre's office, Céline would tell her: 'You know, the Germans are going to lose the war.'

These are not the actions of a man anxious to throw his weight behind the Nazi cause. When the Liberation authorities assessed Céline's guilt they found little to criticize in his deeds. He was tainted by association: his trip to Berlin in 1942 to inspect German hospitals was seen as proof of criminal links with the Nazis. In reality it was an isolated event. Epting testifies that Céline's contacts with the Germans were innocent enough. Socially Céline remained within his pre-war circle of friends – Aymé, Gen Paul and the others. Some of them, like Le Vigan and Ralph Soupault, compromised themselves, but this was not a fascist nor even a political group. Céline shunned the fashionable *tout Paris* of the Occupation. He was too much a 1914 patriot to rub shoulders with German officers. His comment on Abetz made the rounds of Paris – 'a clown for catastrophe', Céline called him.[83] He was scarcely kinder about Alphonse de Chateaubriand: 'if anyone says

Abetz is in the shit-house, Chateaubriand makes a rush for the lavatory seat'.[84]*

In the first years of the war Céline lived like most Frenchmen: struggling to survive from day to day. In June 1941 he wrote: 'One finishes up by shrivelling up like an animal and putting up with almost anything.'[85] Paris life was 'sickeningly difficult'. The lack of transport made moving around 'a torture' and the food problem, which Céline blamed on the 'farmers' greed', was chronic.[86] Like everyone else he intrigued on the black market. His best contact was Mahé, who was supplied by his family in Brittany. Céline's letters to Mahé are full of references to food. In April 1942 he is thanking him for 'the three camemberts which are going to do us immense good'. He does not fail to add: 'If there is any butter there, don't forget.'[87] Usually so ascetic, Céline went into ecstasies over butter: 'Our mouths are watering thinking about that admirable butter.' After one food-parcel he is driven to exclaim: 'At last two weeks of alimentary happiness.'[88] Soap was another problem that took up as much place in Céline's mind as butter. Cold was another. The winter of 1941 was no better than 1940. Fuel and clothing were scarce, so Céline exchanged a dedicated copy of one of his books for a fur-lined jacket. With the help of his Brittany food-parcels he struggled on into 1942. In April he wrote: 'Still here is the Spring after that accursed Winter. Unbelievable sun.'[89]

Céline's mood was not totally bleak. His friends found him gay, full of jokes about the Germans, as helpful as ever. His old comrade from England, Georges Geoffroy, remembers Céline coming to visit him, complete with his 'sheepskin coat and motorcycle goggles', as exuberant as in the old Soho days.[90] Gen Paul would come out into the rue Girardon, call up at Céline's window and tramp with him around Montmartre. On Sunday mornings the two would gather with Aymé, Le Vigan and Ralph Soupault and converse, as they had done before the war. Céline was full of verbal paradoxes. 'I am going to prove Hitler is Jewish,' he said one day.[91] Rebatet, who sometimes dropped

---

* This is about as far as one can go on the broad question of collaboration. The problem of Céline's legal guilt, as Liberation justice defined guilt, and punishment is discussed later. Using 'collaboration' in the wider, non-legal sense, one may conclude that by his writings if not by his actions, Céline did collaborate. He was neither typical nor particularly useful. Once again one may doubt whether he had any real influence. But some aspects of his journalism – particularly his anti-semitism – may be described as supporting the Nazi cause.

in on these Sunday mornings, found him 'welcoming and humorous'.[92] Céline still had his string of protégés. There was Mahé's friend Marcel Plazannet, who was to be sent to Germany on the s.t.o. Céline had to have him exempted. There was a little singer from Brittany, whose house was destroyed in an Allied bombing raid. Céline began a collection for her.

Brittany was becoming more and more important to him. In 1941 and 1942 he went to Saint-Malo for the summer. 'I enjoyed every second of my time,' he wrote on his return.[93] Whenever he could he escaped for a few days to Brittany, his refuge: 'The gateway of the open sea before our windows ... it's better than peace.'[94] He visited Rétiers where Mahé's father lived and where he had analysed the parish priest's water twenty-five years before. He was still friendly with Maria Lebannier, who was helping him obtain his precious butter. He knew all the local girls of Saint-Malo, including Teresa, an Indian beauty, who appealed to his love of the exotic.

Among his Breton protégés was Jef Penven, a young musician who had 'a great knowledge of folklore'.[95] Céline was still delving into Brittany's Celtic past. To him, it was a legend which he had already explored in *Secrets dans l'île* and which offered him a blend of magic and savagery. It also led him into contact with the Breton separatists. He became friendly with Olier Mordrel, former architect and diplomat, who had joined forces with the Nazis in the hope of realizing his dream: an independent Breton state with its own language and culture. Mordrel had been condemned to death in 1940 by a French military tribunal and even his fellow Bretons tended to consider him a traitor. As such, he made a good friend for Céline. Another acquaintance was the Breton historian André Dezarrois, who introduced Céline to the poet Taldir de Carhaix. Taldir was attempting to renew the ancient bardic tradition; but Céline found him 'not very optimistic, alas, about the future of the Breton race'.[96]*

Like the separatists Céline was beginning to feel trapped. There was

* The Breton nationalists had in them a good dose of Celtic sacrificial mania. Mordrel's men fought the Resistance. But many nationalists who did not support Mordrel joined in the fight. They felt that, under the guise of executing Breton collaborators, the *maquisards* were out to destroy Breton culture. Throughout 1943 and 1944, when the Nazis had obviously lost, these men waged their own war with the Resistance. Naturally they paid dearly at the Liberation. In 1943 Céline must have felt quite at home among them.

talk that Mordrel and Taldir might hide him in a remote Breton village.[97] But Brittany was becoming a dangerous place.* By the end of 1942, as threats of an Allied landing mounted, areas of the coast around Saint-Malo were banned to non-residents. Next summer Céline set off again, without bothering to obtain the special visa he needed. He was promptly arrested by the Occupation authorities and held prisoner until a local official – a Gaullist – intervened to have him released.[98]

By 1943 the collaborators' position was transformed. Stalingrad was the watershed. Until September 1942 they were triumphant; afterwards a note of alarm crept in. In one sense their cause had been doomed from the start: it was impossible to convince the French that their real enemies were not the Germans who patrolled the streets, but the English who had killed Joan of Arc. The collaborators had no public: they were politicians without constituencies, journalists without readers. Even the Germans were not very interested in them. Collaboration, declared Goering, was Abetz' policy; as far as he himself was concerned, he just wanted to plunder France.

But, as long as the Reich's armies were triumphant, the collaborators could continue their Tour d'Argent dinner-parties and their anti-semitic press. After the Russian defeats, America's entry into the war and the North African landings, German victory seemed increasingly unlikely. 'September 1943. After the collapse of Italy it is becoming clear that Germany can no longer win the war,' Brasillach wrote in his diary.[99] He left *Je suis partout* and withdrew from politics. Disillusionment mounted among the collaborators. Meanwhile the Resistance was growing into an army. From its tiny beginnings in 1940, it blossomed after the communists hurled their disciplined militants into its ranks. By 1943, swollen by the large numbers of men who fled to the maquis rather than accept the s.t.o., it was a power in the land. By contrast Vichy was declining. Laval returned to office in 1942, but after the German occupation of Southern France Vichy lost the last vestiges of its independence. Most French people were turning their minds to the forthcoming Allied invasion. De Gaulle, unknown in 1940, was a name to be conjured with.

Faced with this startling turn-about the diehard collaborators, com-

* In 1942 Céline made a trip to Berlin; perhaps he was already looking for an escape route.

promised beyond hope of withdrawal, could only trumpet defiance. They did not stop intriguing. Their aim was to force their way into the Vichy government. Shadowy as its power might be, it was real enough for them. Laval did not want them, but the Germans were pressing him. In December 1943 he agreed to take Philippe Henriot and the newest star on the horizon, Joseph Darnand, head of the militia formed to fight the Resistance. He refused to accept Déat, but in March he gave way and Déat became the proud Minister of Labour. The compromised writers soldiered on. *Je suis partout* survived the loss of Brasillach, while radio-announcer Jean Hérold-Paquis continued to begin his broadcasts with the declaration: 'England, like Carthage, will be destroyed.'[100]

No one knew better than Céline that the cause was lost. In April 1942 he wrote: 'I have the impression that the war will last rather a long time.'[101] In the summer he saw trouble ahead: 'The Fritz are stretching their divisions out everywhere ... All this is getting really precarious and dangerous.'[102] He watched the Eastern front with particular care and the hopeful reports in *L'Emancipation nationale* did not deceive him: 'in general the fighting in the east is turning out ugly,' he noted in 1943.[103] He talked of going to battle himself: 'I feel that I am going to pack my haversack for the third time.'[104] But he knew that the war was decided: 'I fear the farce is played out.'[105] His prophecies were about to be realized: the Mongol hordes would descend on France.

Céline had everything to fear from the liberation that the B.B.C. was promising: 'That will really be the start of the troubles,' he predicted.[106] He could not forget that he was marked down for execution. He had now given up sending letters to the press – except for the one to *Germinal* – and he was toiling away at *Guignol's Band*. His period as a pamphleteer was over and he was a novelist again, although *Guignol's Band*, seemingly a book about London in 1915, has much to do with the France of 1943. But Céline could not and did not withdraw quietly from politics. He had to reap the whirlwind he had sown. Not surprisingly one old friend found him 'much less gay ... as if he foresaw already the troubles that were to overwhelm him'.[107] *L'École des cadavres*, banned since 1939, was republished in 1943 to the fury of the Gaullists. Céline was doing nothing to placate his enemies. Geoffroy entertained him along with Lucette and Gen Paul to Christmas dinner in 1943. It was not a festive occasion although Céline, unpredictable as ever, seemed 'happy, relaxed, charming'.[108] But he spent the day telling Geoffroy that the Russians would soon be in Paris.

Céline was now increasingly nervous. The Resistance showed a flair for assassination. In June 1944, Philippe Henriot, the new Minister of Information, was gunned down in public. More executions had been promised and men like Hérold-Paquis went round with armed bodyguards. There was talk within the Resistance of executing Céline.[109] In the flat above him on the rue Girardon lived Robert Chamfleury and the actress, Simone. Chamfleury's flat was a centre for agents parachuted in from England and for young men fleeing the S.T.O. Six members of his group, led by the novelist Roger Vailland, were outraged at the 'collaborationist' gatherings in Céline's flat. They hated to see the cartoonist Ralph Soupault arrive to converse in complete freedom with the monstrous author of *Bagatelles*. They decided to machine-gun the entire nest of vipers on the avenue Junot. The spot was chosen, the time set, the assassin would disappear down the narrow sidestreets. But Vailland's band contained too many intellectuals. Simone started the debate: Céline was the author of *Voyage* as well as of *Bagatelles*. Did they have the right to kill him? Yes, replied Vailland, no said others. The moral theorizing began and action gave way to words. Vailland had to be content with maligning Céline in his post-war *Drôle de jeu*. But the Resistance had more efficient gunmen.

Robert Chamfleury points out that Céline's relationship with the *maquisards* was not as simple as Vailland claims. Céline knew perfectly well that his neighbour's flat was a Resistance headquarters and he never betrayed him. Several times young men lost their way and knocked on Céline's door instead of on Chamfleury's. They were redirected without a word. One night Chamfleury brought down a *maquisard* who had been tortured by the Gestapo. Dr Destouches looked at them, bandaged the man's hand and sent him away. Céline was not trying to buy insurance. He was not imitating the scores of Frenchmen who helped the Germans with one hand and the Resistance with the other. It was his Jekyll and Hyde character that made him treat the wounded *maquisard*.

By early 1944 rumours of Allied landings were circulating openly. R.A.F. planes bombed the Paris suburbs. In April, Denoël published

Guignol's Band. It received an excellent review from Albert Paraz,[110] but few readers had time for novels. Céline's remark about the 'gigantic dishonesty' of the Resistance brought him more publicity. On 6 June the Allies landed in Normandy and the Resistance rose up in the enemy's rear. Railroads were cut, reprisals were severe, France was in a state of civil war. In Paris electricity functioned only a few hours a day, the *métro* stopped and food prices soared. The atmosphere was unreal: a four-year period was dissolving into chaos.

A short piece that Céline published in 1944 gives a clue to his state of mind: the preface to Albert Serouille's *Bezons à travers les âges*. With his unfailing kindness Céline had encouraged Serouille to write the book and persuaded Denoël to publish it. In the preface he sees the history of Bezons as a legend: he dwells on the medieval marquis, who gave his name to the town, and the bridge over the Seine which kings of France had crossed. Such beauty is a 'divine relaxation'.[111] Céline does not forget that legends are cruel, too, and that Bezons' past is full of crimes – 'the web of History is atrocious', he concludes. Contemporary events have brought a new phase of suffering and the bridge, destroyed so many times, was bombed in 1940. Céline, child of nearby Courbevoie, identifies with Bezons' pain: 'from all sides death holds us in its grasp – by hunger, bombings, weariness and hatred'. He seeks a refuge, however fragile, in the past, because he is terrified of the future: 'Our tomorrows are impossible ... hunted, tortured, cursed.' What a contrast with the 'tomorrows full of song' that Louis Aragon was promising the Resistance. The Nazis were in retreat and Aragon's hour had come. Céline, the collaborator, was trapped.

Céline had long been thinking about escape. Brittany was too close and the separatists could offer nothing. He kept his eyes fixed on Denmark where he had hidden his pot of gold. In July he fled. Lucette, whom he had married the previous year, went with him and so did Robert le Vigan. Céline set out for Germany, hoping to cross into Scandinavia. The rest of the hard-core collaborators waited until Leclerc's tanks were in the Paris suburbs. Not so Céline. He was 'the migratory bird who anticipates a change of scenery by flying away first'.[112]

He left the Gare de l'Est wearing a thick overcoat and surrounded by twenty trunks. Terrified of starving to death in the ravished German countryside, he carried cases of farm tools to be exchanged for food.[113] Perched on his shoulder was le Vigan's cat Bébert, destined to become the most famous cat in French literature. The strange cavalcade set out across a country where the Resistance was sabotaging the railways and Allied planes dominated the air. Céline's furniture in the rue Girardon was left to the mercy of all comers. Marie Canavaggia retained the manuscript of *Le Pont de Londres*, which was not to see the light of day for twenty years. Céline's literary interests were entrusted to Denoël, who was shot next year near the Invalides.

The trio arrived safely in Baden-Baden which was an oasis of peace. A spa town, it had escaped the waves of Allied bombers. The Brenner Park-Hotel, where Céline stayed, struggled to maintain pre-war standards of luxury and its huge gardens were green and tranquil. Céline could not enjoy them for long. He pressed on further. When he reached Berlin it was being bombed twenty-four hours a day. Karl Epting met him and they had dinner in 'some sombre restaurant that the bombs had not yet destroyed'. Epting remembers seeing Céline leave with Bébert on his arm 'through the ruins of rows of bombed-out houses'.[114]

Berlin was intolerable. Céline had to wait while the Reich's authorities considered his request for a visa to go to Denmark, but he wanted to find a quieter spot. A colleague, Dr Hauboldt, found him a place in a little village called Kränzlin. It was teeming with refugees and Céline was billeted in a run-down castle. Kränzlin was hardly pleasant, but it was better than Berlin. He later told Marc Hanrez that he was interned there, because he refused to issue propaganda statements for the Nazis. There is no evidence for this. Hauboldt was doing him a service in finding him a refuge that was not being bombed.[115]

Céline stayed there until November. Then he heard that the main body of the collaborators had fled to Germany and established themselves at Sigmaringen. For the time being he preferred to throw in his lot with Frenchmen. He travelled to meet his old acquaintances Rebatet, Déat and the others. And in Sigmaringen, a little town on the Danube, the last act in the drama of collaboration was played out.

The pro-German faction had waited until August, not knowing what to do nor where to turn. Only now were they forced to realize that the Wehrmacht was not invincible. One night, word was handed down from Doriot that flight had been arranged. Hérold-Paquis describes the confusion of the exodus.[116] Along with Rebatet, whom he cordially hated, and Cousteau, he crowded into a lorry on the rue des Pyramides. First it crashed into a parapet on the Quai du Louvre, then it broke down at the foot of the Champs-Elysées. Passers-by looked at them in mocking silence. Finally they were able to go. Huge traffic-jams had formed on the outskirts of the city. The Parisians, awaiting only the Liberation, continued to ignore them. They set out along the road to the east.

They stopped at Nancy where the P.P.F. supporters were housed in a convent. Intrigues were rampant: de Brinon was denouncing Laval, Déat was losing ground to Doriot. While they were at Nancy the editor of the local pro-German newspaper was killed in what seemed like an accident. It heightened the tension. They went on by train to Baden-Baden. The station in Metz had been destroyed and they had to shelter in tunnels from Allied bombers. Only when they crossed the Rhine did they feel safe. At Baden-Baden they split up. The P.P.F. group went to Bad-Mergentheim, the main body to Sigmaringen.

Sigmaringen was a beautiful town built around a Hohenzollern castle. Untouched by the *Hitlerjugend* and the Nuremberg rallies, it regretted the fallen dynasty and the princes who had walked its streets. The castle, which stood on a steep bank overlooking the Danube, was full of rococo furniture. Its library contained first editions of Racine and Goethe. In this fairy-tale setting the collaborators dreamed of impossible German victories. They saw de Gaulle scurrying back to London, themselves parading down the Champs-Elysées.[117]

Not all of them were like this. Brasillach was not even there. He had decided to stay behind in Paris. He hid in a tiny flat and went out as little as possible. At the Liberation he was discovered and thrown into prison at Fresnes. Drieu had stayed behind too, and he committed suicide after two unsuccessful attempts. But the politicians came to Sigmaringen. Pétain, Laval and the Vichy ministers were brought to Germany, with or without their consent. Déat had arrived, Luchaire, Darnand, Constantini, Chateaubriand and the others. Pétain considered himself a prisoner and no longer head of state and Laval, realistic as ever, knew the game was up. But the Paris collaborators went on spinning webs of intrigue.

Doriot had refused to go with the others. He was living at Mainau in a house where Laforgue had once lived. He spent his time organizing his followers into a Committee for the Liberation of France. It had it own radio-station run by Hérold-Paquis and its own agents, who were sent across the French border never to be seen again. Doriot also sent an ambassador to Sigmaringen; but he was coldly received, because Fernand de Brinon had set up a governmental commission which flourished in spite of Pétain's refusal to recognize it. Each of the leaders had his obsession: Darnand, parading around in an S.S. uniform, was pursuing the deserters from the Charlemagne division, formed out of the remnants of the Légion; Luchaire, who had set up a radio-station, was trying to have the rival Hérold-Paquis station banned; Chateaubriand, who was trying to publish French books in Germany, had plans for a three-hundred-page biography of Doriot. Knowing no life but politics, these men continued to buy and sell one another. They devised fantastic schemes for splitting the Russian–American alliance, and no German believed more passionately than they in the new secret weapons. As they plotted they were able to turn a deaf ear to the bombs falling on nearby Ulm.

Rebatet describes Céline's arrival: 'His eyes were still full of the journey across a battered Germany, he was wearing a bluish cloth cap, of the kind engine drivers used to wear around 1905, two or three of his fur-lined jackets with their layers of dirt and their holes, a pair of moth-eaten mitts hanging from his neck, while beneath the mitts, on his stomach, in a rucksack, was the cat Bébert.' The rank-and-file collaborators who had never seen Céline were amazed: was this 'the great fascist writer, the prophet of genius'?[118] Darnand's militiamen could not believe it. Needless to say Céline scorned the politicians' intrigues, which he would later satirize in his funniest book, *D'un château l'autre*. He began work as doctor to the French community.

He found lodgings not with the élite in the castle, but in the Löwen Hotel. It was a tiny, bare room which Lucette, courageous as ever, tried to make into something of a home. At first Céline used to treat his patients there, but then Abel Bonnard found him space in a clinic that belonged to a German doctor away in the army.[119] Food was a grave problem at Sigmaringen and Céline, still terrified of starving, bought sausages and pâté on the black market. This enabled him to shun the thin stews that were standard fare in the castle. Rebatet remembers that one mealtime even Bébert turned up his aristocratic nostrils at the gruel on the table. Céline spent more time in the castle library, reading a set of the *Revue des deux mondes* from around 1880. 'Solid' writing was how he described it to Rebatet, who had given up any thought of politics and was working on his long novel *Les Deux Étendards*.[120] The two men spent much time together. Céline's other companion was le Vigan, who, his face 'half-starved and absent',[121] accompanied him around, interrupting Céline's monologues with anecdotes of his own. They spent the winter quarrelling and making up.

Céline's work as a doctor kept him busy. The undernourished, badly-housed French community – 'We lived worse than pigs and ate much worse'[122] – was prone to disease. There was a plague of lice and the militiamen were riddled with V.D. Céline, with Bébert peeping out from a bag on his shoulder, went around to visit his patients. The winter was cold and the snow thick, but he was not deterred. Simone Mittre relates how he used his own money to buy medicine for his poorer patients.[123] There was only one difficulty: he hated to go to the chemist's because he had to meet the German customers. To remedy this he used to go very early, as soon as the shop opened. He was never – as the Liberation press reported – 'Pétain's doctor and political adviser'.[124] He looked after less illustrious people.

His favourite patient was Madame Bonnard, mother of the Vichy Minister of Education. As she was aged and infirm, she needed frequent care. When Céline visited her she recited to him page after page of Renaissance poetry. 'I was under a spell. I discovered a spiritual universe,' said Céline. 'She would finish a verse and then she would start on another.'[125] Madame Bonnard knew by heart the poems of Louise Labé and Christine de Pisan. While Céline was with her he could forget the chaos of reality for the harmonious sighs of love-stricken heroines. Such poetic magic delighted him.

At other times he was less happy. He was acutely conscious that ordinary life was breaking down in Germany and that his enemies were drawing closer. De Brinon might issue directives in the name of his governmental commission; Céline merely laughed when he saw the signature 'Graf von Brinon'.[126] His sense of humour had not deserted him, but his persecution mania was mounting. He would go a mile out of his way to avoid a car with an unfamiliar number-plate. He blamed his misfortunes on others, particularly on the Germans whose defeat was the cause of his exile. He confided to Rebatet how much he hated them and how proud he was of his 1914 exploit. He kept on describing how he had charged on his fiery steed to save his regiment. In his imagination he had become a lifelong, anti-German patriot, notes the amused Rebatet; no follower of Déroulède was more chauvinist than Céline. He did not even keep his opinions secret. At a dinner to celebrate yet another meaningless Franço-German commission, he lashed out against his Nazi hosts. During the meagre repast of fish and red wine he delivered a furious monologue about how the French collaborators would be severely punished at the end of the war, while the Reich's soldiers would be allowed to return home in peace. The solution, he declared, was to gain favour with the Allies by denouncing the Germans. The Nazi soldiers and officials listened uncertainly and then decided to laugh. Céline was no easy guest, as the Russians had discovered.[127] He was growing more and more eccentric. His health suffered and the athletic friend of Mahé and Aymé gave way to a sombre, broken man.

Later he exaggerated his troubles. He claimed that Doriot's thugs were out to murder him and that the Germans detested him.[128] There is no reason to believe this. To the Germans, he was the writer whose *Voyage* had won European acclaim and whose *Bagatelles* had been praised in the Nazi review *Stürmer*. They did more than ignore his outbursts. The Reich's borders were closed to the flood of people wishing to leave, but an exception was made for Céline. He was granted a visa to go to Denmark.

In March 1945 he set out again. By then the atmosphere in Sigmaringen had worsened. Hope had flickered when Von Runstedt launched his Ardennes offensive in December. Already the collaborators saw themselves back in Paris. But Von Runstedt was halted and the Allied advance continued. In March Déat noted in his diary: 'Time presses on and the counter-offensive has not begun.'[129] In February Doriot had been killed. He was making his way to Mengen to meet Déat in an attempt at reconciliation, when an American plane sprayed his car with bullets. He died instantly and he was buried on a cold morning, while squadrons of Allied bombers thundered overhead. A few of the P.P.F. followers went on intriguing even as the coffin was being lowered. But for Hérold-Paquis, who had struggled to believe in Doriot's destiny, it was the final blow. An unknown man appeared and threw French soil on the grave. Rebatet turned away to walk back to Sigmaringen: 'Everything is finished,' he said to Paquis. 'I don't believe in anything any more, not in an idea nor a man nor a war.'[130]

Next month Rebatet, Bonnard and others stood at Sigmaringen station to see Céline off. The night before he had offered a celebratory round of beer, for which he never paid. Now he stood on the platform with Bébert, whom Le Vigan no longer wished to keep, on his shoulder and his immense passport, stamped with its special *Ausweis*, in his hand. He even had a porter, Chamoin, to help him with his innumerable cases. The train came in slowly. One of the last to function in the Reich, it was burning wood instead of coal. Céline got aboard beaming and waving his passport.[131]

He made his way across a country where the armies of five nations were fighting the most devastating war in history. He saw the ruins of Hamburg bombed into rubble and lit only by the fires of incendiaries. The population lived in air-raid shelters while sirens wailed night and day. It was Armageddon. Miraculously the train went on. According to Céline, there were twenty-seven changes and he had to walk a total of eighteen miles.[132] On 27 March he crossed the Danish border and went on to Copenhagen. He and Lucette made their way, through streets still occupied by Germans, to Karen Jensen's flat. There they hid as Hitler's forces collapsed, the Russians entered Berlin and the war ended.

Céline was lucky. Chamoin returned to Sigmaringen on 31 March to announce that the author of *Bagatelles* had escaped.[133] The others might have been forgiven if they were jealous. Some thought Céline's flight was a betrayal. To Hérold-Paquis it was a repudiation of the pamphlets: 'He was throwing these three books into the fire of his cowardice.'[134] This seems all the more unfair, as most of the collaborators, including Paquis, tried to escape. The P.P.F. and Sigmaringen groups hung on until Allied armies were twenty miles away. Then they fled towards the Italian and Swiss frontiers, away from Leclerc and his dreaded Senegalese troups. North Italy was in chaos. The Americans were in full advance, a few German units and some of Darnand's militia were battling on and the Italian resistants were fighting among themselves. Déat managed to cross the border and find refuge in a monastery. Rebatet also crossed the frontier but was arrested wandering hopelessly around the countryside. Paquis, a long-standing supporter of Franco, was hoping to escape to Spain. He was offered a seat on Laval's plane, but at the last moment there were too many people. He and Cousteau managed to reach Switzerland, where they were interned and returned to France. Laval escaped with Abel Bonnard and his entourage; Maurice-Ivan Sicard also turned up in Madrid. Most of the collaborators were arrested and sent to Fresnes to await trial: Darnand, Luchaire, Constantini, Fernand de Brinon and Chateaubriand all had to face Liberation justice.

Céline was more fortunate, but trouble lay ahead. In April 1945 a warrant had been made out in France for his arrest. In December he was discovered, living in Karen Jensen's flat. The Liberation press was exultant. *Franc-Tireur*, staffed by Céline's former admirer George Altman and by Madeleine Jacob, the Pasionaria of the Liberation, had a huge headline proclaiming that the 'French-Nazi writer', the 'miserable Hitlerite' who had 'sullied and betrayed' France was to be brought to justice.[135] *Samedi-Soir* was delighted that the French ambassador, Guy de Girard de Charbonnière, was trying to have Céline extradited.[136] The Danish authorities, anxious not to displease the French, clapped him into prison to make sure he did not escape.

He remained there from December 1945 until February 1947. Later he described his experiences: 'During my seventeen months of solitary confinement [in the section of the jail reserved for prisoners condemned to death] I was taken out each day for twelve minutes in a cage two metres by two metres ... so that I could take the air. I could see nothing from that cage ... and God knows it was cold in the winter, you can imagine. Exposed to the Baltic cold.'[137] Even allowing for Céline's exaggeration, his year in prison was hard. Lucette, who was held in custody for a short time, was allowed to visit him on condition they spoke English, so that the guards could understand. As she knew little English, this was an added burden. Céline's health grew worse and he suffered from pellagra and mycosis. He did not know when, if ever, he would be released or whether he would be extradited. He did know that Girard de Charbonnière – whom he castigated as an 'ex-Vichyite'[138] trying to cover up his past – was working to have him sent back to France.

He had received two other blows. In September 1944 his name was put on the black-list drawn up by the National Committee of Writers.

The list, which included Drieu, Montherlant, Brasillach and many others, was composed of the writers who had compromised themselves under the Occupation. The National Committee, dominated by communists and fellow-travellers, demanded that their works should not appear in magazine or book form. The second blow fell in December 1945, when Sartre published his *Portrait d'un anti-sémite* which contains the sentence: 'If Céline could support the Nazis' socialist theses the reason is that he was paid.'[139] This groundless accusation could have helped to establish Céline in people's minds as the blackest of traitors. It is thrown as an aside into a brilliant study, but it is surprising that Sartre should have made such a remark without checking his facts.

But then France was in no mood to extend tolerance to collaborators. The purge was in full swing throughout 1945 and 1946. There had been some four and a half thousand summary executions in the months after the Liberation; horizontal collaboration was punished by the shaving of heads and the prison camp of Drancy, which the Nazis had used for Jews, was opened to Vichyites and fascists. The country was eagerly awaiting the trials of the pro-German faction, not just out of a desire for revenge but because they were a 'part of the great task of renewal'.[140] The Liberation was a period of exalted optimism. 'From Resistance to Revolution' was the communist cry. 'The people are under arms tonight because they hope for justice tomorrow,' Camus had written on 24 August 1944 as the barricades went up around him.[141] Having defeated the Nazis, the Resistance hoped to create a new and pure republic. The first stage was the trials, where the country would solemnly renounce the past. They were to be a public cleansing, where the guilt incurred during the Occupation would be washed away.

Not surprisingly the sentences were harsh. Pétain, who had returned voluntarily from Sigmaringen, received the death penalty, although it was rescinded by de Gaulle. Laval, whom the Spaniards had persuaded to return, was executed, as were Luchaire, the dreadful Darnand and many others. The writers fared little better. Brasillach had been one of the first to be sentenced. In spite of Mauriac's attempts to save him, he went before the firing-squad with André Chénier's name on his lips. Hérold-Paquis had time to finish his memoirs at Fresnes before he too was executed. Béraud was condemned to death and reprieved. The old warrior Charles Maurras was sent to prison, proclaiming that here at last was Dreyfus' revenge. Rebatet and Cousteau spent years in jail.

Céline's months in solitary confinement, however unpleasant, were a light price to pay for avoiding Liberation justice. In February 1947 he was released from prison and interned at the Rhyshospitalet. In June he was freed and allowed to go and live in an attic on the Kronprinsessegade. From his window he could look out over Rosenborg park and the palace where the crown jewels were kept. But Céline was not interested in crown jewels. He was now an old man, 'crippled with rheumatism from head to toe',[142] broken in spirit and kept alive by his hatred. He was under the surveillance of the Danish authorities and he could not return to France. He was terrified of being sent back to prison or extradited and his trial was pending in Paris. He had hired a Danish lawyer, Mikkelsen, and two French lawyers, Naud and the star of the far-right, Tixier-Vignancourt. Céline had other troubles. Denoël's death had left the publishing house in a state of confusion. As it had published books like *Les Beaux Draps* and *Les Décombres*, it was under investigation. In any case Céline's books were banned. 'I no longer have any way of earning a living – neither medicine nor writing,' he says.[143] He could not practise as a doctor in Denmark and it was useless for Lucette to try and start a dance school.

Money was a great preoccupation. Céline complained frequently: 'I am poor, I have nothing any more, everything has been taken from me.'[144] Life in Copenhagen was 'too expensive for our non-existent resources',[145] fish was 'exorbitant'[146] and he lived by borrowing from Mikkelsen. How true these statements are is open to question. Céline had money when he left France in 1944 and he had the money from *Voyage* stored in Denmark. His finances are a difficult subject to penetrate, but at least one close friend attests that he was never really poor.[147] What is certain is that he wanted to think of himself as reduced to destitution by his enemies: 'I have been hunted, exiled, sullied, imprisoned, robbed,' he writes in a typical outburst.[148] 'Naturally I am ruined,' he writes to another friend, in a tone of near-complacency.[149] If he borrowed from Mikkelsen – or, more likely, had some arrangement with him – he refused any financial help from his French friends. Even food parcels had to be sent anonymously or he grew angry. He insisted on his independence. When a group of doctors collected twenty thousand francs on his behalf he refused to accept it; the money was returned and the doctors used it to have a party, which amused him.[150] Horrified by Sartre's accusation, he was determined to show that no one could even pretend to be bribing him. As so often with Céline, the cult of independence ran alongside the need to be victimized.

For a year after his release he lived in Copenhagen. A visitor found him in 'a rather shabby attic ... with socks on the table and shirts draped over the furniture'.[151] Céline complained that the roof leaked so badly that mushrooms were growing on his writing-table. Exile he could tolerate, he declared, but not mushrooms.[152] Food was another problem. Because of rationing and his lack of money, Céline lived off potato and leek soup, eating almost no meat and drinking milk. He intrigued to have coffee sent to him from France and even from the U.S.A. His admirer Milton Hindus was a useful supplier, who also sent nylons to be exchanged for food on the black market. There was no question of starving to death, but Céline went on complaining. He resented the way the Danes were behaving: 'My wife and I are treated like pariahs – no contact with anyone.'[153] He dreamed of escaping – to Spain, Canada, anywhere. The trouble was that wherever he went, he would be a fugitive from French justice and in any case the Danes would not let him leave. He talked about going to Greenland as a doctor – that came to nothing. There was a possibility of going to Alaska where there was a shortage of doctors. In Paris the rumour circulated that Céline was about to leave for the U.S.A. He soon set the matter straight: 'No more America than butter in Les Halles.'[154]

He had no choice but to stay in Denmark. René Héron de Villefosse visited him there, making a thirty-hour train journey through the bombed-out towns of Germany. He found Céline at the station, accompanied by Lucette and with the inevitable Bébert on his shoulder. Their attic was bare indeed but scarcely more so, according to Héron de Villefosse, than the rue Girardon flat. One day Mikkelsen took them on a drive to Elsinore. Céline ignored the history museums at which they stopped on the way, but at Elsinore he got out of the car and went on to the terrace overlooking the sea. The mists, the outline of the Swedish coast, the lonely cries of the gulls created a desolate atmosphere. Céline looked at the ocean: 'It's a sea to fish for souls,' he said.[155]

The remark shows a brooding Céline who puzzled over his suffering and was not content with cries of hatred. François Löchen, the pastor of the French reformed church at Copenhagen, saw this hidden side of his character. Céline visited the church in the autumn of 1947 to hear a 'sermon in French'.[156] Löchen, who had been minister at Bezons, became friendly with him and introduced him to Denise Thomassen who ran a French bookshop. Céline and Lucette had Christmas dinner with Löchen and his family and Céline explained, in the course of conversation, 'how there was no suffering to which he was indifferent'. He rejected utterly the Christian notion that suffering could be redemptive; but he was aware of pain as a mysterious entity which shaped the human condition and could not be solved by terrestrial remedies. Löchen felt that Céline was a man 'of deep sensibility, curious, in a discreet, anxious way, about the Beyond'. Unlike Christians, Céline felt that the force controlling the world was 'painful and incomprehensible'.[157] But his sense of life as an agonizing riddle and his sympathy for human misery were the marks of a man who was still, in his own way, searching.

In May 1948 Céline moved to Körsor. Mikkelsen had a summer house which he was lending to him and the countryside would be cheaper than Copenhagen. Céline did not look forward to the change: 'I have a horror of the countryside and the Baltic sea.'[158] He found the grey ocean overwhelmingly depressing and he comments bitterly on 'the thirsty, sandy Prussian plain'.[159] The house had neither water nor electricity and the nearest village was miles away. Céline did find some consolations. One was the druidic circles he discovered in the forest that reminded him of Brittany. Another was the tribe of domestic animals that shared his tiny house. There were cats and dogs, hedgehogs, who came to drink the milk Lucette put out for them, and birds that picked at the crumbs she left on the bird-tables. Céline had a particular liking for refugee animals. One of his dogs was Bessie who had been left behind by a German soldier during the retreat from Denmark. She was difficult to approach and often fled into the forest for days on end. The queen of the tribe was still Bébert, now nineteen years old and as wise as ever. Céline enjoyed the company of animals and he may well have thought them less malicious than humans. But he had no illusions about natural life. One of the things that distressed him in the countryside was the sight of animals devouring one another. He gives a grisly account of how his dog killed and ate a hedgehog.[160]

An old friend who visited him at Körsor in 1948 and 1949 found him a sick man. The chilly house was heated by a peat fire and Céline wandered around in five pullovers. When he went out he put on a long cape, like a mountain shepherd's, and supported himself on a stick. Beside him Lucette was a model of strength: 'At the side of the wounded, sick Ferdinand she retains and increases a supply of physical health and vigour that enables them to survive.'[161] She spent hours each day doing exercises and even in December she went swimming in the sea. Their house was meagerly furnished and on the wall hung a picture of the Moulin de la Galette, a permanent reminder of exile. Céline had not lost his humour: he reminisced about Denoël, the Zola lecture and the evening in Maeterlinck's house. He resented his present position, but at moments he seemed grimly content: 'You get the calvary you can and the stations you find.'[162]

From the time he left prison Céline had been pouring out letters to friends. He wrote to influential supporters like Raoul Nordling, Swedish Consul in Paris, and the Danish critic Ernst Bendz. In particular he wrote to Milton Hindus and to his most devoted supporter Albert Paraz.* Paraz, who had met Céline in 1934 in a café on the rue Lepic, was a novelist and pamphleteer. He had been gassed in 1940 and spent years in and out of hospitals, before going to live at Vence near the Mediterranean. His ill-health did not affect his

---

* These letters are another monument to Céline's will to survive. They may be read as a systematic campaign to win over supporters. Letter-writing was the only form of action left open to him. He made good use of it. His correspondence reveals too his old flair for game-playing. Letters written to different people on the same day show complete switches of style and mood. The letters to Paraz are obviously political. They portray the great patriot and artist Céline, exiled in the snowy northern wastes. With Hindus, Céline is trying to woo a potentially useful supporter. He is patient with Hindus' questions about his writing. He gives the appearance of baring his soul, he even cajoles. With Perrot he allows himself to dwell on happier days in Montmartre; with Eveline Pollet he is occasionally flirtatious. Raoul Nordling was the Swedish Consul in Paris in 1944. It was he who helped arrange the cease-fire between the German garrison and the Gaullists, thus avoiding a battle which would have destroyed much of central Paris. He was now willing to try and arrange a cease-fire between Céline and his enemies. Ernst Bendz was well known in Scandinavia as a critic of French literature. Benjamin Perrot was an old neighbour from the rue Girardon in Montmartre. Milton Hindus was an American academic who tried, rather pompously, to be nice to the pariah Céline. He met with the same fate as the Russians. For his account of the relationship and particularly of his visit to Denmark, see Milton Hindus: *The Crippled Giant*, New York, 1950. For the viewpoint of Céline and his supporters, see Paraz's letter to Marcot, 21.12.1951, *L'Herne*, 5, p. 296.

fighting spirit. Influenced by Céline to the point of imitating his slangy vocabulary and virulent rhetoric, Paraz was an excellent polemist. In 1947 he became convinced that a great writer was being persecuted. He began to correspond with Céline and to look for ways of helping him.

In his letters Céline talks about books, politics, his friends, the past and especially the present. His correspondence is a good guide to his state of mind but there is sometimes a distortion. In particular the letters to Paraz seem to be written with one eye on publication. Céline is harsher than in the letters to Hindus. There is more of the pamphleteer and less of the man, more bitterness and less humour.

In general Céline's state of mind was one of hatred and despair, tinged with mockery. Far from accepting his plight, he railed against it. He never tried to analyse what had happened. He launched into torrents of abuse against his enemies who, he alleged, were guilty of jealousy and malice. When Jean Paulhan hesitated to publish a piece of the unfinished *Casse-pipe* in his *Cahiers de la Pléiade*, Céline concluded that Paulhan was 'secretly jealous ... and only too pleased that I have been shoved into this mess'.[163] Sartre came into the same category: a 'failure' attacking a better artist in order to conceal his own nullity.[164] Céline turned more than ever on those around him. Denoël, no longer there to defend himself, was blamed for re-publishing *L'École des cadavres* in 1943. Mikkelsen was attacked for not defending him better, so was Naud. Even Paraz came under fire: he was not taking Céline's side as forcefully as he might. Hindus received the full blast of Céline's wrath. His book, which Céline had encouraged him to write, appeared in 1949. On discovering that it was not a panegyric, Céline attacked Hindus and encouraged his friends to join in the abuse. Such fury had become a means of survival: 'An immense hatred keeps me alive,' Céline writes. 'I would live for a thousand years if I were certain of seeing the whole world croak.'[165]

He himself was completely innocent: 'All of France has committed treason except me.' The Germans were guilty because they lost the war, the Danes because they persecuted the exile, the French because they rejected the 'number one patriot'.[166] Sartre, Hitler and de Gaulle have replaced the Jews, the Masons and Pétain. The other side of the coin remains the same: Céline was a blameless victim. Like Maurras he saw his situation as 'a Dreyfus case in reverse'.[167]

He talked at length about exile: 'a matter of hatred and poverty and cemeteries'.[168] When Paraz sent him a picture of Courbevoie he was delighted: 'Dear Courbevoie! When they can, old animals come back to die in the place they were born. All I ask is to do the same.'[169] Despite the insults he heaped on the French, he remained deeply attached to France. At no time did he seriously consider settling elsewhere. He raged against his enemies who had cut him off from the French language – 'the real, historical treason'.[170] He listened to the French radio, which gave rise to an amusing incident. A broadcaster, André Gillois, asked for suggestions for improving his programme. Céline wrote offering some. Needless to say Gillois was not interested in the suggestions of a notorious collaborator.[171] But Céline was serious: he wanted better contact with the language. He continued to regard the Danes with deep disgust. They were 'suspicious, sly, cunning'.[172] He never forgave them for his year in prison and he was convinced that beneath their polite exterior – they looked like toy people in shop windows, he grumbled – they were eternally treacherous. Yet Céline was sure he would not be allowed to return to France. Before his mind was the memory of the *communards*, who had to wait ten years for an amnesty. He would not be able to last that long: 'I think I shall croak outside of France, I shall never see my village again.'[173]

When Céline talked about his friends he was disgruntled. He wrote to tell Paraz that he had enjoyed Marcel Aymé's *Uranus*, adding that 'this careful, artistic writing is not at all my kind of thing'.[174] But Aymé himself was 'absolutely ruined by prosperity'.[175] He had become completely bourgeois. The same had happened to Gen Paul who was getting married – 'the kid Paul is under a spell', said Céline with dry amusement.[176] He complained that his friends never wrote to him for fear of compromising themselves. 'He is a Caliban,' he said of Paul, 'really low and treacherous.'[177] The rare mentions of Mahé and Dr Camus were more favourable, or at least neutral. The only old friend Céline talked about with real affection was le Vigan, whom he had left behind at Sigmaringen. Le Vigan had been brought back to France, tried and clapped into prison. 'Poor La Vigue! He's having a taste of it,' said Céline sympathetically, 'he is dying of madness in his cell at Rouen.'[178] On his release le Vigan went to Argentina which, Céline reported, was being invaded daily by boatloads of hostile

Jews. Still Le Vigan managed to make a career by playing death-bed scenes in the cinema. Céline considered this an eminently suitable occupation. 'He has a great future,' he said.[179]

'There are two kinds of Humanity – the one that has been in prison and the other – we do not speak the same language'.[180] This remark sums up Céline's view. Plagued with suffering, he had no patience with men who were comfortable. 'Gide is gone, he has been lucky, a happy life and a happy death,' is a typical comment.[181] Céline could not forget the betrayal of his former friends, who had made a more fortunate political choice. 'You too, Altman,' he wrote wearily after the *Franc-Tireur* articles.[182] He was even harsher on friends in his own camp who had escaped lightly – Karl Epting received a sound rebuke, presumably because Céline felt he should have been kept in prison for longer.[183] Céline had no sympathy for 'Saint-Brasillach'.[184] The regret lavished on the executed author of *Notre avant-guerre* could have been better employed helping living writers – like Céline.

The kindness he had shown his friends had not, however, disappeared. He still had his protégés. A young friend of Mikkelsen wanted to go to France and work in a shipyard; Céline wrote to Löchen to find out what the prospects were. When Paraz asked for advice about his health, Céline replied patiently. His methods as a doctor had not changed. He warned against drastic measures like surgery or new drugs. He advocated abstention: 'Do not move from Vence, no smoking, no sex, drink water.'[185] His repeated comments on sexual restraint must have amused Paraz who was a notorious womanizer.

Céline talked frequently about politics. Although he professed to take no more interest in the affairs of the accursed French – 'What does it matter whether de Gaulle or Thorez becomes Führer?'[186] – he kept a close eye on things. His viewpoint had not changed: France was a rotten country that would soon be annihilated in another war. He repeated his contempt for the Resistance: 'where were they resisting when it was the time to resist?'. Not until August 1944 did the *maquisards* dare show themselves: 'Once the danger was over courage returned! They could hunt down collaborators in safety.'[187] The France of 1947, dominated by the Resistance, was near collapse: 'in this crumbling Republic only the jails and prisons are holding up'.[188] Céline's particular targets were Daniel Mayer, the Jewish Minister of Justice, and Georges Bidault, a Catholic who kept behaving in a most unchristian way. He did not think that the communists would take over the country – 'there will be no Revolution in France. The French are too cunning,'[189] he commented during the 1947 strikes. The danger would come from without.

National problems, even his own, would shortly be resolved: 'the only possible amnesty will be the one on "the Bordeaux road" when the Russian tanks come rolling across the Beauce'.[190] Like many observers, Céline was convinced a third world war was inevitable. He advocated – as in 1937 – that France remain neutral, thus putting himself in the same camp as left-wing intellectuals, including the Le Monde team and the hated Sartre. But he had no hope that his advice would be heeded. He prophesied that when war came the Americans would not fight hard – 'too few men in the U.S.A.'[191] – but would abandon Europe. France would be left to the Russians' tender mercy: 'We will be invaded, moujikized, Lithuanianized in five secs. Amen.'[192] The Eastern hordes remain Céline's principal nightmare. Sometimes they are Chinese, more usually Russian. Either way the French race will be destroyed. The 'deportation of twenty million stupid Frenchmen across the Urals' is only a matter of time.

Céline had not lost his flair for turning on his own side. When the shattered anti-Liberation groups began to reform he denounced them: 'All the so-called anti-maquis papers come from police dens.'[193] Even Rivarol, which was to carry the collaborators' banner into the Fourth and Fifth Republics, earned a rebuke from Céline: 'It stinks of La Gerbe,' he said.[194]

The delicate matter of anti-semitism cropped up frequently: 'On the subject of Jews, I grew to like them a long time ago . . . The Jews have paid like me.' This was the closest Céline ever came to expressing sympathy for the six million Jewish dead. He claimed he was indifferent to no form of human suffering; but this genocide did not weigh heavily on him. He accepted no personal responsibility. Instead he identified with the Jews as fellow-victims of the war. In a bizarre gesture he offered to go to Tel-Aviv and live among them![195] (One might remember that Céline wanted to share the Jewish role of scapegoat.) There is also a current of anti-semitism in the letters to Paraz, because Céline considered himself persecuted by the Jewish-dominated Resistance. 'Just tell me if the communists and the racist Jews are dangerous in Nice,' he writes.[196] This is a minor theme because Céline no longer needed the Jews. Sartre, the Danes and Hitler were more convenient targets. But anti-semitism remained a potential channel for his hatred.

In the letters to Hindus he was more relaxed. He reminisces about his days in Los Angeles and jokes about the pretensions of American universities. He talks more about books. In general he was reluctant to discuss his reading. Rebatet thinks Céline was afraid to praise other writers in case he was accused of imitating them. With Hindus he is more open, although rarely quite serious. He shows that, while he read in a desultory manner and was plagued with prejudices, he did have wide literary tastes.

He had sweeping dislikes. He dismisses the great masters of the twentieth century: Joyce 'goes too slowly', Hemingway he has never read, Dostoyevsky has 'a habit of adoring prisons which I find disgusting'.[197]* Céline denounces the French admiration for American authors in translation: it is a betrayal of the French language. He castigates Faulkner, Steinbeck and Dos Passos – 'we do a thousand times better in form and content'.[198] One wonders who is implied by this 'we' because Céline has only contempt for Malraux and Mauriac. His pet hatred is of course Sartre. Maliciously he reminds Hindus that Sartre, the great writer of the Liberation, played little part in the Resistance and that 'under the "German jackboot" he had his first Paris successes'.[199] Sartre has no talent, according to Céline; this is why he indulges in philosophical abstractions that are out of place in art. The only modern French writers Céline admires are Morand, Barbusse and Ramuz, especially Morand, 'the first man who has written in jazz, so to speak'. Céline considers Morand a 'stylistic innovator'.[200] The contemporary reader may feel that the style of *Ouvert la nuit* is tame alongside *Mort à crédit*, but Céline used Morand as the example of a novelist who had broken free of traditional sentence structure. In the same way he admired Barbusse, who had tried, before *Voyage*, to portray the war from the viewpoint of an ordinary soldier, and Ramuz,

* It is impossible in this correspondence to know where the game-playing begins and ends. Although Céline is trying to please Hindus, one also has the sense that he enjoys writing these letters. For a few moments he can lose himself in discussions about books. One remembers that the United States had a real fascination for him. His comments about literature are a similar blend of pretence and truth. One has the sense that the remarks about Joyce and Dostoyevsky ring less convincingly than the appreciation of Vallès.

who had a primitive touch that was a welcome relief from the over-refinement of Proust and Gide.

In these abrupt judgements Céline reveals the way he read. He picked out the writers he liked and rejected the rest. He judged by instinct and his taste was entirely personal. When the decision was negative he had nothing of interest to say; but he could make incisive comments about writers he admired. He explains to Hindus that he liked American authors who gave a sense of the rough, wild country he considered the U.S.A. to be. Dreiser was one novelist he admired, and he was enthusiastic about Caldwell's *Tobacco Road*. He remembered the Broadway plays he had seen, like George Kaufman's *Dinner at Eight* which had a 'cynical gaiety' that Céline found very American.[201] At the other end of the spectrum he had his favourites among the French classics. As his comments on Madame Bonnard had shown, he loved poetry: La Fontaine as well as Louise Labé and Christine de Pisan. And he had a kindly word for Molière's dance-comedies.[202] Céline tried to introduce dance into his works so he may have seen Molière as a precursor.

A writer he knew well was Jules Vallès. He recommended to Hindus *Le Bachelier* and to Ernst Bendz *La Rue à Londres*, which Vallès wrote while he was in exile after the Commune. Céline had a special sympathy for the pamphleteers because they too were caught up in suffering and violence. When he learned that Léon Bloy had lived in Denmark, he tried to find out more about him, and he was pleased to discover that Bloy had almost starved to death.[203] Céline had a kind word for Bernanos, who had expressed support for him: 'Let all these intellectuals repeat their cowardly words,' he tells Paraz, 'Bernanos was the only one who belonged to my family.'[204] Céline was right. There is an affinity of temperament between him and the other pamphleteers: a revulsion against moderate policies and abstract principles and a need for extremes of emotion.

As well as writing letters Céline went on with his work. He never stopped working, not even while in prison. In 1945 he began to revise *Le Pont de Londres* and he finished a second draft while he was in solitary confinement. But he lost interest in the escapades of Boro and Cascade and turned to *Féerie pour une autre fois*. He began the second part, *Normance*, first. In June 1947 he reported that he had a 'chapter that was quite successful and rather strange – it's about the bombing of Montmartre by the R.A.F. in 1945'.[205] *Féerie* was not completed until after his departure from Denmark. Céline had also written a *Réponse aux accusations* (November 1946), which was to form the basis of his defence, and the vitriolic answer to Sartre, *À l'agité du bocal*, which was published at the end of Paraz's *Gala des vaches*. He reiterated how much he hated to write – 'a nasty disgusting torment', he calls it. He disliked being told to hurry: 'I am much more of a poet than a prose-writer ... People imagine I can pour stuff out like a journalist.'[206] He was outraged when Dr Camus told him that if he would only publish another great novel quickly the French would forgive him his political crimes. He worked on meticulously, puzzling over each word, never hurrying but never stopping writing.

Meanwhile the atmosphere in France was changing. The purge had turned out badly. Seasoned Paris observers like Galtier-Boissière considered the sentences both vindictive and arbitrary.[207] Laval's execution caused general disgust. After a mockery of a trial he was condemned to death. He tried to commit suicide, was revived and dragged off to face the firing-squad. Jean Paulhan felt that writers were being too harshly treated. The businessmen who had built the Channel wall were now building prisons, said Paulhan, to lock up the journalists who had praised the Channel wall.[208] Galtier-Boissière noted that communists like Aragon, who had supported the Nazis until 1941, were lionized, while the rigorously anti-German Béraud was sent to jail. The amnesty extended to Thorez was particularly shocking. François Mauriac, whose Resistance record was impeccable, attacked the purge in the name of Christian charity. Camus opposed him, but he grew disillusioned. Liberation justice never overcame the twin handicaps that it was retroactive and based on instinct rather than on an established body of law. By 1946 it was already evident that the purge had failed in its task of cleansing France. It had merely revealed the degree to which most Frenchmen were tainted, whilst adding the new disgrace of brutal revenge.

The honeymoon of the Liberation was over. In 1946 Jean Paulhan denounced the black-list and he, Mauriac and Schlumberger resigned from the National Committee of Writers. Camus had left already, distrustful of the communist leadership. On all sides the coalition of Resistance forces was breaking up. In January 1946 de Gaulle went back to Colombey. The next year the communists left – or were forced out of – the government. Resistance idealism dissolved into parliamentary bickering. Bidault and Mayer talked like socialists and acted like conservatives. Economic concerns predominated: industrial production lagged behind pre-war levels, prices rose and the working class, so courageous during the Occupation, expressed its resentment in the huge 1947 strikes. Collaboration was less important than the price of bread and the black-list became just a piece of paper. Abroad, the Russian threat grew more menacing. France turned from the 'tomorrows full of song' to dreary, frightened todays.

It was a good moment for *Le Gala des vaches*, which appeared in 1948. Paraz's book, half journal, half pamphlet, sprinkled with the letters Céline had written to him, is a denunciation of post-Liberation France. According to Paraz the contemporary period was 'the most hideous of our history'.[209] The Nazi crimes were being used to justify any and every lawlessness. Paraz attacks 'the terror which reigned in Paris after the Liberation'. He digs up the example of the Resistance leader in the Dordogne, charged with torturing supposed collaborators. He attacks the trials, and wonders if de Gaulle feels any guilt at Brasillach's death. He dislikes the shaving of heads to punish horizontal collaboration. When he turns to the literature of the Liberation, he is contemptuous of 'these receptions where today's triumphant writers drink and hold forth: Fifis, Resistants and men who signed the black-list'. Sartre is no more than an 'imbecile' and Existentialism a mass of unintelligible verbiage. Opposed to such pigmies stands the persecuted giant, Céline.

Paraz has inherited a good deal from Céline, even the desire to be a victim: 'I am aware that I have something in my mug, my smile, my behaviour, my aura which works against me.' Like Céline he does not bother with logic. Instead of noting the differences among de Gaulle, Bidault and Thorez, he makes all three the targets of his invective. He has a flair for comic detail and he tells a wealth of anecdotes about the nurses who looked after him in hospital, about the cinema milieu he moved in, about the hesitant, scrupulous Jean Paulhan. Céline's letters, fierce pieces of rhetoric, provide the 'lead tip' for Paraz's 'club'.

Paraz had begun a campaign to help his friend. He enlisted the aid of Céline's acquaintances like Daragnès, Aymé and Galtier-Boissière who was joining vigorously in the anti-Liberation chorus. The actress

Arletty pledged her support, which may have been embarrassing for she had compromised herself under the Nazis. Painter Jean Dubuffet came forward and Bernanos would have been a mighty voice had he not died in 1948. Attitudes towards collaboration had not changed and few people were convinced by the literary antagonists of the Liberation. But hatred was no longer so sharp and Céline was able to rally support. In 1948 Jean Paulhan risked publishing a piece of *Casse-pipe* in his *Cahiers de la Pléiade* – Céline's only comment was to complain that Paulhan never paid him.[210] Raoul Nordling was using his influence, associations of First World War ex-servicemen came to Céline's aid, even Jewish groups supported him.

Paraz kept up the campaign. In 1950 he published another journal-pamphlet, *Valsez saucisses*, which renews his attack on the Liberation. He begins with the 1944 destruction of towns on the Atlantic coast. Isolated German garrisons were holding out but they were willing to surrender, says Paraz. Instead the Resistance, to prove its paper-heroism, overran them. Paraz returns to the purge, claiming that one hundred thousand Frenchmen had been put to death. Looking at contemporary France, he criticizes the folly of allowing the Communist Party to grow in strength when France might have to go to war with Russia. He directs his wrath against so-called left-wing leaders like Claude Bourdet, former editor of *Combat*, Teitgen, the Minister of Justice, who was unwilling to declare an amnesty, and Madeleine Jacob, a favourite target. Paraz mixes up his satire on Existentialism with ironic comments on doctors who failed to cure his damaged lungs. He denounces publishers and fellow-patients in the same breath. He has picked up Céline's flair for irrelevant onslaughts – there is a long harangue against the Jews who are massacring the Arabs in Palestine, just as the Germans massacred them. Once again, Paraz's verbal skill enables him to turn this stream of invective into a lively, readable book.

Throughout 1949 Céline was preparing for his long-delayed trial. His letters, printed in *Valsez saucisses*, repeat the themes of his *Réponse aux accusations* and of the statement he would make to his judges. His view was simple: 'I did not collaborate, however strange it may appear. My enemies will have to resign themselves to that fact.'[211] Unfortunately the matter is not so easy. An ordinance of 27 June 1944 defined collaboration as any action or writing that aided the Nazi war effort, supported anti-semitism and harmed the Resistance.[212] Céline could not be tried for his pre-war pamphlets, only for his behaviour from 1940 to 1944. Maurice Vanino, a Resistance historian, has analysed the case and he concludes, not surprisingly, that Céline was guilty.

Evidence of collaborationist actions is slight. Vanino is unable to show that the *parti unique* discussions amounted to anything or that Céline's contacts with the German authorities were much greater than his position as doctor and writer demanded. On the question of his writings, Vanino has more to work with. Céline could find no way of explaining *Les Beaux Draps*, except to forget that he ever wrote it.[213] He could explain the re-publishing of *L'École des cadavres* only by blaming it on Denoël.[214] He wanted to forget about his letters to the press on the grounds that they were not really articles. Vanino will not accept this. He singles out the remark about Doriot and the criticism of the Resistance. He demolishes Céline's claim: 'From the time the Germans arrived I took no interest in the Jewish question.'[215] This conflicts with the admiring remark about Hitler and the letter to the organizers of the anti-semitic exhibition. Vanino also digs up the Rouquès matter. In the 1943 preface to *L'École*, Céline attacked Rouquès for the 1939 lawsuit and called him 'the doctor of the international brigades'. This, claimed Céline's accusers, was tantamount to denouncing him to the Gestapo as an anti-fascist. Céline could only reply that Rouquès was known to one and all as a communist sympathizer, so that the preface made no difference. Vanino does not agree.

It is impossible to see how Céline could be found not guilty. One may argue endlessly about the vagaries of Liberation justice. Why was the house of Denoël acquitted on the charge of publishing collaborationist books? If Denoël was innocent how was Céline guilty? There is no obvious answer. But, as the law stood, Céline had committed punishable offences. His claim that he was hated by the Germans, the Vichyites and the collaborators was irrelevant. His writings were sufficient proof of collaboration. The question of to what degree he was guilty is more complex. Vanino considers him a hard-line collaborator, but this is surely exaggerated. Céline had made his main contribution to the Nazi cause before the war. *Bagatelles* and *L'École* were his major works, the wartime writings were slighter. This should have entitled him to a milder punishment than Rebatet or Cousteau. But the arbitrariness of the purge – Hérold-Paquis's typist received twenty years hard labour while Albertini, a leader in the Rassemblement National Populaire, was sentenced to five years in prison – makes such comparisons difficult. If he had been tried in 1945, Céline's fame would probably have brought him a long jail sentence.

As it was, his trial on 21 February 1950 was an anti-climax. *Combat* and *Le Libertaire* had polled their readers.[216] They found that, although most people thought Céline guilty, tempers had cooled since 1944. Among the writers interviewed André Breton and Roger Vailland were anti-Céline, Paulhan, Mac Orlan, Aymé and the inevitable Paraz were for him. Camus declared that, while he loathed the views expressed in the pamphlets, he had lost faith in the trials – 'political justice is repugnant to me'.[217] Other newspapers showed interest. *Radar*, a glossy and sensation-loving magazine, sent a reporter to Denmark. She paints a vivid picture of Céline living in total poverty, a sick man stretched out on a pallet: 'Céline, the swashbuckler, "big mouth" Céline is no more than a poor, broken devil.' *Radar*'s conclusion is that, in spite of his crimes, Céline should be pitied.[218] It is clear that he has become a news item, more bizarre than reprehensible. His picture is in the magazine near photographs of Ingrid Bergman and the boxer Ray Faméchon.

The hearings aroused much interest and little passion. Céline stated, with scant regard for the truth, that he would have liked to attend, but that his doctor had forbidden it.[219] The prosecution read out extracts from *Les Beaux Draps* – sometimes provoking outbursts of laughter from the audience. Naud and Tixier-Vignancourt produced Céline's letter of defence and statements from his friends. Arletty sent a letter which declared that, as Céline had been born, like her, in Courbevoie, he could not have betrayed France.[220] The decision was swiftly reached: Céline was declared guilty and condemned to one year in prison, national unworthiness and the confiscation of half his property. The *Combat* reporter considered this an extremely lenient sentence and Paraz writes gleefully that Madeleine Jacob was blue with anger.[221] Even Céline was pleased. 'I was condemned for *reasons of state*, if they had not knocked me at all they would have disavowed the Resistance,'[222] he said with some accuracy.

But he still had to remain in Denmark or else go to prison. By the next month he had fallen into deep depression. The nervous excitement of the trial had left him exhausted. He was no longer pleased. 'They only half cut my head off,' he writes to Raoul Nordling.[223] Paraz kept up his campaign, urging admirers to plead and petition on Céline's behalf. He began work on a third book, *Le Menuet du haricot*, which renews his attacks on the Resistance – 'made up of very low scoundrels, fortunately few in number' – on Sartre, Madeleine Jacob and, a new enemy, Maurice Merleau-Ponty.[224]

Céline's lawyers were hard at work. In August 1947 an amnesty had been extended to men who fought in the First World War. It might be applicable to their client. Céline was suspicious: 'This so-called Amnesty is only a Resistance trick.'[225] He was sure that, if he returned, he would be clapped into prison. The example of the Commune continued to haunt him: 'They were judging the *communards* in 1880 and harshly.'[226] In December Naud was optimistic, Céline not so. But on 26 April 1951 he discovered that he was pardoned. He could scarcely believe it. Paraz writes that Jules Moch, the socialist Minister of the Interior, granted the amnesty without knowing that Louis-Ferdinand Destouches was Céline; when Moch realized it he was 'mad with rage'.[227] Céline did not delay. In June he took an aeroplane to Nice, leaving behind him a country he had never ceased to castigate. The days of exile were over. He could return to the Paris suburbs he knew so well.

[7]

Guignol's Band

Guignol's Band begins with the Second World War and the chaotic exodus from Paris. Then it moves back to 1915 London. It describes the wounded Ferdinand wandering around the Leicester Square brothels and the East End pubs. He meets the brothel-king Cascade and a more sinister figure: the Russian anarchist Boro, who blows up buildings for no reason and murders his friend, the pawnbroker Van Claben. Ferdinand is drawn into this underworld and he too becomes a killer – he pushes the cripple Mille-Pattes under a train. He flees and meets Sosthène whose aim is to lay bare the secrets of Tibet. The second volume, *Le Pont de Londres*, is even more chaotic. Ferdinand has an intense love-affair with an English child, Virginia; Sosthène works on gas-masks with a mad colonel. Mille-Pattes returns from the dead and drags Ferdinand through a nightmarish orgy in the Touit-Touit club. Finally Ferdinand goes back to the East End and the book ends with a grotesque birthday-party where Cascade presides and the dead return from their graves. This summary is not very coherent, but neither is *Guignol's Band*.

'After *Mort à crédit* I had said everything,' Céline declared not long before his death.[1] The remark contains a kernel of truth. In two long novels he had set out his vision of a tragic, occasionally beautiful universe and he had depicted heroes who came to understand their bitter lot. What else remained? He could repeat himself, which he does in *Guignol's Band*. Here are the same futile wanderings, the same battlefields and brothels. But there is more. Céline could continue to hunt for the beauty that the characters of *Mort à crédit* were seeking in the Passage. To do this, he would have to go deeper into the spirit world that lies behind the so-called ordinary reality. In *Mort à crédit*, the hallucinations and the Krogold legend depicted this other realm; in *Guignol's Band* it is moving closer to the centre of the book. Continuing Bardamu's search on another level, Céline starts to give free rein to his visions.

This is why he needed the experience of the Second World War. All his novels, from *Guignol's Band* on, may be read – like the pamphlets – as attempts to deal with the war. In 1940 the world exploded before his eyes and his hallucinations were acted out on the streets. The waves f bombers that darkened the sky are to his later writing what the Flanders trenches were to *Voyage*. *Guignol's Band* is a first – and ultimately unsuccessful – attempt to put them into a novel.

The introduction and opening chapters are set in the 1940s. At the outset the novelist speaks of himself as the author of *Guignol's Band*. His voice is full of impending doom because it is 1944: 'with things as they are you don't know who's living or dead! Denoël? You? Me?'[2] He has the usual troubles of the Célinian novelist: the public is hostile – 'I give everybody a pain in the ass.' He makes fun of himself by talking about his grandfather, another stylist 'who used to write the prefect's speeches' at Le Havre. Yet he asserts the power of the word. When he publishes a book 'a hundred, two hundred thousand buy it . . . twenty thousand order it, learn it by heart'. There is in life a lyricism that cannot be spoiled. The novelist calls on his readers to be gay – 'Kiss any girl you please!'. He sets himself forward as a joyous master of song:

> Excitement's everything in life!
> When you're dead it's over.

Immediately he shifts to his first chapter, which describes the 1940 bombing of Orléans. Here the theme of *Mort à crédit* is demonstrated with full drama: the man who faces death has insight into beauty. The bombing is a chain of horrors that grow worse until the human mind can no longer contemplate them rationally. This is not an attack by the Germans on the French, but the punishment of mankind by an evil force. The 'devil up there's sore at us,' says Céline. Bombs rain on the bridge, tanks collide with the ambulance, a baby lies roasted on the bonnet of a lorry. People cannot understand what is going on. Conventional values disappear – patriotism, for example, is useless and a colonel vanishes into the river with a cry of 'Vive la France!'. The baby's father, clutching desperately at fragments of ordinary life, keeps asking for something to drink. One woman, Brigitte, has gone mad, which is her way of escaping the pain. At first the narrator tries to make sense of things. That 'must be a reconnaissance flight,' he says, looking up at the sky. 'No mistake! It's getting worse,' he

decides. Later he stops questioning and he too succumbs to madness:
'It's my reason tottering . . . under the shocks of the circumstances.'

'Hell's right here,' says Céline, determined to put everything in a
metaphysical context. The planes are alive and, like demons, they have
'little tongues of fire' which 'shoot forth' everywhere. The narrator
prays: 'We beg the Virgin Mary . . . with big fervent signs of the
cross!.' But his prayers go unanswered since the sky is ruled by the
evil spirits. One bomber is 'an archangel', another is 'hanging from
the angels'. Yet the bombing is seen in aesthetic terms: 'the world
shake-up's musical . . . no stopping the dance'. The Orléans bridge is
compared with the Pont d'Avignon and the thunder of explosions is
'the music of the big slaughter'. The narrator is caught up in the dance:
'the rhythm gets you'. As the crowd and he are 'whirled about in
space' he sees beyond the bombing. A bleeding hand is holding the
universe and drops of blood are falling as joyous birds. Horror and
beauty are mingled in this vision of the 'Palace of Nights'.

Céline switches again. A voice intervenes with an ironic 'Very well
said'. Céline grows calm. He launches into a doggerel poem full of
dire predictions. 'The war's got to start all over,' he says, reminding
us that it is 1944 and France is a battlefield. For a moment he becomes
a pamphleteer again and blames everything on the Jews. This is
Cassandra-Céline, the 'occultist', who will decipher the signs in the
sky. And the signs are bad: 'The stars are dunghill for the Century,'
he laments. He changes his style once more and becomes 'Ferdinand-
child-of-the-Passage' who grumbles about his poverty, his parents'
lower-middle-class ethic and the stupidity of the French footsoldier –
'He wiggles only for the hangmen'. These pages are full of confused
images of hell: men will die 'with frightful choking, a thousand playful
flayings and green contortions of wounds, boiling wax that sticks, torn
apart, muscles in mincemeat'. Céline is obsessed with his own death.
Soon he will succumb 'haggard, swamped, beneath the disgrace, the
repulsion of the righteous'. Yet he still has hopes of joy: man must
'find in his heart the song . . . the gracious secret of the fairies'.

Already the reader is troubled. In these pages, as in the introduction,
Céline is saying that there may be a lyricism which can be enjoyed in the
shadow of death. In the Orléans episode he is saying something more
difficult: that the revelation of death, destroying man's normal nature,
reveals to him a beauty that is inherent in the condemned universe.

Certainly this does not mean that the narrator can give up his struggle and abandon himself to his visions. He must emerge from his madness and go on driving the ambulance, hence the ironic switch of tone. But he is involved in a perpetually desperate situation. He is not plucking the day while expecting the night, nor cultivating his memories as he waits to die. In the difference between these two points of view lies the weakness of *Guignol's Band*.

The London saga is an attempt to recover the origins of the war. Out of the horror of Orléans and the narrator's obsession with the Liberation comes the memory of his youth, which surges back all in one piece, as childhood did in *Mort à crédit*. 1915 is remarkably like 1940. Boro, the first character to be introduced, establishes the link. Like the planes, he is an 'archangel' of destruction who blows up buildings for no reason at all. He too creates beauty, for he charms people with his piano-playing: 'it was really magic the way he had them spellbound'. In London death is everywhere, as khaki-clad soldiers tramp through the streets on their way to Flanders. Contrasts abound: the capital is squalid, full of East End slums and station waiting-rooms; it is also a nightmare where ghosts walk the earth and black masses are celebrated near the Thames. But here again there is lyricism, for Céline describes the songs and dances of the backstreets as well as fair-haired English girls like Virginia.

This London does not seem very different from the Paris of *Voyage* and *Mort à crédit*. These are the same settings of hospitals and brothels and the same cast of pimps, eccentrics and weary doctors. The fighting among the Rancy neighbours is paralleled by the brawling in the pubs. These similarities are only part of the repetition that is an integral feature of Céline's work. He may or may not repeat his motifs and characters more often than other major writers; but certainly it does not reflect any lack of creative power. It draws rather on his concept of the tragic. If all his novels describe a hero who wanders around – whether France, England or Germany scarcely matters – knowing there is nothing to be reached, but that he must carry on just the same, it is because Céline believes there can be no other kind of life. If he creates a long line of rapacious women characters like Pépé, Mimi in *Normance* and Inge in *Nord*, it is because woman's nature leads her to destroy man. Were he to create different kinds of plots and different kinds of women characters, he would be implying that things might be different.

For an artist whose pessimism is rooted, not in any kind of social vision, but in a conception of human nature itself, this is impossible. Women are not malicious because they are French or bourgeois, but because they are women. So each Célinian novel follows the same course: a hero preoccupied with survival, a band of hateful supporting characters, a dash of madness and disgusting sex, the whole circus following a circular structure where the ending repeats the beginning.

This does not mean there is no variety. Céline seizes on different aspects of the tragic in each novel. *Mort à crédit* is less of a legend than *Féerie* which is less comic than *D'un château l'autre*. Céline goes through a definite evolution. Meanwhile the characters vary as the perspective shifts. Let us take, for example, the motif of the cripple – Mille-Pattes in *Guignol's Band*, Jules in *Féerie*, von Leiden in *Nord*. They have in common their ugliness, which in Céline's eyes is the brand of Cain and which makes them bitterly resentful of their existence; but where Mille-Pattes is mysterious, Jules is essentially an artist and von Leiden simply malicious. Each reflects the context of the novel in which he figures. In considering *Guignol's Band* one must look for the differences between this London and the Paris of the first two books.

The young Ferdinand goes through many experiences his elder brother Bardamu had known. He runs away: from the war, from Boro, from Inspector Mathew, from the colonel. His aim is to survive: 'My highest ambition was to get through the war ... without being arrested or hanged.' His preferred territory is the East End, his best friends underworld figures. As the book goes on he commits murder and becomes convinced of his guilt. 'Everything is my fault these days,' he laments. He has fits of madness and dreams of further flights: to America, Australia, the Pacific Islands. All this is familiar enough, but Ferdinand is a slighter figure than Bardamu because he does not learn. He does share Bardamu's curiosity. Having fled from the Leceister Square brothels he yearns to go back and take a look: 'It was crazy and reckless ... and yet I was just dying to do it.' But instead of coming to grips with disease and poverty, as Bardamu did, he falls into greater and greater bewilderment. He is not sure whether the police are chasing him or not, he cannot understand Mille-Pattes' resurrection and he is astonished by the party given for him at the end.

He never faces the problem of Virginia's pregnancy as Bardamu had faced Robinson's death.

The other characters are even slighter, beginning with Boro. Céline does not tell us why Boro wants to blow up buildings or how he spends the rest of his time or what he did before coming to England. Van Claben and Prospero Jim are also foreigners and, as their background is never explained, they seem to the reader to come out of nowhere. Conversely the bevy of pimps, whom Cascade introduces in his first story, disappear from the novel afterwards. The characters of *Guignol's Band* do not belong to any particular social strata and they are not well-rounded. Their chief attribute is that they are mysterious. Céline writes of Clodowitz: 'He had such queer papers, such suspicious stamps on them that they weren't fit to be shown . . . Diplomas that were even more weird.' The reader is left wondering who Clodowitz really is. His identity is as shaky as his papers. At any moment he may be expelled from England and thrust into nothingness. Céline stresses his characters' insignificance by using the puppet motif, both in the book's official title and in the name he gives it in his letters – *Pantin*.[3]

His creatures are like puppets because their actions have no motives. Boro tries to kill Ferdinand before returning ten minutes later to congratulate him on his escape. The colonel, who oscillates between anger and friendliness, is most amiable when he discovers that Ferdinand has been stealing from him. Abrupt changes of character are even more frequent than in *Voyage*: Delphine hovers between affection and murder, Van Claben is transformed by the opening bars of any song. *Guignol's Band* is full of incongruous relationships. La Finette loves fellow-prostitute Fernande who loves their pimp Gros Lard. Joconde and Angèle are both in love with Cascade, who is not interested in either of them. There are no psychological explanations for such behaviour.

Even the theme of hatred has changed. Céline's comment on the dockers applies to all his characters: 'a trifle set them at one another's throats . . . the least ray of sunshine, the slightest break in the clouds had a tragic effect on them'. When two people meet their first reaction is to fight – Boro with Van Claben, Sosthène with the colonel. But they are not consciously malicious – there are no Lavelongues among them. The theme of exploitation of the poor by the rich has been dropped.

There are even characters who are kindly, like Cascade or Virginia. Most of the people do harm by their arbitrariness – Boro is the supreme example. The colonel hesitates between spoiling Virginia and beating her savagely. He is as likely to do the one as the other, and he does not know why he does either. By not explaining how the hatred works, Céline makes it random.

Death is less cruel than in *Voyage* – there is nothing to match the seriousness of Robinson's murder – but it is more bizarre. It is personified in the figure of Achille Norbert, the mummy that is to be put on public display with electric light-bulbs in its eye-sockets. Even the murders do not involve much malice. Van Claben dies as part of a game, played by the intoxicated Boro, and Ferdinand kills Mille-Pattes half-accidentally, on a vague suspicion of treachery. Often it is hard to tell who is alive and who is not. Characters as obsessed with death as the Lady Macbeth-admiring Delphine and the colonel, with his liking for poisoned gasses, take their places alongside the corpses of Van Claben and Mille-Pattes that have returned to haunt the streets.

Not surprisingly, *Guignol's Band* is full of uncertainty. Is Mille-Pattes intriguing against Ferdinand? Ferdinand thinks he is but he is not sure. Why does the colonel suddenly vanish? There is no answer to this and other questions. People and events are shrouded in unreality. Musing over the past Ferdinand says: 'You would think that old Claben had never existed ... nor Delphine either.' He sometimes wonders whether Virginia exists, certainly he never knows who she is. She may be the colonel's daughter or niece or mistress. She is a flaxen-haired angel but she is already 'steeped in depravity'. While Ferdinand pours out his love to her he knows that she is miles away, lost in a world of childish games, cinema and, who knows black magic. The characters may themselves be shadowy, but that does not prevent many of them from worrying about the greater uncertainty in which they move. The principal of authority in *Guignol's Band* is Cascade, unofficial head of the French community. But Cascade is consumed by conjectures about his nephew's death. Again and again he makes Ferdinand tell him how Raoul was shot for cowardice. 'Doubt was undermining him,' says Ferdinand. The problem is illustrated – inevitably – by the London fog which 'rises up from the river, sweeps in from the end of the neighbourhood, takes in all the landings, docks, people and trains ... makes everything hazy and stumpy'. And there is a minor character called Nelson Trafalgar who has a flair for finding his way through the mists. None of his friends can emulate him.

Small wonder young Ferdinand is bewildered. The people around him are being pulled by invisible strings and have no control over themselves. As at Orléans, reason has broken down and many things are quite incomprehensible. So the only explanation is magic. *Guignol's Band* contains magic from all countries and cultures. La Joconde is a fortune-teller, Van Claben an Eastern sorcerer who dissolves his customer's articles into nothing. In *Le Pont de Londres* there are Tibetan gods, ghosts and the mighty Cimetry, death's drummer. Vigginia is a 'fairy' who bewitches Ferdinand, she is also a 'little demon'. Ferdinand has 'the devil inside him' and Sosthène is possessed by Goâ.

Magic is a natural enough theme for Céline to turn to. It is, after all, a primitive science used by peoples who need to explain the phenomena around them, but have no knowledge of physics and chemistry. Having discarded logic, Céline finds himself in a similar position. When they are lost his characters resort to magic. Confronted with the Touit-Touit club Ferdinand exclaims 'It's a black mass' and 'It's unconquerable magic'. Mysterious forces are at work and Ferdinand turns to witchcraft for an explanation.

Magic goes well with another Célinian theme: madness. He is quick to point out that Boro is 'cracked' and La Joconde 'batty'. The colonel is an English eccentric and Delphine plays out theatrical roles in her ordinary life. Ferdinand knows that he borders on madness: 'I went off my nut early.' In *Mort à crédit* Céline shows how such visions may be flashes of truth; here he depicts madness and magic as correct, complementary insights. When he beats out the rhythm for Sosthène's ritual dance Ferdinand is caught up in the magic, but he expresses it differently. 'I was becoming as crazy as my master,' he says. Certain incidents seem to go beyond madness. When Mille-Pattes returns from the dead with Nelson and Bigoudi, Ferdinand says 'they were really present, that was no delusion'. He is clear on that point. On the other hand the Skip Jovil episode seems real enough, but when Ferdinand tells Prospero Jim about it the only reply he gets is: 'Have you been dreaming?'. There is no distinct line between objective and subjective. Ferdinand accepts responsibility for killing Mille-Pattes, but a moment later he claims he is 'the victim of a plot'. Similarly when the characters cannot understand something they attribute it to madness or magic, it scarcely matters which.

The magical episodes cannot be separated from the rest of the book. Mille-Pattes' return to life is no different from Delphine's arrival at the party – 'she came there out of a dream,' explains Ferdinand. There is no one simple level of reality, for Céline continues to interpret phenomena in many different ways. Describing the ships at anchor held by their ropes between land and sea, he remarks: 'miracles are like that'. In this world ordinary events and ghosts come together as they did in *Voyage*, where the Montmartre vision takes its place within the description of Paris life. The change is that in *Guignol's Band*, especially in the second volume, the non-naturalistic elements play a greater role. This forces the characters to delve into magic. The Touit-Touit club and Sosthène's dances take up much of the book and Ferdinand becomes a sorcerer's apprentice in order to fathom them.

Traditionally magic is more than an explanation. It is an attempt to gain control of the irrational forces. If the magician can reduce the supernatural to a series of laws he can intervene and manipulate them. In *Guignol's Band* many of the characters try to do so – Sosthène being only the most striking example. But no one succeeds in escaping from his status as puppet. Mille-Pattes comes back from the dead but, when Cimetry summons him, he has to return to the graveyard. Ferdinand tries to make a distinction between Sosthène's magic – 'black Eastern arts . . . abominable evil spells' and Virginia's – 'I have another kind of magic with me'. But Virginia's sorcery leads him to the Touit-Touit club. The lesson of Orléans is repeated at each new incident: there is no white magic. The forces that control the world are alien to man and they are evil.

This is the vital difference between *Guignol's Band* and the pamphlets. There, there was a magician – the Jew; in the novel no one can pull the strings. One might re-state this in another way: in *Bagatelles* the real magician was the anti-semite who, by his conspiracy theory, avoided the human condition, whereas in *Guignol's Band* all men are struggling hopelessly together. As Céline tells us, 'Everything finishes in the flames . . . all evil spells carry us off into the water, down the pits, into the fire.'

The characters must learn this lesson and none has a harder time than Sosthène. He believes the world is dominated by live and po-

tentially kindly beings that reside in the mountains of Tibet. He has a
hotchpotch hierarchy of gods and demons, who must be prayed to and
placated. Having spent years hunting for gems in Asia – fairy gold is a
motif in *Guignol's Band* – he wishes now to search for the Tibetan
flower the Tara-Tohé, repository of ultimate wisdom. He promises
Ferdinand that he too will be admitted to the secrets of the universe
and the peace that they bring. 'You are, in a word, all music! ...
Harmony,' he exults, anticipating the point Ferdinand will reach when
he becomes a 'Free Man of the Waves'. Sosthène is already in touch
with 'the Waves', the half-physical and half-spiritual forces that
emanate from Tibet. All this reads like a jumbled parody of Eastern
philosophy, but there is more involved. Sosthène's concept of waves
reminds one of Courtial whose supposedly scientific view of the world
had a good deal of magic about it. Both men believe that nature is a
living organism which man can understand. When he does so he will be
freed from his condition and attain the harmony Sosthène mentions.

And therein lies the problem, for throughout *Le Pont de Londres*
Sosthène goes downhill. Although he will not admit it he is meddling
in black magic, for he venerates Achille Norbert and gives himself up
to a 'Cult of the Dead'. Even as he professes to rise above ordinary
mortals, he reveals weaknesses which are all too human: he interferes
with little girls and cadges money from Ferdinand. More important,
his spells turn out to be useless. He enters the colonel's gas-mask
scheme believing that his power will protect him from the poisoned
gas. But it will not. When he tries to prove his witchcraft by using the
demon Goâ to stop the traffic at Leicester Square, he succeeds only in
causing chaos. Aware that everything is turning against him he falls
silent and by the end of the book he has become a passive character.
In a less sensational manner he has gone through Courtial's evolution.

His mistake is not to believe there is such a thing as magic, but to
believe it is beneficent. Interspersed with his harangues is his wife's
story. She has her own spells: Sosthène was a stage-magician and she
was the 'Flower of San Francisco', who won triumphs from Indian
Rajahs. This is more than a mockery of Sosthène's tale. Pépé believes
that her spells are real and that she is a beauty whom no man can
resist. In fact she is a painted hag, but she does have a witch's power
and she is more than capable of debauching young messenger boys.
And her stage magic was real enough to do her harm. She used to dress

as a cadaver and Sosthène would cut her in half. One night he tried seriously to kill her and then began to caress his 'little dead darling'. Without realizing it, she was joining in his 'Cult of the Dead'. Other kinds of magic are clearly authentic, witness the inventions of modern technology which Céline sees – and will persist in seeing – as demonic devices. The electric lights in the Singapore café are, for example, the setting for Sosthène's devilry, the colonel dabbles in crazy science, the Zeppelins are the first angels in the sky. Sosthène uses the telephone to curse people in Goâ's name. Is Goâ's magic less real than the telephone's? asks Céline.

The characters are trapped by this witchcraft. Virginia's sexual magic enables her to cast a spell over Ferdinand but her youth is soon ruined by pregnancy. The explanations that sorcery furnishes are contradicted a moment later: Mille-Pattes is taken away by Cimetry but he soon returns. In one sense magic is no more than a particular illustration of Céline's absurd universe. Yet the sense lingers – largely unfulfilled in *Guignol's Band* – that it may be an avenue to explore. It may offer truth to the searcher who knows he is dealing with evil.

As it is, the characters weave their magic into fantasies about Shakespearean heroines and Tibetan demons. Whether these are true or not they stand as stories, minor works of art. The connection between magic and artistic creation is easily and repeatedly established. Virginia dazzles Ferdinand with tales where she makes the objects in the room – the teapot, table and cushions – walk and converse. 'Everything comes to life ... talks ... laughs,' says Ferdinand. He describes this significantly as a 'magic comedy' and emphasizes that Virginia achieves it 'word by word'. As in *Mort à crédit*, many of the characters are artists. Ferdinand himself is a story-teller who is admitted into the Leicester Square circle because he tells Cascade the tale of Raoul. Delphine is an actress; Mille-Pattes is a cardsharper and a cook; Nelson Trafalgar draws pictures on the pavement. Cascade is a masterly teller of tall tales who enthrals his hearers at the pub: he 'was having a great time! ... So were the customers all around him ... What a brilliant talker.' In *Guignol's Band* Céline allows his characters great freedom to spin out their flights of fancy. His point of view has shifted since *Voyage*. Bardamu looked at his patients' fictions in a moral light and condemned them as lies. In *Mort à crédit* Céline recognized that these tales were an exercise of the imagination and that they had something in common with his own writing. In *Guignol's Band* the moral condemnation is implicit in Sosthène's downfall; but the story of the Tara-Tohé – not the search for it – has some validity as a work of art. Sosthène is creating a new world, which is what a novelist does.

And verbal magic is all that remains of the characters' spells. Sosthène's Leicester Square adventure is a fiasco but, when he recounts it afterwards, it becomes a 'telluric transformation such as had never been seen even in Bengal'. His Eastern lore is real – as a tale that he tells very well. His first speech, delivered in the Singapore, impresses the reader as a glittering monologue rather than a statement of fact. The exotic names – 'Consistoires Brahmaniques, Podages aux jades lazulis, Goupor-Rawhidôr' – are introduced for their own sake. They provide no information but they trigger off the reader's reverie. The same is true of Ferdinand's outbursts. Visiting an antique shop with Virginia he is carried away by the magic of travel, by 'all the countries where strange things happen and wondrous adventures take place'. He knows he will never visit them – 'we won't live long enough to travel, voyage everywhere'. He names them instead: 'Island of Roses, Island of Sapphires, deserted South Sea islands.' He is consciously translating the geography of the Pacific into words.

The entire relationship between Ferdinand and Virginia begins on a verbal level. Ferdinand makes long speeches that are nothing more than words, if only because Virginia is too much of a child to understand the feelings he professes. Interestingly enough, both of them fall silent as soon as her pregnancy has brought real contact between them. But in the early pages of *Le Pont de Londres* Ferdinand escapes from his plight as a hunted fugitive into torrents of pure language. Céline uses the jargon of romantic love – 'I am fire . . . I am light . . . I am miracle'. He switches to a religious vocabulary, letting Ferdinand speak of his 'supernatural emotion'. He punctures the balloon – 'I sigh like three dozen oxen'. He shows how Ferdinand can transform Virginia with words, turning her into a 'cornflower', a 'warbler' and a 'sparrow'. This is a love-story, rather than a love-affair.

But then *Guignol's Band* is made up of such tales. The characters meet, tell each other an anecdote and separate; that constitutes the book's structure. Some episodes are openly presented as story-telling, witness Cascade's account of how the pimps went to war. Here form is much more important than content. The story is a series of variations on a set theme: how Cascade's pimp friends became patriotic and went off to battle leaving him with their girls. The plot is slender but it is made interesting by Cascade's humour, by his *argot* and, once more, by a long string of picturesque names – l'Allumeur, Jojo le Poigne, Luigi le Florentin. At other times the arrival of a minor character like Nelson Trafalgar prompts the young Ferdinand to tell a story about him. Once the older narrator intervenes to promise an account of how he and Boro played the piano on the streets. 'Naturally it turned out badly . . . I'll tell about it later on,' he says. He never fulfils his promise but he has emphasized that *Guignol's Band* is a novel about story-telling. And there is a pub-owner called Prospero Jim to remind us that Shakespeare too wrote a play about play-writing dominated by a king who is a magician.

Many of the relationships among Céline's characters may be seen in author–reader terms. Cascade is Ferdinand's audience and Ferdinand becomes the listener when Sosthène and Pépé begin to speak. Pépé makes advances to him in the middle of the conversation but he pushes her away. 'Really I'm not interested . . . I'm more the curious type.' He wants her to go on telling him about the Flower of San Francisco. Despite this the reader's role is to undermine the author. Ferdinand listens sceptically to Sosthène, while Cascade makes Ferdinand repeat the story of Raoul, because he is never sure that it corresponds to the facts. The best example of snubbing an author is the amazement with which Virginia greets Ferdinand's declamations. He can make no impression on her at all. 'I am grotesque,' he concludes.

The would-be artists' stories stand for a moment and then crumble into the London haze. The problem is best illustrated by the legend within the book, the Véga. This plays something of the role played by the Krogold legend in *Mort à crédit* and there is even mention of a 'chevalier Cwandor' to remind us of the dead Gwendor. The Véga is the book of religion, for it is a 'mass to the spirits of Goâ'. Even more important it is the book of art which outlines the sacred dances and it is described as a 'miniature ballet'. But its ballet remains undanced. Sosthène's ritual ceremony turns out wrong and instead of trapping Ouandor, 'the devil-bird', he captures Goâ. All that remains is the chaos of Leicester Square.

Sosthène fails with his Tibetan epic but Céline succeeds in writing *Guignol's Band*. This is the real legend, complete with demons and ghosts. Its main character is the writer himself, the 1940s Ferdinand who keeps looking back over the young Ferdinand's shoulder. He chooses what we may see: 'I'm not going upstairs ... I'm setting you up on the main floor,' he says as he enters the Dingby Cruise. Already in *Mort à crédit* Céline had separated narrator and actor. This is another form of identity-splitting. It allows Céline to show the different elements in the artist's personality: in particular to show the writing process and the suffering which precedes it. But whereas in *Mort* the narrator vanished after the first fifty pages, he remains dominant in *Guignol's Band*. At the outset he appears as an author arguing with his publisher and with his public. In the Orléans episode he is ambulance-driver and hallucinated chronicler. In London his is the saddened, wiser voice that speaks through young Ferdinand's confusion.

He has taken over the burden of understanding. Having battled through the Orléans bombing and written two novels, he can assess the 1915 experiences. 'I was pretentious then ... I wanted to cut a great figure,' he says severely. He puts things in the Célinian context: 'Truth is death ... I struggled gently against it as long as I could.' He also reminds us that he is remoulding his life to turn it into a novel. He interrupts his narrative: 'Are these memories too personal? Will they spoil my story?' In particular he insists on the difference between his London and the real London. The city of Cascade and Sosthène has vanished, not merely into the past, but beneath the hammerblows of the Luftwaffe: 'it's all smashed at the time I'm writing, gone up in smoke beneath the bombing'. He is 'transposing' it, following the dictum Céline gave in the introduction: 'Transpose or it's death.'

Not that the problem is so simple. There is no question of avoiding death, for it lies in wait at every London street-corner and it gives to the narrator's stories the veracity that Sosthène's lacked. But the narrator's willingness to contemplate it liberates a special beauty. Céline explains himself once more: 'Better the Eternal's rigadoon than the human calamitous Empire, the mammoth scheming molehill.' On the one hand is the absurd attempt to make life seem good, on the other is the acceptance of man's nothingness. The first is a matter of *divertissements* that do not appease and logic that does not work, the second reveals an order which has its own beauty: 'how dazzling it would be if, at that very moment, as we were being nailed up, there should escape, gush from the coffin, the miraculous trill of a flute'. This is

Céline, the 'Troubadour in the Sepulchres', who can enjoy the mad dance of the Touit-Touit club or the 'bewitchment' of a River Thames that is full of rats and corpses. Yet the reader is troubled once again. Elsewhere Céline speaks of memories that 'lie lightly on the years ... they gently enchant you to death'. This is more a matter of nostalgia, of an ageing man reaching back into his youth for happiness. The narrator wants to lose himself in the children's 'impish farandolas'. Certainly death is on his mind but he is pushing it away from him. This concept of beauty is less bold than the notion of the 'Eternal's riga-doon'.

Either way Céline reaches out for the lyricism that the First World War can offer. A few examples may show how he does it, firstly in his portrayal of London. He describes three areas – the East End, Leicester Square and Willesden – but his chosen territory is the East End. Ferdinand is forced to leave after Van Claben's death, but he returns gladly at the end of *Le Pont de Londres*. His description of the dock area combines two quite different elements: the streets are 'dank alleys of despair' which are 'monotonous ... greasy ... sticky with smoke all around'; but they are also an 'elves ball'. Céline stresses the dock-workers' poverty and their fights. He describes the drab brick houses – 'like week-days ... no ends to it' and the rats and the dirt. Yet the East End is full of fair-haired English children – 'Little dreamgirls! ... lively as larks on the wing'. There are dances, songs and barrel-organs on every corner. Nearby is the Thames. 'I wish all roads were rivers,' writes Céline. 'It's magical! ... No denying it! ... A ballet! ... It's hallucinatory.' Water is another form of the movement he loves. The Thames joins with the Wapping streets in a huge dance that banishes poverty. 'All great dreams are born in London,' says Céline who believes that the fog masks another realm, lying beyond the physical world. Such a potrayal of England is not unknown among French writers. Vallès catches something of it in *La Rue à Londres*, which may be why Céline liked his book. In *Beauté mon beau souci*, Valery Larbaud creates a magical Chelsea on the banks of the Thames and a young heroine Queenie Crosland who is not unlike Virginia. But the characteristically Célinian trait is the juxtaposition of the two Londons: the dockers' brawls and the children's songs. He is reminding us that it is he, the artist, who is creating this beauty. He is like 'the fake soot-smeared darkie, harlequin rags ... jigging a sore foot for a penny'.

Like his characters he works his magic, weaving their spells into his. His London is half heavenly and half terrestrial, like the ship on the Thames: 'if the men weren't fighting to hold it back with a hundred thousand ropes, it would drift away, rise naked from the docks, travel up among the clouds, fly to the very top of the sky, a harp, a living harp in the immense sea of blue'.

This incessant creation runs through the Van Claben episode, which moves on two levels. It is the sordid account of a murder: three people beat on old man to death in a jumbled pawnshop. But Céline makes it into a fairy-tale where the transgression of a mysterious law leads to retribution. He gives it something of the splendour which attended Courtial's death. Van Claben is an Eastern potentate dressed in 'oriental fancy dress'. He is mean and vicious but he has one weakness: he loves music and this leads him to his doom for art is very dangerous. When Boro plays the piano Van Claben is hypnotized by his 'magic spell'. Boro has not changed and his 'pixie hands' are equally adept with the piano and the bomb. Delphine is a passionate Shakespearean heroine, now Juliette, now Lady Macbeth, bearing a hair-pin like a dagger. The setting is the pawnshop stocked with exotic objects – 'pyramids of top hats' and 'fans for a thousand tropics'. Outside is the spellbinding Thames.

The catalyst of murder is the cigarettes Delphine receives from the 'Sky Physician'. Here again Céline hovers between the natural and the supernatural. There is a positivist's explanation: Delphine is hysterical and the cigarettes are drugged. But the other interpretation is as plausible. The doctor – a 'bag of bones' – is death's agent and his gift is bewitched. Boro and Ferdinand are warned not to smoke the cigarettes themselves but to save them for the sick Van Claben. They disobey. Immediately they fall into a hallucination where they scatter Van Claben's money on the floor. The 'God of the treasure' takes over and they search greedily for the fairy gold which 'lights up the whole shop'. In a drugged orgy they make Van Claben swallow his coins and then beat his head out on the stairs to recover them. A minor Apocalypse follows when Boro burns down the building. Death has won its inevitable victory but its ritual has an order of its own that delights Ferdinand. He stands for a moment to watch the blaze: 'Nothing's so fascinating as flames, especially flying around like that, shooting, dancing in the sky.'

Many of the adventures in *Le Pont de Londres* follow this pattern.
The Touit-Touit club is a ritual of sex, the party at the end is a grand
reunion of all the characters, whether living or dead. As the book goes
on it becomes more uncertain and more a matter of story-telling.[4]
The narrator digs into his treasure-trove of words to depict his demons.
Already in the 1940s pages he kept switching styles. He goes from
poetry to harangues, sets songs beside rhetoric. In the Orléans episode
he plays with words to show how they can alter the objects they
designate. The bomber is, for example, both a 'devil' and a 'fly', a
'death drum' as well as an 'archangel'.

The style of *Guignol's Band* is different again from *Mort à crédit*.
Céline has not forgotten his revolutionary innovations. To create
emotional immediacy he continues to break up his sentences and to use
slang. But the slang never becomes a torrent of abuse because *Guignol's
Band* is not as horrifying a book as *Mort* – bewilderment is less troubling than pain. The burden of realism has been partially lifted because,
although some of the London descriptions are sordid enough, much
of *Guignol's Band* takes place on the level of fantasy. This allows
Céline to push the language game much further and *Guignol's Band*
is closer to poetry than *Mort* was. Céline wants to show us that language alone can make sense out of the uncertainty. It is the true form
of magic and a pun may provide the connection between two completely different objects.

A device that Céline uses frequently is the recurring metaphor:
images of flowers, birds and water abound. The flower metaphor
shows how he imposes an order on things that have no logical connection. Virginia is a 'cornflower', while the bombs from the Zeppelin
fall in 'baskets of flowers'. Why should the two be described in similar
terms? In one sense Céline is inviting the reader to see links: there is a
danger behind Virginia's innocence and a beauty in the bombing; the
flower image is profoundly ambivalent. Céline brings in other phenomena: the real flowers in Virginia's garden, the flower islands that
Ferdinand mentions. Step by step the reader is led to see the flower as
the incarnation of the spirit world: its 'enchanted perfumes' – here
the drug motif is also introduced – lead one beyond the London
streets. Céline is not just revealing one of the central images of his
writing. He uses extended metaphors in his first two novels – the night
in *Voyage* is only the most obvious example. He is also flaunting his

use of the device. He is displaying his power to rearrange: Virginia, drugs, bombing and travel are all linked. The other images are employed in the same fashion. The bird metaphor connects together the London girls, who are 'larks on the wing', and Ouandor, the 'devil-bird' – a similar ambivalence is present here. Céline is building a new order using words as bricks. To extend it further he makes his images overlap. The flower is also a precious stone: both elements are contained in the entity of the Tara-Tohé. By extension of this image, Virginia may be linked with Van Claben's murder as well as with Sosthène's quest. The hieroglyphics of the universe are being deciphered in a way that Baudelaire and Rimbaud would well have understood. The great variety of *Guignol's Band* – the different kinds of magic, the different commodities in the London docks – represents the book's surface. Underneath is the structure of poetry.

Throughout the book Céline plays with language to show its vast power and its curious limitations. The English setting gives him great opportunities. On the first page he uses the word 'because' as a warning of what is to come. His British characters introduce English terms, like the colonel's 'Brittania rules the gasses' and Delphine's quotations from *Macbeth*. This is less a local-colour device than an attempt to create linguistic confusion. In one sense people have trouble saying anything at all in *Guignol's Band*. The French exiles know a few random phrases of English, Van Claben speaks some 'sort of Yiddish' and Sosthène, who is fluent in Sanskrit, cannot say a sentence in England because he cannot pronounce the 'th'. Bigoudi, who has spent years on the London streets, still knows only her French slang. When she wants to flatter Virginia, she cannot. She is reduced to silence. But the model of incoherence is Skip Jovil. All the reader knows about him – apart from the detail of his crippled arm – is what he says. But, although he struggles to speak English, he comes up with only a few distorted expressions like 'Voyache'. For the rest he spits and emits great grunts of 'Vloaf, Vloaf'.

Language, Céline is saying once more, cannot be used in a propositional manner and cannot provide dialogue. There is an amusing discussion between Cascade and Ferdinand about 'Convictchioun'. Cascade uses the word to impress Ferdinand with his knowledge of England. He does not know what it means and Ferdinand does not know what Cascade thinks it means. But 'Convictchioun' becomes an entity in itself, which strikes terror into Ferdinand.

By wielding language in this independent and triumphant way Céline demonstrates the real magical power: man's imagination. Many of the narrator's stories are, like Cascade's, pure transpositions. The piece on the docks is one of many examples. There is no attempt at realism, at listing quantities and commodities. Céline transforms everything: 'Forests of mahogany in thousands of piles ... rugs enough to cover the Moon ... English sponges to dry up the Thames ... Himalayas of powdered sugar ... Matches to fry the poles'. By jumbling the place names and exaggerating the amounts, he creates a realm of verbal fantasy. Many French writers who come to England describe the London docks and Vallès, for example, does a memorable job. But no one shows Céline's epic flair. His range of styles is equally striking. Cascade speaks a language that the characters of *Mort à crédit* would well have understood, while Sosthène's outpourings are full of rhetoric and mysticism. Ferdinand passes from the high-flown romanticism he uses with Virginia to the Leicester Square slang. Often Céline writes in a style that is removed from everyday life. He gives an archaic touch to his narration by devices like the omission of the definite article – '*du cerceuil miraculeux trille de flûte*'; by inversion of verb and subject, especially where it changes the order of the rest of the sentence – '*Ainsi sera la Mort par vous dansant un petit peu*'; by out-of-date locutions like '*un mouton là gisant*'. He is reminding the reader that he is describing a legendary, hence almost medieval London.[5]

The free use of language, the presence of the magic and the joy of the London streets make *Guignol's Band* into a delightful, zany novel. Delightful and ultimately trivial. Why should this be? On the simplest level it is because the intensity of the Orléans bombing is never recovered in the London chapters. Compared with the slaughter of the fleeing refugees, the escapades of the Touit-Touit club seem tame. And perhaps more is involved than an artistic shortcoming. In the London chapters the presence of death is not real enough. Van Claben's murder is nowhere near as painful to the reader as Courtial's suicide. Except for the rare moments when young Ferdinand is haunted by his memories of Flanders his confusion is not as anguished as the child's. One returns to the difference between the two points of view, outlined both in the 1940s pages and elsewhere. For much of the novel Céline does seem to be spinning out tales, while death lurks in the background but does not play its essential role in their creation. This is why the Véga is a less cruel and hence pale version of the Krogold saga, why Cascade's stories do not have the compelling power that the prison anecdotes will have in *Féerie*, why the magic of London is less sinister and less beautiful than the magic of Brittany will be. In this sense the English adventures are nothing more than a flight from the Orléans bombing and Céline is not yet ready to chronicle the Second World War. *Guignol's Band* is not an attempt to look at the origins of that war or a disguised method of discussing it. It is an escape from it and, as such, an escape from Céline's deeper nature. He does not want to face the knowledge that he is a creature of death and that his art is bound up with evil. *Guignol's Band* is an evasion just like the pamphlets, although of course it is not dishonest and harmful. Céline does not attribute his own dark powers to the Jew; he simply toys with them and then lets them fall. Not until *Féerie* does he become a true visionary.

[8]

Féerie pour une autre fois

Féerie consists of a long, virulent monologue where Céline, speaking from his Danish prison, hurls his defiance at the French nation. He talks of the Liberation massacres and the sufferings he endures in jail. He harks back to his earlier life: to the First World War, to Brittany, to his African travels. He returns constantly to his own innocence and the world's guilt. At the end he switches track and the monologue opens out into an epic. He depicts his fellow-artist, the sculptor Jules, who seduces Ferdinand's wife Lili. *Normance* shows the consequences of betrayal: the Allied bombers are obliterating Montmartre and Jules is waving them in with a magic wand. Ferdinand, now a lowly doctor, battles to survive and to help the wounded. Norbert the actor has a role too and so does the false dancer Mimi. The bombs continue to fall and the world becomes a dance of destruction.

In *Féerie* Céline has taken the plunge. Instead of stopping at the gates of the spirit world he has marched in. He himself describes *Normance* as 'a real event' seen 'in its full dimensions and with its secret significance'.[1] The ordinary world is merely a fragment of death's great whirl. The sordid Paris streets, so precisely delineated in *Mort à crédit*, are destroyed and recreated by explosions. They are cast up into the sky and arranged into new patterns as if by a giant artist, for at the core of *Féerie* and *Normance* stands the artist himself. At the outset he is Ferdinand the scapegoat left to rot in prison. Instead of submitting he transforms his cell into a realm of music and dance. Since artistic creation is what *Féerie* is all about, the best way to approach it is to look at its techniques, particularly at its language. For the universe itself is language: it is woven out of cries of pain.

Céline has written a really important novel about the Second World War. As a chronicler of the war he stands at the opposite end of the spectrum from Albert Speer. Speer sees the fighting in terms of technology. Battles are won and lost in the factories and the decisive element is organization of production. Business management has replaced bravery. War is a rational matter and the more rational side will win. To Céline, war is the most striking manifestation of the evil present in the human condition. It may be viewed – like sin itself – from two different standpoints. It stems from the hatred that Bardamu had observed at Rancy. Such malice has nothing to do with anything as rational as politics. It need not even be directed at the enemy: in *Normance* Jules' dislike of Ferdinand triggers off the bombing. War is also an integral part of the spirit world and quite outside of human control. This is why Céline loves to describe bombing: the explosives fall out of the heavens upon the helpless earth. Ferdinand cannot escape from prison, Norbert cannot make peace. Man is caught up in a cosmic evil to which he contributes but which he cannot alter.

This point of view makes Céline an excellent chronicler of the 1940 war. No longer were men being killed in trenches. Planes descended and devastated whole cities. To describe these mysterious forces Céline uses new techniques. In *Voyage* he had given a realistic setting: the soldiers, the fields, the corpses. In *Normance* he works with myths and magic.

To say that he is a good historian of the war is in one sense to put the question the wrong way around. The war offers the best illustration of his universe. A world in flux, continents wiped out, nations imbued with hatred, this is both the Célinian vision and the reality of 1940. Céline needs the holocaust, even if he cannot face it in the pamphlets or in *Guignol's Band*. The character of Jules shows that Céline even feels he is causing the war by needing it so much.

This is why the conflagration is seen as an artistic process. The Ferdinand of *Normance* describes the beauty in the bombing: 'the bombs are bursting in there like flowers ... carnations'.[2] Céline is not the only writer to take this line. Even Speer has a memorable passage where he stands and enjoys the lights of the explosions which are shattering Berlin. But Céline goes deeper when he views the reshaping of Montmartre as an exercise of the artist's imagination. (He notes elsewhere that Hitler was a failed artist.)[3] This offers him a new insight into the war. It explains why reason should be so useless, why subjective and objective should be meaningless terms. It accounts for the tremendous power that has been unleashed. The tumbling ruins are fragments of reality which emerge from the chaos like images passing through a writer's mind. Then, too, there can be order of a special kind: the planes come and go like motifs in a symphony.

The Second World War is very explicable as a novelist's hallucination.[4]

Féerie is a new kind of novel. It is a long monologue that revolves around a series of anecdotes and is written in a rhetorical style. Every aspect of its form is designed to create the frenzy of anger that is at the heart of war. The monologue is both act and technique. 'The wolf dies without howling, not I,' says Céline. His torrent of words is a kind of defiance. When Ferdinand needs medical attention he cries out: 'If I can't shit, I bay.' He is conducting a dialogue with the 'vengeful reader', his executioner. Sometimes the reader interrupts: 'Shut him up . . . under the marble with the fellow.' Ferdinand carries on. His book is dedicated 'to animals, the sick and the imprisoned' and the only reader from whom he expects anything is the 'collabo', himself a victim. *Féerie* is really a monologue addressed to no one. Céline says of Bébert, 'he doesn't answer questions any more . . . he soliloquizes about himself' and he adds 'so do I'. He tells 'little anecdotes' about Brittany and London. He interrupts himself. 'I'm not going to tell you about my other medical–social endeavours,' he says with mock self-deprecation. But mostly he thunders out his wrath which the monologue form allows him to express directly. This is why *Féerie* maintains an intensity of emotion which is only rarely reached in the earlier novels.

Céline's monologue is very free. It allows him to juxtapose past and present, France and Denmark in a 'confusion of place, time'. It is an ideal form for a writer who does not believe in the scientific universe. Céline does not try to cover the whole area of consciousness. He does use free association of a kind: the rattling of his fever-stricken body in Africa reminds one of the sound the wheelbarrow makes when Sartre and Claudel come to wheel him off to his death. But he uses this device sparingly. He keeps the line of thought clear with recurrent motifs like the ballad of Tante Estrême or the insults hurled at the reader. But the real order comes from his passions. He returns obsessively to the themes of betrayal and hatred. They give force to the anecdotes and structure to his random remarks.

There is no clear line of plot. Céline begins with the story of Clémence Arlon: 'Here is Clémence Arlon. She is about the same age as I am . . . What a strange visit.' In an ordinary novel this would be the start of the plot. Here Clémence vanishes never to return. But the tone has been set. Ferdinand is 'the Montmartre monster' and Clémence's son a would-be assassin. This is 'double Zero hour' and Radio London has condemned Ferdinand to death. Trapped on the Butte he is surrounded by boys with guns and sex-crazed women. The blood-letting of the Liberation is at hand: 'There are four million people in Paris boiling with the same hatred.' There is no question of politics here. It is a mythological struggle.

As the book goes on, Céline leaves his Montmartre flat even further behind. Events shift to Denmark, to the past or into the fantasy of the Ghosts' court. Realistic detail – like Goering's sister and the saucepan – is introduced to provide the comic element Céline needs. He will not allow his spirit world to be dignified. It must contain the ignobility of man's condition, hence the usual insistence on excretion. When Jules appears he is both a demon and a disgusting cripple who squats in his own filth. But, although Céline moves from one reality to another, he remains chiefly on the level of legend.

He uses techniques more often found in poetry: personification and, once more, extended metaphors. *Féerie* moves through a series of short, dramatic scenes like the one at the outset. There are no individual characters because 'almost all humans behave in the same way at the same time'. Instead there are confrontations between figures and images, which represent the various aspects of Céline's vision. During the trial scene the Ghosts embody the France of Verdun which is judging the modern French. In the all-important seduction scene Jules is the evil artist and Lili the dancer, the incarnation of goodness. By painting these characters with simple, bold strokes Céline makes them powers rather than people: Lili is a dancer and nothing else. Things are transformed, too. The cinema is a 'Minotaur of the Caverns' lurking in a den of 'Omni-Film'. From its depths people emerge 'staggering, sleepy ... no longer able to tell North from South'. Seldom has there been a more animated image of nothingness. Throughout *Féerie* Céline crystallizes emotions around such personifications: Radio London is the voice of death and Saint-Malo 'all enchanted ... rising up out of time' is the magic realm. The emphasis is no longer, as in *Guignol's Band*, on the artist giving order to the universe. The images are used self-consciously in the earlier novel; here they emerge from the monologue to give concrete form to Céline's fixations. The tide of Ferdinand's random complaints spills over into the metaphor of the hunt, which depicts his own plight, and of the amphitheatre, symbol of eternal human cruelty. When these references recur the reader is not surprised; they are merely dramatizations of Ferdinand's anger, just as the toboggan image expresses the speed of the monologue as a whole.

Céline's style is still an attempt to 'transpose'. The periods are shorter than in *Guignol's Band* and exclamation marks abound as in *L'École des cadavres*. There is more of the pamphlet in *Féerie* than in any other novel. The staccato rhythm permits great intensity of anger and the hostile 'you', addressed to the reader, turns the monologue into a harangue. Céline's fury drives him beyond prose and into a new tongue – part poetry and part music – to express what he has to say. *Féerie* combines the emotion of *Mort* with the freedom of *Guignol's Band*.

Céline is still fond of neologisms. Frequently they are key words to which he gives as pecial sense: *assasser* is a more casual form of *assassiner*; *étronimes* an even more disparaging version of *étron*, *blavouiller* a comment on the futility of ordinary language. As the sentences are short and the grammar simple, he uses lists of words. One verb can attract another as in '*ça se mugit, beugle, couaque*', where the noises become more animalistic. Sometimes the list parodies jargon in a way that shows Céline's personal slant. He describes himself as '*Génétiste! Anatomiste! Gymnastiste!*' and the juxtaposition of the last term reveals his highly individual view of woman's body. The use of different kinds of words within the list is important, because it shows how the writer can break through conventional language. Often Céline employs rhyme and alliteration, which give to his denunciations the force of a litany: '*crotteux, rateux, ignare, barbare*' is the man who has not read *Féerie*. The description of writers as companions of Sisyphus is strengthened by calling them '*maudits remonteurs de roc*'. Céline can obtain quite different effects. He enhances the charm of the young English girls when he calls them '*mille miss en mollets*', while the phrase '*les égorgements des énormes amours animales*' seems to emphasize the link between sex and bloodshed by its mixture of low and high vowels. Usually Céline's lyricism is black. He alters the names of his tormentors because by deforming their names he can deform them. Aragon is 'Larengon' and Mauriac is '*François en souliers de satin*'. But the chief target is the unfortunate Sartre. He becomes 'Nartre, Bartre' and 'Artrons' – an ingenious mixture of 'Sartre' and *étrons*. In this way he ceases to have any connection with the real-life Sartre and he becomes a creature of Céline's world. The BBC becomes a grotesque *bibibici* which reflects its endlessly shrill broadcasts and *traducteurs* ʋecome *troudoucteurs* to emphasize their nullity.[5]

Prose has been left far behind, as has ordinary reality. Céline is making a conscious attempt to exhaust the possibilities of language. He uses English and German words like 'finish', 'question', 'Maul' and plays with Latin tags. '*Vanitatas! Invidivia! Javalousie!*' he cries, mixing neologisms with alliteration. Alongside this linguistic exuberance runs the sense that language is inadequate and must give way to music and dance. Céline resorts to onomatopoeic sounds: the '*frrt! frrt!*' of the warders' keys and the '*plam! plam!*' of their boots on the floor. He refers to the prisoners by numbers — ninety-two and sixty-eight. There is a whole game of figures in *Féerie* where Céline talks of revolutions as eighty-nine and forty-eight partly to show that only their dates remain. Similarly he tells us that his mother is buried in 'row fourteen, division twenty' of Père Lachaise – the statistic is all that is left of her. Numbers are an alternative to words. The shapes and lines which the planes trace in the sky are yet another form of expression. Céline is showing a world full of signs that the artist must decipher. His wrath unveils to him the mythological significance of life; but he can only express it by becoming a musician. The bars of music that recur in the closing pages are proof of this. All of Céline's linguistic innovations are an attempt to reach the other reality that those few notes contain.

In doing so he lays bare the forces that shape the universe – the cry of pain, the web of time, the dance. In *Guignol's Band* they masqueraded in the guise of Eastern gods. Not so here. Céline does use religious language to describe them. He refers to the Liberation purge as a 'Communion not bread, red hot meat'. He talks of 'dance, my own little religion' and casts Lili as a redeemer: 'Are you Deaf? Dumb? in Chains? Well ... a dancer can save you.' His aim is to create his own theology where murder and ballet are ritual acts.

One may start with the cry. Céline describes the tam-tam as a 'sound like a Cathedral'. It is a religious call, embracing the community and turning it outwards towards the universe. It is greater than man for it emanates from the godhead, the 'Echo's Hollow'. At the heart of life there is this hollow, this nothingness, which the cry must fill. It summons men to murder – victims and executioners being bound together as usual. It is death and life: in the beginning is the word. But the victim has his own cry. Céline cites two examples: the 'hiccup' of the hanging man and the first yell of new-born babies, whose 'little mugs' are 'strangled already'. In this second sense the cry is man's reaction to existence, his sense of belonging to something greater than himself. It is an act, perhaps the only act of which he is capable. Nothing could be further removed from ordinary language, which is a skein spread across existence in order to hide it. The cry is a Dionysian outburst, an expression of mystical oneness with the horrible universe. It is pre-rational: 'at a certain point of their misery people don't care a rap about understanding,' says Céline, 'they just feel'. The 'woufs' that Ferdinand lets out in prison are an example of this primeval feeling. At the other end of the scale the dancer's 'signs' also convey something of the cry because they unveil the spirit universe.

As it comes from the depths the cry allows men to discover what they really are. The normal personality is a mask that slips under persecution: 'all you are is a bundle of remorse swelling up ... swelling up! Remorse for whom ... for what?' Men become themselves when they express their suffering: fear, guilt and hatred, the fundamental emotions, are blended in the cry. But it also contains defiance. Céline cites Roland. By sounding the horn, Roland affirmed to Franks and Moors that he was not dead. Ferdinand's monologue is proof that he is not a submissive prisoner but the only patriotic Frenchman.

In this sense the cry represents individual existence itself. But man is not the only creature who cries out: the entire universe joins in. Bébert makes his 'brrts', the cavalry charge at Longchamps brings a 'lament from the ground'. Céline speaks of 'historic sounds' that have vanished, like the blacksmith striking the anvil. All these cries echo the groans of despair that are heard each night in the prison, and the rumours of hatred that circulate at Montmartre. Ferdinand acts as 'orchestra conductor'. His art consists in transmitting the universal murmur of pain; his stylistic innovations are designed to help him do this. But he is recreating rather than creating. The universe is a giant monologue and hence a work of art. Its creator is something Céline calls 'Time'.

This has little to do with ordinary chronology. Céline has, as usual, no concept of the future. *Féerie* is a backward glance at the war and it ends with the Danish prison and no prospect of release. The past is used in a more complex way. Céline does not see history as a chain of events, leading in some order to the present. The past is the same as the present and history no more than repetition. *Féerie* is full of allusions which portray past events as a series of variations of the executioner–victim motif. Without regard for ideology Céline sees himself as the descendant of Vercingetorix, André Chénier, Blanqui, Oscar Wilde, Jaurès and Sacco. The Liberation massacres repeat the bloodletting of the Revolution and of Saint Bartholomew's Night. In this sense there is no past and hence no movement of time at all. The Célinian universe is eternally static.

But that is objective time, the kind that a detached observer – were such a person possible – would perceive. The narrator does feel the weight of the past on his consciousness. It is inextricably enmeshed with the present. Sometimes it expresses itself as guilt: Ferdinand regrets that he did not help Janine and harks back to London. Often it is a sense of failure like the Rueil experiment which convinces Ferdinand that he will only be unlucky in his medical career. Whatever it is, the past lives on as memory and memory is as real as the present. In his prison Ferdinand relives the pre-1914 parades at Longchamps as well as turn-of-the-century Brittany with its fashionable resorts, parasols and casinos. The monologue of *Féerie* takes place in an eternal present. Later the whole action of *Normance* lasts a few hours but the entire 1939 war is contained within them. This kind of time is best described as a prolonged 'death agony' where everything is dying but cannot quite come to rest. France itself has been declining since Verdun. Clémence Arlon is growing old and is 'almost dead already'. The key word is 'almost', for this state goes on and on. One recalls Beckett's phrase about 'the last but one but one'. 'This time, then once more,' says Molloy, 'I think then, perhaps a last time, then I think it'll be over.'[6] Céline describes women in a similar state of permanent decline: 'they decay like wax, they go bad, melt'. The narrator's hallucinated mind penetrates the death agony. 'In circumstances of real tragedy you see things straightaway ... past, present, future together,' says Céline.

'I televise,' he adds, 'I see into my walls! the future, the past'. The Danish prison becomes the whole planet and Ferdinand roams across it, wandering through space and time. As always in Céline he finds that the world is not made in man's image. He finds that there are forces greater than he. Everything he sees is one fragment of a vast pattern, of the 'Web of Time'.

This sort of time operates behind the eternal present. Frequently it is described with scientific vocabulary. Céline speaks of the 'great jumble sale of universes, supersteinian curves'. He shows by the pun that he knows of the discoveries made about space and time by twentieth-century mathematics. They may, he feels, have something in common with his own notion. Both replace the neat box-like universe of the nineteenth century with a more dynamic concept of matter. Part of the language-game of *Féerie* revolves around scientific terminology and neologisms like '*pathologiste comparatiste*' and '*cosmomédiumnique*' – which sounds like a piece of astronomy jargon, but in fact expresses Céline's view of the writer as visionary. As in *Guignol's Band* he is fascinated by radio, television and photography because they seem to go beyond solid matter. His Ghosts use them: 'Everything is photographed by waves,' he says of the trial. The crimes of the French nation will be revealed as if by camera and their currents of hatred traced as if they were currents of light. 'I pick up the "wavelength" of death agony,' Céline says elsewhere, comparing his perception of the universe with a radio picking up signals.

Time moves through the universe creating and destroying, as planets are shaped and broken by the flux of matter. It can by-pass ordinary reality as easily as television ignores distance. To describe the order Time imposes Céline has recourse to another kind of vocabulary. 'Time's embroidery is music,' he says, implying that the patterns of the universe unfold like rhythms in a symphony. He talks of the 'lace of time', making an analogy with the intricate knots of his mother's work. The universe is a work of art and its structure is that of a dance – or a novel. But there is another element. 'Time's embroidery' is made up of 'blood, music and lace'. The cries were after all cries of pain.

To the ordinary observer, Time's results seem arbitrary. When the English schoolgirls arrive on the Brittany beach they come from nowhere. Until now they have been 'held back somewhere by Time'. Only the narrator knows that they are an integral part of the Brittany dream, their young femininity blending with the charm of the sea to make up a moment of beauty. But such beauty is inseparable from destruction. The blood in the weave emerges as wars which erupt – apparently at any time – to destroy fragile humans. In fact they themselves help unleash them by their hatreds, as the French do by their betrayal of Ferdinand: 'I didn't want to set the forces free, certain . . . forces . . . but you prancing with rage, howling, smashing, you are beyond everything . . . you go outside of Time! . . . break the Web.' As a result they will be annihilated in war. Men who think they live in a solid universe find that their world is a shadow cast by Time. In itself it has no significance: 'Life is filigree work,' says Céline. 'What is written clearly is not worth much, it's the transparency that counts.' The Montmartre flat, the Brittany sea-coast and the Danish prison are temporary realities, which follow one another as Time demands.

The figure who can move inside the dangerous web is the dancer. Described repeatedly as an acrobat – one remembers that Prospero Jim was a tightrope walker – she alone can unveil the universe without smashing it. This is why Lili plays such a crucial role in *Féerie*. There are also many references to music and an attempt to insert melodies into the text. Like Nietzsche, Céline feels that the tragedy he is depicting emerges from a great Dionysian ritual of music and dance. Yet if these are the highest forms of art, they are not – except in one significant sense – different from the others. Céline regards all his own writing as music. Jules plays the bugle and sculpts and he is successful at both. The dancer belongs to a superior order of art, but she is not alien to the writer.

One may begin the discussion of dance by examining the images of soft and hard, static and dynamic, which run through *Féerie* and *Normance*. The soft is abhorrent to Céline. Normance's body is like 'five . . . six eiderdowns'. Why is this so dreadful? The soft has neither shape nor form; it is the antithesis of the sharp lines of the sailing-boat, hence it is ugly. But there is more. If Normance is five eiderdowns then he has no one single identity. This absence of identity is seen in moral terms: the moral consciousness is precisely what makes the difference between man and the universe. Without it man is no longer man. He is like the crowd which sits 'pressed against one another, glued together'. The crowd is cowardly and, while the bombs rain down, it continues to sit like an inanimate object. Ferdinand, beaten to a pulp by Sartre and the others, is 'manure' for the 'leeks'. In an outburst of 'market-garden madness' he is joined with the disgusting earth. Such a death is his worst nightmare and it is to be contrasted with the death of the old lady in *Les Beaux Draps*. Linked to softness is immobility. When Ferdinand is in prison he complains that he has to sit 'with my stool stuck to my ass'. The verb 'to stick' is a key one because it denotes that man belongs to the decaying material world. Céline has a physical revulsion against being stuck and he cannot find language crude enough to express his disgust.[7] By contrast hardness is the mark of integrity: of separation from the universe and of moral freedom. Ferdinand is a 'muscle fetichist', who enjoys the strength of Lili's thighs. By practising hard she has overcome weight and freed herself from her body. But there is another step. Hardness is linked with mobility: the dancer, like the sailing-ship, can move as she pleases. Movement has fascinated Céline ever since he described the whirl of broken crockery in *Mort à crédit*. In *Normance* he watches the furniture fly through the air: 'the chest of drawers waltzed', he says. In doing so it loses its weight and also its function. It goes through the opposite evolution from the crowd. The greater entity of which it becomes a part is not the material decay but the dance that redeems.

Ballet is movement set to music. Like Nietzsche, Céline sees music as the ultimate reality. Nietzsche calls it 'Will' and Céline 'Time'. Nietzsche has a sense of the 'innocence of being' which is quite different from Céline's vision of evil. Yet both feel that music expresses the secrets of the universe.[8] When Ferdinand is in prison his jailers keep him quiet: 'They don't want me to sing,' he says. If he sang, he would escape from his cell into the higher world. The street ballads, scattered through *Féerie*, portray a legend where the sad accoutrements of normality – rationalism, function, prose and pretence – are left behind.

This is the key to Céline's view of music and dance: they are based on loss of self. As his prime interest is neither intellectual nor technical he enjoys all kinds of music. His taste is not highbrow. He is not a lover of classical ballet rather than modern, nor the reverse. It is not even essential to know which dances he likes and why. Despite the long years he lived with ballerinas he does not study methods of choreography. He wants to be emotionally moved. It is not a matter of feeling sorrow or joy, but of being carried off to the sources of sorrow and joy. The parallel with the sexual experience is clear. In his love-making with Sophie, Bardamu has moments that he calls 'erotico-mystical' and Ferdinand goes into a similar entrancement when he contemplates the dancer. Her weightlessness lifts him off the earth. Meanwhile she has been transformed into a 'sylph'. She is 'sinewy', her body is 'way beyond flesh' and she is as free as a 'song bird'. She has conquered her physical nature and sublimated her sexuality. Céline speaks of the 'purity' of ballet and the ballerina, unlike other women, is neither harlot nor murderess. She is solely an artist. There is no question of knowing the dancer from the dance or even of knowing her from the onlooker. Both are caught up in the ecstasy. In dance, man is, to borrow another of Nietzsche's phrases, 'at one and the same time poet, actor and spectator'.[9]

The process of loss and recovery of self is the same as the destruction–creation cycle of Time. Since the universe is a piece of lace-work or a symphony, the artist constructs his forms as part of a greater creation. Ferdinand describes this: 'I do what I like here, I hear everything over again ... I make tropical hurricanes ... I create the charges of the grand manoeuvres.' The memories of his past life are woven into the flux of Time. He reaches out from his prison cell and turns them into a new reality. In discussing the dancer, Céline puts it the other way around. She is transparent: to be 'opaque' is a great crime – and the 'waves' of Time pass through her gestures and reveal themselves to the spectator. In both cases the artist submits to and imposes herself on the universe. Lili's dance is one form of Time's.

Everything about her is associated with her art. When the Danish police interrogate her they cannot break her, for she is 'heroic'. In the midst of the *Normance* bombing she goes up on the rooftops – 'she faced the cyclones', says the admiring Ferdinand. She needs her courage because she is made to suffer. Such suffering is a fundamental theme of Céline's work and in his post-war novels he is more convinced than ever that the artist must pay for his triumphs. The real reason he hates Sartre is that Sartre has not suffered during the war. In *À l'agité du bocal* he claims that Sartre can have no talent because he has not been in prison. 'Look at Shakespeare, schoolboy, three-quarters flute, one quarter blood,' says Céline.[10] Sartre cannot possibly

Céline

be an artist. A philosopher perhaps, but not a writer and certainly not a
musician. 'The Muses are not content with "other people's Blood",'
says Céline, who remembers that Sartre is calling for his head while
sitting comfortably on Saint-Germain-des-Prés. By contrast Lili accompanies Ferdinand on his calvary and is sent to prison in Denmark. To be
deprived of mobility is the dancer's greatest trial and yet she endures it.

Lili is 'reason itself'. When the Danish police interrogate her they
cannot catch her out for she possesses truth. The use of the term 'reason'
is paradoxical because 'she does not think'. As she is a 'sylph' she has
an intuitive understanding of the spirit world. She communicates it
through her movements, which are a living reproach to the writer
because they demonstrate to him the inadequacy of his instrument –
language. When she visits Ferdinand in prison she is not allowed to
speak French; but 'fortunately Lili has signs'. They express in ritual
form what the writer struggles to say with words. 'Just the hands! The
fingers, a gesture . . . The flower of being', sighs Céline.

The dancer is the writer's model; but the only way she is different
from him is that she is absolved from evil. Alone in Céline's world she
is not tainted with original sin. How can this be? How can she participate in the creative forces without becoming involved with destruction?
Can such an artist be a real human being? In fact Lili is a perfect but
incomplete figure. As a character she is ethereal and strangely boring.
Since she has transcended her womanhood there is not much solid
substance left. Whether present or absent she is Ferdinand's companion, seen in connection with him. In the all-important seduction
scene she has no will of her own. She is a prize Ferdinand and Jules
fight over, rather than a separate individual.[11] But then Lili is best seen
as one of the several figures that personify Céline's vision of the artist.

That he should divide the artist's role among different characters is
not surprising. He had already done something similar in *Guignol's
Band* and before that in *Mort*. Here he has taken the process further.
He has abolished the separation between narrator and actor: there are
no old and young Ferdinands. The man who suffers in prison is the
man who tells the tale. This is natural enough: artistic creation has
now become the source of all human activity. But this seeming simpli-
fication masks another kind of identity-splitting. Various figures are
used to portray the artist. In *Féerie*, Ferdinand seems to stand alone;
in fact he speaks with several voices. From the moment Jules enters

there are three figures: Lili, who personifies the artist's triumph, Jules, who is his guilt, and Ferdinand who bears his pain. All three are related: Lili is Ferdinand's wife, Jules is his 'brother' – another 1914 hero. They are also opposites: Jules is ugly, Lili beautiful. Jules, who lives in a dark basement, is jealous of Ferdinand's lofty apartment. Each is attached to the others: Lili pities Jules and even Ferdinand feels sympathy for him – 'just as he is I like him'. All three know they have much in common.

At the outset Ferdinand sits in his cell. He has at least two identities. There is Dr Destouches, the exiled prisoner who is in constant suffering and who faces years in jail. There is the 'ghost' Céline, who is set free by the presence of death.* He is the one who rages against Hortensia, the French ambassador. He is – like his predecessors – near to madness: 'my buzzings are too strong! . . . I'm going dizzy'. Neither the Danes nor the French can harm him for he lives far away in the depths of the night. His writing is an act of vengeance. He will pillory his enemies and fix their names 'in golden letters' on the walls of the Sainte-Chapelle.

This Ferdinand is the friend of the spirits. They guide his steps: 'I, I who am talking to you, I heard "knockings" . . . the next day I'm arrested.' He wins their favour by his willingness to face death. In a frenzied hallucination he describes his murder, seeing it as the symbolic death of France and the French language, piling up the horror. This enables him to turn the tables on his compatriots who have persecuted him without risking their necks. In a spirit trial the Ghosts condemn them to a dance of fire – hellish farandolas and tarantellas. Dr Destouches can be defeated by the Resistance, Céline cannot.

He, not Sosthène, is the true magician. *Féerie* abounds with spells and wizards. Jules has a 'marvellous power of enchantment' and as for Bébert, he is 'sorcery itself'. But Ferdinand is the man who can transform reality with his imagination. He weaves his fantasies: 'I can always laugh by myself . . . all I need is to be left in peace, straightaway a story comes into my head . . . and I split my sides.' His demonic powers run rampant in the Brittany episode. The Saint-Malo of 1900

---

* Dr Destouches is innocent, Céline is guilty. He is guilty because the Resistance has marked him down for execution, which is one way of saying that he personifies death. The real-life Dr Destouches refused to accept any guilt. Here again the novelist probes more deeply than the man.

is doubly dead: lost in the past and destroyed by bombs. Everything has been 'smashed, sent up to the clouds in flames'. Ferdinand re-creates it, presenting it as the eternal Brittany that emerges from the sea as if from Time, a Brittany made out of language. The main theme of these pages is magic itself: Brittany is Merlin's kingdom, the Celtic stronghold. 'No one can escape the enchantment of the emerald bay,' says Céline. Here are the forces of the spirit world: the sea, always in motion, always dangerous; the rose, symbol of beauty – 'from the cradle to the De Profundis the rose is your link with the Heavens'; the leggy English girls and their promise of femininity. Even the satire – the insistence of the fleas swarming over the beaches – adds an element of fantasy. This is an absurd, frightening, beautiful realm.

Céline is asserting Ferdinand's power to intervene with the forces of Time, to create his own reality. This is what he, the author, is doing with *Féerie*. He describes its impact. The Stock Exchange collapses and crowds throng the streets, laughing and singing. Céline is a hero – 'Glory and millions to Ferdinand' – and a new town 'Céline-grad' is founded. *Féerie*, 'the book that rejuvenates your soul', has turned drab post-war Paris into a world of comedy and dance. It remains now to consider how Jules can have turned Montmartre into a conflagration.

During the seduction scene Ferdinand's role changes. He is the long-ruffering Dr Destouches, wrongly persecuted by his neighbours, rather than the creature of the night, Céline. That part is taken over by Jules. He too is an artist – sculptor, painter and musician. He is the antithesis of Lili: she dances on high while he squats, a cripple, in his basement. She moves through the air while he works with earth. She creates precise patterns while his studio is a 'lumber-room'. Jules's art has a random quality. He turns out seascapes, infantas and un-baked clay statues, as the whim takes him. He rushes around the Butte strapped into a box on wheels and he is 'unpredictable'. He has the force of chaos.

He is also the personification of 'Evil'. He hates Ferdinand who is not crippled and whom he regards – in an interesting reversal of roles – as 'spoilt'. But then he dislikes everyone, even the girls who pose for him and the people who buy his work. He is 'full of poison', an exaggerated version of the usual Célinian character. Death hovers around him. He prefers women who are ill like Sarcelle, who has tuberculosis. In the dim light of his basement visitors appear 'neither dead nor alive'. Not surprisingly his art reflects his evil nature. He obtains his clay from one special crevice in Montmartre and bakes it in the oven – two more images of hell. He is the 'Spoiler of the graces' who persuades Lili's pupils not to practise their dances, but to come and pose for him in his basement.

If his creations are ugly they are still art. Céline goes deeper into the artistic process when he describes Jules. Jules keeps looking at himself: 'his little mirror . . . he would look at himself a hundred times a day'. The mirror does not reflect his ordinary appearance, much less his ordinary personality. He is engaged in a self-transformation – 'the true artist creates himself,' says Céline. A man's normal character does not matter much, since it is a fragile thing of pretence. The artist looking into himself changes and projects his personality. This is why he is his own work of art. Jules illustrates the process graphically: he smears his colours all over himself. 'I am a paintbox,' he cries. What he is really doing is realizing his chaotic nature. The notion of self-creation, which entails facing the demonic forces in oneself, helps explain both Céline's aesthetic and the relationship between man and novelist. The doctor gives free rein to the visionary writer, just as the weak cripple Jules becomes a god-like 'Creator'. Looking into his mirror Jules sees himself in different ways: 'I see myself huge! . . . then tiny! like a pea I see myself.' He projects these various selves, as the writer Céline projects the various Ferdinands of his novels as well as the Robinsons and the Juleses. Small wonder that Céline is fascinated by actors whose art consists quite literally in turning themselves into other people.* Once self-creation has been accomplished, the process of imposing one's vision on the world is easy. Time is, after all, working in the same way as the artist.† Jules turns Paris into

* It is here that the artist's creative process becomes a theme in Céline's writing. Jules, the weak cripple, corresponds to the harassed Dr Destouches. In his creative moments Jules looks deep within himself. This process is described later, through the character of Norbert, as a search into nothingness. Out of this metaphysical nothingness—this death, as Céline calls it when he describes his methods of work— comes a new existence, just as the cry comes out of the nothingness of the Echo's Hollow. This destruction and rebirth has all kinds of parallels in mystical experience, not to mention the central mystery of the Resurrection. Out of the calvary of creation comes the triumph of art.

† One could re-state this in another way: the artist is the universe and the outside world is no more than his vision. But throughout this chapter the duality

one of his non-naturalistic paintings. The bombing is described in terms of colour: Jules 'was daubing the sky blue, green, yellow'. He can remould Montmartre with his clay, but first he must seduce Lili.

The seduction is seen in aesthetic terms. There is a political element, for Jules called Ferdinand a 'Boche' and turns the crowd against him. There is a sexual motif too. Jules makes Lili undress and he caresses her. But the sexual act is not completed because Jules' real aim is to capture the dancer, not the woman; here again woman's beauty is a prelude to art.* He makes Lili immobile, first by thrusting his head between her legs and then by persuading her to pose on the couch. He draws her into his vision of the world when he makes her look 'greenish', the colour of death. She has become ugly. But Ferdinand admits that an artistic transformation has taken place – 'there was something aesthetic about it'. Ferdinand is aware too that he is an accomplice to the seduction. He could have tried harder to save Lili. But he has a little of Jules in him and he knows that destruction and chaos are part of art. He takes the painting Jules offers him – thus submitting to Jules' vision – and leaves.

'From that moment on,' says Ferdinand, 'the horrors began.' The seduction is a kind of original sin. Lili, the embodiment of perfection, has fallen victim to Jules. Now his vicious imagination can run unchecked and his reality is substituted for all others. Ferdinand staggers off and the bombs start to fall.

By contrast with *Féerie*, *Normance* is strangely calm. Ferdinand is beaten and insulted but he no longer pours out his resentment. He is the Ferdinand of the Jules episode, who submits bewildered to the chaos, does what he can as a doctor and has occasional moments of hallucinated insight. The frenzied emotions of the first volume have been personified as the Allied bombers. Fear is rampant, but it takes second place to the portrayal of the evil and beauty that make up the

---

has been preserved: artist/Time; Ferdinand's cry/the universal lament; Jules/bombers. This has been done to convey Céline's unfailing sense that there is something in life – whether inside or outside of man – that humans absolutely cannot cope with. This 'otherness' is present in Robinson's death as in Jules' transient triumph.

* Viewed simply in sexual terms this is a piece of voyeurism.

bombing. Ferdinand knows that it scarcely matters what he feels. He can only observe the forces Jules has let loose.

The main characters are titanic figures who do battle together but have much in common. Jules is the demon who orchestrates the bombing. Ottavio, 'the opposite of Jules', is the defender of Montmartre. Mimi is the false dancer with something of Lili's grace but full of malice. Norbert is the actor who creates a realm of calm but then tries to seduce Lili. A struggle goes on between the forces of darkness and of light with Ferdinand, the striving pilgrim, caught in between. But all the characters share a magical power for they are artists constructing their reality. Whether it is good or evil, it is fragile. Jules dominates until he is overthrown by Mimi. Ottavio returns to establish order before he is enmeshed by Norbert. Norbert's realm soon collapses and the bombing begins again. No human, however demonic, can be more than Time's instrument, to be used and discarded. Meanwhile Normance, the character who lacks all magic, is beaten to death. Brutal and cowardly, he represents humanity at its worst, the French nation that has betrayed Céline.

Although the book has some plot its real structure comes from dance. Behind the chaos of the bombing is a series of movements, which seem random but which are variations on a pattern. Ferdinand's wanderings make up a circle. He begins and ends in the same place and in the same state of hallucination. 'This is the exact spot where I was so ill,' he notes in the final pages. In the meantime he has explored and exhausted his circle. He has gone up and down stairs twice, travelling from the sky in flames to the pit in the apartment floor. During this odyssey he has made a number of stops in search of refuge: in his flat, in the doorway, in the pool of blood and in Norbert's dining-room. Each time he is driven out and made to wander on.

Around him everything is in motion: 'the pieces of furniture bump into one another, get entangled, pursue one another around', people collide, Montmartre is turned upside down. Céline stresses that this movement has its own order. The 'surface is doing a polka', he says, and the chest of drawers 'has been waltzing'. The landing outside his flat is a 'landing – dance hall'. As in music there are leitmotifs: Delphine's 'Don't move, André', is one, the cry of 'thirst' another, the *broums* of the explosions a third. Many of the movements have ritual value. Jules' ascent of the mill marks the beginning of his reign.

Mimi's ascent its end. When *Normance* is thrown down the pit, it is in a funeral procession which celebrates the end of chaos and the start of Ottavio's rule. Parallels abound between one kind of movement and another. Ferdinand's manuscripts fly through the air like Armelle de Zeusse's tarot cards. Ottavio carries Ferdinand upstairs at the start and downstairs at the end. In the book as a whole, movement is circular: the planes arrive at the beginning, leave and return in the final pages. There is no sense that any of the movement leads anywhere, but it is internally consistent and hence harmonious.

The book's style marks at least one important difference from that of *Féerie*. There is less rhetoric: fewer personifications and full stops. The narration moves even more quickly because its theme is movement itself. One example will show this: 'the atmosphere vibrates like something solid . . . you feel it . . . it shakes you around, hiccups your whole body . . . charge after charge! Go on lads! no quarter! *bromb*! *rebroum*! *brang*!' The phrases dissolve into individual words and then onomatopoeic expressions. They simply mirror the succession of explosions. The confusion and omission of personal pronouns reveal that there is no detached onlooker and that the individual is only a part of the greater chaos. As in *Féerie* Céline uses sounds – Normance speaks in 'hous' and 'Yrôâs' – to show that language is breaking up, just like Montmartre. But his innovation in *Normance* is to simplify his sentences until the usual burden of language – story and description – almost disappears and all that remains is the rhythm of the dance.

The aesthetic order emerges as a theme in its own right and stands in contrast to the moral, political and physical chaos. In *Normance* the solid universe has been blown apart. Jules rips a hole in the sky with his cane and a chasm appears in the ground. The Butte is a 'crater' and the furniture on the avenue Gaveneau 'flies up into the trails of the aeroplanes'. It is a question of 'God upside down'. But Céline notes that 'even the upside-down explanation does not work, now there are only physical, mathematical and moral surprises'. The universe is constantly changing its shape and Ferdinand is terrified that the ground will open up before his feet and plunge him into an abyss. Time has vanished too. It is neither day nor night and the only light comes from the flames.

Objects are transformed. Sometimes they change roles with men. The 'pieces of furniture become people waddling around', while the crowd is 'no longer people but things'. In the flux of the universe places and men are interchangeable: Montmartre is another Vesuvius, Céline another Pliny. Things lose their function so that the bottles in Armelle de Zeusse's flat are a 'torrential avalanche' and the furniture on the stairs is a 'dance palace'. The planes in the sky become all kinds of creatures, anything except cold machines. They are 'butterflies', 'bats' and trains that go through tunnels. Sometimes they are demons from a fairytale. One of them is 'a giant monoplane stuffed, racked with engines', while others are 'winged monsters'. There is a freedom of invention here which reminds us that Paris is being remoulded by the sculptor Jules.[12] Céline exhausts his vocabulary to find names for the new forms and finally he gives up: 'they don't have names any more,' he says of the planes, 'I'll make them up.'

Meanwhile the people disintegrate. Ferdinand describes their physical break-up: 'you are pulled apart! neck! head! shoulders! feet!' This is a symbol of the break-up of character. People lose their old roles or find strange new ones. Armelle de Zeusse is not in her flat and no one knows where she is. Is she still alive? Elise Nanton does nothing but go around screaming, 'I am a Haitian'. And who is the mysterious 'Eugène's wife', who talks a great deal and whom no one knows? She is a woman without identity created by the bombing and dependent on it for whatever little being she possesses. Other people change drastically under the stress of fear: 'your conscience does a bunk! you turn into someone quite different,' says Ferdinand. Normance grows violent, the crowd gets drunk. Not surprisingly judgements are hard to make and categories confused. Political views offer no guide to what people are like. The Resistance leader Murbate is a blackmarketeer, Crémoïlle, owner of the night-club that caters to the Nazis, is a Jew.

Raymond Depastre and Lutry show what happens when all roles are abandoned. Terrified by the explosions, Raymond forgets who he is: 'he calls himself underneath me ... he is underneath me ... he looks for himself! "Raymond! Raymond! A drink! a drink!" He doesn't know he is himself any more.' The only thing he can do is to cry out. As in *Féerie*, the cry is man's response to death so the whole of Montmartre dissolves into an immense lament: 'the depths of the earth implore,' says Ferdinand. But the cry does not give Raymond an individual existence and Céline, using a familiar expression, describes him as an 'absence'. When his wife devours their marriage certificate, he does not even know whether he is her husband or not. By contrast Lutry is an astronomer who cares nothing for the earth and is delighted with the new, open universe. By a 'pure miracle' he is carried up into the sky. He has lost his old existence and is enjoying a 'celestial experience'. Ferdinand is envious because Lutry has a new identity within the ruptured heavens: he is enjoying the beauty that the bombing has created.

Beauty exists in abundance and Céline announces it in musical and pictorial terms. The nightingale sings, the flames are coloured 'blue . . . orange . . . green', while the searchlights and tracer-bullets form patterns in the sky. He does not forget another of his favourite images, for he tells us that 'the whole horizon is made out of lace'. The incessant transformation of the universe is the mark of artistic creation. But – and this is the lesson of *Mort à crédit* – death is close at hand. The bombs that fall in wondrous shapes look like 'Christmas trees' but they bring 'annihilation pure and simple'. 'Such waves of beauty shake the universe,' says Céline.

One by one the various artist figures impose their version of reality. The most important is Jules who struts on his platform, waving in the bombers. He is a Christ figure in reverse, perpetually thirsty, capable only of 'evil and catastrophe'. At the foot of the ladder people pray to him or for him. He is a magician and his cane a magic wand; but here again sorcery is a metaphor for art. Jules is the 'conductor of the orchestra' who harmonizes the bombing, he is the dancer who balances on high, the painter playing with colour. With a gesture he makes buildings disappear, for Montmartre has become as unpredictable as he. Like God he is creating in his own image.

But Jules is not God. The precise relationship between his gestures and the bombers is not clear. 'It's Jules who is responsible for everything,' says Ferdinand. But the bombers disobey him sometimes. They fly off to the west of Paris to bomb Billancourt. It is a delicate matter to control the spirit forces and even the most agile acrobat cannot hold his balance among them for long. Soon Jules is dethroned, although the bombing goes on. He came to power by conquering one dancer and he is defeated by another. In a display of woman's sexual power, Mimi undresses him and puts her own clothes on him: 'he isn't the little master any more! Mimi, stark naked, takes him in hand. Jules is nothing any longer!' Soon afterwards he comes down from the platform. He is a cripple once again, not a demon.

Mimi personifies woman's spiteful nature. First she fights with her man Rodolphe in a display of hatred that parallels the bombing: 'it's the battle! not in the air any more, the battle no ... under the arch'. Then she climbs the ladder and seduces Jules, using the drug vulnerary as a magic potion. She can now take over the orchestration of the planes. Mimi is a dancer: 'she is so supple, old Mimi! incredibly lithe, old Mimi'. She is also an actress who has been rehearsing a scene with Rodolphe. Later her reign on the platform is described as another rehearsal. She and Jules are practising for an act in Crémoïlle's nightclub, which is called, appropriately enough, the 'Relais des Anges'. Céline is indulging his love of mixing up reality and artifice: the nightclub joins the fairground and the circus as symbols of the aesthetic universe. Like Jules, Mimi belongs to the lower order of artists. She tries to sing but both she and he sing badly, for they are not true musicians. As a dancer Mimi stands far below Lili since she has not transcended her evil nature. She flaunts her sexuality by parading nude on the platform and by abusing men. Naturally her art is destructive.

Her overthrow coincides with Ottavio's return. 'There wouldn't have been any scandal at all if Ottavio had been there,' says Ferdinand. Ottavio would have pulled Jules down from the platform and stopped the bombing. He is Montmartre's defender, who sounds a hand-siren from the top of the Sacré-Coeur. Céline describes him as 'a tiger ... full of sinewy strength'. This is the kind of language used to describe Lili, for Ottavio is in a way a dancer. He controls his body and moves triumphantly among material things and people. He is illiterate because in Céline's world intelligence has small value, but he has something of Lili's intuitive knowledge. He knows, for example, that Ferdinand is not evil and that the crowd is vicious. He has left behind hatred and fear and when he returns from his siren he quickly quells the disorder. He dispatches Normance to hell and quietens the crowd. Like a priest, he calls on the people to make their confession. 'If you don't ask for pardon, there! at once! ... on your knees! I'll chuck you all down the hole,' he thunders. He is repeating the *mea culpa* demand of *Féerie*: the French must accept their guilt and beg forgiveness. But Ottavio does not understand what evil is. He is not demonic enough to cope with the magic around him. When he meets Norbert he goes 'crazy' and falls under his spell. 'This bewitching Norbert would ruin you,' says Ferdinand, who has to drag Ottavio away. Left to himself, Ottavio would wait in Norbert's dining-room until the bombs come raining down again. At the end of the book, as at the start, he goes off to his siren. But he can do little to stop the destruction.

As Ottavio succeeds Mimi and Jules, Normance, who understands nothing of what is happening, submits to the magic. Normance is Ottavio's opposite and the most 'opaque' of men. By contrast with Ottavio's 'real strength' he is a 'heap of flesh', useful only 'as a mass'. Whereas Ottavio mastered his body, Normance is soft and immobile. An entirely physical creature, he weighs twenty-one stone and used to work as a porter in Les Halles. His role is to show what happens to ordinary dull humanity when the spirits are at play.

His refusal to try and understand the bombing is seen in moral terms. Ferdinand watches what is happening through the shattered windows; but Normance huddles in a corner and falls asleep. 'Isn't it cynical to snore like that?' asks Ferdinand. 'He has lost all moral sense,' he adds. Normance is simply an animal – a 'popototam' – or a piece of furniture. He can do nothing but oscillate between fear and hatred. Twice he assaults Ferdinand, hoping obscurely to save his wife or stop the bombs by attacking an innocent man. He is himself mistreated by the crowd, which uses him as a thing to break down the door and cross the crevice. Nothing is achieved by this cruelty, which is simply the crowd's own reaction to the bombing. Normance's head is smashed – it is 'a clot of blood . . . you can't see his eyes any more . . . his mouth is a hole' – and he is blinded. Both are recurrent and ambivalent motifs in Céline's work. Ferdinand lives in constant fear that his head will be crushed, but it is not. The smashing of Normance's head represents the break-up of the material universe. Ferdinand's head, which contains the absurd, magical universe, has already been damaged, but it cannot be destroyed. For Normance, blinding is the culmination of his refusal to understand. For Ferdinand's mother, whose eyes are weakened by working at her lace, it is the sign of greater knowledge, as it was for Robinson. Both themes show the fundamental difference between those who can 'transpose' and those who cannot. Normance is sinful humanity, whom Céline despises and pities. All that remains is for Ottavio to thrust him down the abyss.

Far removed from the confusion stands Norbert, last of the artists.

When Ottavio rescues him from the crowd Ferdinand is dazed. On recovering he finds himself looking into Norbert's dining-room: 'a big clean room . . . nothing smashed'. Norbert is standing in evening-dress amidst elegant furniture before a well-laid table. He has created a realm of calm where the bombing cannot – so it seems – penetrate.

The way he does it provides another example of what art is about. He is compared with Jules: 'he is thinking! creation? . . . creation? what? like the other one up there'. Both are manipulating events, both are engaged in self-creation. Norbert has a mirror and he stands before it: 'he was looking for himself! . . . he was finding himself again! he came and went in himself . . . he built himself . . . rebuilt'. As an actor Norbert is nothing without a part. He searches in his nothingness to find a personality he can become. This process goes on outside of space, for Norbert is not in his own home, and of time for Ottavio has seen him the week before 'in exactly the same pose, motionless'. His particular speciality is to become the personification of silence, to turn nothingness to good account. This is how he made his reputation as an actor. In his films everybody spoke except him; but he dominated the screen. As the 'King of Silence' he is a demonic figure who, like the dancer, has transcended language. In the novel Norbert 'is dreaming' and imposing his dream on Montmartre. He builds 'another world', where Paris is turned into one of his films.

As soon as he speaks he breaks the spell – yet another comment on language. His realm is revealed as a silly fantasy: he is expecting Churchill, Roosevelt and the Pope to arrive for a peace conference. When his reality falls apart he behaves like a classic Célinian maniac – shouting and denouncing Ferdinand. He wants to seduce Lili, so that he can use her magic power to restore his harmony. But he is left alone and impotent, a mere human again, as the bombing restarts. Like Jules he learns that he cannot control Time's patterns. For a moment he is allowed to weave his web and then it is shattered. Indeed the eerie world he creates – as seen by Ferdinand – is quite different from the fantasy he describes. It is an extension, not a transformation, of the horror. There are corpses in the background, quiet corpses, one floating in water, but none disfigured. Danger is present, for Norbert will keep Ferdinand there until it is too late to escape. What he has really done is create a new vision of death. In the Célinian universe nothing is constant: oases of calm are thrown up by chaos, terror gives way to tranquillity and nightmare succeeds dream. Norbert's siren silence is born out of the bombing; it is another of Time's many realities.

Meanwhile there is Ferdinand, who himself speaks with many voices. An established novelist he attacks translations, a child of the Passage he grumbles about black-market butter. He wants to show there is no set subject matter and no set way of looking at it. He doubts the truth of what he is describing: 'Perhaps I only thought I saw Jules.' Is Jules really leading in the bombers? Lili does not think so, Ferdinand is not sure. What level of reality is he perceiving? He says he is 'first and foremost an observer of things.' But he repeats, 'I am hallucinated.' Céline portrays his narrator's mind as a constant flux. Ferdinand forgets to mention Crémoïlle and launches into self-criticism: 'What's the matter with me? A fine thing for me to set myself up as a chronicler! ... I forget whole characters.' His book is the Paris that is being bombed. As in *Féerie* Céline insists that the act of writing and the creation of the universe are one and the same thing. He compares Ferdinand's head with the world outside. 'I feel my head as big as the arch,' says Ferdinand, 'I am like the house when it sways.' At the end of the book the pages of his manuscript are hurled over Montmartre to mingle with the returning bombers. In this sense the narrator is quite different from the struggling doctor and closer to Céline, the ghost of *Féerie*. His is the creation that embraces Lili, Jules and Norbert. He is at one with the 'Web of Time' and he is the most demonic of Céline's fictional selves.

The abundance of creative power makes the book really exciting. Facing up to the worst in himself, depicting the artist's destructive and constructive genius, Céline has written a novel which makes *Guignol's Band* seem tame.* *Féerie* and *Normance* have weaknesses which explain why they have never been considered among his best works. They are too long. The rhetoric of the first and the descriptions of the second tend to be repetitive. But there is a wealth of imagination present. Their bold conceptions – the imprisoned giant who will not be silenced, the seduced dancer as the cause of war – are staggering. The characters, especially Jules, have great vitality and scenes like the Ghosts' trial and Norbert's drawing-room crackle with inventive ability. This may be

---

* Instead of ignoring the evil in the artist's nature – as he did in *Guignol's Band* – or trying to destroy it – as he did in the pamphlets – Céline personifies it through Jules. He shows its necessity and its limitations. He also shows the artist living the consequences of his nature: Ferdinand suffers while Jules reigns.

an imperfect book but to the reader who enjoys Céline it is particularly engrossing. More than anything the language is superb. Céline creates at will, driving his strange novel along. Language is the meaning of the work because it expresses the creative power that is its theme. Here one sees the key difference between Céline and Beckett. Beckett distrusts language and shows its limitations. In a recent piece of writing, *Le Dépeupleur*, he shows himself obsessed with its precision and lack of precision. Perhaps he has taken to heart the Ithaca chapter of *Ulysses*. But Joyce himself, like Céline, went on to create new forms.

At various points *Féerie* reveals one troublesome concern. If the universe is merely Ferdinand's demented imagination, then it can easily vanish. His stories are, after all, 'little anecdotes' and when they dissolve into hot air they take Brittany with them. His manuscript is blown away and with it Montmartre. To put the problem in another way, the destructive element in the universe may complete its work. The violent Web of Time may disintegrate and the cry of pain may be stilled. Jules, Norbert and the others will no longer be able to impose their imagination on Europe and the entire continent will slip into nothingness. The preoccupation with nothingness dominates the last years of Céline's life and becomes the main theme of the trilogy.

[9]

The Hermit of Meudon

When Céline landed at Nice in June 1951 he looked around bewildered. He was returning home with no completed novels, no publisher, no house and no means of making a living. He wondered what to expect. He stood with Lucette beside him and Bébert in his arms, a relic from another age. As an exile in the frozen North he had dreamed of his return. He had talked of the Brittany sea-coast, of the Moulin de la Galette and of hearing French spoken in the streets. Now he felt no joy, only suspicion. He was sure that assassins lay in wait at every corner. 'Oh this amnesty is all very well,' he wrote to Ernst Bendz, 'but the hatred remains . . . vigilant.'[1]

From the airport he went to Menton to stay with Lucette's family. It was an unfortunate arrangement. The hypernervous Céline disliked the bustle of people: 'a household of illiterate, hysterical lunatics', he calls them. Every kindness was a trap, the smallest slight a sword-thrust. 'The refugee stinks,' he repeats. He reacted by turning his back both on Lucette's relatives and his own friends. 'Don't phone me,' he told Paraz who was eager to come and see him.[2] When Dr Camus inquired whether he might visit, Paraz was told to keep him away.[3] Céline's hatred of mankind had never been greater. He talks of the 'physical and moral horror of *Any Human Contact*'.[4]

He could not tolerate his in-laws for long. He accepted the hospitality of Paul Marteau, a wealthy admirer, to whom he gave an early manuscript of *Féerie* written while in prison.[5] This was no better. Céline had less taste than ever for luxury and he disliked being on show. His antipathy to the 'Mediterranean bastards' of the South flared up again and he thought of fleeing to Brittany. 'But the cash,' he asks rhetorically.[6] He felt out of place in a France that had been transformed from the ruined country he had left seven years earlier. He was alarmed at the cost of living and certain that he would finish up destitute. Both he and Lucette were ill, which at least served as a pretext for keeping people away. 'I feel like a Cistercian,' he exclaims in a typical outburst, 'I have nothing to say.'[7]

In August he left the Riviera for Paris. Paraz kept repeating that Céline's friends would provide him with money, cars, contacts. Céline merely grew more agitated. 'I want to disappear,' he insisted.[8] In Paris he planned to meet his daughter and her five children whom he had never seen. He also had to make arrangements to publish his books. For a few weeks he stayed with the Marteaus and loathed it. Then his luck changed. Gallimard made amends for its refusal of *Voyage* by offering him a contract. He accepted. Paraz might castigate the *N.R.F.*, to Céline all publishers were much of a kind: 'The Gallimardites are as good as the others.'[9] He found a house: 25, route des Gardes, near Meudon in the western suburbs. With the advance from the *N.R.F.* and help from Lucette's family, he bought it. Now he could, if he wished, disappear.

Meudon, where Rabelais had once lived, was familiar territory. Céline had been born in nearby Courbevoie. The route des Gardes was a dead-end road that straggled up a hill with grass growing through its cracks. It wound past a few other houses before reaching the Villa Maïtou and petering out further along. The 'villa' was 'a Louis-Philippe-style house standing all askew on the gentle slope of Bas Meudon'.[10] Its appearance was forbidding: 'tall and rough-cast on a grey-stone foundation'. To one visitor's surprise there was no door in the front and he had to go all the way round to the side.[11] The view was extensive. The house looked down to the Seine and the smoking chimneys of the Renault works at Billancourt. In the distance Paris stretched out its rooftops.

The first winter Céline had to toil. The house was in bad condition, so he had to plaster and repair the roof. He complains: 'the dump I live in is huge ... full of holes. Can't be heated ... grotesque.'[12] The cold was terrible, worse than on the Baltic, and he never had enough coal. Shopping was another chore. He hated to go out in the day-time in case his neighbours pointed him out. He went for the groceries in the evenings and returned as quickly as he could. 'It's a torment,' he tells Paraz, 'I have to drag the potatoes, carrots, meat for the animals all the way from Billancourt, more than a mile uphill, it's hard, at sixty-one years of age.'[13] His shopping expeditions would have been more arduous if he and Lucette had not lived off a diet of vegetables and noodles with no meat and only a little fish. Despite the inconveniences, they settled in at Meudon. Lucette began to give dance lessons and her blue plaque was fixed to the garden gate. Near it, more discreet, was another: 'Dr L.-F. Destouches of the Paris Faculty of Medicine, 2–4 P.M. except Friday'. Few patients came at first and the only regular visitors were Lucette's young pupils, who made their way to the upstairs studio watched by her husband's connoisseur's eye.

Some of Céline's old friends came to see him, others did not. A quarrel kept Henri Mahé away, and the friendships with Aymé, Gen Paul and the Montmartre band had lapsed.[14] Paraz came occasionally, but his ruined lungs forced him to spend most of the year at Vence. Héron de Villefosse came to visit Céline 'with his dogs and his bitterness'[15] and Rebatet came with Arletty to sit in the 'untended garden'.[16] The most frequent visitor was Robert Poulet, an old friend from Denoël's publishing house. Poulet, an ex-First World War hero, had been brought up in Belgium and had led a wandering life. He worked as a manual labourer in many cities before becoming a novelist and political journalist. During the Occupation he had edited a magazine in Brussels and, under the strict Belgian laws, had been imprisoned for collaboration. Now back in Paris, he resumed his writer's career and his friendship with Céline.

Like everyone who had known him before the war, Poulet found Céline changed. There was 'something broken, defeated' about him.[17] Céline's health was bad. He seemed frailer, he was always cold, his walk was arthritic and pains in his hands made writing increasingly difficult. Rebatet 'was terribly shocked by his physical decline'.[18] The athlete who loved to sail and walk was replaced by a prematurely aged man fixed to his armchair. Céline was gloomier and his flashes of enthusiasm were rarer. Poulet, who has left vivid descriptions of his visits, describes Céline: 'his face hollow like a weary hermit, his saddened mouth contrasting with his half-closed eyes'.[19]

'The sound of the bell brings a howling mob surging out of the earth and racing down to the unusual barbed-wire fence. An old gardener, who was carting off manure, comes up swearing furiously at the mastiffs. How many dogs are there? Six? Ten?' Such is Poulet's account of the welcome he received one day. There were actually five dogs, along with two cats and innumerable birds that resided in the bathroom. The majestic Bébert had died of cancer at a ripe old age and was buried in the garden. His place as leader of the tribe was taken by Balou, a huge mongrel brought back from Denmark. The dogs, like the barbed-wire, kept the outside world at a distance. They also terrified Lucette's pupils, not to mention Poulet. They were so troublesome that Céline decided to have them castrated. The vet who performed the operation remembers that Dr Destouches looked on professionally, with 'his big cape over his shoulders ... his spectacles perched on his nose'.[20] Céline was no sentimentalist. His devotion to animals deepened as he grew older and his last novel is dedicated to them. But he had no illusions about their loyalty or tenderness. He admired, the vet thought, their 'freedom'.[21] They did not lie like human beings. They had no vanity and made no pretence of virtue. Céline spent hours alone with his pets. He had a parrot whom he tried patiently to teach to speak. When the weather was good he put it out in the garden; but it squawked loudly and the next-door neighbours protested by turning up their gramophone. As Céline would go to any lengths to avoid quarrels, he stopped putting the parrot out.[22]

Once Poulet had made his way safely into the house he would sit with Céline in the living-room on the ground floor. Céline would huddle in his armchair, wrapped in dressing-gowns or in the fur-lined jackets he had worn at Sigmaringen. He was usually unshaven and his grey hair hung down long and unkempt. Another visitor comments on his 'huge feet wrapped up in wool and forced, as if by hammer blows, into felt slippers'. The room itself looked like 'a janitor's lodge'.[23] It was full of 'odd furniture, scattered papers, cushions that have lost their folds'.[24] There was a strong smell of dogs and disinfectant. In one corner was a long table, piled high with sheets of writing and with the legendary clothes-pegs that Céline used to pin his manuscripts together. Sometimes Lucette would come downstairs to hover around her husband, who swore at her affectionately. Their years of marriage had created great intimacy between them, as well as inspiring her with many of his fears. Poulet describes Lucette: 'grace and subtlety incarnated in a weightless body and a finely chiselled face that from time to time broke out into the smile of a malicious nymph'.[25]

After a while Dr Destouches's plaque began to bring him patients. His interest in medicine had not flagged. He was ready to talk about problems, ranging from cancer to the slow rate of heart-beat common among athletes. He kept up with medical literature, although he criticized it when it became too theoretical. He was above all a practising doctor and seeing patients was 'a source of joy' to him.[26]

Sometimes he pretended to despise medicine. He said once that the great diseases like T.B. and V.D. had vanished, carrying off with them the doctor's prestige.[27] This was no more than a piece of Célinian cynicism. He was happy to discover that his evil reputation did not stop patients from coming to consult him. They were the poor people he had always treated. The rich people of Meudon went to fashionable doctors in Paris, the poor came to Dr Destouches, who charged them little.

What of his other vocation – writing? Exile had not stimulated Céline. Between 1944 and 1951 he produced little: a second draft of *Le Pont de Londres*, which he rejected, and unfinished versions of *Féerie* and *Normance*. In order to write he needed the stability of Meudon. In the last ten years of his life he completed five novels and the *Entretiens avec le professeur Y. Féerie* appeared in 1952 and *Normance* in 1954. Céline was beginning the second phase of his novelist's career.

His first two novels were badly received. Even his friends were unenthusiastic. 'No, I don't think Poulet likes *Normance*,' Céline told Paraz with an air of indifference.[28] Poulet did not enjoy *Normance* any more than he had enjoyed *Féerie*. He calls them 'neither wholly successful nor wholly typical works'.[29] Lucien Rebatet was 'discouraged' and wondered whether Céline had exhausted his talent.[30] Paraz, in whose eyes Céline could do no wrong, defended *Normance*; but he knew he was fighting an uphill battle. 'You have to sample *Normance* page by page,' he writes to an unimpressed friend, 'and believe me if Céline had wanted to he could have written another volume of *Guignol's Band*. He has looked for a different form of expression.'[31] It was not the most convincing defence. The reading public showed none of the excitement it had felt for *Voyage*. Céline was no longer a revolutionary novelist to be hated or revered. In 1957 *L'Express* could write that for Frenchmen less than thirty years old he was scarcely a name, and for people older he was a name they preferred to forget.[32] In 1949 Gaëtan Picon had scarcely mentioned him in his *Panorama de la nouvelle littérature française*. *Féerie* and *Normance* did nothing to break the silence.

Céline reacted strongly. He might feign indifference, but he did not feel it. He turned on Gallimard: 'the *N.R.F.* is all enemies, rabbis, villains'.[33] Memories of Denoël's treachery came flooding back to him. He was sure his publisher was working against him. His outbursts reveal the pain he felt. By not reading his books the world was forcing him into oblivion. All his life he had fought against his obsession with the graveyard. He had been haunted by his vision of streets thronged with walking corpses and he had had serious doubts about his own existence. But he had struggled against this. He had travelled, fought in two wars and toiled as a doctor. Now he was menaced by a new kind of death – silence.

When he had returned in 1951 he had expected hostility. To avoid it he had turned in on himself. But how much real persecution was there? There were scribbles, he claimed, on his walls and mutterings from his neighbours. But quarrels over a parrot's squawking do not constitute persecution. Céline was allowed to return and settle in France with no great unpleasantness. None of his fears was realized. He did not fall into destitution – Paraz says, 'Céline doesn't really need money, I don't think.'[34] No ex-Resistance gunmen came out to Meudon to shoot him down. People who disliked his wartime role wanted to forget him. That was the real trouble. Most of the public was truly indifferent, the rest indifferent on principle. But this was what Céline could not tolerate. In the 1930s he had gone to any extreme to incur hatred. Now he would gladly have done the same, but he could not. His refusal to see people, his recluse's habits and his fierce dogs were a way of affirming his existence. Yet no one paid him any heed. He was forced to be the solitary figure he claimed he wanted to be. The only course that remained was to publish his books which, although an investigation of death, bore witness to his will to live. By ignoring *Féerie* the public was carrying out another kind of execution.

This is the battle Céline was waging in the years after his return. He had become the ageing, bourgeois figure that was one of his poses. The Meudon period corresponds in some sense to the years at Rennes: both are Céline's attempt at stable living. In each case he had a home and a wife. But he could not stand it. 'Stability' was a kind of death. Without adventures and hatreds Céline could not feel that he existed. In Rennes it had been a simple matter to flee. Now it was harder. His only weapon was his writing and without the readers he loathed but needed, he could not use it.

To break the silence he published the *Entretiens*, a variant on a well-worn formula.[35] Dismayed by the cold reception given to *Normance* and encouraged by Gallimard to play the game, the narrator Céline holds forth to Professor Y, telling him that he is Europe's greatest writer and, conversely, that he has merely invented one 'little trick'. Mixed with the comedy are nuggets of good sense, which help explain Céline's novels. In particular there is the well-known harangue where he describes his stylistic innovations in terms of a *métro* trip from Montmartre to Montparnasse. Many of the serious things he says have been discussed already. Here the *Entretiens* will be seen chiefly as a book written by the 1955 Céline. He presents himself as a failed author whose novels are not selling. In this way the silence, that hurt him as a man, is exorcised and turned into art.

The narrator sets the traditional interview on its head. An unsuccessful novelist, he is encouraged by his friends to get some publicity. He thinks of television and radio but he can 'neither be listened to nor looked at'. So he has to submit to an interview, that will be published in book form. His friends at the *N.R.F.* are either ill or too busy to act as interviewers. Jean Paulhan, the prime candidate, bows out leaving Céline to the Professor Y, who is not a professor at all but a Colonel Réséda – of the Resistance perhaps? Réséda is terrified that the monster Céline will start talking about politics. He will not ask questions or take notes and he dislikes Céline's novels. He is himself an orthodox writer, with a 'little Goncourt' submitted to the *N.R.F.* and a fervent admiration for Gaston Gallimard. There is no dialogue between the two and the author–reader relationship is shattered. Céline pours out monologues on diverse topics like refrigerators and lending libraries. He repeats himself: 'You're saying the same thing over and over again,' says the colonel. 'I am playing the clown,' says Céline. He talks to fill up the book – 'How many pages is that?' he asks. In the last lines he remarks that 'all this is not very important'.

Such comedy enables him to continue talking. If he were a serious writer, he would despair of himself and his listener. Instead he carries on merrily. He demolishes post-war French society. Everything is 'chromo': 'The taste for the authentic has been lost,' he insists. He denounces vacuum cleaners and popular novels, Renault cars and the Prix Goncourt. The criticism of *Bagatelles* is repeated in an updated 1955 version. In the midst of such falseness there is one striking example of integrity – Céline's writing. Its unpopularity is the proof of its greatness. The clown-author stands alone in a cultureless country.

What is the secret of his art? Céline tells us that he has no idea. His work has only one quality – style. In real interviews given during his last years Céline talked endlessly about style. He maintained that he was concerned with how to say things, not with what he said, and that the characters and plots of his novels were unimportant. His aim, as in the *Entretiens*, was to make a seemingly absurd statement that would puzzle the reader. The real-life journalists reacted with the same disbelief as the fictitious colonel. But Céline was also hinting that writing was important because it was absurd. As a gratuitous act it was superior to manufacturing Renault cars.

In the *Entretiens* Céline does talk about content, especially about death. The *métro* between Montmartre and Montparnasse is the modern artist's inferno, Gaston Gallimard's cellar is the chamber of hell reserved for bad writers. Death is what Céline's work is all about. '*You have to be more than a little bit dead to be really funny*' is how he describes the comedy in his novels. Out of the descent into hell the writer brings a new reality. Denying that he is a realistic novelist Céline calls himself an 'Impressionist', who penetrates beyond the object and offers a new insight. The medium is style, which does not really exist for itself – a well-turned phrase masking a banal idea – but conveys the shock emotional impact that has been Céline's aim since *Mort à crédit*. He explains how the breaking-down of the sentence permits immediacy:

> I carry my whole world off in the subway, pardon! . . . and off I go. I take everyone . . . whether people want to or not! . . . with me! . . . the subway of emotion, mine! without all the hindrances and inconveniences! in a dream! never stopping anywhere! no! on to our goal! on to our goal! direct! in emotion! . . . by emotion! nothing but onward . . . in full emotion . . . end to end!

As in *Guignol's Band* and *Féerie*, the writer is the 'master magician' who can 'read inside his [the reader's] head'. This is the clown's apotheosis. Formerly he talked without a listener and wrote without a subject. Now his reward for the silence to which he is condemned is the vision of another world.

Céline keeps insisting that he is not mad. The colonel considers him a 'maniac', who imagines himself persecuted and has delusions that he is a genius. But throughout the *Entretiens* Céline insists that control is essential. His *métro* train must not 'go off the rails'. He describes how he re-works his language in order to obtain exactly the right effect. Because he has thrown off the straitjacket of orthodox syntax, control is more important to him than to a conventional writer. He must always be on his guard. He uses intellectual terms to define what he does, speaking of 'the refinement of my invention' and 'the cleverness of the work'. One remembers his manuscripts with their innumerable corrections.

By the end of the *Entretiens* Céline has completed his reversal of values. It is the colonel who is mad, not he. Réséda has been exposed as the representative of the 'chromo' world. He is a false professor, a false Second World War hero, who supposedly had a plate set in his head, and a false writer. Céline's bullying breaks through his masks and turns him into a screaming wreck. He urinates wildly, insults Céline and sets off on a hectic race through Paris. He has lost control, whereas the supposedly mad narrator is calm. The colonel buys bouquets of flowers for Gallimard and falls asleep on the paving stones in the front of the *N.R.F.* offices. The sane, who 'play the game' are the maniacs, while the demented Céline, forced into silence, goes off at the end to write the *Entretiens*. The colonel, a false interviewer, cannot write the book himself, so Céline will do it. In spite of the public's indifference he will continue to cry out, because he alone has something to say. This is his defiant answer to the failure of *Féerie* and *Normance*.

The *Entretiens* did little to change Céline's situation. The watershed in his Meudon years came in 1957 with the publication of *D'un château l'autre*. This was a success. Whether because it seems to have the correct political perspective in that it satirizes the collaborators, or because it is easier to read than the surrealistic *Féerie*, or because it is funny, or simply because it is such a good novel, the public decided, after a moment's hesitation, to buy it. Critics laughed particularly at the episode where Pétain and his retinue relieve themselves under a bridge, while Allied bombers thunder overhead. Céline had recovered the fame he had lost. Once again he professed indifference: 'You know, people are lazy and they talk nonsense all the time, they are a bit amused by my book.'[36] In reality he was delighted. His success gave him a new lease of life and his joyous energy was apparent to visitors.

D'un château l'autre aroused controversy. Céline was interviewed by a reporter from *L'Express*, then a left-wing magazine which supported Mendès-France and had not yet been turned, by Jean-Jacques Servan-Schreiber, into a pale imitation of *Time*. It seemed odd that

L'Express should bestow publicity on an ex-collaborator and that Céline should give an interview to a leftist review.[37] As in the 1930s, he was about to show that he belonged to no political camp.

He began by playing games. The reporter, Françoise Giroud, kept on putting leading questions and Céline kept on talking about his pet subjects – pure style and the yellow peril. She wanted him to say that the content of *D'un château l'autre* was significant; he affirmed that, 'My goodness, the story is very much a sideline. It's the style that is interesting.' He insulted his readers – 'I don't write for someone ... You write for the writing itself' – and did not forget his favourite targets, like Sartre and the *N.R.F.* printers who butchered his punctuation. He was determined to talk on his own terms.

The trouble arose when he discussed politics. He fell back into the victim's role that he loved. 'I yielded to a sacrificial mania,' he says about the pamphlets. He had never been a collaborator and at Sigmaringen he had been 'in prison, in a cell'. The Germans hated him. 'Hitler, if he had lived, would certainly have had me shot.'

This might have appealed well enough to *L'Express*'s readers. But Céline spiced the brew with other political judgements. The Reich, he claimed, was defending Europe, its army was the only barrier against the Asiatic hordes. Hitler might have been 'an idiot', but 'he was doing something constructive, he was building Europe'. Germany's defeat marked the end of the western world. Céline went on to demolish the Resistance view, that France had struggled bravely against the Nazis. France had been soundly trounced. All the Resistance had done was to create a new myth: 'De Gaulle triumphant, etc., heroes everywhere ... It's just a myth.' He went out of his way to be irritating: talking of his Flanders' exploits he mentioned another 1914 hero – Joseph Darnand.

Turning to contemporary France, he continued in the same vein. He reiterated that the nation was falling apart from over-eating, smoking and alcoholism. He remembered to criticize the Fourth Republic's contribution to public morality: the closing of the brothels. This, apparently, was another proof of decadence. Céline showed a marked nostalgia for the pre-1914 era. He praised the old French army: 'It was a real order. There's no more order.' Such militarism shocked Françoise Giroud, who could not understand why he applauded discipline. He did not bother to explain. Instead he admitted that French shortcomings did not much matter, because the Chinese would soon be arriving. In a quip on his old enemy Aragon he concludes that 'for the white race there are no tomorrows full of song'.

None of this was new. Céline had said it all before and he would say it again, with suitable variations. The novelty lay in making these statements in 1957 to a mass, predominantly left-wing audience. *L'Express*'s readers were taken aback. Many protested that the interview should never have taken place.[38] This pleased Céline who confessed that he had been giving a performance 'like a pig wallowing in its filth'.[39] He had praised Hitler and Darnand in order to display his full 'disgustingness'.[40] His only worry was that he had not gone far enough. 'I only get two or three letters a day which means the *Express* interview did not make people so mad,' he laments. 'Sagan would have got them much more publicity'[41] – Françoise Sagan being another of his favourite dislikes. Still, he was not displeased and he admits proudly that he has become a 'fashionable news-item'.[42]

The sharpest protest came not from the left but from the right: from the hallowed halls of *Rivarol*. *Rivarol* was the rallying-point of former collaborators who had never accepted the Liberation view of the war. Proclaiming its purity it condemned everything that had happened since 1944. It loathed the Fourth Republic – 'hideous System born out of the Resistance'[43] – and would be equally contemptuous of the Fifth Republic, headed by its arch-enemy de Gaulle. In 1957 *Rivarol* was flourishing. It offered its readers a rich diet of anti-communism, anti-parliamentarianism and support for Algérie Française, the whole mixture flavoured with virulent rhetoric. Tixier-Vignancourt, Céline's former lawyer and future presidential candidate, was idolized, Mendès-France, the betrayer of Indo-China, execrated. In *Rivarol*'s ranks were several of Céline's old friends. There was Pierre-Antoine Cousteau, his fiery spirit undimmed by his years in prison, Lucien Rebatet and Pierre Dominique, who was to heap praise on Céline in his book on the pamphleteers. Albert Paraz, now an Algérie Française supporter and still attacking Madeleine Jacob, did the column on radio and Robert Poulet wrote the book reviews. But *Rivarol* had no use for *L'Express*, which symbolized the triumphant spirit of the left that had committed the Liberation crimes and was now selling-out in Algeria.

Cousteau considered Céline's interview a betrayal. Talking to

L'Express was the first crime, denying his anti-semitism and collaboration was the second. Cousteau had emerged from prison convinced that the only absolute virtue was loyalty to one's friends. Now he was horrified. On 21 June, one week after the interview, he published an article which juxtaposed Céline's *L'Express* comments with quotations from *Bagatelle..* Céline might claim he was a victim, Cousteau would show he had been a diehard Nazi supporter. Cousteau concludes simply that Céline is a 'turn-coat'.[44]

The article triggered off a crisis of conscience within *Rivarol*. On 27 June Paraz defended Céline, claiming that he had been making fun of *L'Express*.[45] Cousteau countered with a satirical piece in which he wonders why Céline does not claim to have been a leading resistant, instead of merely a victim.[46] The other newspapers watched this heart-searching with huge amusement. *Le Canard enchaîné* published an article lamenting that Céline could please no one, whatever he did.[47] The excitement continued in the next issues of *Rivarol* where Poulet gave *D'un château l'autre* a sympathetic review,[48] while Cousteau, who had now found time to read the book, expressed fresh outrage. Not only had Céline talked to *L'Express* but his novel was another proof that he had changed sides. He had delivered up 'to the mockery of our new Lords and Masters the poor, hunted devils of Sigmaringen'.[49]

Céline was taken aback by this onslaught from an unexpected quarter. To make amends he wrote a short piece for *Rivarol* called *Vive l'amnistie, monsieur*, which attacks the French government for not granting a general amnesty to men who compromised themselves under the Occupation.[50] In his letters he was less conciliatory. Cousteau is 'stupid, phoney, a blackballed politician'.[51] 'My God, what a Gaullist he would be if de Gaulle could have me guillotined,'[52] Céline tells Paraz. He resented attacks from the right as much as from the left and his last novels are sprinkled with insults. In *D'un château l'autre* there is an unkind comment on Altman 'who treats me now like a piece of dirt, like an obscene traitorous monster'. This is balanced by a thrust at Hérold-Paquis, whose condemnation of Céline's flight to Denmark had not been forgotten. He is 'as shameless a liar as Tartre'.[53] Céline never forgave nor forgot an enemy. He continued to attack Cousteau long after his death in 1958. In *Rigodon* Cousteau is dismissed as 'a first-rate shit'.[54]

But the *L'Express* controversy served Céline well. From 1957 on, visitors flocked to Meudon. Some of them were familiar faces: Poulet, Rebatet and Arletty. Paraz was conspicuously absent. He died in September 1957 losing his long struggle against T.B. Younger admirers came, undeterred by Céline's sinister reputation and witnesses to his recovered popularity. There was Dominique de Roux who was to edit the *Cahiers de L'Herne*, Marc Hanrez who wrote a study of Céline's work and Jacques Darribehaude who wanted to make a film about him! Journalists came in increasing numbers and not just from literary periodicals. *Le Monde et la vie* published an interview, *Qui êtes-vous M. Céline?*, in the middle of articles about Aristotle Onassis and Brigitte Bardot.[55] *Télémagazine* sent a reporter to find out which were Céline's favourite television programmes.

He reacted in various ways. Sometimes he sent his visitors away – Jacques Darribehaude was not admitted on his first trip because Céline distrusted film-makers. Sometimes he complained about the waste of time, and invariably he was suspicious of his visitor's motives. But he usually agreed to talk. He harangued the reporters, avoided answering their questions and repeated things they already knew. Soon they realized what to expect. Céline would sit in his armchair, wrapped in his ragged overcoats, and talk about his harsh childhood, the publication of *Voyage* and the Baltic cold. Delivering these monologues was more important than their content. One listener states that beyond what Céline was actually saying was 'a constant effort to go on forward'. Céline hesitated, found a new topic and continued. He talked like 'a broken text'. Silence threatened but he always overcame it. 'He would talk by himself. Our questions do no more than modify the composition of his speeches which our presence allows to unfold but which our interventions do not shape.'[56]

Céline did not talk as energetically as he had done at Rennes. He did not invent so freely and he did not grow excited. He had less energy to spare. But talking was a more serious matter than it had been then. Now it was his only defence. So he rambled on, telling his stories like the Ferdinand of his last novels. Of course that Ferdinand is still a more extreme figure. Silence and words are all he knows. But Céline was himself not so far from that point, not so far either from the Ferdinand of the *Entretiens*, who must break through the Professor's indifference. Céline's many selves were merging again. Fact and fiction came together as he struggled to hold on to life.

'When you don't have the strength you have to play the clown'[57] – the clown image recurs in Céline's Meudon conversations. He acted out the role of the monster, who loathed what good men admired. He posed as the martyred victim. He invented tales about his youth. He performed as people expected. Sometimes he added something new. Had he always attacked Proust? Well, now he would declare that *À la recherche du temps perdu* was a great novel. Did journalists ask why he was a writer? It was easy to reply that he wanted to 'make the others seem unreadable'.[58] Like his monologues, these games were simpler than they had been in the 1920s. Then many roles had been open to him: doctor, bohemian, voyeur, traveller. Now his universe had narrowed down to the bare minimum. He had to take the parts he was offered.

Sometimes the game-playing was grotesque. *Noir et blanc*, which specialized in nudes, crimes and the English Royal Family, published an article called *Les Célébrités de Paris aiment la campagne*. It quoted from Maurice Chevalier and Charles Aznavour, who had moved to the country and were going into ecstasies over verdant meadows. At the end came the necessary discordant note. The only celebrity who was not happy was the black-hearted Louis-Ferdinand Céline, who dared to declare: 'I am not interested in trees'.[59] *Télémagazine* had a worse shock. Jacques Chancel apologizes profusely for including the 'traitor Céline' in his survey. True to form, Céline told him that television was 'a force for stupidity' and that he never watched it. For no particular reason he went on to attack Françoise Sagan and the Abbé Pierre. Chancel concludes piously that Céline disliked television because he had turned his back on the world.[60] Two years earlier Céline had neatly disposed of another of post-war France's hallowed institutions: holidays. Mere decadence, he said. France was indeed a pleasant country for vacations, he told a startled *Arts* interviewer, the trouble was that other people thought so too. While the French were basking on beaches the 'Manchurian armies were dreaming of Touraine'.[61]

Céline assimilated everything to himself: the whole world existed to provide material for his clowning. In 1959 he gave an interview on Rabelais where the author of *Gargantua* was turned into a figure remarkably like the author of *Voyage*.[62] 'What's good about Rabelais is that he put his head on the block, he took risks. Death was watching him and death is an inspiration.' Céline demolished the view of

Rabelais as a merry, hard-drinking friar. 'He spent his time trying to avoid being burned at the stake,' says Céline. In case the reader misses the point he adds: 'I have spent my time too putting myself in desperate situations.' Céline and Rabelais do have much in common. They are both great stylists who revolutionized the language of their day. When Céline says that in Rabelais 'language, only language' counts, he is making an interesting, if one-sided, comment. But his aim was to remodel Rabelais entirely in his own image. 'Rabelais didn't pull it off. He failed,' says Céline. Shades of the failed narrator of *Mort à crédit*!

Journalists were happy to cooperate. They had come to Meudon to listen to the reprobate and they could not return without words of heresy on their tape-recorders. Like Professor Y they did not distinguish between games that were games and games that were serious. There was no reason why they should. But there were two recurrent themes in Céline's conversation that go deeper than comments on Françoise Sagan: the decision to make his past life into a legend and his profound rejection of contemporary France.

Detail by detail he filled out the myth of the victim. He dwelt on his deprived childhood, replete with noodles and smelly feet. He talked of his parents' poverty and of the cruel shopkeepers he had worked for. He told with excited gestures how he had been wounded in the head in 1914. He repeated that he had never wanted to be a writer. He had published *Voyage* in order to make money to buy a flat, but then Denoël had cheated him of his royalties. Politically the tale was the same. He had been trying to save the ungrateful French from massacre. They turned on him at the Liberation, as had the Germans and the Danes. Now he wanted only to retire. He would gladly stop writing, except that he owed money to Gallimard who was exploiting him. Occasionally he embellished the story with new examples. 'Last week they threw me out of a café in Paris,' he said once.[63] He gave no reason and the reporter expected none. Another time he remarked that his ambition had been to become the head of a lunatic asylum – a fascinating possibility, this.[64] Naturally 'they' had not allowed him to realize it. Even Hanrez and Poulet wrote down parts of this extraordinary tale, although Poulet understood what Céline was doing. Not everything was false, but the total impression was quite wrong. Céline was selecting the elements in his life that made him seem a scapegoat. Why should he do this? An artist to his fingertips, he was turning his existence into fiction. The strong self-destructive urge in his character made him create a legend in which he was destroyed by his enemies. He then substituted this crucified Céline, a much less interesting figure, for the vigorous Destouches.

'There are cars, "fridges", steak and chips, holidays all through July and August for everyone.'[65] This is a typical comment on the France of the 1950s. Céline's pet aversion was the Renault car, symbol of the country's new prosperity, which was produced beneath his eyes at Billancourt. Having formerly loved to walk, he despised cars. Writing to Paraz he says that in cars people's 'heads have disappeared ... and their legs too'.[66] Feminine beauty had declined. Women had been more attractive under the Occupation when they had to walk; now they were overweight. As for himself he had no chance of becoming a successful doctor because patients respected no one who did not own a car. Céline found materialism rampant. 'The French are only refined when it comes to guzzling ... There we are champions', such is his backhanded compliment to French cooking.[67] By contrast the pre-1914 era had been a world of brave soldiers and skilled craftsmen. The French army had stood firm at Verdun, while Madame Destouches wove her exquisite lace. It was a far cry from the parades at Longchamps to the chimneys of Billancourt.

His remarks on politics were equally scathing. His great enemy was de Gaulle, whose return to power in 1958 seemed to him, and to *Rivarol*, the ultimate consecration of the pseudo-Resistance. In *Nord* Céline identifies de Gaulle with the comic-strip character Tintin. (De Gaulle also compared himself with Tintin in a conversation with André Malraux.[68]) 'Little Tintin,' says Céline, 'condemned to death, to save honour and his own skin jumped on a plane for London.'[69] Once more this is an interesting reaction against a man, whose concept of France's destiny was the exact opposite of Céline's. De Gaulle's success as a writer was another cut: the '27 million francs' his *Mémoires* had earned jarred with the failure of *Féerie*.[70] He must be cut down to the parody of himself – to Tintin, the little man with delusions of grandeur. De Gaulle's vision of France's world-wide role seemed to Céline to be mere castles in the air. That de Gaulle himself frequently felt this and that he judged his own efforts harshly and his compatriots even more harshly, did not interest Céline. To him Tintin with 'his statues everywhere'[71] was anathema.

In general, post-1944 French history was a series of murderous struggles. 'The '54 war is finished. When will the next one start?'[72] is Céline's response to the Geneva agreements. He still considered war the expression of man's natural hatreds: 'You would only have to re-open the amphitheatre and there would be no more Algerian problem'.[73] All battles must end with France's defeat at the hands of the foreigner. The F.L.N. could be cast in the role of barbaric invader, after Suez Nasser was another candidate. Céline's fear of Russia declined, especially when Khrushchev came to power. He felt an aristocratic contempt for this Ukrainian peasant: 'He doesn't behave properly, don't you think, he tells dirty stories like a commercial traveller.' The Chinese had become the great threat and Céline expected them to come swarming, at any moment, over the Meudon hill. At other times he felt that even they were decadent. There would be no conquerors, only general chaos: 'the wildest armies . . . by the time they arrive at Cognac they'll be so broken down, they'll have started to like cognac and then they'll have eaten so much'.[74]

Céline was re-fighting the battles of the 1930s. The *deux chevaux* had replaced the *apéritif* and the Chinese the Jew; but materialism and murder were still two sides of the same coin. Despite his clowning, Céline was still engaged in culture criticism. Europe, he declared, lacked 'faith'. It had lost 'that gratuitous element which made possible the great mystical civilizations'.[75] Without unselfish emotion man was no more than a truncated body sitting in a car. Individualism, moral honesty and physical grace were lost. Céline's alienation from the standardized world of industry remained with him to the end. Only the tone of his criticism had changed. In the 1930s it was virulent, now it was quietly mocking or else querulous. He was reduced to attacking television instead of the Communist Party. He was playing the same tune in a minor key, because he knew that it was all quite hopeless and in any case he did not care.

Death was drawing closer and the web of irony was a fragile defence. Céline talked more than ever of death, which was less a future event than a part of his daily consciousness. 'I don't know how to enjoy life. I don't live. I don't exist'[76] is a characteristic comment. He dreamed of tranquillity: 'Happiness consists of being alone on the seashore and being left in peace.'[77] He talked of going to Le Havre, where he could walk on the harbour and read the newspapers without being recognized. Yet he continued to need the naïve young reporters and the feuds with Cousteau. Death came in different disguises: Meudon's solitude protected him against his nervousness, its boredom paralysed his spirit. Lucette's vigour was one defence, the animals were another, humour a third. He loved to mock: Poulet says that Céline's imitations of Gallimard and Paulhan were both hilarious and surprisingly accurate. He laughed at his own frustrations: 'I was sure that I would be awarded the two Nobel prizes: for peace and literature,' he wrote after *D'un château l'autre*.[78]

Religion might have been another defence, but Céline refused it to the end. He insisted that he was a positivist and he grew angry when Poulet talked about his religious temperament. Still, another friend described him as 'irreligious but mystical'[79] and no one could have been more conscious of the absence of God than this ascetic recluse, who lived in his shabby dwelling on the hill and looked down on Paris, the modern Babylon. Céline said that 'there is in men's hearts a need for God';[80] but he remained obstinately certain that there was no God to satisfy it.

So he sat in his armchair and faced the fact of his growing weakness. His doctor says that, 'if illness had made him physically feeble,' he was 'always very alert, curious, witty, sometimes mocking and extremely well-read'.[81] When Jean Ducourneau, who was also a Balzac scholar, came out to discuss 'the last little trivialities' of the Pléiade edition, he and Céline talked about Balzac, who had lived at Meudon. Céline even wrote to Héron de Villefosse to ask questions about Balzac's stay, but nothing could be discovered.[82] Another friend brought him a thesis written on the Napoleonic cavalry: 'He devours it, reads and reads it. He is delighted – he does not stop talking to me about it: "I was in at the end of all that." '[83] Such outbursts of enthusiasm grew rarer. When Marc Hanrez came to visit him in the autumn of 1960, Céline sat in the kitchen with two of his dogs asleep at his feet. Lucette gave her lesson upstairs and Céline aroused himself to cook a piece of fish for their dinner. He was tired and Hanrez left early. Céline was losing the fight. He was 'merry and full of anecdotes until dusk. Then the wolves came out of the woods. Céline's face grew haggard, he battled with his headaches. Paris, his city, was lighting up and Céline was fading away.'[84]

What remained was his writer's vocation. 'I work,' he said not long before his death, 'it's my life. The sheet of white paper is my tombstone. "Here lies the author".' [85] In 1960 he published *Nord*, the second novel of his trilogy. Immediately he went to work on *Rigodon*, although his arthritic hands were now very painful. Already he was planning yet another book – it was to be called *L'Ambassadrice*.[86] Meanwhile he toiled to finish his chronicle of Nazi Germany's collapse. In this trilogy Céline confronted death more calmly than he had ever done before. A dying man, he looked back coolly at the destruction he had seen.

A draft of *Rigodon* was completed on 1 July 1961, the day he died. He collapsed of a brain seizure and expired in Lucette's arms. He was not true to his legend. He was not executed by communists, he was not bombed by the Luftwaffe and he was not the victim of an assassin's bullet. It had been a very hot day and he was tired from working. He died quietly.

His death was kept secret and was announced on the French radio three days later, the day of the funeral. The parish priest of Meudon had refused to allow Céline to be buried on consecrated ground – would he have wanted this? – so the funeral was to take place in the municipal cemetery. It too was a closely guarded secret. 'There won't be anyone at that funeral; everyone will be very pleased, I more than anyone,' Céline had said.[87] Fewer than thirty people attended. Lucien Rebatet had received a telephone call from Poulet: 'Bardamu, Céline. Died yesterday. It's strictly secret. But you have the right to know!'[88] Rebatet made his way to the funeral. He found the Meudon house as untidy as ever. One of Céline's fur-lined jackets was hanging from a peg. It was raining as the small cortège set out for the graveyard.

Hemingway, who had died the same day, was monopolizing public attention. That week he made the front cover of *Paris Match*, while Céline was relegated to an inside page. Aymé dismisses Hemingway as 'a greater hunter than a writer';[89] Céline would have said it was another triumph for translations over French writing. Meanwhile the group of friends stood round the grave. Arletty describes the scene: 'I remember his wife, a doctor and a cat that circled his grave. He wanted a holly-tree, a holly-tree was in flower; a young child with a chequered apron straight out of a 1912 catalogue was watering the flowers on the next grave. The child, the animal, the flower he liked, this was how he finished his journey.'[90]

The Hermit of Meudon

After the funeral Lucette went back to the route des Gardes and her dance-lessons. Controversy continued. There were squabbles over Céline's estate, as his daughter, who had taken little interest in his work, disputed Lucette's rights. Colette withdrew hurriedly in 1963 when a bombshell exploded. Gallimard was sued by the Germans who were the models for the Schertz family in *Nord*. They had not after all vanished behind the Iron Curtain. They were alive and well enough to press their case. 'Isis' led the attack, claiming that Céline had transformed her family into a band of degenerates. The suit dragged on and attracted to the family more publicity than they would ever have received from *Nord*. In 1965 they won. Céline's estate was fined and *Nord* had to appear with the names changed.[91]

In 1964 *Le Pont de Londres* turned up. When Céline had fled twenty years earlier he had entrusted the manuscript to Marie Canavaggia. Then he did a second version before and during his imprisonment. But in March 1947 he abandoned it for *Féerie* 'which is eating at me'.[92] Nothing remains of the second version. After his return to France Marie Canavaggia mentioned the first manuscript but he had lost interest in it. Perhaps, too, he was anxious to keep up the legend of all the manuscripts his enemies had destroyed. Marie Canavaggia and Lucette were hardly friends and it took three years after Céline's death for *Guignol's Band II* to find its way to Meudon. The task of preparing it for publication was entrusted to Robert Poulet. He discovered that there were two drafts of the story, the second more polished but incomplete. He decided to tack the ending of the first on to the second, which seems a reasonable enough solution. Naturally he did not escape criticism – how could he in Céline's circle? When Jean Ducourneau edited the novel for the *Oeuvres complètes* he was loftily condescending towards Poulet's work. He also criticized the title *Le Pont de Londres*, which was added in 1964. A 'dull choice', says Ducourneau.[93]

Céline's ghost was walking the earth. In May 1968 Paris flared up. Students rioted in the *quartier latin* and the Billancourt factory was occupied by the workers. At Meudon a sudden fire ravaged Céline's house and reduced it to a shell. Lucette, advised to abandon it and move elsewhere, refused. She had the house rebuilt and she stayed on.[94]

Surely the fire had ended the matter of unpublished manuscripts. Not so, for in 1969 *Rigodon* came out, eight years after Céline had 'finished' it. After his death Lucette had photocopied the pages and stored them in a huge trunk. Still plagued, as her husband had been, by security, she handed them over to Céline's former lawyer Naud. Two other lawyers, Gibault and Damien, prepared the manuscript for publication. It was no easy task because the weakened Céline had not re-copied each page, but had left it a jumble of crossed-out lines with words written in above. And why, wondered the Paris literary world, were mere lawyers entrusted with this complex task? Years went by and *Rigodon* did not appear. Céline's punctuation baffled Gibault and Damien. Finally the book came out, to be greeted with howls of criticism. The uncertainty of the text made people ask whether *Rigodon* was not an unfinished work. Ducourneau, mentioned in the text as a 'Balzac scholar ... very serious',[95] has a low opinion of the lawyers' edition.[96]

Finished or not, Céline's last book was, in one sense, true to its creator. On the first page he attacks the faithful friend of his last years, Robert Poulet: 'I can see that Poulet is not friends with me ... Poulet Robert condemned to death ... he never talks about me any more in his columns ... before I was the great this ... the incomparable that ... now an occasional little mention by chance, rather scornful.'[97] This gratuitous onslaught – Céline claims that his friend neglected him because he denied any interest in religion – distressed Poulet. 'It hurt,' he says with a shrug of his shoulders. He knew Céline too well to expect much else, or to take it too seriously.[98]

The saga of this posthumous existence is not finished. In the conflict-ridden circle of Céline's friends there must be secrets that will still emerge. There may be other manuscripts, perhaps even the Krogold legend ... Céline left behind a merry history of discord that must be amusing his mocking spirit. His confused lawsuits and jumbled manuscripts are one more way of avoiding death. He is continuing the fight beyond the grave.

[10]

D'un château l'autre,
Nord and *Rigodon*

Céline's last novels describe his wanderings at the end of the war. *D'un château l'autre* takes place at Sigmaringen. It has a cast of historical characters – Pétain, Laval and the others – whose dreams gradually fade away. *Nord* begins in Baden-Baden where the Simplon hotel is itself a dream that is shattered by the anti-Hitler plot. Ferdinand goes on through a ruined Berlin to Zornhof. The village has a close-knit circle of characters bent on destroying one another and themselves. As they battle, Berlin is being wiped out. In *Rigodon* Ferdinand travels again, still with Lili and Bébert: to North Germany, back briefly to Ulm and Sigmaringen and then on. The towns are all bombed and empty, only names remain: Oddort, Hamburg, Flensburg and finally the safety of Copenhagen. Meanwhile Céline flits to and fro between Meudon in the present and the Germany of 1944. In Meudon he has enemies too, he tells stories, he refuses to die.

These novels reflect the dry humour of Céline's old age. Ferdinand – whether in 1944 or in 1956 – is weary. His world has shrunk to a house in Meudon and a Germany in ruins. He does not want to understand like Bardamu, and he does not go through a frenzy of creation like Jules-Lili-Ferdinand. He still switches his roles but his overriding mood is one of detachment. It is not hard to see why. Faced with nothingness – the obliteration of the Reich and his own death – he has gone beyond lamentation and hatred. All 'the sensational things are only a prelude', he notes.[1] Around him the artist figures work their magic, but they are unable to net reality. Le Vigan is a mere shadow of Norbert and the new forms that the bombing creates are short-lived. As the trilogy goes on Ferdinand diminishes still more. In *D'un château l'autre* he is mocking, in *Nord* he is bitterly defensive. But in *Rigodon* he is no more than mildly and calmly suspicious.

A slighter figure than the imprisoned 'collabo' of *Féerie*, Ferdinand is spending his last hours telling stories. Naturally enough they form a lament: 'Frankly, just between you and me, I'm ending up even worse than I started.' Ferdinand is sixty-three, he has no patients and his books lie forgotten in his publisher's cellar. His mother is dead, Denoël is dead and his suits are worn out. Violence is all around him. He discusses various kinds of suicide and concludes it is best to blow out one's brains with a shot-gun. He watches the motorists speeding along the road, urged on by a death-wish. Despite the violence Ferdinand thinks he will die a 'natural death'. He will disintegrate slowly, until he is just not there any more.

Around him the Paris he knew as a child has faded away, along with the Dreyfus case and Impressionist painting. His cancer-ridden patient Madame Niçois is already 'absent' and as for her house, it is 'a miracle that it's still standing'. Nearby is a once famous restaurant, the 'Pêche Miraculeuse', which is now 'not much more than a memory'. And as the capital totters, so does western civilization itself. There is a threat of nuclear destruction but it is more probable that the whites will simply be absorbed by the Asian hordes. 'The white man is dead! he doesn't exist any more,' Ferdinand tells Poulet. The Chinese invaders are depicted as an anonymous menace; they have blank faces and they feel nothing. They epitomize the non-human. 'The earth just doesn't want men,' says Ferdinand.

But he is defiant. 'Another Spring . . . two . . . or three . . . I won't be here any more,' he says, clinging to his sense of 'the last but one'. Similarly Achille, although so frail that 'when you open the door, you've got to hold him . . . or the draft would blow him away', survives to torment his authors. Céline admits that he is repeating himself: 'can I help it if I'm senile and repetitious?' He has no choice because there is nothing new to say and he is not willing to fall silent. So he talks on and on – about his childhood in the Passage, the plundering of his rue Girardon flat, Sartre's iniquities, anything at all.[2] Repetition is a way to keep talking. For Ferdinand does not really want to die. The first pages of *Rigodon* are a litany of resistance. His visitors want him to deny himself. Poulet asks him to admit that he believes in Christianity, Cambremousse that he will work for a revival of French grandeur. Ferdinand is obstinate: Stalingrad was the end of Western Europe. To admit to optimism would be to share the illusions of modern France and to renounce his own past. This he will not do. The greatest temptation comes from the mad priest – there is one in each novel of the trilogy – who arrives at Ferdinand's door over Christmas to beg forgiveness for insulting him. Ferdinand rejects him: guilt and evil cannot be wiped out.

This is *Voyage* reduced to a miniature. In the same way Ferdinand asserts truth by undergoing the hardships of the war. Instead of sitting back like his compatriots, who wait to be liberated and then call themselves heroes, he fights and speaks out, until he is punished by Germans and Allies alike. He is the symbol of the real, beaten France: 'Sold out,' he says bitterly, 'I'm like France ... sold out bag and baggage.' He is detested at Sigmaringen as at Zornhof because he bears witness to defeat. *Bagatelles* was the 'scapegoat book' which brought down on him the wrath of the French. They blamed Céline, the arch-collaborator, for the Occupation, thus depicting themselves as innocent. They betrayed him as they did their country. The novelist, however, does not, like the pamphleteer, transfer the blame or escape into hatreds of his own. He does no harm. Ferdinand shows a doctor's pity to Madame Niçois as to the idiot children of *Rigodon*. But his pity comes from despair, which is the source of his grievance against the Abbé Pierre. Ferdinand resents him, not just because the Abbé is popular, but because he practises pity without falling into nihilism. He retains his belief in divine grace and the possibility of human goodness, both of which Céline considers delusions.

This sense of nothingness is never absent from Ferdinand's mind. It drives him across Germany and shapes the stories he tells. He describes how death accompanies him through the Berlin streets: he drags 'a double around with me, a kind of dead man, a stiff with canes and worries'. By projecting death as a *Doppelgänger* he gains a certain freedom, which he uses to take on various identities – rather as le Vigan searches desperately for a role. Once again there are several Ferdinands: the Meudon novelist, the struggling fugitive, the visionary of the Hanover pages, the clown who is ready to agree with Laval and Abetz. Each is a circus figure that Céline sets up in order to survive a little longer.

In one sense the trilogy's main theme is the decline of Ferdinand's creative power. The Charon vision, which is actually one of Céline's finest pieces of writing, poses the problem. Already Ferdinand has been telling stories and then debunking them – rather like Molloy.*

* The Meudon sections of the trilogy are very Beckettian: an ageing narrator

He interrupts to remind us that what he is doing is very trivial: 'Maybe I'm going to bore you ... something funnier? ... more titillating?' By the end of the trilogy he is juggling memories. The smell of burning in Hanover reminds him of the fresh tar on the turn-of-the-century Paris roads. Such free association enables him to build some sort of novelist's world. But he ends with some reflections on Balzac. Ducourneau has been making attempts to discover traces of Balzac in Meudon. He has failed. Balzac has vanished, just like Céline who is being buried in the Pléiade editions, vault of dead writers. Literature is itself dying.

Céline's style reflects this. It stands in marked contrast to the flamboyant rhetoric and game-playing of *Féerie*. It is a sober style, simple in syntax and vocabulary. In *D'un château l'autre* Céline is familiar. He uses lots of 'frankly', 'to tell the truth' and 'in fact'. He is playing his role as a minor story-teller. When he uses the jargon of the theatre to describe Sigmaringen, he does not let it build up into extended images. 'Pétain had nothing to do on stage,' he says and then moves on. *Nord* is even more sober for it is a grimmer book. Céline begins with short paragraphs instead of a rambling monologue: he has less to say now. At Zornhof he sets out the tiny details of Ferdinand's life: the exact road he takes to the shops, the trouble he has getting a cup of coffee. He starts to punctuate his text with questions. Of the Berlin cane-shop he asks: 'Where can it be now? ... What zone? ... What's happened to it?' In *Rigodon* there are many more questions and scarely any answers: 'it's the same with all declining countries ... you'll see tomorrow how it will be ... London? ... Prague? ... Moscow?' The sentences do not explode into onomatopoeia, as they did in *Normance*; they drag on repetitively: 'they are not ugly, they have no age, so to speak, they are outside of age'. The 'so to speak' is characteristic, for the deliberate vagueness is growing. *Rigodon* is full of 'I think' and 'It seems'. The vocabulary is narrower than in any other Célinian novel and the sentences are barer, often mere lists. Céline can do no more than jot things down. In all

---

who has nothing to say but will not be silent. Having gone beyond the 'sensational things' of *Féerie*, Céline has rejoined Beckett. But the focus is still somewhat different. The pain that Molloy and L'Innomable suffer is less acute because Ferdinand knows that he can still create if only in a minor vein. Then he turns back to Germany and lets his imagination run free, which L'Innomable is not allowed to do.

three novels there are flashes of his old inventive self. After the brick incident *Rigodon* changes: there are metaphors, alliteration. But it soon slows up again, held back by the narrator's 'I forgot to tell you', 'nearly', 'almost' and the like. This slowness is the most important feature of *Rigodon*'s style. Movement – the essence of Céline's art – is growing weaker, the dance is drawing to a close.

As a chronicler of the war Céline has shifted his focus. He no longer sees it as a creative–destructive process, presided over by the demonic artist. Now it is a march – inevitable and self-willed – into nothingness. Céline is describing the Reich's last hours: the orgy of self-hatred that led to Hitler's collapse. The period suits him well. The German nation, which is helplessly awaiting defeat, is a good example of Célinian man.

One of *Féerie*'s paradoxes remains: war is a cosmic force that ignores mankind, war is the expression of human hatred. Throughout the trilogy runs the sense that collaborators and Germans alike have no control over what is happening to them. Céline uses images of gambling to convey this: 'matter of luck! … the wheel turns, the stakes are down'. Elsewhere he describes bombing as a 'lottery'. There is no question of politicians making decisions that will affect the outcome: 'it's not the marshals or diplomats that dictate peace, it's fleas and rats' – the comparison with a plague is revealing. This view fits the concept of history outlined in *Féerie*. Céline laughs at Marxists who detect an order in what happens: 'the trend of History through the asshole', he scoffs. Reverting to the scientific language he loves, he describes events moving in 'atomic tremors from year to year, through mutations and myths'. History pursues its own road to chaos. So the war just goes on. The bombers fly overhead and the Germans have neither fighters nor anti-aircraft guns to challenge them.

To the throngs of displaced people, travelling around on the trains in *Rigodon*, the war is a metaphysical mystery. Céline has caught the viewpoint of the ordinary man, who suffered, without understanding, as his normal world fell apart – in part Ferdinand himself is such a man. Céline demolishes rational explanations, particularly the notion that the war is a crusade by brave Allies against evil Nazis. To blur this picture he depicts the hostility the Germans feel towards the collaborators: 'the real hatred of the Germans, I might say in passing, was directed against the "collaborators" … not so much against the Jews'. Such preposterous statements do more than irritate the reader; they introduce an element of absurdity. Céline loves to confuse categories by describing Sigmaringen as a ghetto or by comparing Laval with Mendès-France. Another tactic is to create mysteries, as he does in *Nord* which is full of unanswered questions. How does Madame von Dopf's fan turn up in Faustus's flat? Why does the Russian kill von Leiden? Who are the pierrots Kracht and Ferdinand meet in the darkness? The reader does not know. And this is how Céline uses the motif of the anti-Hitler plot. Ferdinand is told on the Ulm train to deliver a message in code to one of von Runstedt's staff. There is some conspiracy afoot, some evil in the air. But he is not sure what it is.

Conversely there is a sense that everything is known. Harras is a fountain of knowledge who comes to Zornhof at the end, knowing precisely what has taken place in his absence. When Hoffman meets Ferdinand in the Ulm train he greets him like an old friend. Restif is aware in advance that they are all to be killed at Oddort. What the reader is not told is how Restif obtains his information, which adds to the uncertainty. But the feeling that everything has been foreseen hangs over the trilogy. It stems from Céline's fatalism but it also expresses the inevitability in 1944 of an Allied victory.

The destructive process is in full swing. In Céline's novel there is a fine balance between self-hatred and hatred of others; here both are rampant, especially the first. Germany is in 'a nihilistic rage', says Ferdinand as he watches the riots on the railway stations. There are concomitant signs that the end is near, like the uncontrolled sexuality and hysteria that break out in Baden-Baden on the rumour of Hitler's death. Aside from the devastation of the bombing, the Germans are tearing one another apart. At Zornhof the battles are not fought out among different groups, least of all pro- and anti-Nazi. Marie-Thérèse hates Inge who loathes her husband and so on. The village wants to destroy itself. One remembers how Hitler demanded that German towns be laid waste before they were conceded to the enemy. The Nazis – of whom more later – wanted their *Götterdämmerung*. Céline was there to observe it.

Beyond *Götterdämmerung* there lies quite simply extinction – a universe returned to atoms, to nothing at all, where creative power has failed. In the trilogy Hitler, the former housepainter, is no longer able to impose his vision on Europe. It slips from his grasp and disintegrates. In *D'un château l'autre* the collaborators' imagination runs riot but it has nothing to do with their situation. In *Nord* and *Rigodon* the topsy-turvy world of the bombing fades away. Several new forms remain. The reader does not see them being shaped, for there is no Jules to wave his wand. They stand there: the last oases of reality, strange, fragile realms. Some are in Berlin – the shop, the Steinbeck hotel and Faustus's flat. They have been created and populated by the war; they did not exist before and they will vanish as the bombs complete their task. In *Rigodon* there remains only the Hamburg vault – a realm as surprising as Norbert's, but exceptional and surrounded by ruins. Céline is describing the Germany that the war left behind. He has seized on the utter sterility of Hitler's rule.

In *D'un château l'autre* the Charon vision is the key episode, for it is both the gateway from Meudon to Sigmaringen and the flash of privileged insight into life. It follows on the Montmartre vision of *Voyage*, the boat hallucination of *Mort à crédit* and the profusion of creation in *Normance*. Many of its elements are familiar. Ferdinand rejects any notion of the supernatural – 'I'm positivism personified' – and yet describes supernatural events. He wonders whether he is mad or at least 'kind of groggy' and does not decide one way or another. By offering several interpretations of what he sees, none of them complete, he is blurring the various levels of reality. Is the vision to be read in the same way as the description of Meudon? Perhaps, since le Vigan speaks in his usual slang. But it is a legend, too, for le Vigan's gold coins are the *oboles* of Greek mythology. Time is as arbitrary as ever for the boat is a pre-1914 *bateau mouche*, the riverside is Meudon 1956 and le Vigan is associated with the war. The vision encapsulates the book.

It portrays life as a fragile kind of half-death. Charon is a monster 'part ape ... part tiger' who smashes men's heads with an oar. Like Cimetry in *Guignol's Band* he is a personification of death, but he is not complete extinction. His river is the Seine, but instead of rowing across it he goes perpetually up and down. The death he offers is like a continuation of life: beatings and oppression. For Emile death and life are much the same thing. Returning from the Legion of French Volunteers he was beaten to a jelly by a crowd at the Liberation. After his burial he rose up – a parody of the Resurrection – and went to work on Charon's boat. He is not an isolated example, for he has himself seen other men emerge from their mass graves on the Russian front and go out to fight and be killed again – one remembers the vanishing corpse in Clichy. Emile is neither man nor corpse, but a 'monstrous insect' who has some strange existence. He lives at Charon's command and carries on from day to day, not knowing what will become of him.

Le Vigan is a more complex figure. He has a precarious existence as Charon's cashier and his pouch of coins is another form of fairy gold that is tainted with death. He is dressed as for one of his roles – 'a kind of clown–gaucho–boy-scout, well, somebody in disguise' – so that his work is a piece of artistic creation. His account of his experiences with Charon is mixed up with descriptions of his films, which are in turn mixed up with his life in Argentina. He was playing the part of a gaucho when Perón fell and so he had to leave. He escaped across the pampas with the help of gauchos who admired his acting. Le Vigan's life – like his present half-death – is made from his own inventions. After talking to him Ferdinand turns his back on the river and flees. Determined as ever to survive, he will not wait for Charon. But le Vigan has set the tone. Ferdinand is taken back to Sigmaringen where the collaborators fantasized as long as their Charon – Leclerc – would allow.

'The Chancellery of the Greater Reich had worked out a certain mode of existence for the French in Sigmaringen, neither absolutely fictitious nor absolutely real ... half-way between quarantine and operetta.' The ingredients of this existence are the collaborators' wild fantasies juxtaposed with their hopeless positions. They are more ambitious than le Vigan, but they achieve no more. As the war draws to an end even they become aware of this. Behaviour grows more extreme, witness the evolution from the Hilda to the Frau Frucht episodes. Madness breaks out and hatred becomes violent. Finally, in the Hohenlychen section, life itself is very tenuous.

At the outset illusion is rampant. Céline uses theatrical vocabulary to describe the castle. It is 'super-Hollywood', 'stucco and *papier-mâché*', like something out of an 'operetta' – 'you're waiting for the sopranos, the lyric tenors'. Beneath this surface, the castle is evil itself – the stronghold of the Hohenzollern dynasty, full of portraits of emperors and executioners, 'more and more treacherous ... more and more cruel ... grasping ... monstrous'. It is a true image of Céline's absurd universe, for its corridors form an endless labyrinth where everyone – except Lili the dancer – gets lost. And the castle itself is dying, waiting to fall into its own Styx, the Danube, haunted by its ghost, the last of the Hohenzollerns, Princess Hermilie. Here the difference between illusion and truth is explained and the uncertainty of *Guignol's Band* is left far behind.

'Man is first a dreamer! a born dreamer,' says Céline. Most of the fantasies are familiar. There is Bichelonne, obsessed by the triumphal return to Paris – 'on the double beside Laval, triumphant . . . Arch of Triumph, Champs-Elysées.' There is Abetz, who clings to his role as ambassador – 'ambassador of what?', wonders Ferdinand. Not only does he refuse to face the German defeat but he has forgotten all about the war. His obsession is a huge statue of Charlemagne to be built as a symbol of Franco-German friendship in the reoccupied Paris. Beside it will stand statues of Roland, von Runstedt and Darnand. Abetz spends his time reconstructing his Paris, a never-never city. Another imaginary realm is Switzerland, the neutral haven of freedom. In fact its border is thronged with policemen who beat Papillon very badly when he tries to escape. Switzerland too must remain a dream. Raoul Orphize introduces a more complex kind of illusion when he comes – from Dresden of all places – to make a film of Sigmaringen around the *Kraft durch Freude* motif. He and his wife, elaborately dressed, have turned into the glorious figures they intend to portray. As he walks around, he transforms all Sigmaringen into the ideal fascist community of his film. Naturally he does not survive long. Most of the others fare no better for they run the usual gamut of Célinian horrors.

Alphonse de Chateaubriand provides a fresh example of the 'maniac' type. He arrives at Sigmaringen 'like a character in his novel', full of plans to obliterate the Allies with a new spiritual weapon – 'a stupendous moral bomb'. As soon as his dream is shaken he begins hurling crockery, like young Ferdinand's father in *Mort à crédit*. 'He, always so precious, ceremonious, well-mannered . . . all of a sudden I saw him! a total barbarian,' says Ferdinand. Delaunys goes even further and becomes an 'exile'. He and his wife illustrate another of Céline's eternal themes – the break-up of the so-called normal world of pre-1914. Delaunys, a hard-working musician, is imbued with memories of Gabriel Fauré and Florent Schmidt. Confronted with the craziness of Sigmaringen he falls apart. He takes refuge in a dream: to be first violinist at a concert to celebrate von Runstedt's retaking of the Ardennes. Far removed from violence, he withdraws into the castle's music room where he eats, sleeps and rehearses.

Even he is less extreme than the mad bishop of Albi, who looks back to Fleury in *Mort à crédit* and forward to pastor Schroeder in *Nord* and even to le Vigan's Christ role. For Céline madness and Christianity go together, because the strain of believing in an ultimate harmony is too great. The Christian juggles pain and redemption until he can stand it no more and becomes the maddest of all men, victim of his fellows. As an Albigensian the bishop has much experience of suffering – 'persecuted since 1209', he says, corroborating his creator's view of history. But he believes in a communion that goes beyond hatred and, for a few short moments, he imposes this vision on those around him. He ends the violence of the Strasburg refugees and saves Clotilde. Later in *Nord* Schroeder will use the shattered Nazi planes as aviaries, symbols of plenty. He too believes in harmony: 'the sky belongs to God! God created the bees! His will be done.' Both priests are treated badly. Schroeder is driven out of Zornhof; the bishop of Albi is packed off to hell, which in this case is called 'room 36'.

Not surprisingly, sexual activity is frenetic in Sigmaringen. It centres around the station: a medley of soldiers on their way to battle, swarms of women, many already pregnant, precocious young girls like Hilda. Sex and war go together as they did in *Voyage*. The descriptions of the pregnant women copulating with soldiers are among the most disgusting in Céline's writing; and yet beauty is present. There is a piano in the station and the endless refrains of *Lili Marlene* are played without a 'discordant note'. Hilda personifies Céline's old ambivalence. She is 'really a beautiful Boche animal', a model of physical perfection who is 'gifted in bitchery' and eager for debauchery. Frau Frucht has no such redeeming virtues. She is ugly, sexually aggressive and enamoured of cruelty. She entertains selected groups of young men and beats her women servants. When Ferdinand visits her he is struck by her eyes – 'her eyes? . . . glowing coals! . . . the fire of live volcanoes . . . dangerous'. 'Is she going to rape me?' asks Ferdinand. Nothing so simple. It is Lili she wants and, in a really grotesque moment, she offers Ferdinand a big plate of ravioli if he brings Lili to her. Even Frau Frucht is, however, less dangerous than Aïcha von Raumnitz who is woman at her most destructive. An 'Oriental horsewoman' with her riding boots and dogs, her task is to drive men down into room 36. Both women are minor versions of Mimi, who take advantage of the chaos to impose their tyranny on men.

Room 36 has a particular importance in the novel. Sigmaringen is full of violence. The Strasburg refugees, who want to beat Clotilde, are trying to find an outlet from their fear. Head-smashing is another familiar motif, exemplified by the unfortunate Papillon. But room 36 means total disappearance. People who enter are just never seen again. Aïcha's genius is to create a void around her: the refugees are swept away and the landing is suddenly bare. Sigmaringen is a 'half-way' life, but nothingness is very much present. Throughout the novel people vanish. Neureuil wanders off into the night and Alphonse de Chateaubriand just leaves. 'I never saw dear Alphonse again,' says Ferdinand, stating one of the trilogy's main themes. The collaborators talk and dream but their deepest desire is 'not to be'. They are all like Fernand de Brinon who has lost interest in politics and 'didn't want to get mixed up in anything any more'. Like the ageing Ferdinand in Meudon, Sigmaringen will end quietly, for death is not as spectacular as in *Féerie*. Not surprisingly the arch-assassin Restif is an ordinary man: 'attentive, discreet ... nothing special about him'. Although his task is to purge France when the collaborators return – 'a hundred and fifty thousand traitors! all to be liquidated in three months' – he treats murder as a matter of technique. He has perfected a trick to cut throats, just like a workman who has learned to clean a car engine. Restif has no ideas and no emotions. Himself a vacuum, he exists to create other vacuums.

The Hohenlychen episode, where Sigmaringen does disintegrate, is introduced in a disjointed way. The narrator does not tell us he is going on the trip and then he describes it as a passenger. This jars the reader, separates these pages from the rest and creates a mystery that is only resolved at the end. The journey to Bichelonne's funeral begins as make-believe. The ministers set out in the Shah of Persia's pre-1914 train. They wrap themselves up in the Eastern hangings in order to keep warm, so they soon look like a theatre cast. As their journey goes on it becomes vague. Place and time are confused: 'we were floating forward as if in a mirage,' says Ferdinand, who wonders whether they are not already in Russia. When they arrive there is no town, no church and almost no service except a last piece of make-believe – the tricolor flag. On the way back their clothes are torn off by a band of wild children: that strips away the last shreds of pretence. There is snow everywhere, the days drift by and they return to an Ulm which has been completely destroyed: 'there wasn't any station ... gutted sheds all around us'. This foreshadows the future: 'there won't be any peace in the world until all the cities are razed'.

This is not Céline's last word – not yet and not even in *Rigodon*. The temptation of nothingness is great and it recurs throughout the trilogy. Like Fernand de Brinon, Céline wants to have done with everything. He is horrified by the spectacle of life going on and on, in a weary succession of *divertissements* and brutalities. In the middle of an empty Ulm he laments that all is not over because 'there'd always be the S.S. and the S.A.'. In connection with Abetz he remarks on 'the continuity of Power', on the arrivistes, courtiers and clowns who dominate life and are 'reborn from century to century'. Sigmaringen offers him a flagrant example of men who persist in fighting over prestige long after they have none. Small wonder that Céline, the severe moralist, should want to put an end to such wicked nonsense. He welcomes the destruction of Germany, just as he looks forward to the atomic war which will terminate the foolish delusions of modern France. Yet the other side of his nature asserts itself: he will face the worst and go on living. The half-life of Sigmaringen – provided it is recognized as such – is worth something.

Its value is assessed by the book's ending: the labour pains of the refugee woman and the arrival of Madame Armandine. Narrator Ferdinand sets the Sigmaringen follies in context, as he did at the beginning. The Hohenlychen episode finishes with the woman who is about to have her baby. Ferdinand takes her off the train and into his makeshift hospital. Babies are a recurrent theme in the trilogy. In *Nord* the young Thomas, 'a strong kid', survives the trip in the trunk of Harras's car and crows healthily when he is picked up. In *Rigodon* the baby abandoned in the train carriage is sturdy and tough. It would be ludicrous to see this as a great symbol of 'Life', a dramatic onrush of optimism and confidence. In one sense Céline is doing no more than saying that babies, like the S.S., will always be with us and that, as they cannot reason, they are well equipped to live in a ridiculous world. But in *D'un château l'autre* he presents the motif a little differently. The woman is brave – 'she complains, but not very much' – and Ferdinand returns to the hospital, despite his fatigue, to look after her. Céline is asserting that humans want to survive. Death is something alien and the death-wish an ugly thing. Both patient and doctor fight against them.

The ending of the Meudon section shows how the struggle is carried on. When Madame Niçois returns to see Ferdinand she is half-paralysed and completely silent. Ferdinand himself is weak: 'you're never really awake, you're always dozing,' he says of his Meudon life. Death is on his mind and he harks back to the Dreyfus case, remembering Major Henry who committed suicide. But there is no peace for him, because with Madame Niçois comes her friend Madame Armandine who is 'definitely cracked' but full of 'vigour'. She was a cancer patient but she has recovered. Now she laughs and talks all the time. She has the gaiety of old people who know they are near death and have gone beyond fearing it. Her strength comes from her ability to play games: she makes up her face like an actress and goes outside to pirouette like a dancer. She does a 'complete backbend' with her leg in the air 'like the Eiffel Tower'. Grotesque as she is, she displays, in the minor key characteristic of the trilogy, something of Lili's art. She reminds the reader of Madame Bonnard, who keeps death at bay in Sigmaringen with the fragile stanzas of Christine de Pisan.

So one comes back to the artist, the weary narrator Ferdinand, who spins out his stories, going nowhere, no different at the end from at the outset but still surviving. He knows he is another Madame Armandine: 'get up on those ropes you old clown', he tells himself. His point of view on the collaborators is an unusual one. To him their extravaganzas are material for writing, fictions that provide him with his own 'half-life' at Meudon. He has explained his perspective, while discussing the pre-1914 stage-shows he used to go to as a child. He and his grandmother sat enthralled through dramatic representations of Indian onslaughts or the siege of Peking. But the audience could distinguish illusion from truth. When Louise Michel appears on the stage his grandmother tells him: 'That's not Louise Michel my boy . . . it's not her nose or her mouth!' Ferdinand adds: 'you couldn't fool my grandmother'. Having lived through the repression of the Commune she remembers the real Louise Michel and knows she is dead. This is the artist's viewpoint in *D'un château l'autre*: he tells his tales and undercuts them, he listens to Abetz and laughs. From the very waning of his power he draws a new creative force – comedy.

This is why *D'un château l'autre* is Céline's funniest book. The humour is essentially the same as in *Mort à crédit*; but it plays a more important role. It is born, here again, of despair. When Ferdinand returns from Hohenlychen he talks to Lili: 'I tell her about our expedition ... for the laughs ... we laugh ... one more hope gone'. If he hoped, he would be angry; as it is, he can laugh. To him the war is a jumble of disorder, occasionally beautiful and always amusing. His amusement comes from the gulf between one's picture of reality and reality itself, or the lack of it. He makes fun of Abetz and his statues but he is also making fun of himself and his novel.

Even more than *Mort à crédit*, *D'un château l'autre* has the structure of a Molière farce. Instead of plot there is calculated disorder: 'I was supposed to go to Laval's and I took you to Abetz' ... forgive me.' In the Pétain episode Céline has fused two separate stories: the confrontation at the castle and the bombing of the bridge. There is no connection between them, except that they display the same brand of humour. Céline moves from anecdote to anecdote: the Pétain escapade gives rise to the Corpechot saga, a meeting with Abetz is the starting-point of the Alphonse de Chateaubriand outburst. Like the Meudon section, Sigmaringen presents a series of variations on the motif of illusion – very much like *Les Fourberies de Scapin* or, a more sophisticated example, *Le Malade imaginaire*.

The Laval episode shows how the technique works. Ferdinand arrives to play his role as listener: 'he didn't ask anything of me ... except to listen, that was enough!' Laval delivers a long speech about Franco-German cooperation, which Ferdinand greets with irony. Then in the first development he attacks Laval, claiming that the former Prime Minister did favours for his friends but nothing for him. This provides the delighted Laval with another opportunity and he launches into a tirade of self-denigration. Ferdinand applauds: 'Bravo Mr Prime Minister.' Laval shifts again and starts to defend himself before his imaginary judges; this third speech is an appeal to the High Court. To make the whole piece of oratory even more ridiculous Céline punctuates it with Bichelonne's agitated comments about his shattered pane of glass. Finally Ferdinand pushes the fantasy to its breaking-point by demanding and being given the governorship of

Saint-Pierre and Miquelon. Of such nonsense is *D'un château l'autre* made. The book seems as if it could go on for ever with stories about Pétain, Brinon and company; but in fact it stops and a very different novel begins.

The trilogy's chronology is not that of Céline's life. Céline went to Baden-Baden and Berlin before Sigmaringen. In the novels the Sigmaringen story comes before the journeys – or else outside of them – except for the brief return visit to *Rigodon*. The lack of clear order in the sequence of places and the abrupt ending in a park in Copenhagen give the trilogy its air of mystery. Yet the aesthetic order is clear enough. Although *Nord* describes the first part of Céline's wanderings, it continues the *D'un château l'autre* theme of illusion: Baden-Baden is a minor version of Sigmaringen. Then the mass bombing of Berlin puts an end to all fictions and prepares for the nihilistic hatreds of Zornhof.

Baden-Baden is a 'dream', says Madame von Doph, uncrowned queen of the Simplon Hotel. She herself lives on incongruous memories of gallant duels and balls in a pre-war never-never land, and of a husband who had gone to China to train the troops of Mao Tse-Tung. She takes Ferdinand to a Russian Orthodox church in the hotel grounds, where the faithful await the return of the Tsar. She jests: 'the Hotel Simplon is asleep and its guests . . . under a spell! . . . only a bomb can awake them'. But of course the illusion crumbles like the Hollywood setting of Sigmaringen. The rumour of Hitler's assassination provokes fighting and orgies. Even at Baden-Baden nerves are 'shot to hell' and the French collaborators, Nazi officials and German officers react in true Célinian manner. There is nothing political about it, for they all behave in the same way. It is just real human nature showing through. After one decadent night the hotel is cleared out. Ferdinand is sent on to Berlin, Madame von Doph is dispatched to a lunatic asylum. The whole community disappears: 'I never saw any of those Baden-Baden refugees again,' says Ferdinand. How is this vanishing act carried out? Schulze, the Reich's representative, must have received instructions to weed out suspected anti-Nazis. This explanation is hinted at but not stressed. Céline does not want explanations. He wants to present the demise of the Simplon Hotel as a metaphysical event: a fragile reality broken up into chaos and absorbed by nirvana.

Berlin is even more fragile. Ferdinand is puzzled: 'you think a street exists, it's not there any more'. The bombing is killing the town. Through it runs the Spree, 'that Teutonic Styx', and above is a 'sky that will never smile'. Céline makes comparisons with Hiroshima, which to him represents complete extinction. Berlin has not quite reached this point. Céline describes it in theatrical language: 'the city was all stage sets ... whole streets of façades, the insides had caved in'. Something remains of the recreation that went on during the Montmartre bombing. On the pavements old women are constructing castles out of fallen bricks. Buildings that remain standing are changed by the destruction around and within them. The shop, where Ferdinand buys his cane, has 'counters full of nothing' and is staffed by senile salesmen. On the fourth floor, amazingly, is a whole department full of walking-sticks. It is an oasis of abundance, as if designed for the cripples the war has created. Ferdinand himself becomes a new man once he has his canes. He is full of 'delirious joy' because now he can hop around among the ruins. The hotel presents another example of a new form which has emerged from the bombing. On both sides is a 'void' and the building is tottering – 'the walls and partitions give way'. It stands there with new passages created by explosions and bedrooms littered with rubble. Everything about it is artificial – even the coffee is 'false' – and temporary, but it is real enough for Ferdinand. Its proprietor is a Russian who spends his time eulogizing Siberia. What is he doing in Berlin? No specific explanation is needed. The war has created its own population to inhabit its reshaped cities. Berlin is full of 'Sub-Hebraics, Semi-Latvians, Triestines, Africano-Czechs'. They are displaced persons moved from other long-since-destroyed towns, living in air-raid shelters and underground stations, speaking no particular language.

An even greater miracle than the hotel is Faustus's flat. An 'aerial mezzanine', it has been thrown together by the explosions and 'the ceilings, the partitions are from other buildings ... across the street'. Cooperating with the Allied planes, Faustus has furnished his flat with furniture 'from other destroyed neighbourhoods ... especially Alt Köln', and smothered it in flowers, those ambivalent images of beauty as precarious as the flat itself. He is yet another of Céline's artist figures – how many of the collaborators were artists, witness Alphonse de Chateaubriand, Orphize, Delaunys! – and he is creating a world out of the war. Parallel to his flat he builds a Nazi myth: every day the doors of the Chancellery open, Hitler appears, the crowds cheer. Ferdinand, the supreme realist, soon debunks this. When he is taken to the main square he realizes that Faustus is seeing things: 'there's nothing . . . absolutely nothing! . . . the square is deserted . . . all the shops closed . . . and he sees Hitler!' Ferdinand knows that Faustus is another maniac and he leaves as quickly as he can. Faustus is left in Berlin to await the final Allied onslaught.

A 'big stone rectangle, something like granite . . . but more dismal than granite . . . more funereal'. This description of the Chancellery stands as an epitaph on the Reich. In *Nord* Céline has more to say about the Nazis than elsewhere. He depicts two party leaders – Schulze and Harras – as well as an S.S. man, Krachtt; he offers some insight into how Nazi philosophy works. His analysis of Nazism can scarcely be separated from his account of the war, because he is describing the final hours of both. But there are particular features of Hitler's régime that fascinate and repel him. His view as novelist differs from his view as pamphleteer. In *L'École des cadavres* there was a superficial, although misleading, admiration for the New Order – Aryan purity and other nonsense – and a more real enthusiasm for Hitler, the great anti-semite. Céline, driving himself to extremes, admired a man who had gone further than he. But in his novels Céline has gone further again and he now looks back on Nazism with contempt. His deep sense of evil enables him to penetrate this most hateful of régimes; but he has no sympathy for it – except perhaps for Harras's mocking nihilism. From the dry, quietly despairing standpoint of the ageing Ferdinand the Reich's antics in 1944 were the futile panderings of men who had wanted to remould Europe, had failed and were now desperately trying to give their death a significance it did not possess.

Faustus's vision of the Führer saluted by his Volk is only one of the Nazi illusions that Céline shatters. He loves to make fun of the master race theory. The only character threatened by the laws on racial purity is Bébert, who risks being put to sleep because he is 'without pedigree' – on one level this is comic, on another Céline is deadly serious: the Nazis show their brutality by trying to exterminate the cat, the creature who understands, as among humans only Lili the dancer can understand, what life and beauty are all about. Céline is indulging in his favourite sport of ridiculing ideologies. Berlin, the Aryan stronghold, is populated with Slavs of uncertain racial origins. Hitler has supposedly done away with the gypsies, but they have a flourishing community at Zornhof. Here again Céline overturns the contemporary French view of the Nazis: far from being inhumanly efficient they blunder around like everyone else. The magistrate who comes to Zornhof was a ladies' hairdresser before 1933 and cannot possibly deal with the situation. Most of the people Ferdinand meets are not party members at all and they loathe Hitler. But that is part of Nazism.

Harras explains to Ferdinand how things work: 'This Reich owes its survival to hatreds.' The Ministry of the Interior is militantly anti-Nazi, the Berlin prostitutes despise all males, Zornhof is a model for the nation: 'all these people denounce, plot . . . and rave'. Nazism has given free rein to the natural human desire to hate. Although it offers all kinds of targets – Slavs, Jews and foreigners – they are not enough. Even the war is not enough, so the Germans end up loathing one another. To achieve their ends the Nazis have unleashed an energy they cannot control. And behind all the rage is the instinct of self-hatred, which leads the country to strike at its leader. At Baden-Baden quarrelling among the various clans goes together with joy at the reported death of their Führer, who is supposed to embody the nation. Nazi Germany has sunk much lower since the Isherwoodian decadence of 1933. The horde of syphilitic prostitutes wandering around the countryside is the concrete manifestation of the base instincts that have been unleashed. But there is no Wagnerian grandeur in all this. By describing a small village Céline turns the Reich's downfall into a squalid affair. Two deranged women, Inge and Kretzer, burning down the house is nothing more than a mockery of *Götterdämmerung*.

The Nazi leaders have trouble maintaining control. Schulze, the party representative at Baden-Baden, is a familiar figure. As the Reich collapses he is preoccupied only with the preparation of his *bouilla-baisse*. Concentration on a trivial matter may be a form of madness, but it helps him avoid a greater madness. Göring does the same at the end of the book when he loses himself in the reconstruction of Napoleon's retreat from Moscow. Kracht does not have this outlet. Perverse as ever, Céline makes the S.S. man a sympathetic figure, who saves Ferdinand when Léonard and Joseph are plotting against him. But Kracht is horrified by the growing hysteria. As the book wears on he turns 'green and yellow . . . all shrivelled up'. When Kretzer yells her insults at the Führer's portrait he does not know what to do. He shaves off his Hitler moustache and then re-grows it. He threatens to commit suicide.

Official Nazi order is breaking down, but Harras reasserts his brand of control. He returns to Zornhof after the murders to set things straight: 'Nazi administration! ... high-powered and meticulous! philosophic-accelerated', he tells Ferdinand mockingly. It consists of putting the murderers Léonard and Joseph in charge of the estate. Inge, Kretzer and the Countess Thor von Thorfels are packed off regardless of their innocence or guilt. The two French prisoners start to run the farm efficiently because Harras has warned them: the slightest mistake and they will be hanged. He has used the technique of playing off one hatred against another. Morality is not his concern. What matters is that Zornhof should give no trouble and that the farm should be run as usual.

Harras's strength springs not from any belief in the justice of Hitler's cause but from a limitless pessimism. No one is more certain that the war is lost. The 'Russians will go as far as Berlin,' he says. He does not need to analyse the fighting rationally, for he is guided by a truly Célinian sense of absurdity. The vast, empty plains of Prussia are a void, which is the natural home for the nameless, faceless hordes of the Red Army. Harras feels this. He has 'absences', where he enters a 'mystic trance' and joins with the nothingness to come. He takes Ferdinand to a former Huguenot village near Berlin and muses on vanished civilizations. He does not hate, for what would be the use? He does have an obsession: medical cooperation between France and Germany. He wants Ferdinand to help him write a study on some obscure German doctors who worked at the universities of Paris and Montpellier. But when Ferdinand produces nothing he does not mind. He has some magic power for his Zornhof cupboard is an Ali Baba treasure trove, which remains full of delicacies no matter how often Ferdinand raids it. But Harras does not really need his cupboard. He is charmed by the absurdities of the Reich's last days, oscillating between 'serene wisdom' and 'spells of buffoonery'. He knows that his underground headquarters at Grünewald are a parody of the New Europe. He is delighted to use all the Berlin searchlights to look for Bébert or to fly off to Lisbon where he confers with Allied doctors about the dangers of plague. Such irrational acts are born from and reinforce his nihilism.

Officially he is a Nazi party member and politically he is a heretic. Is he in some deeper sense a Nazi? The link between nihilism and fascism is clear. Camus, for example, criticizes his German friend because he so 'readily accepted despair'.[3] Not that Harras's extreme pessimism is the springboard to fanatical belief. He has no use for jackbooted Stormtroopers. But it does set him above moral laws. It permits him to put murderers in command. It leaves him free to choose arbitrarily between good and evil, to like the French and loathe the Slavs. After all, why not? If asked his opinion Harras could make no objection to the concentration camps. Meanwhile he himself stands outside the human condition. He lives luxuriously while ordinary people go hungry and he shelters in Grünewald while Berlin is destroyed.

On both counts he is arrogant. It is a more subtle arrogance than the banal Nazi assumption that they represented Europe and with their downfall European culture ended. But Harras is pleased with the collapsing world, unlike Ferdinand who is equally pessimistic but does not share – or want to share – his protector's lawless freedom. Of course Harras's reign as king of the absurd does not last long. When Ferdinand meets him again in *Rigodon* he finds that Harras 'wasn't laughing any more'. Already in *Nord* Ferdinand notes that he 'came to a bad end ... bound to ... a lot worse than me'. Presumably Harras was high on the Allied list of war criminals. But Céline does not tell us what happened because he prefers to let Harras sink into oblivion – like Nazi Germany itself.

It does not matter, then, that the von Leiden family is aristocratic and not overtly Nazi. In the violence of its hatreds it is Germany in miniature. By concentrating on a small village not directly affected by the war, Céline is showing the intrinsic evil in each man that causes destruction. At the same time references to the bombing of Berlin show the greater forces at play. Céline presents the Zornhof episode in almost Balzacian manner: Harras describes the cast of characters and Ferdinand meets them all in the first few days; then the tension rises until it erupts into the murder and arson which conclude the book. Once again the psychology is familiar – perhaps all too familiar: a few surviving illusions, the collapse of pre-1914 normalcy, mutual loathings followed by madness, sexual excess and violence.

Most of the characters at the manor house are still living in the aristocratic, pre-Nazi world. Baron von Leiden harks back to the gaiety of Paris which he knew before the 1870 war; the Landrat seems to Ferdinand like a figure out of the Russian ballet; Countess Thor von Thorfels remembers the Bois de Boulogne and the battle of flowers. But it is too late for such fantasies. Madness is everywhere: Kretzer provides a female example when she bursts into hysterics and denounces both the evil French and Hitler. Other people go even further. Like Delaunys, Hjalmar is the 1914 man of duty unable to cope with this greater war. He goes around every day beating his drum to warn of air raids, although no bomb has fallen on Zornhof. Baron von Leiden is cast in similar mould because he goes off on his horse to fight the Russians, as he had done thirty years before. In *Nord* hatred is more gratuitous than in any of Céline's novels. Ferdinand provides a target for the patriots Léonard and Joseph, for Kretzer, for the village. Hatred comes as first reaction to the younger von Leiden. As a cripple he makes contact with life through his deformity, so he immediately loathes it in blind self-defensiveness. Ferdinand is the object of his dislike but his feelings run deeper. Similarly the Landrat 'doesn't like the French at all, or the Russians, or the Nazis, or the Poles'. In his case his hatreds are an all too obvious form of self-hatred because they lead to his murder. The several killings result from the Zornhof atmosphere rather than from specific motives. It is not clear, for example, why or how the Russian kills von Leiden. There is little individual psychology left because, feeling themselves close to death, the characters respond with naked human emotion. Their actions are quite explicable in Célinian terms. The Berlin prostitutes who beat the Baron to death are following in the tradition of Célinian woman who is intent on destroying man. Inge, in attempting to poison her husband, is doing the same. And her final outburst where she tries to set fire to the manor is nothing more than an expression of the death-wish that haunts all Germany.

Meanwhile the other war goes on and the bombers thunder overhead to destroy Berlin, just as the von Leidens are destroying Zornhof. The Allies could obliterate the village any time they wished to – 'one hand-grenade would do it'. This fear haunts all the characters, breaking Kracht's morale and provoking Kretzer's hysteria. The rhythms of the explosions punctuate conversation. Ferdinand notes that 'the manor house never stopped trembling' and that 'the lukewarm soup in the dishes rippled and trembled'. Zornhof is caught up in the conflagration, a mere point on the roulette wheel of war. Its hatreds have a metaphysical as well as a personal dimension. Looking back from his post-war vantage point, Céline sees that all these things were signs of the end: 'all these people I'm talking about must be ghosts ... they were even then'.

So narrator Ferdinand writes down the events of his shrunken world. However malicious von Leiden might be, he does not have Jules' stature; Countess Thor von Thorfels' dreams are not as colourful as Abetz'. Ferdinand has less scope for comedy or rhetoric, hence the simplicity of his narration. The problem is vividly illustrated by the figure of le Vigan who is both Ferdinand's *alter ego*, as Robinson was Bardamu's, and the descendant of the artist figures of *Féerie*. Le Vigan can remain alive only by finding a role. As Charon's gaucho-moneytaker he had some tenuous existence; now things are even worse.

When he arrives in Berlin no one recognizes him, which to le Vigan is the equivalent of death. In the passport office he rants on about his flight from Paris with the *maquisards* at his heels. Still no attention. He is willing to catch at any straw as Ferdinand later explains: '"Le Vig", you could say, "you killed your mummy!" ... that turned the trick ... he'd change before your eyes.' Without a part he bursts into hostility – convinced that the people in the passport office are spies – or else slumps into a daze.

In the course of *Nord* he does find several roles and he leaps from one to another like a frantic acrobat – to borrow one of Céline's favourite images. The part he prefers is Christ: the suffering, triumphant Christ of the Passion. At Grünewald he stands crucified with the two Polish girls at his feet. By playing Christ he can give some shape to his misfortunes: he is redeeming the girls. This also allows Céline to make another of his ambivalent comments on Christianity: only a Christ could make the war meaningful and the only Christ is the mad actor Le Vigan. Frequently he flies to the other extreme and, despairing of his divinity, adopts the role of the 'man from nowhere'. This marks no triumph, but it does give form to the half-life he is leading. Does he wander hopelessly around Germany? Well he is a true man from nowhere. At another moment he is Molière's misanthropist, which is a relevant role at Zornhof, for it enables him to avoid the seething hatreds and it gives meaning to his loneliness.

These extreme points of view are le Vigan's only defence against the war. There is no question of self-control or logic: 'No use trying to reason with le Vigan, the "man from nowhere" . . . a waste of time.' He has to 'create himself' an identity. As the murders pile up he has less material to work with. He retreats into silence and utters only a soft 'broum' at each bomb explosion. He is being drawn into the destruction of Germany. H existence slides away as he forgets what has happened to him – the Steinbock Hotel and Grünewald disappear into nothingness. Only desperate measures remain. He goes into a dream of happiness which he substitutes for Zornhof: 'I'm in the middle of a dream . . . don't bother me! . . . you'll be in it too! and Lili! and Bébert! . . . all four of us in a dream.' Pathetically he offers this non-reality to Ferdinand, who is too weary to challenge him but too sceptical not to mock. Then in front of the magistrate le Vigan breaks his silence to leap forward and shout: '*Ich bin der mörder*'. Is he expressing some universal guilt or is this the only possible role? Le Vigan, the proud actor, is breaking down. Is he mad or is this an ultimate piece of pretence? With him 'you could never tell', says Ferdinand. But at the end of the book le Vigan has exhausted the resources of his imagination.

This is the starting-point of *Rigodon* where le Vigan, completely defeated, drops out of the struggle. Ferdinand continues, although he too is being worn down. As he puts it, he and Lili are 'more and more simple travellers, more and more modest tourists – we would finish up on all fours'. His artist's power has waned still further. Corresponding to the Charon hallucination is the Vaudremer vision. The presentation of death is different here. Charon was a monstrous figure and his speciality was head-smashing. Vaudremer is quieter. He stands there 'greenish' like a 'sort of ghost'. He does not reply to Ferdinand and he vanishes after a moment. The spectacle he conjures up is not violent. It is the aftermath of the 1940 defeat, the refugee camp at Saint-Jean d'Angéley. The German tanks are watchful but not aggressive. The French are sinking slowly into the mud where they will rot peacefully. This vision is presented quickly as one of the opening chapters. It is on a par with the others and it does not make an exceptional impact on the reader. The role of the visionary artist is hence reduced – just as in the vision itself there is no Le Vigan to assert the imagination.

In *Rigodon* the illusions of Sigmaringen and the hatreds of Zornhof are replaced by a haphazard vagueness.[4] There is even less plot: just Ferdinand's travels around Germany. His eyes are fixed on Denmark but he has to go where he can. He is stopped at Warnemünde by soldiers. Who are they? They are neither S.S. nor S.A. Are they really guarding him? It is not clear, but Ferdinand submits to the compulsion they represent. Then the train stops at Moorburg, although it is supposed to go to Berlin. The Sigmaringen trip provides another detour. When the train is stopped under mountains Ferdinand does not know where they are or where the other passengers hope to go. Even after he turns north again it takes him several trains and several accidents to get to Denmark. Images of nothingness surround him. Even the enemy is absent. The R.A.F. planes ignore Ferdinand's train and as for the Russians, 'we talk about them all the time but we never see them'. Céline does not want to present conflict because it interferes with his theme of human life just disappearing. He makes frequent references to the Third World War when death will come suddenly from the outside, like the hand of God. The 'next one, the atomic one' will be soon over, says Ferdinand; a 'continent to be wiped out? ... matter of two ... three minutes'. But in the meantime fragments of Germany remain.

As Ferdinand travels he meets the familiar Célinian figures, most of them shadows of their former selves. Instead of the vindictive von Leiden there is the English cripple at Hanover; Harras reappears but he is pale and worried now. The characters resort to the same desperate stratagems in order to stay alive. Felipe follows Schulze and Göring in fixing on one simple idea: he wants to return to his boss at the brick factory at Magdeburg. For him 'the war wasn't something you bothered about ... the war was going on somewhere else'. He has to hold on to a kind of normalcy, because the cataclysm is too great for him to comprehend. At Rostock there is Dr Haupt, perhaps the last Nazi, who runs things as Harras did in Zornhof. He lays out the wounded in the snow: the strong get up and walk, the weak die. This grotesque parody of Nietzsche is all that remains of the Reich's philosophy. Proseïdon is a recognizable figure of a different kind. A Greek doctor with a French wife who spent years in the Soviet Union, he is accustomed to horrors. His solution is to remain silent. He keeps to himself, saying nothing and munching on black bread – he is a model for the suspicious Ferdinand.

Other characters have been broken by the war. When Ferdinand meets von Runstedt he is amazed to find no trace of the feared tank commander. Undisturbed by Le Vigan's outburst, von Runstedt speaks absentmindedly to Ferdinand, strokes Bébert and leaves. Céline is showing that the notions one has of reality are false. The von Runstedt of the Ardennes campaign does not exist – or at least not any longer. People do not have permanent personalities but, instead of going from passion to passion as in the earlier novels, they slump into nothingness. A more extreme example is the ironically named Siegfried, who is the sole and useless survivor of Ulm's one hundred and ten firemen. Siegfried, obsessed with suicide, has forgotten his name and his age. His profession and past life have vanished along with his home town.

Not surprisingly the 'I never saw him again' refrain runs through *Rigodon*. The symbolic example is von Lubb who slips off the train in the tunnel and is lost. His men look for him but they cannot find him and the train leaves. 'Marshal von Lubb? – did he even exist?' muses Ferdinand. Perhaps Ferdinand invented him in order to create some sort of reality; but, if he did, he cannot keep him in being. Proseïdon and his grave-digging lepers are sent off across the snow to Stettin. Naturally they vanish: 'In fact we never saw them again, or heard anything about them ... nothing about the leper colony or Stettin ... towns and villages have changed their names, so it seems.' Restif, even quieter than in *D'un château l'autre*, disappears after the Oddort shootings: 'I never saw Restif again ... neither in Germany, nor in Denmark ... nor later on here.' Ferdinand keeps meeting people – like the Rostock wounded – who may be alive or dead or even something else. As he flees from Oddort he sees 'forms ... they looked like forms, darker than shadows'. We are never told who or what they are. The uncertainty in Ferdinand's description is characteristic: it may be that the forms do not exist or that he cannot describe them or, most probably, both of these things. Over the waiting-room in Flensburg station hovers a 'bluish glimmer ... you can't see very well whether these people are dead or not'. By the time Ferdinand reaches Hamburg it scarcely matters, for his entire chronicle is fading away.

This is really what *Rigodon* is all about. Neither the people nor the places are described in any detail. They stand as lists of names, each town being a variation on the theme of near-nothingness. They have no connection with one another, for that would imply some order and there is none. They reveal different kinds of destruction which Ferdinand notes down and puzzles over. That is all there is to it. At Rostock the hotel is deserted and it offers none of the surprises of the Steinbock. Soon the town will be empty: 'There will be no one left in Rostock,' says Ferdinand, introducing another *leitmotif*. Warnemünde presents a characteristic play on the real and the unreal. It is described like theatre décor: 'baroque chalets ... the "frivolous German" style'. Ferdinand's hopes rise and he thinks of escape, for beyond Warnemünde lies the sea. But the sea merely mirrors the North German plain: 'a grey platitude ... the sky, the little pebbles, the water ... they all blend together out there, far away'. This is an image of death and any notion of escape is fallacious. On again to Ulm which is completely empty. The buildings have been razed, the people have fled, even the incendiaries have disappeared. 'Death is only a cleaning machine,' says Céline. Oddort is another variation. In peacetime it was not a town at all. Now it has been created by the Reich's war-machine as a place of death. Its population waits to be shot down. In true Célinian manner, neither murderer nor murdered knows who the other is nor why the killing is taking place. And so the list of towns goes on – to Hanover which is reminiscent of the Berlin of *Nord*. It has 'ex-mansions' and what is described as a 'street, at least it looks like a street'. Some forms can be distinguished among the rubble and it is here that *Rigodon*, for a while at least, changes direction.

By this time le Vigan has gone. In *Rigodon* he is slumped in despair like a 'dime-store Hamlet'. Not until Ulm does he find his last role. He dresses up in Siegfried's fireman's uniform to hunt for incendiaries. But the part is not complete: 'he would like to see himself like that as he is ... all decked out ... but there's no mirror'. Without it le Vigan cannot be sure that he has created a new identity, that he has projected himself. He wanders down the street unhappily: as Ulm is empty there is no one to recognize him and make him real. Then he meets the French workers who are delighted to welcome the famous actor. Their admiration gives him the strength to play a great role: he leaps out into the road to challenge the German army. He hurls his defiance at von Runstedt: 'No longer will you go to France.' A moment later 'he doesn't even remember it any more'. The Germans are not upset since the time for patriotism is long past. Le Vigan returns to apathy and soon after he seizes the chance to leave for Rome. Reverting to his Christ role, he abandons Ferdinand and sets out on his ridiculous quest.

But the artist's power to transform is not quite eclipsed; at Hanover Ferdinand has a last hallucination. As usual there is a positivistic explanation – his head is struck by a brick – and as usual it does not account for everything. In his hallucination Ferdinand enters into the chaos around him and ceases to think of himself as a puzzled observer. The distinction between subject and object, which is never marked in Céline's writing and which is so easily blurred by the ambiguous references to the narrator's head, is abolished. Ferdinand plays with grammatical forms, juggling 'a brick hit you on the head' with 'I've been hit by a brick'. He is putting the brick and himself on the same level. At once he begins to see a magical order behind the chaos. Felipe makes bricks in Magdeburg so he must be responsible for the one that fell on Ferdinand. Perhaps he is a sorcerer. This is a very minor version – almost a parody – of the bold interpretations of *Normance*. But another theme is more important: Ferdinand begins to see beauty in the war.

This theme has not been completely absent from the trilogy. In *D'un château l'autre* Ferdinand enjoys the spectacle of the station: 'poetry ... flesh was made to be on the move! the perpetual coming and going isn't just in the sky ... same on the rails!' From his artist's perspective he can forget the embittered crowds and appreciate the universal movement. The beauty of the creative–destructive process is shown again in *Nord*, witness the reshaping of Berlin. At Hanover Ferdinand begins to use aesthetic terms to describe what is happening to and around him. He hears 'the air as of a symphony over this ocean of ruins'. It is he who is 'composing' the music, although 're-composing' would be a better word, for artist and universe are one. Germany is caught up in a great dance which Ferdinand, determined to invoke all the arts, describes in a curious mixture of words. The 'houses are like pictures,' he says, 'they hang over and buckle.' He reintroduces the upside-down motif, when he sees a huge engine perched on its head in a heap of scrap metal. Like the houses it has lost its function and it remains as a shape. When he arrives in Hamburg he sees the entire harbour upside-down and all the ships 'with their noses stuck in the mud'. And, inevitably, the image of flowers recurs: the bombs that fall on the Kiel canal explode 'like giant blossoms green ... red and blue'.

This is a world of colours, shapes and sounds. Ferdinand ceases – although not completely – to worry about Denmark and gives himself up to enjoying it. Other people do not share his vision, but that is because they are not artists or because they are not mad. To Ferdinand, author of *D'un château l'autre*, North Germany has become vastly comic: 'it makes me laugh,' he says. As he surveys the ruins and the pitiful train with its drunken engine-driver, he sees the war as a huge farce: 'I start laughing again, I can't stop myself.'

Appropriately enough he is surrounded by a throng of idiot children who are also enjoying the war. Children play the part in the trilogy that Courtial's band played in Blême-le-Petit. Since they take the world as it comes, without expecting it to make sense, they thrive amidst chaos. In *D'un château l'autre* the refugee youngsters tear the clothes off the ministers and create havoc in the train. In *Nord* the Russian children, who play in the manor gardens, are quite heedless of the plotting within. In *Rigodon* Céline has taken the theme still further, for these children are exiles who know nothing of fear or pain or normal human expectations. They 'are going in the same direction as life'. So they rampage with delight across ruined Hamburg. Céline reasserts the theme of *Mort à crédit*: madness and art go together. Lili moves 'like an acrobat' through the rubble, Ferdinand is still laughing. They are spiritual parents for the children: 'We are as idiotic as they,' says Ferdinand, who also puts it the other way round: 'they knew as much about things as we did'. The cortège visits the underground cavern which is Céline's last miracle.

This is both a kind of hell, littered with corpses, and a wondrous realm created by the bombing. It is 'a phenomenon hard to imagine outside of very special circumstances ... the elements, finally, gone quite beyond themselves'. Everything is topsy-turvy but shops are maintained intact. Inside them shelves of food are stacked up in neat order as they were in Harras's cupboard. The idiot children run amok amidst the crevices and Bébert and Lili find their way around easily. By comparing it with Notre-Dame Ferdinand invites the reader to see it as a monument of the war-torn twentieth century. But it is doomed: 'the giant arch ... wouldn't last long'. Already it is unique in Hamburg, soon it 'would crumble away'. Ferdinand is anxious to leave and he drags the children off. By the time the train reaches Flensburg his head is better and his visions are over. He is thinking about escape again.

Finally he reaches Denmark. Copenhagen is a haven, for it has not been bombed and there is plenty of food. Ferdinand finds a hotel and walks through the tranquil streets. But this is a half-reality. It is a 'charm', some frail invention that is man's last refuge. Ferdinand at least is not deceived, for he knows his true position: he is a notorious collaborator wanted by the French police. Soon he will be tossed into prison. He feels that 'nothing here is for us ... we are not all in our place'. Behind Copenhagen's calm lies the inevitable violence: nightly police raids on the waterfront and cries of pain from the town's prison. In any case Denmark will disappear as Germany has done: 'everything will vanish soon and collapse: décors, streets, the hotel and us beneath'.

In another of his circular twists of chronology Céline is taking the reader back to an early incident in *D'un château l'autre*, which was also set in Denmark. Ferdinand was working as a helper in the hospital. His 'presence there was very fragile'. He was busy with the cancer patients: when they died he wheeled them out to the morgue. To the doctors he said 'never a word'. But even this tenuous existence was stopped when a guard entered, 'strong but quiet', and took him back to the total silence of prison.

The same sense of void hangs over the Hellenrup park episode. Ferdinand and Lili know one moment of reality. They take out their passports and marriage certificate which prove that they exist. Significantly these documents are bundled up with a tube of cyanide. Death is very close now and life can persist only by magic. In the trees are rare birds, which have escaped from the Reich's zoos. Lili and Ferdinand are 'bird charmers' with whom these other refugees feel safe. For a while they sit there, the dancer and the writer, surrounded by beauty, at one with their war-torn world. Then Denmark gives way to Meudon, the vanished Balzac, the Chinese armies and nothing.

To write three long novels about a writer who has less and less to say and a Europe that is going under is a tremendous gamble. It does not entirely work. The Zornhof pages in *Nord* can be tedious and *Rigodon*'s vagueness is an artistic shortcoming as well as a theme. But in all three novels the sense of 'otherness' is strong. The metaphysical nothingness is Céline's last vision of death and it is certainly as compelling as the bloodshed of Flanders. It shapes the entire trilogy and explains its curious simplicity. *D'un château l'autre* is particularly comic because laughter is all that is left to Ferdinand. *Nord* is particularly grim because the Zornhof hatreds are all he has to jot down. But in both novels the 'otherness' is vivid: Leclerc's Senegalese and the air-raids on Berlin. In *Rigodon* it has taken over almost completely. Yet Céline's last word is survival. The Chinese are coming but they have not yet arrived. The old clown is still up on the ropes, resenting it but creating. Around him, in concentric circles, his various selves are dancing. They are protecting him against death, helping him in the fight from beyond the grave. The dance is still going on.

Conclusion

While this book was being written the Passage Choiseul was being rebuilt. The shabby old shops were torn out and shiny new boutiques put in. The lighting is better and the walls gleam with paint. There is no lace-shop but there is a 'sex-shop' and a store selling Mary Quant make-up. The Passage has been brought into the 1970s. The restaurant at the corner has discarded its *art nouveau* décor and replaced it with garish plastic. Nothing could better illustrate Céline's remoteness from the Europe of today. Last year Arthur Koestler went back to the places in France where he had hidden during the chaos of 1940. He found them smug and prosperous, almost unrecognizable. Koestler seemed bewildered. The world he had known had disappeared. Similarly, Céline felt in the last years of his life that he belonged to another Europe: a continent of wars and ideologies, of frontiers that were jealously patrolled, of communists and fascists. It was quite different from the Europe of the Common Market. Paradoxically Céline owes his posthumous recovery of fame to the very fact that his Europe has gone under. A younger generation can look more calmly on his political views. And yet when reading Céline one must make an imaginative leap backward: to the Gare de l'Est and the Popular Front and, still further, to the Dreyfus case and the not so *belle époque*. Céline lived his age to the full. France's defeat in 1940 was a personal defeat, industrialization was a direct insult. He belonged to the *bureaux de tabac*, the neighbourhood restaurant and the glorious French cavalry.

When one thinks of him as a Frenchman one comes back, hauntingly, to de Gaulle. The comparison seems strange at first: the triumphant world-statesman and the shabby, tormented writer. They have the similarities of opposite extremes: they are equally removed from the self-satisfied France over which Pompidou now rules. But there is more. De Gaulle's vision of '*grandeur*' has the same metaphysical dimension as Céline's obsession with France and the graveyard. Both had religious temperaments. France is not the sum of its citizens and certainly not the total of their economic wealth. God has given it a special destiny – to be exceptionally great or exceptionally miserable. Both believed that they alone possessed truth and they refused all compromises. Both incarnated their France. In 1940 de Gaulle continued the struggle in the name of the nation, Céline assumed the burden of the defeat. De Gaulle, too, throve amidst catastrophes. He returned to power during the Algerian war; in the late 1960s he seemed to grow bored with peace. He may have believed that France was eternal but he was deeply conscious of death. Like Céline, he was shaped by the early years of the century and he distrusted the modern world. In the 1930s he was a prophet and his message was the same as Céline's: France would lose the war. In the 1950s Céline withdrew to the solitude of Meudon – his Colombey – and waited, like de Gaulle, for disaster. Both men had a low opinion of their compatriots – de Gaulle's comment about their 'grumbling, griping and groaning' has a very Célinian ring. Naturally they encountered great hostility. De Gaulle had almost the entire country against him in 1940, Céline in 1944. De Gaulle was condemned to death by Pétain, Céline was forced into exile, both risked assassination. They gave themselves up to their destinies and by the end they had little personal life: they were legends already. Today the Cross of Lorraine towers over the hillside at Colombey while there is still no plaque in the Passage. But even that continues the parallels. De Gaulle in his simple French army overcoats and Céline in his old dressing-gowns are two images of a former France.

What remains alive of Céline? When one looks beyond his period and beyond all the different roles he played, what remains of the man and his work? His life was dedicated to probing the pain that men feel at their contact with the world. Each person knows, as he goes about his daily round, that one part of himself does not join in. It remains outside, permanent and untouched. One tries to ignore it but it is there. It was Céline's destiny to face this 'otherness': to look hard at it and to liberate it. It rushes out in his work as fear: the fear of man abandoned to himself. In Céline's vision this fear engulfs all existence. It expresses itself in many ways: as pain, loneliness, hatred and pity. These are the guiding demons of Céline's work – inseparably interwoven. But beyond all of them is this fundamental and total fear. It explains why reading Céline is such a shattering experience. It is not that fate dominates or that death lies in wait. It is that at every moment the 'otherness' is rampant. It runs around screaming that the nightmare is real and the waking hours only a dream. It imposes on the reader a very special kind of pain – reminiscent perhaps of Shakespeare's wildest moments in *King Lear*. This note runs through the narrator's comments at the beginning of *Mort à crédit*, through Céline's letters from Denmark, through his conversations with Pastor Löchen. This is Céline's wisdom.

Small wonder that his achievement is caught up with evil. How could he have analysed hatred so well if he had not felt in himself an infinite need to hate? In the pamphlets he gives himself up to his destructive/self-destructive passion. This particular strain is part of the psychology of fascism. It is present in Hitler's character as well as in the movement as a whole – Hitler's flair for attracting enemies equalled even Céline's. In the pamphlets Céline gives way to it.

But in the novels he does not. Not only does he suffer through his nightmare, but he brings out of it his wonderful cascade of language, a monument to the human greatness he so strenuously denied. These two things account for his importance as a writer: his vision of catastrophe and his style. All else is secondary. His understanding of human psychology is great, he creates characters who live, he makes innovations in the structure of the novel. But his books are dominated by two images: the graveyard and the dancer. The beauty that Elisabeth and Lili attained through movement he will recreate through language. From the depths of the night he returns with the gift of tongues.

This accounts for his unique place in modern writing. Who are his forerunners? His place in the Augustin–Pascal–Baudelaire lineage has been discussed, his role as a *voyant* in the Rimbaud tradition has been mentioned. But in twentieth-century France no one – except for Bernanos and Beckett – has anything of his tragic vision. For this reason alone *Voyage* is a landmark. Nor does any novel written since 1932 catch its special brand of pain. What of the second element – language? Céline's contribution is certainly original and if he has ancestors they are poets, not prose-writers. The question of his influence is more complex. From the late 1950s on, French writers have paid eloquent tribute to Céline. Alain Robbe-Grillet calls him the greatest writer of the period between the wars and a major influence on the *nouveau roman*. But in practice Céline's influence is a negative one. By breaking down barriers he made possible the stylistic experiments of Robbe-Grillet and Butor. He showed that rounded periods were not necessary and he introduced new kinds of vocabulary. He made traditional French writing seem obsolete. For this reason he is admired too by Roland Barthes and the theorists of *Tel Quel*. But Céline's style is not negative or anonymous. Its most important characteristic is its incessant creative drive – the so-called language-game. Few writers have followed him down this path. Le Clézio asks how one can write differently from Céline. But he does not himself write like Céline. The epic quality has been lost.

Outside of France, who has taken on Céline's mantle? The most obvious claimant is Henry Miller who repeatedly told Lawrence Durrell how much Céline meant to him. Miller too tries to unleash the hidden side of human nature and his style has the torrential flow of *Mort à crédit*. But his vision is more optimistic and – a strange word to apply to the author of *Tropic of Cancer* – more innocent. He does not have the Célinian sense of evil. In this respect Faulkner is closer to the creator of Robinson. The beat writers who have been compared with Céline – Ginsberg, Kerouac and company – seem like children beside him. Somewhat closer stands John Hawkes whose fictional landscapes catch something of the hallucinatory quality that is found in Céline's London or Berlin. In Germany, a case could be made for Günter Grass – at least as far as language is concerned. It is interesting that Ralph Manheim who translates Céline also translates Grass. And in Britain one might have to go back to Joyce, who is the only writer who can really match Céline's command of language but whose achievement is much different. One could go on with these examples but perhaps there is no one who writes like Céline. His style is the mirror of his temperament. It shapes and reflects the dreadful adventure that was his life. He stands on the very limits of literature, at a spot where he cannot be annexed or tamed. He is still out in the depths of the night.

Notes and References

1 THE FIRST FORTY YEARS

1. Robert Poulet, *Entretiens familiers avec L.-F. Céline*, Plon, Paris, 1958, pp. 19 ff. and Max Dorian, 'Céline rue Amélie', in *Les Cahiers de l'Herne*, 3, *L.-F. Céline*, pp. 25–7.
2. Poulet, op. cit., p. 19.
3. Ibid., p. 31.
4. Jeanne Carayon, 'Le docteur écrit un roman', *L'Herne*, 3, p. 32.
5. Dorian, op. cit., p. 26.
6. Georges Geoffroy, 'Céline en Angleterre', *L'Herne*, 3, p. 12.
7. L.-F. Céline, *Oeuvres complètes*, vol. 1, Gallimard, Paris, 1969, p. 26. The editor, Jean Ducourneau, provides here a 'Chronologie' (pp. 21–32) which lists accurately the known facts of Céline's life.
8. Poulet, op. cit., p. 3.
9. Lucien Rebatet, 'D'un Céline l'autre', *L'Herne*, 3, p. 42.
10. These reviews are reprinted in 'Dossier de presse du *Voyage*', *Oeuvres complètes*, vol. 1, pp. 777–815.
11. Note to 'Correspondance L.-F. Céline – Lucien Descaves', *L'Herne*, 3, p. 115. For a vivid, partisan account of the Prix Goncourt controversy see Jean Galtier-Boissière *Mémoires d'un Parisien*, vol. 2, Paris, 1961, p. 278 ff.
12. Jeanne Carayon, op. cit., p. 24.
13. *Entretiens avec le Professeur Y*, *Oeuvres complètes*, vol. 3, p. 354.
14. Elisabeth Porquerol, 'Le temps comme il passe. Céline il y a trente ans', *Nouvelle Revue française*, September 1961, pp. 550–57.
15. Note to 'Correspondance L.-F. Céline – Georges Altman', *L'Herne*, 5, p. 134.
16. Marcel Brochard, 'Céline à Rennes', *L'Herne*, 3, p. 14. A good friend of Céline, Marcel Brochard was an ebullient man with a passion for pursuing large animals and young women. His account of Céline's childhood is engaging but not necessarily reliable. He did not know Céline at the time and, in his attempt to demolish the myth of the 'victim', he gives way readily to cynicism.
17. Louis Montmourcy, 'Monsieur Destouches', *L'Herne*, 3, p. 9.
18. Brochard, op. cit., p. 14.
19. Ibid.
20. Ibid., p. 13.
21. Poulet, op. cit., p. 3. When he described his childhood to Poulet, Céline was constructing the legend of the victim. Poulet knew this, but he wrote it down as the version that the ageing Céline wanted people to believe. His book

should be read as a portrait of Céline in his last years, rather than as an attempt at biography. [From an interview which I had with Robert Poulet.]

22. Quoted by Poulet, op. cit., p. 3.

23. Marc Hanrez, *Céline*, Gallimard, Paris, 1961, p. 226. Hanrez was also a frequent visitor to Meudon and the biographical details in his study come from Céline. The same distortion is present as in Poulet's book. For another example of the victim legend see Henri Mondor's Preface to the Pléiade edition of Céline's works.

24. Céline describes this in the *Hommage à Zola*, *Oeuvres complètes*, vol. 2, p. 503.

25. Poulet, op. cit., p. 71.

26. Ibid., p. 56.

27. Hanrez, op. cit., p. 44.

28. 'Des pays où personne ne va jamais', Céline interviewed by Jean Guénot and Jacques Darribehaude, *L'Herne*, 3, p. 185.

29. Poulet, op. cit., p. 74.

30. 'Des pays où personne ne va jamais', p. 187.

31. Brochard, op. cit., p. 14.

32. 'Des pays où personne ne va jamais', p. 186.

33. Marcel Aymé, 'Sur une légende', *L'Herne*, 3, p. 217. This comment must be treated with reserve. Aymé did not know Céline until about twenty-five years later. By this time Céline had been through the trenches and had ample reason to dislike the Germans. In any case, the supposed horrors of Diepholz provided him with material for a good story, another important point.

34. Brochard, op. cit., p. 14.

35. 'Des pays où personne ne va jamais', p. 188.

36. Ibid. This comment – like the next one – is characteristic of the ageing Céline's view of his early life. It should be read with the appropriate circumspection.

37. Poulet, op. cit., p. 77.

38. Brochard, op. cit., p. 14.

39. 'Carnet du cuirassier Destouches', pp. 9–11.

40. 'Entrevue avec Claude Bonnefoy', *Arts*, August 1961, p. 5.

41. André-Louis Lejay, 'Temoignage', *L'Herne*, 5, p. 281.

42. Reprinted in *Oeuvres complètes*, vol. 2, p. 22.

43. Aymé, op. cit., p. 217.

44. Ducourneau, 'La fin d'une légende', in *Oeuvres complètes*, vol. 1, pp. 35–40.

45. Brochard, op. cit., p. 15.

46. Geoffroy, op. cit., pp. 11–12.

47. Ducourneau, 'Chronologie', in *Oeuvres complètes*, vol. 1, p. 26. This is a good example of the dearth of information on the young Céline. Throughout these years Céline must have written to parents and friends. None of these letters has been preserved. In an upper-class, literary milieu, like André Gide's, such letters would have been carefully arranged in the family archives; Céline did not move in such circles.

48. Ducourneau's notes to *Mort à crédit*, *Oeuvres complètes*, vol. 2, p. 712 ff.

49. Poulet, op. cit., p. 77.

50. Ibid., p. 77 ff.

Notes and References

51. Céline to Milton Hindus, 18. 7. 1947, 'Correspondance Céline – Hindus', *L'Herne*, 5, p. 85.
52. Poulet, op. cit., p. 77.
53. Ibid.
54. Henri Mahé, *La Brinquebale avec Céline*, La Table ronde, Paris, 1969, p. 212.
55. 'Chronologie', *Oeuvres complètes*, p. 24.
56. Brochard, op. cit., p. 16.
57. Céline to Albert Paraz, 19.6.1957, 'Correspondance Céline – Paraz', *L'Herne*, 3, p. 157. The 'Correspondance Céline – Paraz' is strewn among five books: Paraz's three journal-pamphlets, *Le Gala des vaches*, *Valsez saucisses* and *Le Menuet du haricot*, and two volumes of *L'Herne*.
58. Brochard, op. cit., p. 14.
59. Guy Morin, 'Destouches médecin', *L'Herne*, 3, p. 18.
60. Ibid.
61. Brochard, op. cit., p. 15.
62. See André Lwoff, 'Quand Céline était "chercheur" à l'Institut Pasteur', *Le Figaro littéraire*, 7.4.1969.
63. Brochard, op.cit., p.16. Brochard knew Céline well at this time. His opinions on the Rennes period have more value than his comments on Céline's childhood.
64. Ibid.
65. Ibid., p. 15.
66. '*La Vie et l'oeuvre de Philippe Ignace Semmelweis*', *Oeuvres complètes*, vol. 1, p. 603.
67. Ibid., p. 617.
68. Brochard, op. cit., p. 16.
69. Céline to Paraz, 19.6.1957, *L'Herne*, 3, p. 157.
70. Poulet, op. cit., p. 57.
71. Céline to Eugène Dabit (undated), 'Correspondance Céline – Dabit', *L'Herne*, 3, p. 89.
72. 'Des pays où personne ne va jamais' *L'Herne*, 3, p. 188.
73. Céline to Hindus, 19.7.1947, op cit., p. 86.
74. 'Chronologie', *Oeuvres complètes*, vol. 1, p. 24.
75. 'La Médecine chez Ford' *Oeuvres complètes*, vol. 1, pp. 709–720.
76. Céline to Dabit (undated), op. cit., p. 86.
77. Céline to Hindus, 22.8.1947, op. cit., p. 92.
78. Ibid. (undated), p. 100.
79. Ibid., 23.8.1947, p. 92.
80. 'Préface pour *Bezons à travers les âges*', *Oeuvres complètes*, vol. 2, p. 511.
81. Jeanne Carayon, op. cit., p. 20.
82. Ibid.
83. Ibid.
84. Céline's favourite term for her.
85. Brochard, op. cit., p. 17.
86. Mahé, op. cit., p. 27.
87. Jeanne Carayon, op. cit., p. 21.
88. Mahé, op. cit., p. 27.
89. Céline to Hindus, 2.9.1947, op. cit., p. 94.
90. Ibid. (undated), p. 96.

91. Jeanne Carayon, op. cit., p. 21.
92. Mahé, op. cit., p. 68.
93. Jeanne Carayon, op. cit., p. 23.
94. For an analysis of the link between role-playing and artistic creation see Erika Ostrovsky, *Voyeur Voyant: A Portrait of Louis-Ferdinand Céline*, Random House, New York, 1971, p. 115 ff.
95. Mahé, op. cit., p. 24.
96. Rebatet, op. cit., p. 45.
97. Mahé, op. cit., p. 11. Mahé tells innumerable, improbable tales of the Clichy clinic. His book is a series of disorganized reminiscences, some having nothing to do with Céline, many based on letters which he received from Céline and which he prints, usually in fragments and without dates. Mahé does not allow historical accuracy to stand in the way of a good story. Yet he certainly knew Céline well and some of his more interesting remarks – about Céline's sexual habits, for example – can be supported from other sources. He depicts a bohemian Céline who enjoyed himself with great gusto. Although Mahé is clearly out to create a new legend, his Céline is at least as true a portrait as the Poulet–Hanrez version and it serves to counterbalance it.
98. Quoted by Pierre Monnier in 'Residence Surveillée', *L'Herne*, 3, p. 164.
99. Hanrez, op. cit., p. 227.
100. 'Préface inédite de *Semmelweis*', *L'Herne*, 3, pp. 163–4.
101. '*La vie et l'œuvre de Philippe Ignace Semmelweis*', *Oeuvres complètes*, vol. 1, p. 587.
102. 'Les assurances sociales et une politique économique de la santé publique', *Oeuvres complètes*, vol. 1, pp. 721–30. This article may be read as a continuation of 'La Médecine chez Ford'.
103. Erika Landry *née* Irrgang, 'Céline et une jeune étudiante allemande', *L'Herne*, 5, p. 37.
104. Mahé, op. cit., p. 11 ff. This is one of Mahé's characteristically fanciful tales.
105. Céline condemned the mask of respectability worn by middle-class people, while himself playing with masks of all kinds. The difference is that he knew he was playing.
106. Erika Landry, op. cit., p. 35.
107. Ibid., p. 36.
108. Ibid., p. 38.
109. Céline to Erika Landry (undated), 'Correspondance Céline–Erika Landry', *L'Herne*, 5, p. 41.
110. Céline to Mahé, quoted by Mahé, Mahé, op. cit., p. 47.
111. Ibid., p. 58.
112. Céline to Eveline Pollet, 25.10.1938, 'Correspondance Céline-Eveline Pollet', *L'Herne*, 3, p. 106.
113. Mahé, op. cit., p. 146.
114. Mahé, op. cit., p. 140.
115. See André Brissaud, 'L.-F. Céline a terminé son voyage au bout de la nuit', *Carrefour*, 5.7.1961, p. 22.
116. Céline to Hindus, 28.2.1948, op. cit., p. 104.
117. Céline to Mahé quoted by Mahé, op. cit., p. 33.
118. Ibid., p. 47.

119. Mahé, op. cit., p. 33.
120. Ibid., p. 39.
121. Céline to Hindus, 28.2.1948, op. cit., p. 104.
122. Ibid.
123. Hanrez, op. cit., p. 225.
124. For another viewpoint on Céline's relationships with women see Erika Ostrovsky, op. cit., p. 66 ff.
125. Céline to Eveline Pollet, 29.6.1933, op. cit., p. 99.
126. Charles Baudelaire, *Journaux intimes*, Crépet et Blin, Paris, 1949, p. 95. There is another of Baudelaire's pithy sayings that Céline might have liked: 'The taste for intelligent women is the taste for pederasty.'
127. Brochard, op. cit., pp. 16–17.

2 *Voyage au bout de la nuit*

1. With the exception of this and the long quotations on pages 53–54 and 111, translated by P.McC., references are to *Journey to the End of the Night*, translated by John H. P. Marks, New Directions, New York, 1960.
2. The quotation is from *L'Eglise*: 'He was a lad of no collective significance, just an individual.' The Céline–Sartre relationship is a dialogue of the deaf. Céline never made any attempt to read Sartre. One wonders whether Sartre ever appreciated the theme of evil – not of absurdity – in *Voyage*. The anguish of the Sartrian character, confronted with a painful liberty, is quite different from the wild panic with which the Célinian character reacts to life. Later – as described in Chapters Five and Six – Céline's anti-semitism turned the two men into enemies. The gulf that separates them illustrates the point discussed here.
3. Samuel Beckett, *Molloy, Three Novels by Samuel Beckett*, Grove Press, New York, 1965, p. 133.
4. Baudelaire; 'Le Voyage', *Les Fleurs du mal*, Crépet et Blin, Paris, 1942.
5. Poulet, *Entretiens familiers avec L.-F. Céline*, Plon, Paris, 1958, p. 98.
6. Céline's strong self-destructive urge is, however, controlled in his novels. This preface may be found in *Oeuvres complètes*, vol. 1, p. 5.
7. Baudelaire, *Journaux intimes*, Crépet et Blin, Paris, 1949, p. 79.
8. Ibid., p. 38.
9. Ibid., 'Le Vampire', *Les Fleurs du mal*, p. 34.
10. Baudelaire, *Journaux intimes*, p. 7.
11. Baudelaire, 'Hymne à la beauté', *Les Fleurs du mal*, p. 25.
12. Baudelaire, *Journaux intimes*, p. 92. This frantic fear of women must of course have played a role in Céline's life. But it would be more than usually foolish to interpret his relationships with women through the attitudes of his fictional selves.
13. Baudelaire, 'La Chevelure', *Les Fleurs du mal*, p. 27.
14. Baudelaire, 'Le Beau Navire', *Les Fleurs du mal*, p. 56.
15. Here, for example, one is tempted to resort to legends. It is a commonplace of most mythologies that the willingness to confront death brings liberation from death. To quote an example Céline might have known: the Breton sailor, who rows the souls of the dead from the mainland over to the île de

Sein, knows that he will be the first man to be drowned the next year. He accepts this. This is not quite the same thing as Céline is saying, but it is similar. And of course Christianity invites the faithful to think at every moment about death, which will come like a thief in the night. But the faithful are not encouraged to take on themselves the guilt and evil in the world. Still, Céline's theme of deliberately incurring guilt has something in common with Baudelaire's determination to be conscious of evil.

16. Quoted by Hanrez in *Céline*, Gallimard, Paris, 1961, p. 276.

3 *Mort à crédit*

1. 'Dossier de presse de mort de crédit', Céline, *Oeuvres complètes*. M à vol. 2 pp. 731–60.

2. References are to *Death on the Installment Plan*, translated by John H. P. Marks, The Bodley Head, London, 1966, except for the long quotation on page 111, translated by P.McC.

3. Anissimov: 'Préface à la traduction russe de *Voyage au bout de la nuit*', *L'Herne*, 5, pp. 165–72. For other Marxist critics see Maxim Gorki: *Conférence des auteurs*, quoted in *L'Herne*, 3, p. 336, and Sartre's friend Paul Nizan: '*Voyage au bout de la nuit*', *L'Humanité*, 12.9.1932.

4. Solipsism is a temptation for Beckett too, as he shows in *Murphy*. Like Céline, he rejects it. In the pamphlets Céline does fall into solipsism because he severs the link between himself and the political reality he is supposedly talking about.

5. On a more general level the Krogold legend may be read as a prophecy of the impending conquest of Europe (Christiania by Krogold) by Hitler. It invites comparison with Louis MacNeice's vision of a new Ghengis Khan and with Yeats's sense of the anarchy loosed upon the world. But the Krogold legend must be seen in the context of *Mort*. Céline is not giving way to a self-destructive fascist dream. He describes the legend with calm irony and separates out the various elements of majesty and murder. Moreover, as is shown in these pages, the legend can be recaptured only by living through the squalor of the Passage. In Céline's novels the dream is always an extension of reality. It is the failed artists, like Ferdinand's father, who try to separate the two.

6. Céline to Elie Faure (undated) *L'Herne*, 5, p. 48. In the Zola lecture Céline uses similar language. He employs the term 'nightmare' and he rejects the objective, documentary approach – 'We work from the inside,' he says.

7. Céline, 'Hommage à Zola', *Oeuvres complètes*, vol. 2, p. 503.

8. Poulet, *Entretiens familiers avec L.-F. Céline*, Plon, Paris, 1958, p. 99.

9. Céline: 'L'argot est né de la haine. Il n'existe plus', *Arts* 6.2.1957. The quotations that illustrate stylistic points are left in French where the English translation loses the point in question.

10. Céline, 'Entretiens avec le Professeur Y', *Oeuvres complètes*, vol. 3, p. 357.

11. Céline, *Bagatelles pour un massacre*, p. 146.

12. 'Entretiens avec le Professeur Y', op. cit., p. 359.

13. Céline to Pierre Audinet, 'Dernières Rencontres avec Céline', *Nouvelles Littéraires*, 6.7.1961.

14. Céline to Albert Paraz, 10.9.1949, *Valsez saucisses*, Amiot-Dumot, p. 315.

Notes and References

4 NOVELS AND POLITICS: 1932–40

1. Céline to Eveline Pollet, *L'Herne*, 3, p. 102.
2. Ibid., June 1933, p. 98.
3. Ibid., 28.6.1933, p. 98.
4. Céline to Hindus, 28.7.1947, *L'Herne*, 5, p. 87.
5. Henri Mahé, *La Brinquebale avec Céline*, La Table ronde, Paris, 1969, p. 130.
6. Céline to Marie Canavaggia, 15.5.1936, *Oeuvres complètes*, vol. 2, p. 719.
7. Céline to Mahé, Mahé, *La Brinquebale avec Céline*, La Table ronde, Paris, 1969, p. 76.
8. Reproduced in *L'Herne*, 3, pp. 165–6.
9. Céline to Eveline Pollet, 28.9.1933, op. cit., p. 101.
10. Mahé, op. cit., p. 161.
11. Céline to Mahé, Mahé, op. cit., p. 101.
12. Mahé, op. cit., p. 163. Céline probably met Abel Gance through Elie Faure. Gance's films are still shown in revivals of 1930s cinema. He had a taste for long, epic subjects. One is amazed that *Voyage* has never been filmed. All it needs is the right director. Ken Russell perhaps?
13. *Secrets dans l'île*, *Oeuvres complètes*, vol. 1, pp. 565–70.
14. Ibid., p. 569.
15. Céline to Mahé, Mahé, op. cit., p. 97. Jacques Deval was a popular 1930s author. His best-known work is the play *Tovarich*.
16. Mahé, op. cit., p. 97.
17. Céline to Hindus, 18.6.1947, *L'Herne*, 5, p. 85.
18. Ibid., 24.10.1947, p. 100.
19. Ibid., 23.8.1947, p. 92.
20. Céline to Eugène Dabit, October 1933, *L'Herne*, 3, p. 88.
21. Céline to Eveline Pollet, 14.9.1933, op. cit., p. 101.
22. 'Hommage à Zola', *Oeuvres complètes*, vol. 2, p. 506.
23. Ibid., pp. 505, 503.
24. Pierre Monnier, 'Résidence surveillée', *L'Herne*, 3, p. 78.
25. Céline to Mahé, Mahé, op. cit., p. 177.
26. Marie Canavaggia, 'Mlle Marie ma secrétaire', *L'Herne*, 3, p. 31. Marie Canavaggia replaced Jeanne Carayon as Céline's secretary and confidante. She remained his closest – and only – helper right up to his death. No one knew more about his fanatical striving for perfection, about his jealousy and suspicion of publishers, critics and other writers. Much of this she inherited from him.
27. Mahé, op. cit., p. 140.
28. Céline to Dabit, 1934, op. cit., p. 86.
29. Céline to Eveline Pollet, 29.6.1933, op. cit., p. 99.
30. 'Pour tuer le chômage tueront-ils les chômeurs?', *Oeuvres complètes*, vol. 1, p. 733.
31. Ibid., p. 735.
32. Céline to Eveline Pollet, March 1933, op. cit., p. 97.
33. Céline to Mahé, Mahé, op. cit., p. 169.
34. Céline to Eveline Pollet, February 1939, op. cit., p. 107.
35. Ibid., p. 96.
36. Céline to Dabit, June 1933, op. cit., p. 87.

37. Céline to Erika Landry (undated), *L'Herne*, 5, p. 43.

38. Ibid., April 1936, p. 46.

39. Céline to Dabit, 1937, op. cit., p. 86.

40. Mahé, op. cit., pp. 125–6.

41. Céline to Mahé, Mahé, op. cit., p. 89.

42. Mahé, op. cit., p. 91.

43. Céline to Mahé, Mahé, op. cit., p. 101.

44. Mahé, op. cit., p. 102.

45. Céline to Mahé, Mahé, op. cit., p. 96.

46. Ibid., p. 103.

47. Jeanne Carayon, op. cit., p. 23.

48. Mahé, op. cit., p. 103.

49. Céline to Mahé, Mahé, op. cit., p. 103.

50. Céline to Erika Landry, 1934, op. cit., p. 50.

51. *Oeuvres complètes*, vol. 2, p. 505.

52. Céline to Dabit, 1.9.1935, op. cit., p. 88.

53. Elie Faure to Céline, 30.7.1935, 'Correspondance Céline – Elie Faure', *L'Herne*, 5, p. 59. Elie Faure was a historian of art, of religion, a philosopher and a prolific writer. Céline liked his books on art. He probably saw in Faure's imaginative recreation of past epoques a kind of legend. Faure was delighted with *Voyage* but he wanted to teach Céline to emerge from his pessimism, as Faure himself had done. For a longer, if partisan, account of the friendship see the chapter 'Une Amitié météorique' in Paul Desanges's *Elie Faure*, Geneva, 1963.

54. Céline to Faure, 2.3.1935, op. cit., p. 57.

55. Ibid., undated but written after the February riots, p. 53.

56. Ibid. (undated), p. 52.

57. Ibid. (undated), p. 53.

58. Faure to Céline, 30.7.1935, op. cit., p. 61.

59. Note by Paul Desanges to 'Correspondance Céline – Elie Faure', Desanges, op. cit.

60. Céline to Dabit (undated), op. cit., p. 86.

61. Céline to Eveline Pollet, 16.8.1933, op. cit., p. 100.

62. Céline to Mahé, Mahé, op. cit., p. 58.

63. Céline to Faure (undated), op. cit., p. 55.

64. Mahé, op. cit., p. 61.

65. Ibid., pp. 181–2.

66. Rebatet, 'D'un Céline l'autre', in *L'Herne*, 3, p. 50.

67. Céline to Mahé, 2.6.1937, Mahé, op. cit., p. 181.

68. Marcel Aymé, 'Avenue Junot' in *En Arrière*, Paris, 1950.

69. Ibid., p. 117.

70. René Héron de Villefosse, 'Prophéties et litanies de Céline', *L'Herne*, 3, p. 33.

71. Mahé, op. cit., p. 98.

72. Ibid., p. 137. Le Havre is not of course in Brittany. This is a piece of Célinian geography. See below.

73. Céline to Hindus, 23.8.1947, p. 92. The 'Breton prophet' is a role that Céline assumed, rather than an influence that he absorbed. He spoke no Breton and rarely went to the Breton-speaking area further out on the peninsula. Saint-Malo was very frenchified, even in the 1930s. Nor is it certain that

Notes and References

Céline's family came originally from Brittany, much less from the Breton-speaking part. He claimed Breton descent. But his mother's side of the family can be traced no further than Paris and his father's side goes only as far west as Le Havre. Le Havre is close enough to Brittany for Céline to transfer his grandfather across the border. On the other hand he may well have had Breton blood. He certainly had blue eyes. Either way he clearly wanted to see himself as a Celt.

74. Céline to Mahé, Mahé, op. cit., p. 59.
75. Mahé, op. cit., p. 137.
76. Ibid., p. 91.
77. Céline to Mahé, Mahé, op. cit., p. 78.
78. In 1956 Eveline Pollet published a novel called *Escaliers* which (according to Erika Ostrovsky, *Voyeur Voyant: A Portrait of Louis-Ferdinand Céline*, Random House, New York, p. 347) is a fictional account of her affair with Céline. He appears as the tall, dark stranger of women's magazines. He arrives, seduces and leaves; she remains in Antwerp, faithful and imploring. This is one point of view. One might note, ungenerously, that Eveline Pollet was married with a child and that she was playing games of her own: she could be a secure housewife and the mistress of a famous novelist.
79. Rebatet, op. cit., p. 45.
80. Céline to Hindus, 17.5.1948, op. cit., p. 109.
81. Mahé hints at this, op. cit., p. 118; see also Erika Ostrovsky, op. cit., p. 100.
82. Céline to Erika Landry, 3.10.1933, op. cit., p. 43.
83. Ibid. (undated), p. 41.
84. Ibid. (undated), p. 43.
85. Ibid.
86. Ibid., 1932, p. 42.
87. Céline to Eveline Pollet, July 1933, op. cit., p. 99.
88. Ibid., 6.8.1933, p. 100.
89. Ibid., 31.1.1937, p. 103.
90. Ibid., 25.10.1938, p. 106.
91. Céline to Mahé, Mahé, op. cit., p. 127.
92. Céline to Erika Landry, 13.5.1936, op. cit., p. 46.
93. Erika Landry, op. cit., p. 40.
94. Poulet, op. cit., p. 52.
95. Céline to Lucien Descaves, 25.9.1936, quoted in *Oeuvres complètes*, vol. 3, p. 570.
96. André Pulicani, 'Chez Gen Paul à Montmartre', *L'Herne*, 3, p. 38.
97. For a brief discussion of when Céline began *Casse-pipe* see Ducourneau's note in *Oeuvres complètes*, vol. 2, p. 723. Mahé mentions Céline's plans for a London novel, p. 125.
98. Céline to Paraz, 15.3.1948, *Le Gala des vaches*, Éditions de l'Élan, Paris, 1948, p. 214.
99. Rebatet, op. cit., p. 44.
100. Céline to Eveline Pollet, 31.1.1938, op. cit., p. 105.
101. Céline, *Oeuvres complètes*, vol. 3, p. 336.
102. Céline, Réponse aux accusations', *L'Herne*, 5, p. 321.
103. Céline to Dabit, 1937, op. cit., p. 89.
104. Poulet, op. cit., p. 51.

105. Ibid.
106. Mahé, op. cit., p. 123.
107. Céline to French Consul in Jersey, 29.1.1938, *L'Herne*, 3, p. 94.
108. Céline to Paraz, 18.5.1951, *L'Herne*, 3, p. 148.
109. Céline to Guy Morin quoted by Morin, op. cit., p. 19.
110. Mahé, op. cit., p. 172.
111. Note to 'Correspondance Céline–Consul de France à Jersey', *L'Herne*, 3, p. 93.
112. Céline to French Consul in Jersey, 29.1.38, op. cit., p. 94.
113. Céline to Eveline Pollet, 3.2.1938, op. cit., p. 105.
114. Ibid., 5.9.1938, p. 106.
115. Ibid., February 1939, p. 107.
116. Ducourneau, 'Chronologie', *Oeuvres complètes*, vol. 1, p. 27.
117. Céline to Eveline Pollet, 29.5.1939, op. cit., p. 107.
118. Mahé, op. cit., p. 193.
119. Céline to Dr Camus, 9.1.1940, *L'Herne*, 3, p. 114.
120. 'Chronologie', *Oeuvres complètes*, vol. 1, p. 28.

5 CÉLINE THE PAMPHLETEER

1. The problem of modernity in twentieth-century France is discussed by Stanley Hoffman in 'Paradoxes of the French Political Community' in *In Search of France*, Harper & Row, New York, 1963.
2. *L'École des cadavres*, Denoël, Paris, 1938, p. 148.
3. *Bagatelles pour un massacre*, Denoël, Paris, 1937, p. 165.
4. Ibid., p. 14.
5. Ibid., p. 99.
6. *L'École des cadavres*, p. 237.
7. Emmanuel Mounier, '*Bagatelles pour un massacre*', *Esprit*, March 1938, reprinted in *L'Herne*, 5, pp. 341–2. Maurice Vanino, *L'École d'un cadavre*, Editions Creator, Paris, 1952, pp. 6–7.
8. *Mea Culpa*, *Oeuvres complètes*, vol. 3, p. 345 ff.
9. De Gaulle, *Memoires de guerre*, Plon, Paris, 1954, p. 1.
10. *Stürmer*, 27.7.1939.
11. The relevant section of this essay, the 'Portrait d'un anti-sémite', appeared in December 1945 in *Les Temps modernes*. It is very much a Liberation piece of writing. References are to this version: pp. 442–70.
12. Ibid., p. 462.
13. Pierre Monnier, 'Résidence surveillée', *L'Herne*, 3, p. 77. The story was told to Monnier by Céline, Monnier himself did not witness it.
14. This is surely the answer to what Erika Ostrovsky seems to be saying, in *Voyeur Voyant: A Portrait of Louis-Ferdinand Céline*, Random House, New York, 1971, p. 146 ff.
15. 'Les Juifs, Céline et Maritain', *L'Herne*, 5, p. 335.
16. Emmanuel Mounier, op. cit., p. 341. This is the dehumanization discussed in Chapter One. It was the only way Céline could escape from the prison of Bardamu's lucid pity.
17. De Gaulle, op. cit., p. 1.
18. Maurice Clavel – *Arts*, 12.7.61 – thinks that Céline had no influence at all.
19. Interview with Dominique de Roux.

Notes and References

6 OCCUPATION AND EXILE: 1940–51

1. Marcel Aymé; 'Sur une Légende', *L'Herne*, 3, p. 217.
2. Interviewed in *L'Express*, 14.7.1957, p. 17.
3. Céline to Eveline Pollet, 17.2.1941, *L'Herne*, 3, p. 108.
4. Ibid., 15.4.1941, p. 109.
5. For an account of daily life under the Occupation by one of Céline's acquaintances, see Jean Galtier-Boissière, *Mémoires d'un Parisien*, vol. 3, La Table ronde, Paris, 1961. See also Gérard Walter, *La vie à Paris sous l'Occupation*, Paris, 1960.
6. Jean Hérold-Paquis: *Des illusions ... désillusions*, Bourgoin, Paris, 1948, p. 125.
7. First published in *Nouvelle Revue française*, May 1941, reprinted in Drieu la Rochelle, *Sur les Écrivains*, Paris, 1964, pp. 291–5.
8. *La Gerbe*, 13.2.1941.
9. *Au pilori*, 14.3.1941.
10. 'Réponse aux accusations', *L'Herne*, 5, p. 325.
11. Robert Brasillach, *Notre avant-guerre*, Paris, 1941, p. 276.
12. Ibid., p. 236.
13. Robert Brasillach, *Journal d'un homme occupé*, Les Sept Couleurs, Paris, 1945, p. 183.
14. Brasillach, *Notre avant-guerre*, p. 189.
15. Lucien Rebatet, *Les Décombres*, Denoël, Paris, 1942, p. 573.
16. Ibid., p. 539.
17. Drieu la Rochelle, op. cit. p. 183.
18. Ibid., p. 185.
19. Rebatet, 'D'un Céline l'autre', *L'Herne*, 3, pp. 45–6.
20. In *La Gerbe*, 13.3.1941. For an examination of the collaborationist press see Michèle Cotta, *La Collaboration 1940–44*, Colin, Paris, 1964.
21. *La Gerbe*, 11.7.1940. Before the war Bernard Fay had been a good critic with a particular interest in the United States. As a reward for writing articles like this one he was made director of the Bibliothèque Nationale.
22. *La Gerbe*, 8.8.1940.
23. *Pays libre*, 5.4.1941.
24. *La Gerbe*, 10.10.1940.
25. *L'Appel*, 12.6.1941.
26. *Pays libre*, 3.5.1941.
27. *La Gerbe*, 8.8.1940. *La Gerbe*, which published Giono's declaration of support for Vichy, was particularly keen on honest toil, traditional rural values and the like.
28. *Pays libre*, 12.4.1941.
29. *L'Appel*, 6.3.1941.
30. *Les Décombres*, p. 566.
31. *Au pilori*, 12.7.1940. Even by the standards of the collaborationist press *Au pilori* was a hard-line paper. Its first editor Henri-Robert Petit went too far in his attacks on Vichy and was forced to resign in September 1940.
32. *Révolution nationale*, 12.10.1941.
33. *L'Appel*, 3.4.1941.
34. Ibid., 13.3.1941.

35. *La Gerbe*, 8.8.1940. Bonnard was a flamboyant homosexual whom the Vichy government, in a fit of foolishness, appointed Minister of Education.

36. *L'Appel*, 3.4.1941.

37. Brasillach, *Journal d'un homme occupé*, p. 203.

38. Rebatet, *Les Décombres*, p. 622 ff.

39. See issues for November 1941.

40. *L'Appel*, 7.8.1941.

41. 'Lettre ouverte à Pétain', *Au pilori*, 12.7.1940.

42. Ibid., 8.1.1942.

43. Constantini had anticipated the Riom trials by a year. His article appeared in the first number of *L'Appel*, 6.3.1941.

44. See *La Gerbe*, 13.2.1941.

45. 'Prologue du parti unique', 11.12.1941.

46. 'Vers le parti unique', 25.12.1941.

47. 'Entretien avec Céline', *L'Émancipation nationale*, 21.9.1941. pp. 1–3. Sicard had been writing for *Le Petit Crapouillot* when Galtier-Boissière attacked the Rosny brothers.

48. Céline, 'Qui détient le Pouvoir?', *L'Appel*, 9.4.1942.

49. 'Céline nous écrit', *Révolution nationale*, 5.4.1942.

50. 'Acte de Foi de Louis-Ferdinand Céline', *La Gerbe*, 13.2.1941.

51. Céline to Lucien Combelle, 20.4.1941, *L'Herne*, 5, p. 65.

52. 'L.-F. Céline nous écrit', *l'Appel*, 4.9.1941.

53. Céline, 'Vivent les Juifs', *Au pilori*, 2.10.1941.

54. *L'Émancipation nationale*, 21.9.1941.

55. Robert Chamfleury, 'Céline ne nous a pas trahis', *L'Herne*, 3, p. 66.

56. Maryse Desneiges, 'D'une Française ... à L.-F. Céline', *Pays libre*, 22.3.1941.

57. Another headline in this issue runs 'Mourir en Combattant'.

58. 'Louis-Ferdinand Céline répond au *Pays libre*', 5.4.1941.

59. 'L.-F. Céline nous écrit', *L'Appel*, 4.12.1941.

60. Céline to Combelle, 12.2.1943, op. cit., p. 65.

61. Céline, *Vivent les Juifs*, op. cit.

62. Céline to Combelle 20.4.1941, op. cit.

63. 'Céline s'explique', *Au pilori*, 8.1.1942.

64. 'Acte de Foi' de Louis-Ferdinand Céline, *La Gerbe*, 13.2.1941, p. 1.

65. 'L.-F. Céline répond au *Pays libre*, *Pays libre*, 5.4.1941.

66. 'Acte de Foi' de Louis-Ferdinand Céline, op. cit.

67. Rebatet, 'D'un Céline l'autre', *L'Herne*, 3, p. 47.

68. 'Une Lettre de Céline', *Germinal*, 28.4.1944.

69. Céline to Lucien Combelle (undated), op. cit., p. 65.

70. Céline to Paraz, 5.5.1948, Paraz, *Le Gala des vaches*, Éditions de l'Élan, Paris, 1948, p. 238.

71. Ibid. [November 1949], Paraz, *Valsez saucisses*, Amiot-Dumont, Paris, 1950, p. 332.

72. Ibid., 5.10.1948., Paraz, *Le Gala des vaches*, p. 278.

73. Saint-Paulien, *Histoire de la collaboration*, Paris, 1964, p. 257 ff. A fugitive from French justice, Sicard lived in Spain for many years after the war. He published this book under a pseudonym but reveals his identity in the introduction.

Notes and References

74. Interview with Robert Poulet.
75. 'Réponse aux accusations', op. cit., p. 332.
76. Maurice Vanino, *L'École d'un cadavre*, p. 32.
77. Rebatet, 'D'un Céline l'autre', *L'Herne*, 3, p. 48.
78. Saint-Paulien, op. cit., p. 276.
79. Maurice Vanino, op. cit., p. 28. He is quoting a letter from Céline to Capitaine Sezille.
80. Ibid., p. 32.
81. Karl Epting, 'Il ne nous aimait pas', *L'Herne*, 3, p. 57.
82. Simone Mittre, *L'Herne*, 5, p. 283.
83. Céline to Hindus, 20.9.1947, op. cit., p. 94.
84. Céline to Paraz, 28.2.1951, *L'Herne*, 5, p. 120.
85. Céline to Eveline Pollet November 1941, op. cit., p. 110.
86. Ibid., 15.8.1942.
87. Céline to Mahé, 24.4.1942. Mahé, *La Brinquebale avec Céline*, La Table ronde, Paris, p. 208.
88. Ibid. (undated), p. 210.
89. Céline to Eveline Pollet, 17.4.1942, op. cit., p. 110.
90. Geoffroy, 'Céline en Angleterre', *L'Herne*, 3, p. 12.
91. Marcel Brochard, 'Céline à Rennes', *L'Herne*, 3, p. 16.
92. Rebatet, 'D'un Céline l'autre', *L'Herne*, 3, p. 48.
93. Céline to Mahé, September 1942, Mahé, op. cit., p. 212.
94. Ibid., 1943, p. 230.
95. Mahé, op. cit., p. 267.
96. Céline to Mahé, 1943, Mahé, op. cit., p. 244.
97. Mahé, op. cit., p. 227.
98. 'Réponse aux accusations', op. cit., p. 321; see also Mahé, op. cit., p. 258 ff. There is a difference between the two versions. Céline does not mention that a special visa was needed. He gives the impression that the Nazis arrested him out of spite. This was not the case. It was simply a bureaucratic matter.
99. *Journal d'un homme occupé*, p. 249.
100. Céline calls him 'the Great Destroyer of Carthage!' – *Castle to Castle*, Delacorte Press, New York, 1968, p. 211.
101. Céline to Eveline Pollet, 17.4.1942, op. cit., p. 110.
102. Céline to Mahé, Mahé, op. cit., p. 211.
103. Ibid., p. 245.
104. Ibid.
105. Ibid., p. 257.
106. Ibid., p. 237.
107. Morin, op. cit., p. 19.
108. Geoffroy, op. cit., p. 12.
109. Robert Chamfleury, op. cit., pp. 60–66.
110. *L'Appel*, 20.4.1944.
111. Céline, *Oeuvres complètes*, vol. 3, p. 511 ff.
112. Robert Aron, *The Vichy Régime*, Putnam, New York, 1958, p. 513.
113. Rebatet, 'D'un Céline l'autre', L'Herne, 3, p. 50.
114. Epting, op. cit., p. 59.
115. Céline told the same story to Paraz (Paraz, *Le Gala des vaches*, p. 237). But Rebatet refutes this version (Rebatet, op. cit., pp. 49–50).

116. Jean Hérold-Paquis, op. cit. This is a graphic, eye-witness account of the exodus. It was written in Fresnes where Paquis was waiting to be executed.
117. Paquis, Saint-Paulien and others have described these fantasies in colourful detail. Aron gives a more sober account of Sigmaringen.
118. Rebatet, op. cit., p. 51.
119. Abel Bonnard, 'À Sigmaringen', L'Herne, 3, p. 67.
120. Rebatet, op. cit., p. 52.
121. Simone Mittre op. cit., p. 284.
122. 'Réponse aux accusations', op. cit., p. 323.
123. Simone Mittre, op. cit., p. 282.
124. Samedi-Soir, 16.2.1946.
125. Poulet, Entretiens familiers avec L.-F. Céline, p. 70.
126. Céline to Galtier-Boissière (undated), L'Herne, 5, p. 138.
127. Rebatet, op. cit., p. 53. Rebatet sees a dramatic change in Céline at this time. It was now that he began to lose his old vigour and to become the Céline of the last years. Poulet, Aymé and other friends testify to the difference between the pre- and post-war Céline.
128. 'Réponse aux accusations', op. cit., p. 324.
129. Marcel Déat, Journal, 16.3.1945, in L'Herne, 5, p. 143.
130. Paquis, op. cit., p. 114.
131. Rebatet, op. cit., p. 54.
132. Céline to Dr Camus 30.6.1947. 'Lettres d'Exil' in Écrits de Paris, October 1961.
133. Déat, 31.3.1945, op. cit., p. 144. Chamoin is an intriguing figure. He had a double dose of the difficulties that Céline underwent.
134. Paquis, op. cit., pp. 125–6.
135. Franc-Tireur, 19.12.1945.
136. Samedi-Soir, 16.2.1946.
137. Céline to Eveline Pollet, August 1947, op. cit., p. 111.
138. Céline to Paraz, 19.8.1947, Paraz, Le Gala des vaches, p. 111.
139. Sartre, Portrait d'un anti-sémite, Les Temps modernes, December 1945, p. 462.
140. Peter Novick, The Resistance versus Vichy, Columbia University Press, New York, 1968, p. 38.
141. Reprinted in Albert Camus, Resistance, Rebellion and Death, Modern Library Books, New York, 1963, p. 28.
142. Céline to Hindus, 31.4.1947, op. cit., p. 74.
143. Céline to Eveline Pollet, 23.7.1947, op. cit., p. 111.
144. Céline to Pierre Monnier, quoted in 'Résidence surveillée', L'Herne, 3, p. 79.
145. Céline to Hindus, 17.12.1947, op. cit., p. 104.
146. Céline to Benjamin Perrot (undated), L'Herne, 5, p. 127.
147. Interview with Robert Poulet.
148. Céline to Pierre Monnier, loc. cit.
149. Céline to Eveline Pollet, 1948, op. cit., p. 112.
150. Paraz to Marcot, 22.3.1949, L'Herne, 5, p. 228. Marcot was another Céline supporter whom Paraz had enlisted in his campaign.
151. René Héron de Villefosse, 'Prophéties et litanies de Céline', L'Herne, 3, p. 34.
152. Céline to Hindus, 5.12.1947, op. cit., p. 102.

153. Ibid., 10.8.1947, p. 90.
154. Céline to Paraz, 19.8.1947, *Le Gala des vaches*, p. 111.
155. Héron de Villefosse, op. cit., p. 34.
156. Céline to Pasteur Löchen, *L'Herne*, 3, p. 132.
157. Note by Pasteur Löchen to Céline's letters, op. cit., p. 131.
158. Céline to Hindus, 17.12.1947, op. cit., p. 104.
159. Céline to Dr Camus, 'Lettres d'exil' in *Écrits de Paris*, October 1961, p. 107.
160. Ibid., 15.6.1948.
161. Pierre Monnier, op. cit., p. 73.
162. Céline to Pierre Monnier (undated), op. cit., p. 80.
163. Céline to Paraz, 19.8.1947, *Le Gala des vaches*, p. 111.
164. Ibid., 13.11.1947, p. 145.
165. Ibid., 1.6.1947, p. 86.
166. Ibid., 5.10.1948, p. 278.
167. Céline to Ernst Bendz (undated), *L'Herne*, 3, p. 124.
168. Céline to Dr Camus, 15.10.1948, op. cit., p. 108.
169. Céline to Paraz, 25.12.1947, *Le Gala des vaches*, p. 155.
170. Ibid., 22.5.1949, *Valsez saucisses*, p. 329.
171. Paraz, *Le Menuet du haricot*, Paris, p. 59 ff.
172. Céline to Perrot (undated), op. cit., p. 128.
173. Céline to Paraz, 17.1.1948, *Le Gala des vaches*, p. 163.
174. Ibid., 16.7.1948, p. 260.
175. Céline to Perrot (undated), op. cit., 5, p. 127.
176. Ibid. (undated), p. 126.
177. Céline to Hindus, 30.6.1948, op. cit., p. 110.
178. Céline to Perrot (undated), op. cit., p. 127, 131.
179. Céline to Paraz, 17.3.1951, *L'Herne*, 3, p. 147.
180. Ibid., 21.11.1948, *Valsez saucisses*, p. 328.
181. Ibid., 24.2.1951, *L'Herne*, 5, p. 119.
182. Céline to Georges Altman (undated), *L'Herne*, 5, p. 135.
183. Céline to Paraz, 5.4.1948, *Le Gala des vaches*, p. 224.
184. Ibid., 17.3.1951, *L'Herne*, 3, p. 146.
185. Ibid., 25.9.1948, *Le Gala des vaches*, p. 277.
186. Céline to Hindus, 24.10.1947, op. cit., p. 100.
187. Céline to Paraz, 5.7.1949, *Valsez saucisses*, p. 241.
188. Céline to Raoul Nordling, 27.10.1949, *L'Herne*, 3, p. 137.
189. Céline to Paraz, 29.11.1949, *Le Gala des vaches*, p. 151.
190. Ibid., 25.5.1949, *Valsez saucisses*, p. 337.
191. Céline to Hindus, 5.12.1947, op. cit., p. 101.
192. Céline to Paraz, October 1947, *Le Gala des vaches*, p. 145.
193. Ibid., 17.3.1948, p. 220.
194. Ibid., 28.2.1951, *L'Herne*, 5, p. 120.
195. Ibid., 15.3.1948, *Le Gala des vaches*, pp. 213–14.
196. Ibid., 17.4.1950, *L'Herne*, 3, p. 143.
197. Céline to Hindus, 23.8.1947, op. cit., p. 94.
198. Céline to Paraz, 16.7.1948, *Le Gala des vaches*, p. 260.
199. Céline to Hindus, 24.9.1947, op. cit., p. 97.
200. Ibid., 2.10.1947, p. 98. Poulet thinks that Céline merely pretended to have been influenced by these three authors. It was just something to tell the

journalists. On the other hand Poulet believes that Céline genuinely admired La Fontaine.

201. Ibid., 12.6.1947, pp. 79–80.
202. Ibid., p. 81.
203. Céline to Paraz, 25.7.1947, *Le Gala des vaches*, p. 88.
204. Ibid., 19.8.1947, p. 112.
205. Céline to Hindus, 11.6.1947, p. 79.
206. Céline to Paraz, 11.9.1949, *Valseẓ saucisses*, p. 319.
207. *Mémoires d'un Parisien*, vol. 2, p. 130 ff.
208. Quoted by Peter Novick, op. cit., p. 157.
209. Paraz, p. 88.
210. Céline to Paraz, 29.3.1948, *Le Gala des vaches*, p. 222.
211. *Valseẓ saucisses*, p. 238. In these pages Céline and Paraz discuss Céline's defence.
212. The legal basis of the purge is discussed by Peter Novick, op. cit., p. 79 ff. He concludes that Liberation justice was not very just.
213. The 'Réponse' makes no mention of *Les Beaux Draps*.
214. Letter to the court quoted in *Combat*, 22.2.1950. Céline's statement runs: 'I am not proud of republishing it in 1943. Denoël wanted to compromise me.'
215. 'Réponse', op. cit., p. 319.
216. *Combat*, 21.2.1950; *Le Libertaire*, 13.1.1950. Both newspapers had their roots in the Resistance.
217. *Le Libertaire*, 20.1.1950.
218. *Radar*, 5.3.1950.
219. Letter to the court, op. cit.
220. *Combat*, 22.2.1950.
221. Paraz to Marcot, 1.3.1950, op. cit., p. 291.
222. Céline to Paraz, 23.2.1950, *Valseẓ saucisses*, p. 358.
223. Céline to Nordling, 10.3.1950, *L'Herne*, 3, p. 139.
224. *Le Menuet du haricot* was not published until after Paraz's death in 1957.
225. Céline to Bendz (undated), op. cit., p. 127.
226. Céline to Paraz, 8.11.1950, *L'Herne*, 5, p. 145.
227. Paraz to Marcot, 1.5.1951, op. cit., p. 294.

7 Guignol's band

1. 'Sa dernière interview: L.-F. Céline', *Arts*, 1.7.1961, p. 3.
2. References to *Guignol's Band* are to the New Directions edition, translated by Bernard Frechtman and Jack T. Niles, New York, 1954. References to *Le Pont de Londres* are to Céline's *Oeuvres complètes*, vol. 3. For convenience' sake the second volume is called by its own title – *Le Pont de Londres*. One must not forget, however, that the two volumes make up one novel – *Guignol's Band*. The same method is used in the next chapter where *Normance* is called by that name, although it is better considered as the second part of *Féerie pour une autre fois*.
3. Céline to Marie Canavaggia quoted by Ducourneau in *Oeuvres complètes*, vol. 3, p. 566.

Notes and References

4. One must not forget either that *Le Pont de Londres* is a first draft which Céline did not intend to publish. Had he revised it for publication he might have solved some of the riddles. But this is not probable. For details of publication see Chapter Nine.

5. Céline resorts to this 'archaic' technique in the gayer moments of his work. It is not always very successful. He uses it in the dance-world pages of *Les Beaux Draps* but it sounds artificial and fails to convince.

8 *Féerie pour une autre fois*

1. Robert Poulet, *Entretiens familiers avec L.-F. Céline*, Plon, Paris, 1958, p. 46.
2. References to *Féerie* and to *Normance* are to *Oeuvres complètes*, vols. 3 and 4.
3. Milton Hindus, *The Crippled Giant*, Bear's Head Books, New York, 1950, p. 56.
4. This unpolitical view of the war follows on the unpolitical depiction of society in *Mort à crédit*.
5. Céline's use of names merits another book. Sometimes the games he plays are simple: the initials of *Guignol's Band* stand for Great Britain. Often a name reveals a character: Cascade corresponds to his flow of language, Yudenzweck means 'Jewish purpose' in German, Normance = no man. Céline likes unpleasant or obscene connotations: Fort-Gono in *Voyage* invites us to read it as Fort-Gonorrhoea, Bragamance in *L'Église* is a play on *braguette*, the French word for 'prick'. Other names refer to different works: Prospero to Shakespeare, Robinson perhaps to Defoe, La Joconde is a parody on Leonardo's ideal of beauty. In this way Céline can introduce new levels of meaning and new ranges of association. He is also revealing every time the artist's power to distort and recreate. He is not unique in this, for many writers do the same. Joyce turns Bloom into Boom, Flower and the like. Beckett has a penchant for obscenities: the names of places in *Molloy* are Shit, Hole, etc. To name or to rename someone gives the artist, as stated here, power over the person in question. Once again this is a common belief of primitive mythology: the enemy who knows your name has an advantage over you. In this case Céline is stripping Sartre of his identity. On a larger scale Beckett does the same with his fictional selves. After a series of deliberately banal variations on the letter M – Molloy, Moran, Malone – he arrives at the Unnamable. The value of these techniques depends on how they are used. Paraz picked up the habit from Céline but he employs it simply to insult people. What counts is the richness of the associations aroused – the relationship of the *Tempest*'s Prospero to Prospero Jim – or the context – the *Oddort*, 'odd place', of *Rigodon* is a one-line joke; but set in between Ulm, Hanover and Hamburg it acquires an extra dimension; they too have become 'odd places'. To see the savour that the names add to a Célinian text one need only compare the original names in *Nord* with the names that had to be inserted after the lawsuit: Isis, the Egyptian goddess-queen, becomes a stunningly banal Inge; Schertz – 'joke' in German – becomes von Leiden, and so on.
6. Samuel Beckett, *Molloy, Three Novels by Samuel Beckett*, Grove Press, New York, 1965, p. 8.

7. One returns to Céline's fundamental horror of the flesh. In *Mort à crédit* being stuck is associated with other forms of physical unpleasantness: excretion and sex. Young Ferdinand's bottom is eternally sticky. Madame Gorloge, while seducing him, presses her fat, soft body on him so that he cannot move.

8. Nietzsche's phrase '*die Unschuld des Werdens*' is more precisely translated as 'the innocence of becoming'. Céline knew of Nietzsche's interest in dance. He quotes with approval Nietzsche's remark about refusing to believe in a God who cannot dance – Céline to Hindus, 12.6.1947, *L'Herne*, 5, p. 81.

9. Friedrich Nietzsche, *Die Geburt der Tragödie*, *Sämtliche Werke*, Band 1, Alfred Kröner Verlag, Stuttgart, p. 72.

10. À *l'agité du bocal*, Oeuvres complètes, vol. 3, p. 417.

11. Céline might have disagreed violently with this. But the fact remains that both Lili and the 'good' women characters of *Voyage* are boring. This is not because they are women. Céline's 'bad' women are brilliantly drawn – Lola, Madame Gorloge and the others. All writers have trouble portraying 'good' characters. But Céline has a particular problem since evil occupies such a large part of his vision. A 'good' character must lack the common clay of life, must be ethereal.

12. This draws on the technique used in the Orléans pages of *Guignol's Band*.

9 THE HERMIT OF MEUDON

1. Céline to Ernst Bendz, 1.23.1951, *L'Herne*, 3, p. 130.
2. Céline to Paraz, 10.7.1951, *L'Herne*, 3, p. 150.
3. Ibid., 15.7.1951.
4. Ibid., 19.7.1951, p. 151.
5. Erika Ostrovsky, *Voyeur Voyant: A portrait of Louis-Ferdinand Céline*, Random House, New York, 1971, p. 245. Paul Marteau had made a fortune out of tarot cards.
6. Céline to Paraz, 10.7.1951, *L'Herne*, 3, p. 150.
7. Ibid., 19.7.1951.
8. Ibid.
9. Ibid., 11.9.1952, p. 152.
10. Robert Poulet, *Entretiens familiers avec L.-F. Céline*, Plon, Paris, 1958, p. 1.
11. Jean Guénot, 'Voyage au bout de la parole', *L'Herne*, 5, p. 256.
12. Céline to Paraz, 14.1.1953, *L'Herne*, 3, p. 153.
13. Ibid., 26.6.1953.
14. Aymé did come to Meudon but the friendship was not as strong as before the war.
15. Héron de Villefosse, 'Prophéties et litanies de Céline', *L'Herne*, 3, p. 34.
16. Rebatet, 'D'un Céline l'autre', *l'Herne*, 3, p. 54.
17. Poulet, op. cit., p. 4.
18. Rebatet, op. cit., p. 54.
19. Poulet, op. cit., p. 1.
20. Jean Pommery, *Bestiaire de Céline*, p. 301.
21. Ibid., p. 305. This may seem harsh. Both Lucette and Céline were animal lovers. They looked after their pets and found them a protection against

loneliness. Céline felt great pity for animals because, like himself, they were exposed to human malice. But there was little of the conventional dog-lover in him. Animals, he felt, knew intuitively what life was about, hence Bébert's role as the dancer's companion. He enjoyed his dogs' wildness because he thought it reflected life in its savage state. Of this, suffering was a part. Once again there is a difference between Célinian pity and mere sentimentality.

22. Poulet, op. cit., p. 6 ff.
23. Jean Guénot, op. cit., p. 248.
24. Poulet, op. cit., p. 1.
25. Ibid.
26. Dr R.B., 'Le Médecin de Meudon', *L'Herne*, 3, p. 81.
27. 'Des pays où personne ne va jamais', *L'Herne*, 3, p. 185.
28. Céline to Paraz, 20.7.1954, *L'Herne*, 3, p. 156.
29. Poulet, op. cit., p. 34.
30. Rebatet, op. cit., p. 54.
31. Paraz to Marcot, 24.11.1954, *L'Herne*, 5, p. 297.
32. *L'Express*, 14.6.1957, p. 15.
33. Céline to Paraz, 18.1.1954, *L'Herne*, 3, p. 156.
34. Paraz to Marcot, 16.3.1953, op. cit., p. 296. Lucette claims too – in articles written in recent years – that they were persecuted. But the examples she cites are not convincing. Maurice Clavel notes that Céline was allowed to resettle in France with no great difficulties. This is not to say that Céline did not torment himself with fears of persecution. But Sartre's form of enmity – absolute silence – was a far more dangerous threat than scribbles on walls.
35. *Oeuvres complètes*, vol. 3, pp. 356–411.
36. Céline to Paraz, 19.6.1957, *L'Herne*, 3, p. 159.
37. *L'Express*, 14.6.1957, pp. 15–18.
38. Letters to the editor the next week ran about equally for and against, on the issue of publishing the interview with Céline.
39. André Brissaud, 'Voyage au bout de la tendresse', *L'Herne*, 3, p. 226.
40. Interviewed in *Arts*, 19.6.1957.
41. Céline to Paraz, 18.6.1957, *L'Herne*, 3, p. 157.
42. *Arts*, 19.6.1957.
43. *Rivarol*, 27.6.1957, p. 5.
44. Ibid., 20.6.1957, p. 5.
45. Ibid., 27.6.1957, p. 15.
46. Ibid., p. 5.
47. Le Canard enchaîné, 28.8.1957, p. 4.
48. *Rivarol*, 4.7.57, p. 13.
49. Ibid., 11.7.57, p. 5.
50. Ibid., 11.7.1957, p. 7. An expanded version of this article is printed in *L'Herne*, 5, pp. 28–30.
51. Céline to Paraz, 19.6.1957, *L'Herne*, 3, p. 15.
52. Ibid., 22.6.1957, p. 159.
53. *Oeuvres complètes*, vol. 4, p. 272 and p. 357.
54. Ibid., vol. 5, p. 338.
55. *Le Monde et la vie*, November 1960, pp. 46–7.

56. Guénot, op. cit., pp. 251–2.
57. Céline to Paraz, 19.6.1957, *L'Herne*, 3, p. 15.
58. Pierre Audinet, 'Dernières Rencontres avec Céline', *Nouvelles Littéraires*, 6.7.1961, p. 4.
59. *Noir et Blanc*, 14.3.1958, pp. 176–7.
60. *Télémagazine*, 25.1.1958, pp. 47–9.
61. *Arts*, 'Le guide noir des vacances', 8.8.1956.
62. 'Rabelais, il a raté son coup', reprinted in *L'Herne*, 5, pp. 19–22.
63. Pierre Audinet, op. cit.
64. *Arts*, August, 1961, p. 5.
65. *Arts*, 8.8.1956, p. 1.
66. Céline to Paraz 22.12.1953, *L'Herne*, 3, p. 154.
67. Guénot, op. cit., p. 257. The relish with which Céline made comments like this one does not mean that he necessarily enjoyed being interviewed. He did not. He wanted to be left alone and he resented having to pose as a clown. The fact that he needed journalists was enough to make him dislike them. Even now Céline was not a simple man.
68. André Malraux, *Les Chênes qu'on abat*, Gallimard, Paris, 1971, p. 52.
69. *Nord*, p. 11.
70. 'Vive l'amnistie', *L'Herne*, 5, p. 30.
71. *Nord*, p. 11.
72. Céline to Paraz, 20.7.1954, *L'Herne*, 3, p. 156. The Geneva agreement ended the Indo-China war as far as the French were concerned.
73. *Le Monde et la vie*, November 1960, p. 47.
74. Guénot, op. cit., p. 257. This comment on the Chinese finds its way too into the last paragraph of *Rigodon*: Céline was still talking novels, trying out his narrator's stories in his conversations. Decidedly life and fiction were drawing together.
75. *L'Heure de Paris*, 13.2.1958, p. 24.
76. *Arts*, 12.7.1961, p. 3.
77. 'Des pays où personne ne va jamais', op. cit., p. 189.
78. Céline to Raoul Nordling, *L'Herne*, 3, p. 140.
79. Dr R.B., op. cit., p. 82.
80. *Le Monde et la vie*, November 1960, p. 47.
81. Dr R.B., op. cit., p. 81.
82. Note by Ducourneau to *Rigodon*, *Oeuvres complètes*, vol. 5, p. 512. The Balzac matter also found its way into the novel – *Oeuvres complètes*, vol. 5, p. 499. Céline was as anxious to be included in the Pléiade edition as he had been to win the Prix Goncourt with *Voyage*. So much for the writer who cared nothing for success.
83. Jean Pommery, op. cit., p. 304.
84. Ibid.
85. *Le Monde et la vie*, November 1960, p. 46.
86. Pierre Audinet, op. cit., p. 4.
87. Ibid.
88. Rebatet, op. cit., p. 55.
89. Aymé, 'Sur une légende', *L'Herne*, 3, p. 214.
90. Arletty, *L'Herne*, 3, p. 197.
91. Note by Ducourneau to *Nord*, *Oeuvres complètes*, vol. 5, p. 503 ff.

92. Céline to Marie Canavaggia, 5.3.1947, quoted by Jean Ducourneau *Oeuvres complètes*, vol. 3. p. 566.

93. Note by Ducourneau to *Le Pont de Londres, Oeuvres complètes*, vol. 3, p. 565 ff.

94. Erika Ostrovsky, op. cit., p. 366.

95. *Rigodon, Oeuvres complètes*, vol. 5., p. 499.

96. Notes to *Rigodon Oeuvres c nplètes*, vol. 5, p. 509. Doubts about the book's authenticity were expressed by several reviewers. Céline's political sins had not been forgotten either. For the reaction of France's leading left-wing magazine see Jean Frustié: *La Pavane du collabo* in *Le Nouvel observateur*, 17.2.1969.

97. *Oeuvres complètes*, vol. 5, p. 336.

98. Interview with Robert Poulet.

10 *D'un château l'autre*, *Nord* and *Rigodon*

1. References to *D'un château l'autre* are from the translation by Ralph Manheim, *Castle to Castle*, Delacorte Press, New York, 1968. References to *Nord* are from the translation by Ralph Manheim, Delacorte Press, 1972. References to *Rigodon* are to *Oeuvres complètes*, vol. 5.

2. This is very much like the real-life Céline. But Ferdinand's situation is simpler and more desperate. He does not possess his creator's wide range of moods.

3. Albert Camus, *Resistance, Rebellion and Death*, Modern Library Books, New York, 1963, p. 21.

4. Despite the doubts about its authenticity *Rigodon* fits the pattern of the trilogy: it follows naturally down the road to complete destruction. But Céline, had he lived, would probably have made changes in the style to strengthen, not to change, the impact of vagueness.

Bibliography

WORKS BY L.-F. CÉLINE AVAILABLE IN ENGLISH

Death on the Installment Plan, translated by John H. P. Marks, The Bodley Head, London, 1966; translated by Ralph Manheim, New Directions, New York, 1966.

Castle to Castle, translated by Ralph Manheim, Delacorte Press, New York, 1968.

Guignol's Band, translated by Bernard Frechtman and Jack T. Niles, New Directions, New York, 1954.

Journey to the End of the Night, translated by John H. P. Marks, New Directions, New York, 1960; Penguin Books, London, 1966.

North, translated by Ralph Manheim, Delacorte Press, New York, 1972.

Rigadoon, translated by Ralph Manheim, Penguin Books, New York, 1974.

WORKS BY L.-F. CÉLINE IN FRENCH

À l'agité du bocal, P. Lanauve de Tartas, 1948.

Bagatelles pour un massacre, Denoël, Paris, 1937.

Ballets, sans musique, sans personne, sans rien, Gallimard, Paris, 1959.

Les Beaux Draps, Nouvelles Editions françaises, Paris, 1941.

Casse-pipe, F. Chambriand, 1949.

D'un château l'autre, Gallimard, Paris, 1957.

L'école des cadavres, Denoël, Paris, 1938.

Entretiens avec le Professeur Y, Gallimard, Paris, 1955.

L'Église, Denoël, Paris, 1933.

Féerie pour une autre fois, Gallimard, Paris, 1952.

Foudres et flèches, C. de Jonquières, 1948.

Guignol's Band, I, Denoël, Paris, 1944; *Guignol's Band II*, Gallimard, Paris, 1963.

Mea Culpa, suivi de La Vie et L'œuvre de Semmelweis, Denoël, Paris, 1936.

Mort à crédit, Denoël, Paris, 1936.

Nord, Gallimard, Paris, 1963.

Normance, Gallimard, Paris, 1954.

Oeuvres complètes, Bibliothèque de la Pléiade, Gallimard, Paris, 1962. This contains only *Voyage au bout de la nuit*, and *Mort à crédit*.

Oeuvres de L.-F. Céline, edited by Jean Ducourneau, André Balland, Paris, 1966–69. This contains all of Céline's works except *Bagatelles pour un massacre*, *L'école des cadavres* and *Les Beaux Draps*.

La Quinine en thérapeutique, Doin (ed.), bibliothèque de la Faculté de Medecine de Paris, no. 85. 131, 1925.

Rigodon, Gallimard, Paris, 1969.

Scandale aux abysses, F. Chambriand, 1950.

Secrets dans l'île, in *Neuf et une*, Gallimard, Paris, 1936.

La Vie et l'oeuvre de Philippe-Ignace Semmelweis, thesis for the Faculté de Médicine de Paris, no. 161, 1924.
Voyage au bout de la nuit, Denoël, Paris, 1933.

WORKS CONTAINING ARTICLES OR LETTERS BY L.-F. CÉLINE
OR INTERVIEWS WITH HIM:

L'Appel, 4.12.1941, 'L.-F. Céline nous écrit'; 9.4.1942, 'Qui détient le Pouvoir'.
Arts, 8.8.1956, 'Le Guide noir des vacances'; 19.6.1957, 'Entrevue'; 12.7.1961, 'Sa dernière interview'; August 1961, 'Entrevue avec Claude Bonnefoy'.
Les Cahiers de L'Herne: Louis-Ferdinand Céline, vol. 3 and vol. 5, Paris 1963 and 1965. These two volumes contain numerous articles by Céline, almost all of which have now been included in the *Oeuvres complètes*, and letters by him to Eugène Dabit, Léon Daudet, the French Consul in Jersey, Eveline Pollet, Dr Camus, Lucien Descaves, Ernst Bendz, Pastor Löchen, Raoul Nordling, Albert Paraz (vol. 3); and Erika Landry, Elie Faure, Lucien Combelle, Milton Hindus, Denise Thomassen, Benjamin Perrot, Galtier-Boissière, Georges Altman, Albert Paraz (vol. 5). These two volumes also contain a good selection of critical articles.
Brasillach, Robert, *Notre avant-guerre*, Paris, 1941; *Journal d'un homme occupé*, Les Sept Couleurs, 1945.
Écrits de Paris, October 1961, 'Lettres d'Exil' (Letters from Céline to Dr Camus).
L'Emancipation Nationale, 21.11.1941, 'Entretien avec Céline'.
Europe-Amérique, 11.8.1949, 'Entrevue'.
L'Express, 14.6.1957, 'Entrevue'.
La Gerbe, 13.2.1941, 'Acte de Foi de L.-F. Céline'.
Germinal, 28.4.1944, 'Une lettre de Céline'.
L'Heure de Paris, 13.2.1958, 'Entrevue'.
Le Monde et la vie, November 1960, 'Qui êtes-vous M. Céline?'.
Noir et Blanc, 14.3.1958, *Les Célébrités du Tout-Paris aiment la campagne: L.-F. Céline*.
Nouvelles littéraires, 6.7.1961, 'Dernières Rencontres avec Céline'.
Paraz, Albert, *Le Gala des Vaches*, Éditions de L'Élan, Paris, 1948; *Valsez, saucisses*, Amiot-Dumont, Paris, 1950; *Le Menuet du haricot*, Paris, 1958. (Letters from Céline to Paraz.)
Pays libre, 5.4.1941. 'L.-F. Céline répond au *Pays libre*'.
Petit Crapouillot, February 1958, 'Réponse à Roger Vailland'.
Au pilori, 2.10.1941, 'Vivent les Juifs'; 11.12.1941, 'Prologue du parti unique'; 25.12.1941, 'Vers le parti unique'; 8.1.1942, 'Céline s'explique ... à propos de la saisie des *Beaux Draps*'.
Radar, 5.3.1950, 'Entrevue'.
Révolution Nationale, 5.4.1942, 'Celine nous écrit'.
Télémagazine, 25.1.1958, 'Enquête sur la télévision: L.-F.Céline'.

SELECTED LIST OF WORKS ON CÉLINE HIMSELF OR ON HIS AGE
Altman, Georges, 'L.-F. Céline ou le "Râleur grandiose"', *Lumière*, 9.1.1937.
Arland, Marcel, *Essais et nouveaux essais critiques*, Gallimard, Paris, 1952.
Aron, Robert, *The Vichy Régime*, 1940–44, Putnam, New York, 1958.

Bibliography

Aymé, Marcel, *Le Passe-Muraille*, Le Club du meilleur livre, Gallimard, Paris, 1943; *En arrière*, 1950.

Barjavel, René, *Journal d'un homme simple*, Chambriand, Paris 1951.

Bernanos, Georges, *Le Crépuscule des dieux*, Gallimard, Paris, 1956.

Le Canard enchaîné, 28.8.1957, 'Un traître nommé Céline'.

Combat, 21–23 February, 1950 – on Céline's trial.

Cotta, Michèle, *La Collaboration 1940–1944*, Colin, Paris, 1964.

Cousteau, Pierre-Antoine, *En ce temps-là*, Librairie française 1958.

Crespelle, J.-P., *Montmartre vivant*, Paris, 1963.

Debrie-Panel, Nicole, *L.-F. Céline*, Éditions Vitte, 1961.

Defence de l'Occident, July–August 1962.

Desanges, Paul, *Elie Faure*, Geneva, 1963.

Dominique, Pierre, *Les Polémistes français depuis 1789*, Editions la Colombe, Paris, 1962.

Drieu La Rochelle, *Sur les écrivains*, Paris, 1964.

Epting, Karl, *Frankreich in Widerspruch*, Hanseatische Verlagsanstalt, Hamburg 1943.

Franc-Tireur, 19.12.1945, 'L'Écrivain franco-nazi'.

Freustié, Jean, 'La Pavane du collabo', *Le Nouvel Observateur*, 17.2.1969.

Galtier-Boissière, Jean, *Mémoires d'un Parisien*, La Table ronde, Paris 1961.

Guénot, Jean, 'De la parole à l'écriture', *Le Monde*, 15.2.1969.

Halperine-Kaminski, E., *Céline en chemise brune, ou le mal du présent*, Editions Excelsior, 1938.

Hamilton, Alistair, *Appeals of Fascism: A Study of Intellectuals and Fascism*, Macmillan, New York, 1971.

Hanrez, Marc, *Céline*, Gallimard, Paris, 1961.

Hérold-Paquis, Jean, *Des Illusions . . . désillusions!* Bourgoin, Paris, 1948.

Hindus, Milton, *The Crippled Giant*, Boar's Head Books, New York, 1950.

Jamet, Claude, *Images mêlées de la littérature et du théâtre*, Editions de L'Elan, Paris, 1947.

Le Clézio, J-M-G., 'Comment peut-on écrire autrement?', *Le Monde*, 15.2.1969.

Legris, Michel, 'L'Antisémite', *Le Monde*, 6.7.1961.

Le Libertaire, January–February 1950 – on Céline's trial.

Lwoff, André, 'Quand Céline était "chercheur" à l'Institut Pasteur', *Le Figaro*, 7.4.1969.

Mahé, Henri, *La Brinquebale avec Céline*, La Table ronde, Paris, 1969.

Morand, Jacqueline, *Les idées politiques de L.-F. Céline*, Librairie générale de droit et de jurisprudence, Bibliothèque constitutionnelle et de sciences politiques, no. 46, Paris 1972.

Nadeau, Maurice, 'Céline', *L'Express*, 6.7.1961.

Nizan, Paul, '*Voyage au bout de la nuit*', *L'Humanité*, 12.9.1932.

Les Nouvelles littéraires, 6.2.1969, 'Le Testament d'un maudit' – interview with Madame Céline.

Novick, Peter, *Resistance versus Vichy*, Columbia University Press, New York, 1968.

Ostrovsky, Erika, *Céline and his Vision*, New York University Press, 1967; *Voyeur Voyant: A Portrait of Louis-Ferdinand Céline*, Random House, New York, 1971.

Paris-Match, 15.7.1961 – notice of Céline's death.

Céline

Paris-Soir, 8.12.1932 – on the Prix Renaudot.

Pia Pascal, '*Rigodon*', *Carrefour*, 12.2.1969.

Pican, Gaëtan, *Panorama de la nouvelle littérature française*, Gallimard, Paris, 1951.

Pollet, Eveline, *Escaliers*, La Renaissance du livre, 1956.

Porquerol, Elisabeth, *Le Temps comme il passe: Céline il y a trente ans*, Nouvelle Revue française, September 1961, pp. 550–57.

Poulet, Robert, *Entretiens familiers avec L.-F. Céline*, Plon, Paris, 1958; 'Une Oeuvre retrouvée de Céline', *Rivarol*, 6.2.1964; 'Le Pont de Londres', *Rivarol*, 30.4.1964.

Rebatet, Lucien, *Les Décombres*, Denoël, Paris, 1942.

Rivarol, June–August 1957 – on the *D'un château l'autre* controversy.

Sartre, J.-P., 'Portrait de l'antisémite', *Les Temps modernes*, December 1945.

Schwob, René, 'Lettre ouverte à L.-F. Céline', *Esprit*, no. 6, 1933.

Sérant, Paul, *Le Romantisme fasciste*, Paris, 1959.

Sicard, Maurice-Ivan. (Saint-Paulien), *Histoire de la collaboration*, Paris, 1964.

Télémagazine, 5.4.1969, 'Madame Céline raconte son mari'.

Thiher, Allen, *Céline: The Novel as Delirium*, Rutgers University Press, New Brunswick, 1972.

Vailland, Roger, 'Nous n'épargnerons plus Louis-Ferdinand Céline', *La Tribune des Nations*, 13.1.1950.

Vandromme, Paul, *Céline*, Editions Universitaires, Paris, 1963.

Vanino, Maurice, *L'Affaire Céline*, Editions Créator, Paris, 1952.

Walter, Gérard, *La vie à Paris sous l'occupation*, Paris 1960.

Index

* People who are real and who also appear as fictional characters in Celine's novels are listed only when they are referred to as real people.

Index

Brinon, Fernand de, 173, 187, 195, 196, 197, 200
British Broadcasting Corporation (B.B.C.), 171, 191, 243
Brochard, Marcel, 28, 30, 37, 47
Butor, Michel, 318

Caldwell, Erskine, *Tobacco Road*, 211
Camus, Albert, 7, 56, 57, 173, 201, 212, 216
  La Peste, 57
Camus, Doctor, 38, 45, 128, 208, 212, 264
Le Canard enchaîné, 275
Canavaggia, Marie, 121, 194, 283
Candide, 13, 83
Capone, Al, 46
Carayon, Jeanne, 15, 36, 37, 38
Carel, Alexis, 29
de Carhaix, Taldir, 189, 190
Cartier, Jacques, 136
Céline, Louis-Ferdinand, his works
  À l'agité du bocal, 168, 212, 249; *L'Ambassadrice*, 282; *Bagatelles pour un massacre*, 8, 16, 19, 42, 87, 132, 133, 135, **139–69**, 175, 180, 183, 185n., 186, 187, 192, 198, 199, 215, 270, 275, 287; *Ballets sans musique, sans personne, sans rien*, 157; *Les Beaux Draps*, 133, 144, 157n., 163, 163n., 164, 166, 167, 171, 175, 176, 179, 180, 181, 182, 183, 186, 202, 215, 216, 248; *Casse-pipe*, 132, 133, 206, 214; *D'un château l'autre*, 8, 9, 97, 168, 196, 222, 272, 273, 275, 281, **285–314**; *L'École des cadavres*, 13, 133, 137, 142, 147, **159–63**, 166, 187, 191, 206, 215, 301; *L'Église*, 33, 34, 117, 122; *Entretiens avec le Professeur Y*, **268–72**, 276; *Féerie pour une autre fois*, 9, 39, 49, 63n., 81, 154, 168, 211, 215, 222, 237, **238–63**, 264, 268, 269, 271, 272, 279, 283, 288, 289; *Guignol's Band*, 9, 25, 49, 50, 91, 132, 133, 167, 191, 193, **218–37**, 239, 242, 246, 250, 262, 262n., 268, 271, 291, 293; *Mea Culpa*, 132, 133, 135, 139, 142, 143, **144–7**, 157, 163, 164; *Mort à crédit*, 7, 8, 9, 16, 17, 18, 21, 27, 49, 50, 73, 81, 82, **83–116**, 117, 120, 121, 126, 131, 132, 133, 142, 146, 147, 148, 155, 158, 166, 168n., 210, 218, 219, 221, 222, 228, 230, 231, 234, 236, 238, 242, 248, 250, 258, 271, 278, 293, 294, 298, 312, 317, 318; *Nord*, 81, 222, 279, 282, 283, **285–314**; *Normance*, 48, 211, 238, 245, 247, 248, 249, **254–63**, 268, 269, 272, 313; see also *Féerie*; *Oeuvres complètes*, 8, 24, 139, 283; *Le Pont de Londres*, 194, 211, 218, 227, 232, 234, 268, 283; see also *Guignol's Band*; *Réponse aux accusations*, 212, 214n.; *Rigodon*, 275, 282, 283, 284, **285–314**; *Secrets dans l'île*, 119, 189; *Vive l'amnistie, monsieur*, 275; *Voyage au bout de la nuit*, **7–9**, 11, **12–16**, 25, 31, 37, 38, 41, 42, 43, 47, 48, **49–82**, 84, 88, 91, 92, 94, 95, 100, 105, 107, 110, 111, 117, 118, 120, 122, 123, 124, 125, 128, 132, 139, 143, 144, 167, 168, 169, 175, 181, 192, 198, 202, 210, 219, 221, 223, 224, 228, 234, 239, 265, 268, 276, 277, 278, 287, 294, 317
Cervantes, Miguel de, 11
Chamfleury, Robert, 182, 192
Chamoin, 199
Chancel, Jacques, 277
Chaplin, Charlie, 27, 154, 156
Chateaubriand, Alphonse de, 176, 187, 188, 195, 196, 200
Chénier, André, 201, 245
Chevalier, Maurice, 277
Churchill, Winston, 175, 261
Cive, Jean, 123
Claudel, Paul, 16, 148
Clavel, Maurice, 45n.
Clémenti, Pierre, 176, 183
Clichy Municipal Clinic, 12, 15, 17, 36, 39, 42, 118, 126, 136
Cocteau, Jean, 16
collaboration, 149n., 188n., 190, 214, 215, 289

Index

Index

Index

Index

Index

Index

A Penguin Book

"A remarkable feat of getting inside another man's skin, of seeing his works from an interior vantage point"—Richard R. Lingeman, *The New York Times*

Céline is the dark genius of French literature—a novelist whose art was fed by tainted streams of madness and nightmare. He was at once kindly doctor and rabid anti-Semite, patriot and Nazi collaborator, meticulous writer and master of the century's most delirious style. In this acclaimed biography, Patrick McCarthy follows to the end the haunted corridor of Céline's life, giving us an unforgettable picture of a brilliant mind devoured by the specters of death and nothingness.

"McCarthy's book is to be recommended highly on both its biographical and critical sides. . . ."
—Anthony Burgess, *Harper's*

"His critical discourse displays many fine discriminations and . . . a powerful gift of synopsis. . . . [McCarthy] has done a fine, firm job."
—John Updike, *The New Yorker*

"Excellent"
—Larry McMurtry, *Washington Post Book World*

Cover design by Neil Stuart

Biograp
ISBN 0 1
00.4534

$3.50